Archetypes in Religion and Beyond

Archetypes in Religion and Beyond
A Practical Theory of Human Integration and Inspiration

Robert M. Ellis

SHEFFIELD UK   BRISTOL CT

Published by Equinox Publishing Ltd
UK: Office 415, The Workstation, 15 Paternoster Row, Sheffield, South Yorkshire S1 2BX
USA: ISD, 70 Enterprise Drive, Bristol, CT 06010

www.equinoxpub.com

First published 2022
© Robert M. Ellis 2022
All rights reserved. No part of this publication may be reproduced or transmitted in any form or by any means, electronic or mechanical, including photocopying, recording or any information storage or retrieval system, without prior permission in writing from the publishers.

British Library Cataloguing-in-Publication Data
A catalogue record for this book is available from the British Library.

ISBN-13 978 1 80050 076 1 (hardback)
978 1 80050 077 8 (paperback)
978 1 80050 078 5 (ePDF)
978 1 80050 167 6 (ePub)

Library of Congress Cataloging-in-Publication Data

Names: Ellis, Robert M., author.
Title: Archetypes in religion and beyond : a practical theory of human integration and inspiration / Robert M. Ellis.
Description: Sheffield, South, Yorkshire ; Bristol : Equinox Publishing Ltd, 2022. | Includes bibliographical references and index. | Summary: "This multi-disciplinary book weaves together religious studies, ethical philosophy, the psychology of bias, the neuroscience of brain lateralisation, the linguistics of embodied meaning, the feedback loops of systems theory, with a lifetime's experience of Buddhist practice and appreciation of symbolism in the arts: all with the aim of producing a fresh understanding of the role of archetypes in religion and beyond, that can also be directly applied in practice"-- Provided by publisher.
Identifiers: LCCN 2021039517 (print) | LCCN 2021039518 (ebook) | ISBN 9781800500761 (hardback) | ISBN 9781800500778 (paperback) | ISBN 9781800500785 (epdf) | ISBN 9781800501676 (epub)
Subjects: LCSH: Archetype (Psychology) | Religion--Philosophy.
Classification: LCC BF175.5.A72 E45 2022 (print) | LCC BF175.5.A72 (ebook) | DDC 155.2/64--dc23
LC record available at https://lccn.loc.gov/2021039517
LC ebook record available at https://lccn.loc.gov/2021039518

Typeset by S.J.I. Services, New Delhi, India

Contents

List of Figures	vii
Acknowledgements	ix
Introduction	**1**
1. What is an Archetype?	**10**
a. The Experience of Archetypes	10
b. The Universality of Archetypes	16
c. Archetypes as Embodied Schemas	20
d. Archetypes as Metaphors	25
e. The Baggage of the 'Collective Unconscious'	31
f. The Baggage of Platonism	37
g. Archetypes and Religion	43
h. Archetypes, Tradition, and Modernity	49
i. Evidence and Testability	56
2. The Projection of Archetypes	**62**
a. The Projection Process	62
b. Reactive Projection	68
c. Projection as Metaphysical Belief	72
d. Projection as the Denial of Embodiment	77
e. Projection as Left-Hemisphere Over-Dominance	81
f. Projection as Bias	86
g. Projection as Reinforcing Feedback	91
h. Projection as Power	96
i. Projection as Evil	100
3. The Integration of Archetypes	**105**
a. The Middle Way and the Integration Process	105
b. Integration and Mindfulness	111
c. Integration and the Arts	117
d. Critical Universalism	124
e. Working with Traditions	131

4. Categorization of Archetypes — **136**
    a. The Basis of Archetypal Categorization — 136
    b. Variations of the Four Archetypes — 142
    c. The Hero and the Ego — 147
    d. The Anima/Animus, Sex, and Specialization — 153
    e. The Shadow, Death, and Suffering — 162
    f. God and Religious Experience — 169
    g. The Middle Way Archetype — 178

5. Archetypes in Religious Traditions — **186**
    a. Ethnic and Universal Religion — 186
    b. The Buddha — 190
    c. Mahayana Symbology — 196
    d. Hinduism: The Great Appropriation — 204
    e. The Archetype of Nature in China — 210
    f. Yahweh, Idolatry, and Literacy — 217
    g. Graeco-Roman Tradition — 224
    h. Christ — 229
    i. Christian Mythology — 235
    j. Christian Mysticism — 242
    k. Islam: The Tawhid — 247
    l. Islam: Jihad and the Satanic Verses — 252
    m. The Kabbalah — 257

6. Archetypal Function in 'Secular' Concepts — **263**
    a. Nature — 263
    b. Goodness — 268
    c. Truth — 273
    d. Beauty — 278
    e. Rationality — 283
    f. Humanity — 288
    g. Democracy — 292
    h. Health — 296

Conclusion — **301**

Bibliography — 308

Glossary — 318

Index — 325

List of Figures

1.	Maslow's hierarchy of needs (diagram by factoryjoe)	13
2.	Mahavajrabhairava (unknown Tibetan sculptor)	16
3.	Table of relationships between archetypal functions, values, and psychological stages (by the author)	54
4.	Zeno's paradox: Achilles and the tortoise (diagram by Daniele Pugliesi)	84
5.	Reinforcing and balancing feedback loops (diagram by the author)	92
6.	Satan's rebellion (Gustave Doré)	103
7.	The two mules (pacifist poster)	107
8.	Meditator (Mokoti Tonn)	112
9.	*Ecstasy of St Francis* (Sassetta)	122
10.	The three axes creating archetypal categorization (diagram by the author)	140
11.	Snake (David Clode)	143
12.	Cave painting of hunt from Cueva Manos, Argentina	148
13.	Virgin Mary and angels from the *Wilton Diptych* (unknown artist, England)	157
14.	The Skiff – *La Yole* (Pierre-Auguste Renoir)	159
15.	Milton's heroic Satan (Gustave Doré)	165
16.	*Hell* (Hieronymous Bosch)	167
17.	The Buddha (Gandhara sculpture)	171
18.	Green Tara mandala from Ladakh (unknown artist)	174
19.	Buddha leaving his family, fresco from a temple in Sarnath, India (unknown artist)	182

20. Buddha leaving the ascetics, fresco from a monastery in
    Laos (unknown artist) — 182
21. *Holy Family* (Andrea del Sarto) — 183
22. The Buddha accepts food to end his aceticism (unknown
    Indian sculptor) — 192
23. Buddha Shakyamuni (Kawanabe Kyosai) — 194
24. Thousand-armed Avalokiteshvara (unknown Tibetan
    artist) — 197
25. Mahakala (unknown Tibetan artist) — 201
26. Padmasambhava image at Tsozong Gongba Monastery
    (unknown Tibetan sculptor) — 202
27. Shiva-Shakti statue (unknown Indian sculptor) — 207
28. Shiva Nataraja from Tamil Nadu (unknown sculptor) — 209
29. Xi Wangmu (unknown Chinese artist) — 214
30. *Moses Receiving the Law* (William Blake) — 218
31. *The Judgement of Paris* (Anton Mengs) — 226
32. *Miracle of the Bread and Fish* (Giovanni Lanfranco) — 232
33. *The Conversion on the Way to Damascus* (Caravaggio) — 237
34. *The Vision of St Bernard* (Domenico Puligo) — 244
35. Islamic prayer (Rumman Amin) — 248
36. The *sefirot* (diagram by the author) — 259
37. *Nature* (sculpture by Ruggero Rovan) — 265
38. *Truth Presenting a Mirror to the Vanities of the World*
    (unknown artist) — 274
39. *Allegory of Humanity* (sculpture by Jan Štursa) — 289
40. *Hygeia* (Peter Paul Rubens) — 297

Acknowledgements

The author would like to thank the following people for reading the manuscript and offering invaluable suggestions prior to publication: Erik D. Goodwyn, Miranda Gill, Viryanaya Ellis, Susan Averbach.

Figure 27 (Shiva-Shakti statue) is reproduced by kind permission of Lotus Sculpture Inc, and Figure 38 (*Truth Presenting a Mirror to the Vanities of the World*) by kind permission of the Ashmolean Museum, Oxford. The remaining illustrations are all public domain or creative commons pictures, as credited in their captions, apart from those produced by the author. Some creative commons pictures that are included are reproduced under share-alike licences, indicating that the picture (only) can be freely reproduced under the same terms: these are noted in their captions where relevant.

Introduction

Why write about archetypes today? I want to write about them because they are very practically relevant. The archetype is a crucial concept that can allow us to resolve a quite unnecessarily polarized discourse about religion – as well as about any other sphere in which humans have ideals.

Archetypes can have a central place in helping us understand why religion can remain *inspiring*, and why this inspiration is needed, even though it has no necessary relationship with religious beliefs as widely understood. As well as being practically valuable, I think archetypes can be rigorously theorized, without any of the speculative metaphysics that has sometimes become attached to them.

In writing about archetypes, of course, I am also motivated by my own experience of finding them inspiring, not because I 'believed' in them, but because I engaged with their meaning. Probably my earliest experience of that comes from fiction – for instance the works of J.R.R. Tolkien, which I read at an early age. Tolkien's work for me still provides a central example of the separability of archetypal meaning from belief. One can find Middle Earth overwhelmingly meaningful, in all its detail and all its interplay of heroic, attractive, wise, and dark forces, but still not use it directly as a basis of judgement in one's own practical life. I don't expect to meet Gandalf in my local pub, but nevertheless his perspective is added to the internal voices available to me. As Tolkien also pointed out,[1] this is not at all because his kinds of stories are 'untrue'. Rather, I would argue, the perspective of belief is not relevant to them, and we need to hold them in a balanced, agnostic position that is meaningful without being assumed either 'true' or 'untrue'.

That this perspective should also be applied to religious symbols is something that has gradually become more apparent in my personal experience as well, even though I'd admit that the actual overwhelming weight of the conventional association of religion

1   Tolkien (1964).

with absolute belief has to be constantly acknowledged. One breakthrough moment for me in this respect came at the funeral of my father – a Christian minister – where I anticipated a habitual alienation from the service, but then realized that I could put archetypal meaning to work in my active interpretation of every aspect of the ritual. That experience was remarkably liberating, and has done a lot to help form the perspective expressed in this book. Absolute belief, as I shall argue, is closely associated with projection and conflict, but this is not an inevitable effect of religious or any other archetypal symbols. We can be deeply inspired by their meaning without that conflict, and let go of it without taking sides.

The concept of archetype is indelibly associated with the work of Carl Jung: a rich resource to which anyone who writes about archetypes should acknowledge their debt. Jung has provided us with the core idea of functional similarities across cultures that can be recognized through the role of symbols. He saw these symbols as fulfilling universal psychological functions for each individual experiencing them. He also saw that these functions could be displaced, or *projected*, as a kind of delusion in which the psychological function is believed to be fulfilled by an external object: for instance, that mere devotion to a feminine image can meet our need for feminine qualities. Without the interference created by projections, however, we are much better able to allow those psychological functions to operate helpfully in relation to each other (to integrate them).

I am already paraphrasing Jung here, trying to draw out the general practical significance of what he wrote rather than using his own preferred language. However, the above offers a summary of the Jungian concept of archetype that shapes this book. There are issues about all the key terms here – the symbol, the function, the projection, and the integration – that will be explored, but these are nevertheless the central ideas that I believe still have huge potential to resolve our confusions about religion.

Unfortunately, the practical relevance of these core ideas has been obscured for many people. It's been obscured by unnecessary intellectual baggage on the one hand, and on the other by a failure to synthesize our understanding of archetypes with lots of other interests – meaning, the body, metaphor, bias, critical thinking, and mindfulness amongst them. Archetypes are a feature of human experience, and a conceptual tool for everyone. They should not be associated only with the discourse of a small tribe of Jungians.

Jungians should be credited with keeping the flame alive, but they have also sometimes obscured it in the process.

Archetypes are no more Jung's sole property than gravity is Newton's, or (as I've argued elsewhere) the Middle Way is the Buddha's. To make a discussion of archetypes into a mere scholarly discussion of Jung or his successors would potentially distract from an understanding of their relevance and importance in relation to wider human experience and practice. Instead, this book offers a wider theory of archetypes, justified in relation to a range of evidence and argument in the context of human experience in general, not solely in relation to the authority of the master. To idealize Jung's authority, indeed, would in my judgement be contrary to the central insights of his archetypal theory.

For that same reason I have dispensed with baggage that many Jungians still seem to regard as necessarily attached to the concept of archetypes, but that, starting with their practical function, I find unhelpful and distracting. This baggage is associated particularly with the concept of the 'collective unconscious' in Jung, and also with the Platonic interpretations that Jung tended to attach to the archetypes. I will give some, though not too much, space in this book to explaining these judgements. However, my main focus is a positive one: that of explaining the positive value of archetypal theory without this baggage, and applying it to aid our understanding of religion and of symbolic culture beyond religion. We do not need to know what archetypes 'really are', whether they 'exist', or how they originated, to use them helpfully as a concept. Instead we just need to stipulate clearly what we mean by them, and then show the helpfulness of the concept by applying it to interpreting a range of human experiences.

My definition of an archetype may at first sound technical, but please be assured that the terminology I am using has a practical purpose, and will become familiar. An archetype can be defined as a *diachronic schematic function*. The term 'function' may sound reductive to some ears, but it is not here: it is just a common name for a huge spectrum of identifiable tendencies for parts of a system to organize so as to achieve an apparent goal for that system. One can see a 'function' at work in the coagulation of oil droplets that seem to seek each other out in water[2] at the most simple extreme, to the

[2] This is an example of molecular self-organization: see Capra and Luisi (2014) pp. 145–9.

immense and mysterious complexity that is the human relationship with God at the other. In human experience we tend to see functions as purposes or motives, whilst in observed inanimate things the scientifically inclined are more likely to assume that they are determined events that merely appear motivated. It does not matter for our purposes whether or not functions in any context are causally determined (we could never know in any case). In practice, we can let go of that, and just note the systemic relationship of 'function' that we observe. By acting in a particular way, parts of the system benefit the whole.

An archetype, however, is a very specific kind of function. It is a human function that benefits us in our whole complexity, in both our psychological and cultural context. It is *schematic* because it consists in a set of basic associations that make symbols meaningful to us. It is *diachronic* (from the Greek for 'through time') because it is specifically the type of schema that helps us to retain the awareness required to maintain a function *over time*. We are forgetful creatures, and archetypes have the function of reminding us of what we find most meaningful in the *long-term*. Cultural expressions of archetypes are interdependent with their psychological functions so as to create these reminders.

Such a definition of archetypes may sound superficially like reductionism or 'murdering to dissect' to those who have an immediate and intuitive relationship with them. It is not. Just because we recognize a function does not mean that we claim to know exactly what it ultimately *is*, which is what reductionists claim to know. An account of what archetypes *do* can be helpfully precise without posing any threat to our appreciation of the profundity of archetypal experience, because it does not involve any assertion that archetypes are *just* anything. Archetypes have the function of being *inspiring*, meaning that they provide us with ongoing motivation for developing beyond our limitations at any given point, but along with that function comes the profound experience of being awed and challenged. So we can see archetypes as *both* profound experiences for individuals, *and* at the same time phenomena whose structure and functioning can be clearly theorized, observed in individual experience, and potentially also tested scientifically to some extent (see 1.i).

This account of archetypes as diachronic schematic functions, which will be explored more fully in the course of this book, is consistent, I believe, with how the notion of an archetype *helpfully functions* in Jung's work. It does not fully accord with how Jung defined them, which combined both Platonic and biological features in uneasy relationship. Rather than maintaining the purity of Jungian doctrine, then, I am much more interested in synthesizing Jung's insights with those I have found in other areas.

In particular, that includes the embodied meaning theories of George Lakoff and Mark Johnson, which can offer great illumination of archetypes in relation to the schematic development of meaning for human beings in their embodied interaction with their environment. In their account, our experience of meaning as association through embodied schemas is then extended by metaphor, so I will be discussing archetypes in relation both to schemas (1.c) and metaphors (1.d).

The chief practical value of the idea of archetype consists in the way in which it can help us distinguish between deluded projection and valuable meaning. This is a distinction that strongly parallels the Middle Way of the Buddha (as well as the Middle Way found, in a less developed form, in Jung's own work[3]). The way that archetypal projection and integration can be traced in mindfulness and meditation practice can provide a clear practical starting point to working with archetypes that can also be applied in the context of any tradition.

Archetypal projection and integration also have a crucial relationship to systems theory, where the concept of a function is found. Although it is humans that project or integrate archetypes, these responses to them correspond to the two types of feedback loops in systems theory – closed, 'positive', or reinforcing on the one hand and open, 'negative', or balancing on the other (see 2.g). To project an archetype is to continue repeating your current way of trying to fulfil a function regardless of the circumstances, but to integrate it is to adjust the way we relate to it. As humans, our great evolutionary advantage is adaptability, but we constantly tend to lose that advantage through rigid projection of the archetypes. Absolutizing religion and its conflicts are good immediate examples of this bloody-minded loss of balancing awareness that we are so prone to. We could parallel this to rigidity in any system: for instance, the feedback loops of accelerating climate change that have been set off

---

3   This is the subject of Ellis (2020).

by our own psychological feedback loops of projected 'reality'. As long as we believe that God commands us to do as we wish with the earth's infinite resources, for instance, the feedback loop of projection can continue to ruinously feed non-sentient feedback loops in our environment.

The relationship of the archetypes to the massive amount of work on biases that has been accomplished in cognitive psychology is also striking. In this book I will argue that biases and archetypal projections are equivalent (2.f). Our work in overcoming projection and integrating archetypes can thus support the overcoming of bias – provided that the areas of cognition and emotion are no longer falsely separated. For instance, a prejudice against someone is also a projection of the shadow archetype. To assume that someone, say, of a different race must be a threat, is also to substitute a simplistic concept of evil for our complex experience of a person.

Far too much of Jungian discussion of archetypes seems to neglect the critical thinking that we need to stop projecting those archetypes – something that I mean to remedy in this book. Critical thinking needs to be *combined* with the deep intuitive cultivation of imaginative associations, not separated from intuition as an either/or choice. To stop the projection we make when we fall in love, for instance, so as to recognize the qualities of our beloved in a more realistic and balanced fashion, we need to be able to *think* through the way we are using that archetype. This involves avoiding the 'halo effect' by which one attractive quality leads us to unthinkingly attribute lots of other good qualities. This is an archetypal projection that can also be aided positively by cultivating our relationship to the archetype represented by the beloved. For instance, a man who can positively recognize and celebrate Mary, or the Buddhist figure Tara, *as an aspect of his own experience* is far less likely to treat a woman deludedly as though she possessed all those qualities.

The first three sections of this book, then, are concerned with a general theory of archetypes. I explain what they mean and imply (or do not imply) on the most helpful model, how they are projected, and also, crucially, how they can be *integrated* as a crucial aspect of personal religious or spiritual practice. The value of discussing archetypes is so that we can recognize and celebrate archetypes as part of ourselves, rather than projecting them.

After these initial sections, I then go on to the categorization of archetypes (section 4), which is another vexed subject. What are 'the' archetypes? Can there be such a thing as a complete list? To get too hung up on archetypal taxonomy, I argue, can be an unhelpful distraction from the ways that the concept of archetype can be helpful to us. However, a fourfold analysis of the chief archetypes – hero, anima/animus, shadow, and God – in my view puts a necessary focus on the *functions* of archetypes in our experience. Jungians and New Age archetype enthusiasts often talk about a whole range of archetypes: for instance the lover, magician, trickster, mother, child etc. In my view this puts insufficient emphasis on the core inspirational *function* of the archetype – though that doesn't imply that these subsidiary archetypes, along with many other possible variants, cannot be helpful and inspiring. I argue that the functions of self and other, attraction and repulsion, integration and conflict, can help us to identify the chief archetypes. In each case, though, we also need to distinguish those archetypes themselves from other distracting associations that are largely products of the *projection* of the archetype. This account of the four main functional archetypes gives us *four types of inspiration* (an earlier candidate title for this book).

It is this general discussion of archetypes and their function that lays all the groundwork for the subsequent discussion of archetypes in religion (section 5). Here, by analysing selected aspects of the world's religious traditions, I will trace how the four types of inspiration have been cultivated in many different contexts. In the process, I will also need to distinguish between the helpful and integrated use of archetypes as a source of inspiration, and their common projection, which can then turn the archetypes instead into a source of repression and conflict.

Though I argue that there are four basic types of inspiration, I also suggest a fifth that can be distinguished in some respects but not others: the Middle Way archetype. This inspires us not only through a vision of potential integration, but also to focus simultaneously on our current non-ideal situation and continually work with the tension between ideal and actuality. The Buddha gave the most explicit account of the Middle Way, but it also emerges implicitly in the incarnation of Christ, and even potentially in the Muslim vision of worshipping God without idolatry. The Middle Way, then, has a hybrid archetypal status, somewhere between God and the hero, reminding us not to project either of them. The positive function of religion for many, then, is as a source of inspiration for balanced spiritual development in which different human functions remain in tension with each other. The implications of that development are also not merely individual, but need to be applied in the judgements made by religious groups and organizations.

Archetypal religion, then, consists in an interpretation of religion that fully acknowledges the power of these archetypal functions in it. However, it also applies critical thinking to maintain the awareness that absolute religious 'beliefs' are not only unnecessary to this archetypal function, but also in conflict with it. There is no shortage of evidence and argument available on the negative effects of absolute religious belief, particularly as assembled by atheist thinkers. However, the unnecessary association between recognizing these negative effects on the one hand, and beliefs about the *non-existence* of the projections (particularly God) on the other, is one of reactive projection (see 2.b). Projection can be just as much a matter of believing that our own assumptions 'don't exist' beyond us as that they 'do exist'. We do not resolve a projection by just introducing a contradiction, but by recognizing and avoiding the projection. At the same time we can positively cultivate an integrated relationship with the archetype. I thus argue that the practice of archetypal religion is one that requires rigorous agnosticism – agnosticism of a kind modelled to some extent by religious mystics as well as by the most reflective secular thinkers.

The apparently non-religious, 'secular' cultures of the classical and modern worlds also have other ways of projecting absolute ideas and forming beliefs about them. These are primarily conceptual rather than visually symbolic, but another of my quests in this book is to argue against conceptual exceptionalism. Abstract concepts can operate as symbols fulfilling archetypal functions just as visual symbols can. For instance, the widespread uses of the concepts of 'Nature' and 'Truth' in scientific culture can fairly, I argue, be seen as archetypes of science. The issues are the same as those of religious archetypes, in the sense that these archetypes can be projected and become the basis of beliefs, or they can be recognized as inspirational ideals and celebrated as such. A good many other 'secular' qualities have been allegorized as figures as well as being reified in conceptual beliefs – including goodness, beauty, rationality, humanity, and democracy.

Once we consider these 'secular' archetypes and how much they have a similarity of function with religious archetypes, the grounds for over-strong popular distinctions between 'religion' and 'science' (or other 'non-religious' areas) rapidly disappear. We all have the same problems as well as the same kinds of inspirations: these problems and inspirations are human, not just 'religious'. One major message of this book is thus that the false boundaries put around religion by those who think of it only in the light of its 'beliefs' can and should be eroded. In the light of the erosion of religious 'belief' amongst Western populations, the revival of its function for human beings surely lies in an archetypal interpretation.

1. What is an Archetype?

1.a. The Experience of Archetypes

> *Hold fast to dreams,*
> *For if dreams die*
> *Life is a broken-winged bird,*
> *That cannot fly.*
> Langston Hughes

What is an archetype? How do you recognize one? One point that Jung was very clear about is that you should not mistake an archetype for its appearance: 'they can be recognised only from the effects they produce'.[1] We can't describe an archetype only in terms of a particular concrete or representational form. For instance, the hero doesn't even have to be human, let alone always male or always carrying a sword. Nevertheless, archetypes are only relevant to us because they appear in our experience. They appear on each occasion as a *symbol* or a *motif*.

A *symbol* is an ambiguous and multifaceted representation, distinguishable from the deluded univocality we attribute to a *sign*. A sign is supposed to mean one thing, as a red traffic light means 'stop', but even a red traffic light is also a symbol, depending on the range of association we have with it (it could also mean traffic, frustration, impatience, danger, and many other things). Anything that provokes a sense of meaning (both 'cognitive' and 'emotive') within us can be a symbol – an object, a person, a picture, a model, a sound, a smell, a word, a sentence, a gesture, a colour, a tune. When any of these things evokes other ideas beyond the mere sensual experience of the object itself, it becomes symbolic – and thus potentially also archetypal. The archetype does not reside in the form of the object itself, but in what it means for us.

A *motif* is a symbol that has some consistency over time and space, but not an absolute consistency. For example, the colour white is associated in Western culture with purity and virginity. Brides wear white, blank pieces of paper are white with unrealized potential,

---

1   Jung (1958) §222, note 2.

and the innocent are described as 'whiter than white'. This *motif* holds within a certain cultural sphere: but beyond that sphere the meaning may change. For example, in India, white is associated with mourning. So, the appearance of a *motif* is not itself an archetype, but it is nevertheless a sign of consistent human energies associated with the *meaning* of the motif. Whatever you may think about the moral implications of them doing so, people often tend to care about their concepts of purity and virginity in one form or another, even if they express them in different ways.

In this sense, archetypal meaning is no different from other sorts of human meaning. There can be no meaning unless we are prepared to direct energy and attention towards an object that we find meaningful. When we do so, that meaning arises, not *in the object*, but *in us* – specifically, *in our bodily experience*. The more meaningful we find something, the more obviously our bodies respond to it – for instance in the nervous agitation of excitement or the heat and directedness of anger. Even when there is no strong 'emotional' response, meaning provides new neural connections that sensitize us to similar stimuli when we meet them again next time.[2]

So, the appearance of archetypes is their appearance *in us*, not in the object that forms the symbol. Nevertheless, there is a (limited and contingent) cultural consistency in the kinds of objects that tend to produce the same sorts of meaning. What makes them archetypal is not that limited cultural consistency, but rather the nature of the response. The patterns of meaning that archetypes have *for us* is what I call their archetypal function.

Each time we encounter a stimulus that we symbolically associate with the archetype, we have our experience of that meaning reinforced. Our neural connections are renewed and strengthened in relation to it, and our bodies respond in accordance with that meaning. We have a sense of satisfaction, even of enjoyment, as those connections are re-forged, and a new energy surges through our systems in response to the meaningful stimulus. We feel our lives are given a little more shape and purpose, our energies gathered and applied, as we encounter this meaningful connection.

We could say this about a lot of things that induce a response in us – often an apparently automatic one: food, drink, sexual opportunities, threatening behaviour or danger, illness or injury. It is

2 See Johnson (2007) chs. 1–4.

important that we do not completely separate archetypal symbols from these biological imperatives, so that we recognize that in some ways they are simple, basic, and universal. At the same time, however, it's important that we don't reduce them to a set of biological determinants. Determinism is crude and unjustified enough even when applied to the movements of planets, let alone the experience of meaning in humans. That's because it involves a premature certainty that we can even potentially capture all events in descriptive laws – one that ignores the complexity of the universe and the limitations of our own perspective.[3] Archetypal meanings should not be understood as biological determinants, but we do need to understand that they can hit us in the gut in the same way. If you've ever been hungry or sexually aroused, you already know what archetypal meaning is like. It may not be entirely compulsive, but it's not simply optional, either. You don't 'choose' it in some abstract or instantaneous way, as though it was a matter of indifference. It arises out of the conditions of what it means to be you, inhabiting your body, and you can only potentially influence it through long-term planning.[4]

Later in this first section of the book I will go into the workings of embodied meaning, and of how archetypes can be understood in relation to the schemas and metaphors that structure that modern understanding of meaning. Embodied meaning is built up in our bodies in response to the ways that we interact with our environment from early infancy. Some things are more important than others even then – perhaps because they've been supported by instinct, perhaps because of their importance in our environment. Mother is likely to be important, but whether trees, cats, or snow are meaningful to you depends on how important they are in your environment.

Archetypal function is an aspect of that embodied meaning. Some things are more important to us than others, but some things are always reliably important because of our human needs. Those needs have been analysed by Maslow in his well-known hierarchy of needs,[5] working up from our most basic physiological require-

3   See Ellis (2015a, 4.c) for a fuller argument.
4   Haidt (2012, ch. 3) summarises the psychological evidence that although most of our judgements are intuitive, intuitions can also be shaped by judgements: he compares this to riding an elephant.
5   Maslow (1943).

ments to the refined needs he refers to as 'self-actualization' (**figure 1**). Some of these needs are immediately satisfied without any great need to turn them into symbols: for instance, we see some food and eat it, without any great need for reflection or conceptualization. However, our distinctive abilities as humans seem to include the capacity to symbolize longer-term needs, not only to make plans about how to fulfil them, but also to continue to inspire and motivate ourselves with regard to them. That is where archetypal functions become important. As suggested in the introduction, these are *diachronic, schematic* functions. Their diachronic aspect means that that they create *symbolizations of our long-term embodied needs*, of a kind that would not be fulfilled without symbolic motivation.

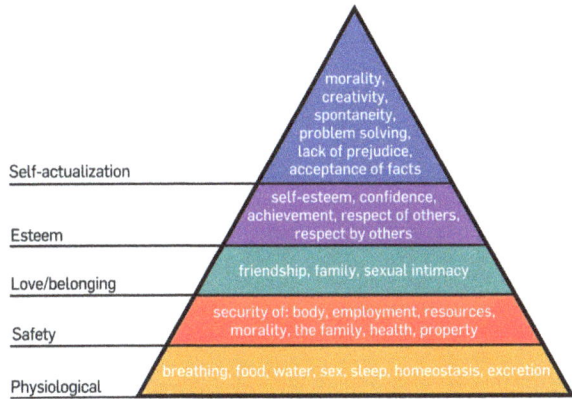

Figure 1. Diagram of Maslow's hierarchy of needs, by factory-joe (Wikimedia Commons).
Creative Commons Attribution Share-alike 3.0 Unported license.

Let's take the example of any long-term plan, such as for instance the plan to write a book such as this one. To carry out such a plan, I obviously need relatively precise symbols (of the kind we are likely to interpret as signs) representing what I am going to do – a set of intentions and an outline of what the book will look like. To actually put that plan into operation, however, I am going to need motivation. That motivation does not come solely from the kinds of motives that are likely to arise in my everyday life otherwise. To be inspired to sit down and devote the required time to writing the book, I will also need symbols of my longer-term motives, so that their meaning engages my attention and reminds me of the need to keep working on the book, rather than being distracted by more immediate goals.

It is these kinds of longer-term motivating symbols that are archetypal in function. In the case of a long-term project the archetypal symbols are likely to be heroic in nature, reminding me of the possibility of reaching a larger goal despite the obstacles. For example, if when taking time out from writing I watch a film in which a hero reaches a goal by overcoming obstacles, this may well help me to recall my own goals and the need to overcome obstacles in reaching them through persistent effort.

Our longer-term needs are also the ones that keep more immediate needs in perspective, preventing them from conflicting with each other. We need to be frequently reminded of these needs and their importance, so that they are not eclipsed by more immediate needs and desires. Our longer-term needs may involve following sustainable principles that we can share with others, developing more fulfilling relationships, finding new meaning by bringing together different aspects of our experience in creative activity, or developing more long-term understanding of the conditions around us so that we can make more appropriate judgements about it. These needs are often known as morality, love, art, and wisdom: all spheres in which archetypal symbols are very common. These spheres also tend to coalesce in the larger sphere commonly known as religion (I will return later [1.g] to the question of what 'religion' means).

It is in these distinctively human, long-term-orientated areas of our experience that the archetypal functions become important. Throughout this book, I will be working with an analysis of four archetypal functions:

1. To live and develop as human beings in the long term we need the ability to make plans and see them through to fulfil goals. This is the *heroic* function.
2. We need to be able to identify and avoid or eliminate long-term threats. This is the *shadow* function.
3. We need to be able to develop relationships with those who are different from us, but who may have complementary qualities. This is the *anima/animus* function.
4. Most of all, we need to be able to maintain a vision of the possibilities for our own individual long-term development and that of our communities, keeping ideals in mind for how things could be as well as how they are. This is what I will call the *God* function, though other labels are of course possible.

In section 4 of this book I will be saying more about the ways that these four functions create the four most important types of archetype. Here it needs to be noted that this is one analysis, but any cake can be cut in lots of different possible ways, and the complex phenomena we are dealing with could be analysed in lots of other ways. This approach is primarily justified over other possible ways of analysing archetypes by its helpfulness, though the four key archetypes identified are also ones that Jung emphasized in places.[6]

Our ability to reflect on long-term goals, threats, relationships, and potentialities, however, is double-edged. On the one hand, we can respond more effectively to all these things if they remain strongly meaningful to us. On the other hand, however, that meaning can easily become fixed in an inflexible response. We then mistake the form it has taken for the archetypal function itself, and fail to adapt the function into a different form for different circumstances. The biggest issue that this creates is the rigidifying of the God function into a set of *beliefs* about God that dominate the world religions – but this is only the most obvious of the ways that rigidification of archetypes can betray their functions. The idealization of a lover, the demonization of an opponent in politics or business, and obsession with impossible goals are all common examples of such rigidification in relation to the other archetypal functions – all of which can also feed into religion.

I will be discussing the process of rigidifying (or projecting, or absolutizing) archetypal functions in more depth in section 2, but then also the positive, integrative role of archetypes in our lives when we have overcome this projection in section 3. Although the opponents of 'religion' in its easily criticized absolutized version may see it as essentially rigidified, my case is that religion is a much more complex phenomenon than that. It also offers many resources for overcoming that projected form. Once we are able to combine critical thinking with positive appreciation of the archetypes, we are much more free to unlock their potential for positively symbolizing the long-term needs in our lives. We easily forget how easily we forget those long-term needs, and there lies the delusion of those who dismiss archetypes as unimportant.

---

6 E.g. the four opening chapters of Jung (1959b) and throughout Jung (2009).

1.b. The Universality of Archetypes

If a story is not universal, it has failed.
Nathan Englander

How do we know that archetypes are universal? Could they not be a construction of Western culture, created in its terms, but not recognizable in other cultures unless our understanding of them is formatted in those terms? Confirmation bias leads us to find what we're looking for and see what we want to see. So, for instance, if we find an apparently devilish figure in a new culture, we may conclude that it represents the shadow function. But surely we could have completely misinterpreted it, not understanding the whole system of symbols in which that figure is found? Even in, for instance, Tibetan Buddhist culture, apparently fearsome figures like Mahavajrabhairava (**figure 2**) that may seem to be representations of the shadow often turn out to have a protective function: their fearsomeness just makes them into better security guards. If we can make these mistakes even in Buddhist culture, which has a lot of links with the West going back to ancient times, surely we could make much bigger ones in more remote and relatively unknown cultures?

Figure 2. Mahavajrabhairava, Tibetan sculpture, 16th–17th century. Photo by Gautier Poupeau (Wikimedia Commons). Creative Commons Attribution 2.0 Generic license.

Like many of the questions that have been raised about archetypes, I think that this is one that does not need to be answered in full. That's because it is grounded in a scientific query about the general truth of archetypal theory as an explanation of symbolic phenomena, rather than a practical concern about how helpful the concept of archetypes can be for us. That practical concern does not mean that we abandon indications of the facts in favour of wishful thinking. Rather it means that we adopt a likely indication of the facts over a less likely one, because that would also be the practically responsible course, but without being too obsessively concerned with 'the facts' for their own sake.

We do not *know* that even our concept of practicality is not culturally limited – that is, we cannot have complete justification showing that it must be true. We only have likelihood. We can have confidence that archetypal analysis is *likely* to apply to all human beings, because all human beings are subject to the same basic needs that create archetypal functions. The evidence for that comes not from analysis of their symbols and how they appear to us, but rather from their functional similarities to other humans. It seems very *likely* that all humans have the four archetypal functions, because they all have goals, threats, relationships, and potentialities, plus the ability to develop symbols so that they can be reminded of those functions over the long term.

Practical judgement does not have to be preceded by certainty, and the practical value of archetypes no more requires certainty about archetypal theory than any other practical judgement does. Before we set off in a car, we do not ask whether we have total certainty about the engineering principles with which it was created. Rather, we have *sufficient confidence* in the machine, based on past experience of its probable performance in relation to our needs, to be prepared to use it. There are doubtless some conditions (extremes of heat or cold, for instance) in which the car could not function, even if we can only recognize where the boundaries of these are in vague general terms. Similarly, we can place our confidence in archetypal ideas based on experience of them aiding us in understanding the conditions of religion and making them work helpfully. To do this, we do not have to have more than a very rough idea of the boundaries of where those ideas would cease to operate so effectively.

The concept of universality, far from being a description of proven ubiquity, can instead operate as a crucially necessary *practical* element in our understanding of archetypes. In this practical sense, universality does not involve a claim about what must be actually ubiquitous, but rather an aspiration for consistency and sustainability. We have a responsibility to develop maximal consistency and sustainability, so as to make our theories maximally adequate in different conditions. We also have a responsibility to note their limitations. Given that we are so subject to confirmation bias, we need to have maximally helpful default settings. It is better to see consistency and sustainability where they may not exist than not to see them where it does, because in that way we are more likely to be able to act on joint aspirations to consistency and sustainability. If we assume that the default is that other cultures do not have the archetypal functions that we would generally attribute to humans, we are much more likely to treat them instrumentally – either as means to fulfil our own goals or as threats – and thus end up with conflict, repression, or both. The opportunity for each culture to develop by learning from the other will have been lost.

To illustrate this, imagine that we have just encountered a race of intelligent aliens from outer space. Imagine that we work on the assumption that they have archetypal functions, and that they do likewise. That means that they are capable of considering the possibility that we are not just either an immediate threat or an immediate opportunity for exploitation. Rather, they can be reminded by symbols around them that in the longer term they do not know what potentialities there might be in a partnership rather than a conflict: they might learn much that benefits them in the longer term, and so might we. Whether they are heroically engaged in a long-term plan, or are trying to avoid long-term threats, or are interested in long-term relationships, or just have a wider awareness of unknown potentialities in the encounter, they will need archetypal symbols, and it is these that provide the best possibility of avoiding the zero-sum bets of game theory. Game theory predicts the results when we are fixated on certain narrow goals, rather than recognizing wider possibilities. Before we destroy the aliens, or they destroy us, we need to be able to bet on those wider possibilities by assuming the universality of archetypes.

Of course, in many cases that doesn't happen. At the time of the European invasion of the Americas, the dominant paradigm for the Europeans was that Native Americans did not have symbols that Europeans recognized as maintaining what they understood to be right universal values (in other words, implicitly, archetypes, although no concept of archetypes existed yet). Archetypal functions were assumed to reside only in the culturally specific symbols themselves, rather than in the human meanings of those symbols. Thus, cultural chauvinism could fuel cultural destruction, even genocide. Even at that time, though, there were a few people who were willing to appreciate common humanity, one of the foremost of these being Bartolomé de las Casas. De las Casas shifted his position to oppose his compatriots' slaughter and exploitation of native Americans because he recognized the value in common humanity between both racial groups as more important than the culturally specific value of Christian symbols. For him, then (especially later in his life when he became a Dominican friar), the most valuable specific symbol epitomizing the highest values (the Christian God) came to include and imply the value of common humanity.[1] Humanity as an aspect of the God archetype is something I will discuss further in 6.f below. Implicitly, then, he was applying a universal archetype rather than a specific symbol, and his mind was opened as a result.

The concept of universality, indeed, can itself function in an archetypal way. Like many other symbols that draw our attention to commonality and shared value (such as God, the good, humanity, rationality), it functions schematically so as to inspire us over time to apply those values consistently. Archetypally, too, it can be projected, so that we start to assume that universality resides in the world itself rather than in our own application of consistent values. We can thus understand the universality of archetypes by adopting a practical standpoint on the meaning of universality in its functional impact on our judgement, as opposed to a merely abstract metaphysical one (see 2.c).

A wider and more adequate understanding of archetypes, leading on to a wider education in them, has the potential to harness peoples' attachment to archetypal symbols in a way that avoids merely projecting them onto culturally specific forms. Genuine and practical universality is the product of reflectiveness. That reflectiveness includes critical reflectiveness on the limitations of our identification with specific archetypal symbols, but that criticality alone is not sufficient. We also need a positive recognition of the vital function of archetypal symbols in fulfilling their central sustaining function.

1   Carozza (2003).

1.c. Archetypes as Embodied Schemas

I'm a fountain of blood. In the shape of a girl.
Björk

The embodied meaning theory of George Lakoff and Mark Johnson[1] is a formative influence on the perspective of this book, alongside that of Jung himself. That theory has offered a radically new and far more adequate understanding of meaning – and hence of many other concepts dependent on meaning – since the 1980s. Rather than thinking of meaning as dependent on a relationship with a hypothesized reality, and dividing it falsely between cognitive and emotive types, as mainstream Western thought has done, it begins with meaning as we experience it in our bodies and connects it to the process of learning. This also has huge implications for how we understand archetypes.

Embodied meaning is something that we develop by association, as we interact with our environment from early infancy.[2] As we do so, we associate those interactions with symbols, and so create new neural connections. If those neural connections get sufficiently reinforced, we will recall the symbol in relation to the experience, and the experience in relation to the symbol. That symbol, as already noted, could be any kind of object, but can also include visual representations, sounds, and of course language.[3]

Embodied meaning theory implies de-privileging language and showing that it does not have a unique representational relationship with reality, even if it is more complex in its functioning than other kinds of symbols. To do that it sets out to explain how even the most abstract and advanced language remains dependent on basic associations with embodied experiences. There are two main concepts it relies on to do this: *embodied schemas* and *metaphors*.

An embodied schema is a basic and early association between a type of embodied experience and a type of symbol. It is a root association that can then be elaborated so as to associate further experiences and symbols. It is not a specific symbol, but rather, one could say, a *symbolic function*. For instance, the container schema is a general association between the experience of containment and the

---

1 Detailed in e.g. Johnson (2007), Lakoff (1987), Lakoff and Johnson (1980), as well as other works by Lakoff and Johnson and their followers.
2 Johnson (2007) ch. 2.
3 Ibid. chs. 10, 11, 12.

most basic language of containment – for instance the preposition 'in'. The experience of containment might come very early from the experience of eating, when the food goes 'in' the body, but the concept is flexible enough to also be recognized when a cow is *in* a field or a brick is *in* a box. Indeed, the understanding of terms like 'field' and 'box' thus comes to depend on this schema. We see a 'field' or a 'box' as primarily a container that other things can be 'in'.

An embodied schema of this kind, interacting with many other such schemas, forms the basis of a wide variety of proliferating meaningful language through the development of metaphor. Once we have the idea of a 'field' as a container, for instance, we can then apply it to an academic 'field' by extension. The idea of movement into a container is also basic to our understanding of an abstract term like 'incorporation' – the etymology providing a clue to this, as it has developed from the idea of making something part of a body.

I have already argued that archetypes are the expressions of a relationship between an archetypal function and a specific symbol, so that the symbol is meaningful to us in a specific kind of way because of the archetypal function. It thus becomes evident that *archetypal functions are embodied schemas.* Just as the container schema provides a general association between a certain range of experiences and a certain range of symbols, so an archetypal function provides a general relationship between certain kinds of experiences and certain kinds of symbols that are associated with those experiences. The general, schematic relationship that creates the basis of an archetypal function does not involve specific symbols, as we would expect those to vary in different cultural circumstances. However, it does provide the *meaning* of the symbols as it impacts on our minds and bodies.

Let's take the example of the heroic function. If the heroic function is a type of embodied schema, its meaning arises from an association between a set of symbols on the one hand and, on the other, the experience of making plans and seeing them through to fulfil our goals in spite of obstacles. Whenever we encounter a specific symbol that we have associated with the heroic function, then, some of the same synaptic links will be activated as those involved in actually carrying out a plan despite obstacles. This is not just a short-term experience of effort, but an experience of reflectively maintaining an effort over a period of time, when the reminder of our purpose makes the crucial difference, as we would otherwise give up. So hero archetypes are not simply complex metaphors built up on a schema of associations with the experience of effort, but sets of associations that evoke the greater awareness required to *sustain* effort in the face of setbacks.

The archetypal function of the hero as a schema can then be associated with a wide variety of possible symbols. Most immediately this may be with a person (perhaps a parent) who shows this quality, or even with an idea of one's own past application of it ('I did it then, so I can do it again'). However, the heroic function has an especially potent relationship with storytelling, and it is likely to be associated with a variety of fictional, mythical, or historical characters who succeed against the odds from an early age, whether it's Odysseus, Frodo Baggins, or Robert the Bruce. The symbolic 'hero' could also be female, or even an animal. Storytelling is more potent than the mere evocation of the name of the hero, because it leads us to re-create that experience of struggle over time, together with the suspense of uncertain outcomes. Every time we experience symbolic re-creation of the heroic function, we re-create it *in our bodies* as an embodied schema. As we listen to the story of the hero's struggle, we go through a mild version of the physical states that the hero himself goes through as he struggles: the tensing of muscles for the threat, the surge of relief as it recedes, and the dopamine hit of reaching the goal.[4] As Ben Bergen argues, supported by neuroimaging studies, 'we understand language by simulating in our minds what it would be like to experience the things the language describes.'[5]

A similar account can be made of the other archetypal functions as embodied schemas. The shadow function is our instinctual response to threat, but developed for long-term purposes. To avoid a threat in a sustainable way, it's not only the ability to recognize it immediately and go into fight-or-flight mode that we need. We also need a longer-term awareness of the kinds of phenomena that might be associated with threat[6] – whether it's the pawprints of a big carnivore, or the signs of dangerous insecurity in a partner. For this we need to be able to link the *meaning* of these threats with the right sorts of symbols – not always exactly the same symbols, but a field of symbols. As our fellow humans have become far more of

---

4   See Hyden (2013) on the role of the body in narrative.
5   Bergen (2012) p. 13, quoted by Johnson (2017) p. 25.
6   Schlund et al. (2013).

a threat to us than wild animals, our shadow symbols have gradually become more closely associated with signs of long-term human unreliability such as cruelty, rigidity, and obsessiveness, in addition to signs of more immediate threat.

The anima/animus function is an attraction to something other than us that may be beneficial – often though not always by offering sexual and reproductive possibilities. The function is, again, not merely an immediate sexual response to a sexual stimulus, but rather a longer-term association between a set of 'attractive other' meanings (with their capacity to gain our attention) and particular kinds of symbols that can remind us of the attractive other. Such a symbol is not even necessarily an icon, but perhaps even an oblique reminder – a comb or a stream. Our capacity to *symbolize* the attractive other in relation to more subtle kinds of arousal than the obviously sexual can be understood in terms of the *sublimation* of sexual energies.[7] Sublimation channels energy that may initially be seen as sexual towards non-sexual channels: a process that has been evidenced, for instance, in relation to creativity.[8] A sublimated energy will obviously be directed towards a symbolic object that is not simply a sexual stimulant, but rather a longer-term and more subtle anchor for emotional responses.

Finally, the God function relates to our long-term symbolization of open potentialities. We may have more or less profound experiences of such potentiality through 'flow' states, mindful states, and even ecstatic religious experience accompanied by stimulation of the temporal lobe (see 4.f). However, these experiences of greater potentiality are rarely sustained for very long, because they are dependent on particular changing conditions in the brain. The God function is a set of meanings that we can associate with these sorts of experience and their accompanying access of meaningfulness, deep security, creativity, and insight. In general, this set of meanings becomes associated with a set of symbols – some of which involve 'God' in an explicit sense, but others of which, depending on the cultural context, may involve the symbolism of enlightenment, of mysticism, of artistic profundity, and of empowerment. The use of the term 'God' here does not in any way require that symbolism of God as such is necessarily associated with the God function, any

---

7   The mention of sublimation here does *not* imply a Freudian theoretical framework in which all energies are necessarily seen as sexual.
8   Adair and Shimkunas (1973).

more than any other specific symbol *must* be used in relation to any other embodied schema. 'God' is the dominant symbol associated with this function in a pre-modern Western and Middle Eastern context, but the God function is merely a label for a field of meaning that could also be associated with entirely 'secular' symbols.

The element of reflectiveness and sustainability between these four archetypal functions also makes them cumulative, in the sense that the God function can incorporate the others. As we become more reflective, open, and long-term in our thinking through the use of archetypal symbols for the hero, shadow, and anima/animus functions, these functions may increasingly come to be associated with a wider potentiality. The longer-term and the more enlightened our plans become, the more open does our understanding of their fulfilment need to be – so the heroic function gradually develops into the God function. The more subtly we come to recognize potential threats, the more we are likely to realize their complexity and the ways that they are interdependent with us, leading us to see potentiality even in our sources of anxiety. The more sophisticated and sublimated our relationship with objects of attraction becomes, the more we are likely to understand the ways that they elude our possession, and the more likely we are to find an open potentiality in that relationship rather than only a craving.

It is understanding the God function in this way, as continuously connected to our most basic embodied experience, yet also marking an increasing openness and reflectiveness in relation to that experience, that seems to me to be the basis of the way that we can depolarize our relationship to religious symbols. To be reminded of that, we need to be able to move up and down a column of reflectiveness between our most basic embodied experiences on the one hand – even those of fear and lust – and our most refined and abstracted symbols on the other. This idea is reflected in Buddhist tradition in the idea that the lotus, blooming with its purity of colour, nevertheless has its roots in the mud. If we study symbols whilst forgetting their embodied schemas, our understanding of human meaning will lack roots.

1.d. Archetypes as Metaphors

You must be rich with metaphors,
Like an ore of gold waiting to be mined,
If you are to digest my words
When they're fresh.
                Jalal Ad-din Rumi, Divan 981

If archetypal functions are embodied schemas, the other side of the archetype – that is, the specific symbolic form taken by an archetype in a given case – must be metaphorical. In this, I draw heavily on the account of metaphor developed by Lakoff and Johnson,[1] which I am simply applying to archetypes. In their account, most language, not just certain selected 'literary' language, is metaphorical, because it depends on an associative parallel between an embodied schema and some other context. As we have already seen, an academic field, or a process of incorporation, or any of a great many other metaphors that rely on the container schema, *is like* that basic container schema. It is only for that reason that we can relate more abstract conceptual language by association to embodied experience. It is only by making some sort of link from embodied experience to symbol, however abstract the symbol, that we 'understand' it.

Metaphor, then, should not be contrasted with 'literal' language. The whole idea of literalness is misplaced, because it depends on there being a direct representational relationship between language and a state of affairs that it refers to. This involves a basic misunderstanding of the operation of meaning in the body, ignoring the way in which meaning requires processing through the body and brain as a whole, and instead focusing only on the type of meaning associated with the 'linguistic' area of the left pre-frontal cortex (known as Broca's Region). It is this area that matches meaning with states of affairs that we believe to be true, assuming that the meaningfulness of the language is dependent on its relationship with these states of affairs. This area of the brain tends to assume its autonomy, believing that the meaning it processes has somehow been directly created from the world.[2] However, this ignores the ways that meaning relies on sensual experiences, schematic bodily responses to those experiences, and the development of those responses through metaphor.

1   Lakoff and Johnson (1980).
2   McGilchrist (2009) pp. 49–51.

All of this is reliant on the right hemisphere and the wider neural system rather than only the left pre-frontal cortex. In this 'literalist' tradition, even metaphor itself is understood in a way that is subservient to this dominant model, being assumed to be an elaboration of 'literal' (i.e. representational) language.[3]

Metaphor is, instead, the unacknowledged way in which most of our language is made meaningful, even the 'literal' language. A sentence like 'the meeting went on until 8 pm' sounds 'literal' enough, but 'literally' the meeting did not go on anywhere – the idea of 'going on' in space is applied metaphorically to time, with a later time being further along the spatial route. We are able to understand the progression of time in the meeting by relating it to our schema of moving along a path through space. As Lakoff and Johnson document, much of our language is made up of such metaphors, even though we are no longer aware of them – they are thus 'dead' metaphors embedded in a cultural context.[4] A typical 'literal' statement is simply a dead metaphorical statement, in which etymological analysis can reveal successive layers of metaphorical relationship. Even the word 'metaphor', for instance, is itself revealed by etymology to be metaphorical, coming from the Greek to 'carry across'. The deadness of a metaphor means that we only primarily process it through our left pre-frontal cortex as part of an assumed representation, but that representation only remains meaningful in dependence on successive layers of association in the rest of the brain.[5]

These points about metaphor are essential for understanding the relationship between archetypal function and specific archetypal symbols. That relationship has been frequently misunderstood, because archetypes have been treated as representations of some kind – only perhaps a kind of variant representation that reflected 'the unconscious' rather than the rest of the world. This is just as misleading as a way of understanding archetypes as it is to see metaphors as optional elaborations on 'literal' language. Instead, we need to recognize that archetypal symbols operate as metaphorical expressions of archetypal functions – that is, they offer ways of re-enacting a set of associations that evoke those functions for us. The

---

3   E.g. Sperber and Wilson (2008).
4   Lakoff and Johnson (1980) ch. 5.
5   McGilchrist (2009) pp. 115 ff.

difference between archetypes and other metaphors, though, is the reflective long-term nature of the functions they serve.

This might become clearer if we compare the archetypal function of the hero to the specific forms the hero might take. The hero takes a particular form depending on the cultural context, but expresses the heroic function regardless of that context. In a dominant culture, for instance, the hero is more likely to be an establishment figure (say a king), but in an oppressed culture, he or she is more likely to take the form of a trickster figure who breaks the rules. In English legend, the heroism of Henry V, hero of wars against the French, represents the confidence of medieval Anglo-Norman culture at a point of success against the rival French. A couple of centuries earlier, though, Robin Hood is a trickster figure who breaks the rules, showing continued Anglo-Saxon resistance against Norman dominance. Either Henry V or Robin Hood can equally be a metaphor for the heroic function, reinforcing our awareness of the need for sustained perseverance and reflection to achieve long-term goals.

In the same way, the quests of both of these figures are metaphorical extensions of the embodied schema known as source-path-goal. We have a basic experience of following a path towards a specific physical goal, and extend this metaphorically in all sorts of ways. A quest is a path, through both space and time, in which the goal is something more complex than just a particular point in space, but nevertheless we understand its meaning through an association with the process of moving on a path through space. For Henry V, the quest was to conquer France, whilst for Robin Hood, it was to bring justice to the poor. Without the quest, there could be no hero, so one metaphorical structure builds on another – however, the archetypal function depends for its meaning not just on the source-path-goal schema, but also on the experience of reflectiveness in relation to that schema that allows us to maintain a sense of it over time.

Just as metaphors die when they are habitualized and 'literalized' by the left hemisphere,[6] so can archetypes. Even when 'dead' they are still present, in the sense that we can only understand them through implicit previous layers of metaphorical extension from embodied meaning. They do not cease to be archetypes, but they no longer offer the wider awareness with which the archetypal

6   Mashal et al. (2007).

function was previously associated. Instead, this awareness is substituted by a symbol that has been flattened into a sign. We hear the story of the hero, but are no longer aware of its relationship with our own experience. So we demote it to a marginal role, and give it whatever reduced function we can think of – perhaps just telling the stories of the hero to children for no better reason than that we want to keep them amused. This deadening of the archetype is associated with its projection, because the archetype has not disappeared: I just start to relate to it only in some context that is separated from my experience of long-term motivation. I may believe, unrealistically, that I can keep a risky business going, or that a politician will make my nation great again, but I am no longer sufficiently in touch with the experience of the hero to reflect on the fuller range of difficulties confronting him. My heroic confidence then becomes brittle, sentimental, decontextualized, and under-informed.

Once again, the same pattern can be applied to the other three archetypal functions. They can be expressed in different ways as metaphors of an embodied schema. Just like such metaphors, they become dead as they are projected. This means that the sources of meaning that they rely on are no longer acknowledged, and only the connections with a representational context are understood.

In the case of the shadow function, a wide variety of symbolic forms can be associated with our long-term awareness of what we need to avoid, from Satan to a noisy next-door neighbour. While that archetype remains 'live', and we remain aware of its connection to our own experience, some wider perspective will remain on that negativity, and we will at least recognize that it is for a specific purpose. If the noisy neighbour ceases her noise, we may be able to resume friendly feelings towards her. Once the shadow archetype becomes part of a settled representational system, though, there is no longer any check on the cyclic proliferations of hatred. The archetype becomes dead, because we will only see it as part of a representation of fixed state of affairs. Rather than a symbol of the suffering we want to avoid, we are likely to instal Satan as a fixed supernatural agency of pure evil, with which we identify other hated objects. We are then likely to become concerned with the 'existence' of Satan, making him a matter of belief rather than only of meaning, and this habit of 'belief' may become culturally entrenched as the default for a group. As a meaningful archetype, he is valuable because we are able to put him in a wider context in which no evil is pure – but as an entity that is the object of belief, he becomes an excuse for simplistic demonic projections and thus a recipe for conflict.

In the case of the anima/animus function, a wide variety of forms can represent our long-term awareness of the attractive other, most but not all of them recognizably sexual sublimations. A feminine anima figure (primarily for men), for instance, may take the form of a mermaid, a nixie, a fairy, a mother, a child, or perhaps just an enticing landscape. In all of these, it is the deep otherness combined with a deep attraction that takes it beyond the level of a simple and immediate sexual response, leading to a search for qualities like nurturance, innocence, playfulness, and beauty that sublimate that sexuality. All of these can thus be seen as specific cultural or personal metaphorical expressions of the anima function. The metaphors remain alive as long as we remain aware of their relationship to our own experience. This awareness that may be prompted by the changeability of these objects of fascination, or by them showing other, more masculine qualities that do not fit the archetypal function. The dead metaphor, however, is a projected archetype, in which, for instance, a man insists on seeing only his anima in a woman, repressing all alternative possibilities. The projected anima is then just part of a represented state of affairs protected by an intractable confirmation bias. Again, an archetype that could be highly meaningful is deadened when it becomes an object of belief rather than simply a meaning.

In the case of the God function, the metaphorical forms can most obviously take the form of God, but may also be associated with ideals of enlightenment, truth, nature, empowerment, integration, total love, or total wisdom. Here there are very obviously deep cultural differences between the ways the God function has been interpreted in the monotheistic religions, in the non-monotheistic Chinese and Indian traditions, in the pre-monotheistic pagan context of Greek and Roman civilization, and in the modern post-monotheistic context. But there are also personal differences in the metaphors we are likely to favour and adopt, dependent on the potentialities that matter most to us. Is it God the father, the pursuit of truth, the ideal society, integration of humans with nature, the wise old man or woman, or the integrated psychic state symbolized by the mandala? These metaphors remain live as long as they are connected to our own spiritual development, so we are engaging with new potentialities and adjusting our responses in relation to them. However, they die when they are projected into a state of affairs in which God, truth, nature etc. becomes an entity with a particular metaphysical status. This metaphysical status can also operate just as strongly in theoretical denial. The atheist ignores the meaningfulness of God, and also confirms the deadness of the metaphor through which he is seeing her, in his haste to deny God's 'existence'. Denying God's existence no more removes the God function than denying Robin Hood's heroic status removes the heroic function, or denying the attractions of Marilyn Monroe removes the anima function.

Putting together Jung's insights with those of Lakoff and Johnson gives us an extremely powerful model for reconsidering the deadening assumptions through which not only religion, but much of the whole of the rest of human culture, have been interpreted. Religious archetypes are not 'just' metaphors, when we understand the power and significance of the schemas *of which* they are metaphors. Our understanding of neuroscience can also play a role in helping us understand the nature of 'dead' metaphors and the relationship between these and projected archetypes. Such liberating synthesis is long overdue as the standpoint from which we can start to see religion in its full power as meaning, rather than in its deluded form as projected belief.

1.e. The Baggage of the 'Collective Unconscious'

My guess is that Jung would not have wanted a legacy of a group of followers who look upon his theories with reverence rather than with a critical eye. Jung was well aware of the intellectual atrophy that developed in psychoanalysis because of this problem.
Andrew Neher, 'Jung's Theory of Archetypes: A critique'

This chapter and the following one are solely concerned with addressing traditional Jungian ways of discussing archetypes to show why they are unnecessary. If you are only interested in the positive theory in this book rather than its relationship to Jungian ideas, you might prefer to skip them.

The belief that the archetypes are definitively 'archetypes of the collective unconscious' is the legacy of Jung's formulation. In his formulation, the unconscious parts of the psyche are divided into two parts: the personal unconscious, containing 'forgotten or repressed' contents that were formerly conscious, and the collective unconscious, which is inherited.[1] Archetypes then amount to 'definite forms of the psyche which seem to be present always and everywhere'.[2]

In my view this formulation is one that is both unnecessary and problematic. Both elements of the term 'collective unconscious' can be dispensed with and yet we can still have an account of archetypes with the same, or better, practical justification and purpose. It needs neither to be 'collective', nor to be 'unconscious'. That's not because these terms didn't originally have some justification, but that this justification can be fulfilled much more effectively by alternative formulations. Jung's formulation violates a principle of theoretical economy: do not posit more theoretical entities than are necessary to specify the helpful theoretical structures that are needed.

The most important part of this Jungian formulation is the idea of archetypes being a product of the 'unconscious' – a central concept for the psychoanalytic movement. As a concept, however, it was only made necessary in the first place by the overwhelmingly Cartesian assumptions with which post-enlightenment Westerners have tended to view the mind. For Descartes, 'the mind' is defined as something we are clearly conscious of, with an accompanying

1   Jung (1959a) §88.
2   Ibid. §89.

assumption that the distinction between conscious and unconscious is binary and absolute.[3] A thought, a feeling, or a sensation is 'conscious' *if we are aware of it*, and what we are not aware of is 'unconscious'. This binary distinction created the conditions for another common fallacy: that what we are clearly aware of must be true. Freud and Jung stretched this model only by insisting that 'the mind' also contained another element, the 'unconscious', which took a mental form but could not be examined directly whilst it remained unconscious. In Jung's approach this 'unconscious' is 'psychic', rather than merely part of the wider physical world, *because* it is capable of being examined in conscious awareness at some point.

This model has always been a simplistic one, artificially imposed on our experience of consciousness. One experience that is likely to challenge it for an increasing number of people in modern society is that of meditation. In meditation you learn how scattered your awareness habitually is: that you can be 'conscious' of both your mental states and your goals at one moment, but the next unexpectedly realize that this consciousness has been overthrown, and that you have been carried away on a train of thoughts and feelings quite separate from this intention. This underlines the ways that Descartes' way of thinking was simply not diachronic enough, not taking into account the variations in our mental states over even a very short period of time. Am I simply flipping between 'conscious' and 'unconscious' states over this short, distractable period of time? No – it is more that in some respects I remain 'conscious' and in others 'unconscious', and my *desire* to label it all as 'conscious' is the result of the wishful thinking of the part of myself (commonly called the ego) that thinks of itself as fixed and stable.

As in many other areas, 'consciousness' is a matter of degree, but has been unhelpfully seen in terms of a binary absolute to serve egoistic purposes. Rather than a searchlight, consciousness is more of an *edge* of awareness passing through time. The edge has no thickness because it is an aspect of an experience of awareness that is always *of something*. Although the concepts we use to talk about the objects we are aware of seem definite and stable, the actual aesthetic experience of being aware of them, either through our senses or internally, is more that of moving over an ever-changing texture. We can experience that particularly in the process of meditation,

---

3   Descartes (1968) *Meditation 2.*

because it tends to take as an object of attention something that is aesthetic or experiential rather than conceptual: the breath, a flame, the sounds of certain words, an emotional state. We cannot hold that experience still: rather the experience of the object *moves through* the shifting edge of consciousness.

Some neuroscientists have argued for a distinction between consciousness and attention, but the need to make this distinction appears to be due to an incremental model being used for attention whilst a non-incremental model is used for consciousness. For example, things that we glimpse for less than 120 milliseconds, or that form an afterimage, may grab our attention, even though we are 'unconscious' of our attention being directed.[4] If we adopt an incremental model of consciousness that also encompasses attention, however, we can alternatively describe this as an example of becoming conscious of an object *to some degree*, in some respects and not others.

The things that 'I am conscious of' take only an edge rather than a period of time as the object of consciousness. I might also claim to be conscious of what I have just experienced, or of the whole object that I am considering, or even the whole situation. If I am sitting in meditation, I might also be 'conscious' of the distraction that I just overcame, of the intentions of the practice, and of the position of my body as I sit – but only in the sense that I could recall them if I wished. Other things that I might claim to be 'conscious' of could readily be accessed: I might immediately be able to tell you where my keys are, where I parked my car 20 minutes ago, or what the capital of Germany is (if I have not 'forgotten' these things). But if being 'conscious' just means having the capacity to recall something, it is a much weaker requirement than actually experiencing it at this moment. What, then, about the things I could recall with an effort, or would fail to recall if asked, but might suddenly recall unprompted then minutes later? Are these 'unconscious', or are they just less conscious?

So, if I am surprised in the way that psychoanalysis describes, for example by a dream, is the dream 'unconscious'? No, for as soon as I talk about it, it is 'conscious' – and then it fades again, unless I write it down to reinforce it. Dreams can certainly be illuminating, but only because they remind us of longer-term material of which

---

4   Koch and Tsuchiya (2007).

we are less aware. They arise from the depths of the less conscious, and from the processes of our bodies: the complex synaptic links of our brains and nervous systems, influenced in turn by all the other processes in our bodies.

So, 'unconscious' is a very unsatisfactory term for the phenomena that Jung wanted to draw our attention to. The things he wanted to draw our attention to were valuable, but the conceptual equipment was deficient. To begin with, it uses a binary term for phenomena that are incremental. Secondly, it attributes to the 'mind' phenomena that are just as much aspects of the 'body'. The Cartesian legacy leaves us flailing around in binary assumptions about the mind and the body, with absolutizations of the conscious mind on the one hand and reductivist absolutizations of the body as explaining everything 'physically' on the other.

However, what we *need* to be able to talk about are not minds or bodies, consciousness or unconsciousness, but *degrees of awareness* in a context that is based in the conditioning effects of the body. We can also become *more aware* not just through intensity of awareness, but also through extending that awareness over time. This is reflected in the practical usefulness of two Buddhist terms for 'mindfulness': *sati* and *sampajana*. *Sati* is awareness at one time and *sampajana* is awareness over time.[5] Both are a matter of degree, not a matter of being 'conscious' or 'unconscious'.

This takes us to the question of what Jung meant by the 'collective' unconscious. As already mentioned, he distinguished this from the 'personal' unconscious because he thought of it as not dependent on personal experience, but rather on innate features of human genetic inheritance. Since the time he was writing, however, the scientific perspective on genetic inheritance has moved on considerably, with many phenomena recognized as epigenetic – i.e. due to stable non-genetic conditions that lead some genes to be expressed rather than others, not genes alone.[6] Andrew Neher also points out that even in Darwinian terms, genetic modification involves constant variation, but the theory of the collective unconscious does not take this into account.[7] The boundary between 'nature' and 'nurture', always a false dichotomy, has thus become even more blurred than it was.

---

5   On this account of *sampajana* see Sangharakshita (2003) pp. 13 ff and Lomas (2016).
6   See Goldberg et al. (2007).
7   Neher (1996).

Epigenetic features may be much more limited in their distribution than genetic ones, not being a necessary part of human status, but nevertheless part of one's basic constitution rather than one's personal experience. They may be shared with all humans, or only a few humans. If 'collective unconscious' means 'genetic inheritance', then, we can no longer be sure of such a distinction, if we ever could.

Jung's claims about the 'collective unconscious' as an origin for archetypes are thus speculative, out-of-date, and uninformative. They are also irrelevant to the practical application of the concept of archetype. In order to apply the concept of an archetype, we need to identify what the archetype *does* rather than what it ultimately *is* or what its origins are. The question of what an archetype ultimately *is* may be a fruitless metaphysical one. Understanding of their origins may help us in understanding archetypal phenomena up to a point, but only before the potential answers become speculative. Most likely any answers will be more complex than we think, and may involve a mixture of genetic, epigenetic, and non-genetic factors.

If we think, instead, about the phenomenal experiences that are addressed by the ideas of the unconscious and of collectivity, these are experiences of diachronic meaning. An 'unconscious' process is not one that we are *never* aware of, but rather one that we become aware of at one point that we also take to have been influencing us at others. Its practical value comes from the extent to which we can become more fully aware of it and acknowledge it. The deeper an archetypal experience lies, the more likely it is that we will have to use special techniques or practices (such as therapeutic dialogue, dream interpretation, or free association) to become more aware of it. However, these techniques do not reveal a wholly unconscious archetype and make it wholly conscious: rather they help us to trace the importance of the archetype to us, the forms it takes, and its degree of projection.

The experiences that lie behind the idea of the collectivity of the archetypes are ones either of symbolic similarity or of similarity of function. At the most superficial level, this will involve a direct commonality of symbols: if two middle-aged men both dream about alluring nymph-figures, for example, it is not difficult to judge where the commonality lies. Where the symbols differ, however, it also involves our experiences of commonality of function: for instance, a Christian and a Muslim may at first assume that they worship different gods with different names, until they examine more closely the similarity of role that God plays in each of their lives. No top-down deduction of absolute commonality from a certified innate universal is needed to find such commonality, because its practical benefit comes from the extent to which we can actually discover it in experience. We discover it, not just in direct talk with others, but also through experiencing that commonality of function at the level of story, at the level of mythological systems, or even at the level of anthropological theory. If at any point the common function is no longer evident, it ceases to have a practical effect so is no longer relevant. However, the paths of humans in different cultures evidently lie together a long way, when understood in functional terms.

Rather than adopting a top-down approach to archetypes by assuming that they are innately present in the 'collective unconscious', then, I suggest that we need to take them as theory of a kind that can helpfully structure our experiential interpretation. If we define archetypes as diachronic schematic functions, the diachronicity fulfils the helpful aspects of what Jung meant by 'unconscious', and the schematism the helpful aspects of what he meant by 'collective'. We then need to look, in the case of each archetype, at the specific ways that they help to stimulate our awareness over time, and at the ways that the schema concerned sets up a basis of meaning in relation to our embodied experience. For example, the hero archetype functions by stimulating our awareness of the sustained effort required to complete a task over time, and depends on the schematic experience of effort. Effort involves changes in our whole bodies such as tensing of muscles and mobilization of the nervous system. This way of structuring our understanding is not unique to the kind of archetypal theory I am proposing, but can be shared and developed by embodied meaning theory, neuroscientific theory, and cognitive psychological theory. Jung used the resources of his own time to try to provide a theoretical account of archetypes, but these badly need an update. The theoretical structure should be subsidiary to the practical end that it serves – that of integrating archetypal phenomena and thus improving our judgement in relation to them.

1.f. The Baggage of Platonism

It is important to appreciate that there are two Jungs – the one with an open epistemology and Socratic ignorance, and the other Jung who, following Gnostic epistemology, was, in fact, essentialist and universalist.
  Renos Papadopoulos, 'Jung's epistemology and methodology'

'"Archetype,"' Jung tells us, 'is an explanatory paraphrase of the Platonic εἶδος', which he identifies with 'images that have existed since the remotest times'.[1] Plato's term εἶδος is usually now translated as 'Form', and refers to an essential meaning for a term – one of an entirely abstract, metaphysical kind, distinct from all specific instances. For example, the Form of the man is the ideal man, free of the contingent imperfections of actual specific men, but providing the basis on which specific men can be identified as such. The relationship between this idea of Platonic Form and archetypes is far from clear: as one commentator puts it 'archetypes are not easily recognizable in the Platonic corpus in the way in which Jung meant them'.[2] Perhaps the clearest academic analyst of this issue, Jean Knox,[3] makes a good case that this is a matter of distinct ideas being unhelpfully conflated in Jung's mind. If we try to isolate the function that this Platonic element plays, however, it turns out to be that of universality: one that can be much better fulfilled in other ways.

The biggest and most obvious problem with the idea of an archetype as an essential meaning is that it involves thinking of the archetype in terms of its explicit represented form, rather than in terms of the function behind that form. An essential meaning of the kind Plato seems to have been discussing in the idea of 'Form' is explicit and conscious, being reached through a process of definition and analysis that culminates in an entirely rationalized dialectic. The education of Plato's idealized philosopher-kings involves training in five mathematical disciplines as the foundation for the dialectic through which the Forms can be grasped, all of which ignores the question of how these disciplines actually function, and focuses on rational abstraction, on the assumption that this will necessarily help to resolve conflicts in beliefs.[4] The essentialism that Plato assumes is

1   Jung (1959a) §5.
2   Nagy (1991) p. 157.
3   Knox (2003) pp. 23 ff.
4   Plato (1987) §521c–534e.

also linguistically naïve when compared even to later forms of representationalism, such as nominalism, let alone to embodied meaning: a word does not have an 'essential' meaning, but rather the meaning we give it in a particular circumstance.

When seen in relation to embodied meaning, the error can be seen even more clearly as that of assuming that meaning is found in the relationship between linguistic forms and some form of actual or hypothetical reality, rather than in embodied experience. In a masterly deconstruction, Lakoff and Johnson show how Plato's essentialism is made to look plausible through a series of metaphors: that ideas are objects, that knowing is seeing, that essences are ideals, and that degrees of knowledge are degrees of being.[5] Jung is not the first or the only thinker to be seduced by this rationalized Platonic structure into the belief that the Forms have some underlying relationship to experience, but both he and others fail to recognize that Plato's approach involves a constant attempt to transcend the world of experience by absolutizing the independent dominance of left-hemisphere dominated abstract representation.[6] Far from representing the power of the 'unconscious' to shape our experience, the Forms indicate the apotheosis of deluded conscious reasoning, falsely separated from all the gestalt experiences that provide us with wider awareness.

Jung seems to have been attracted by the idea not only that archetypes are essences of conscious meaning, but also that they were simultaneously metaphysical, existing in some timeless form beyond their specific manifestations in time. In this he was influenced by Schopenhauer as well as by Plato, with both having an idealist belief that timeless immaterial principles are somehow responsible for events in time.[7] Jung's ideas about synchronicity are used to support this, interpreting coincidences in experience as an indication of metaphysical organizing principles in the universe that are only accessible to the unconscious. Knox points out the important flaw in this approach:

His view was partly based on a misunderstanding of mathematical probabilities; he failed to appreciate that our sense that coincidences are meaningful is an illusion produced by the fact that non-conscious attention highlights certain chance

5   Lakoff and Johnson (1999) pp. 364–72.
6   McGilchrist (2009) pp. 285–9.
7   Nagy (1991) p. 165; Knox (2003) p. 34.

occurrences precisely because they are meaningful to us. Statistically these coincidences have no significance, but humans do seem to have a poor intuitive sense of probabilities, with a marked tendency to underestimate the likelihood that two events will occur together by chance.[8]

The assumption that coincidences are the result of underlying metaphysical principles is, indeed a betrayal of Jung's insights in his theory of archetypes, because it involves a projection of power and reason from our own archetypal God function onto the universe itself. Projection occurs whenever we believe that our own archetypal functions are occurring independently of us, and this whole line of Jungian thinking is a projection in this sense.

Jung's attraction to Platonism is also probably evident in his attraction to Gnosticism, with these two related traditions sharing the idea of hierarchies of essential being. Jung's use of Gnosticism is extensive in the *Seven Sermons to the Dead* that are included in the *Red Book*,[9] and elsewhere I have discussed the conflicts this shows in Jung's philosophical approaches.[10]

Whether the Platonic understanding of archetypes is interpreted as essential meaning or as an independent metaphysical principle, this is entirely inconsistent with the idea of an archetype either as a biological principle or as schematic framework, as Knox points out.[11] However, none of these four versions of the Jungian archetype focuses sufficiently on the *practical* role of the archetype and how it functions. If Jung had subjected his Platonic interpretations to any kind of functional analysis, it would surely have become clear to him that they are, at best, irrelevant for understanding the role of archetypes, and at worst, a major distraction (as they have proved for many Jungians). Metaphysical constructions are projections maintained by speculation and dogma (see 2.c), and linguistic essentialism is a tool of power that is frequently used to try to rigidify a debate into binary terms according to the bias of those who seek to control it (e.g. either you're a 'true Christian', according to an essential definition, or you're not).

To think more positively about what attracted Jung to Platonic interpretation, however, it might help to review its appeal in the Socratic dialogues. Plato's dialogues are built initially on the

8   Knox (2003) p. 36.
9   Jung (2009) pp. 346 ff.
10 Ellis (2020) ch. 11.
11 Knox (2003) pp. 23-37.

teachings of his teacher Socrates, who is scarcely recorded elsewhere, and gradually diverge from them until Socrates becomes merely a mouthpiece for Plato's doctrines. Strangely enough, the Forms emerge gradually from the early Socratic insistence on the value of defining our terms, and indeed, critically examining our assumptions about essential meanings. The following passage from 'Euthyphro' can illustrate the point. Socrates has met Euthyphro, whom he is astonished to find is prosecuting his own father for manslaughter on the grounds that it is 'holy'. Euthyphro is rather over-confident about his knowledge of what is holy, and Socrates seeks to subject this to critical examination:

> SOCRATES: .... Euthyphro, you think that you have such an accurate knowledge of things divine, and what is holy and unholy.
> EUTHYPHRO: Why Socrates, if I did not have an accurate knowledge of all that, I should be good for nothing....
> SOCRATES: Then tell me. How do you define the holy and the unholy...?
> EUTHYPHRO: Well then, I say the holy is what I am now doing, prosecuting the wrongdoer who commits a murder or a sacrilegious robbery, or sins in any point like that, whether it be your father or your mother, or whoever it may be. And not to prosecute would be unholy....
> SOCRATES: ... At present try to tell me more clearly what I asked you a little while ago, for, my friend, you were not explicit enough before when I put the question 'What is holiness?' You merely said that what you are now doing is a holy deed, namely, prosecuting your father on a charge of murder.
> EUTHYPHRO: And Socrates, I told the truth.
> SOCRATES: Possibly. But, Euthyphro, there are many other things you will say are holy.
> EUTHYPHRO: Because they are.
> SOCRATES: Well, bear in mind what I asked of you was not to tell me one or two out of all the numerous actions that are holy; I wanted you to tell me what is the essential form of holiness which makes all holy actions holy. I believe you held there is one ideal form by which unholy things are all unholy, and by which all holy things are holy. Do you remember that?
> EUTHYPHRO: I do.
> SOCRATES: Well then, show me what, precisely, this ideal is, so that, with my eye on it, and using it as standard, I can say that any action done by you or anybody else is holy if it resembles this ideal, or, if it does not, can deny that it is holy.[12]

Socrates is asking here *what the essential form of holiness is*, but it is not he, but Euthyphro, who claims to know what that essential form

12 Plato (1961) 'Euthyphro' 4e–6e.

is. Socrates is actually going through a process of making Euthyphro aware that what he thought was a universal meaning for holiness is actually a more particular one, by testing it against the standards of universality. Socrates here does not claim to know what that universal standard is, but merely acts sceptically to deflate people's assumptions about what it is. Thus, the universality of holiness acts as a notional measure (what Kant would call a 'regulatory idea') that provides a standard by which we can recognize its absence in any specific case.

The gradual process by which this merely sceptical perspective of Socrates changes into a dogmatic essentialism and metaphysical absolutism is not one that I will chart further here, though I have written about it elsewhere,[13] and it has also been discussed by others.[14] The key point is that an aspiration for universality is required for a critical perspective on particularity. It is also too seldom remarked that the process of mistaking the particularity of one's own beliefs for a universal truth is the familiar Jungian one of projection (discussed further in section 2). The rationalist tradition that Plato began turns this projection into a supposed metaphysical truth by attributing it to the universe as a whole. Jung was evidently taken in by this projective tradition, perhaps because it was so imbued in the idealist philosophy he admired as a young man. However, the function of the archetypes that Jung identified, prior to that projective process, is much better illustrated by the early, sceptical Socrates we have seen illustrated above than by the later, dogmatic one that Plato constructed as his mouthpiece.

The holiness that Euthyphro feels so strongly about is an archetype – I would suggest, a version of the God archetypal function. In section 6 of this book I will be exploring the impersonal, 'secularized' forms that the God archetype can take at times, 'Holiness' being but one of these along with other universal abstractions such as Nature, Truth, and Rationality. Euthyphro insists on projecting that archetype as being an essential truth of the universe that he is merely obeying by prosecuting his father, but recognized prior to that projection it is, instead, a meaningful symbol expressing a diachronic schematic function. Euthyphro remains inspired by that archetype, but since it has probably taken various symbolic forms in

13 See Ellis (2001a) 3.d; Ellis (2001b).
14 E.g. Soloviev (1935).

his experience, it is not very surprising that he struggles to 'define' it convincingly. Socrates, in his irritating role as gadfly philosopher, requires that definition of his victims even though he cannot offer one himself. However, we could also see him in the role of therapist: by questioning Euthyphro he seeks to relieve him of his inflated projection (though, in the text, he does not succeed).

As I argued above in 1.b, archetypal functions need this universality. Plato was the first major figure in the Greek tradition to argue systematically for such universality, and it is quite likely that the Forms did have archetypal value for Plato. However, the subsequent role of Plato has been as a source of rationalizing projection in Western thought, and Jung seems to have been subject to that too. It may be helpful when thinking about the significance of archetypes to recall their Socratic roots in the universalizing demand, but not to project that universalization into a Platonic metaphysics, as Jung ended up doing. The Platonic legacy is overwhelmingly unnecessary baggage, but perhaps the Socratic legacy that precedes it is not.

1.g. Archetypes and Religion

The opposite of faith is not doubt, but certainty. Certainty is missing the point entirely.
                    Anne Lamott, *Plan B: Further Thoughts on Faith*

The archetypes potentially provide us with a new practical understanding of religion: one that is not based on 'beliefs' but rather on a widespread human search for meaning. In an age where ever-increasing numbers of people simply find religion irrelevant because they assume it is a matter of 'belief', and where those who are still attached to religion use it to justify intractable dogma and conflict, this perspective is of immense relevance. Religion is a dimension of human experience, and cannot be so easily cast aside, but without the successful popularization of a more helpful understanding of it, it often remains destructive and regressive.

Jung talked of a 'religious function' in human experience, and made a vital contribution to opening up the possibility of an archetypal account of religion, but his insistence on the baggage discussed in the last two chapters has become part of the problem. The 'collective unconscious' is an object of suspicion for theologians and scientific naturalists alike, whilst Platonism takes us straight back into the realm of absolute belief. In the place of this vocabulary I want to propose an understanding of religion in accordance with the *functions* of the archetypes. Fortunately, some of Jung's ways of talking about the archetypes do emphasize these functions. The key Jungian feature of religion is defined by Frieda Fordham as 'to give conscious expression to the archetypes'.[1] This understanding of religion can also be amplified by Jung's attempt to define it:

> *A peculiar attitude of mind which could be formulated in accordance with the original use of the word 'religio', which means a careful consideration and observation of certain dynamic factors, that are conceived as 'powers'; spirits, demons, gods, laws, ideals, or whatever name man has given to such factors in his world as he has found powerful, dangerous or helpful enough to be taken into careful consideration, or grand, beautiful and meaningful enough to be devoutly worshipped and loved.*[2]

Jung here goes well beyond merely *expressing* the archetypes. The 'careful consideration and observation of dynamic factors' suggests

---

1   Fordham (1959) p. 71.
2   Jung (1958) § 8.

that religion draws our attention to underlying factors in a process of change. The 'powers', however, are aspects of our own power – as long as we do not project them as other.

So, I want to propose a clarification of Jung's rather lengthy definition of religion – one that better fits his remarks in other contexts about 'activating' the archetypes.[3] Religion, I want to suggest, is the *practice* of integrating the archetypes. To integrate the archetypes, we recognize and accept that they are *our* functions (whether at an individual or a social level) and cease to project either their presence or their absence elsewhere. This recognition is not merely an intellectual process of using critical awareness to puncture the illusions of projection (important though this is) – it also involves a positive celebration of the archetypes as meaningful in their own right: even 'devoutly worshipping and loving them'. Devout worship and love is already a well-established feature of religion, but the critical awareness of projection is much more limited in religion as a whole. As I will be arguing, whenever that critical awareness emerges it has a tendency to be re-appropriated by projective religion. Nevertheless, it is essential for the *function* of religion that the critical combines with the celebratory. The diachronic function of the archetypes cannot operate effectively if we assume that our beliefs about (for instance) 'God's will' at one point are the whole story – that they do not need to be reconciled with the critical voices that will come either from ourselves or from others at other points.

The whole idea that religion is a *practice*, although consistent with the form religion has taken from early times, conflicts with the post-enlightenment worldview of those who wish to see it in terms of beliefs alone. The 'believers' are supported by the conventional establishment not only of religious authorities and institutions, but even of lexicographers when they define 'religion', and (even more ironically) anti-religious campaigners, who enter an unholy alliance with religious dogmatists to keep 'religion' dogmatic as an easy target. Even Religious Education (if not very carefully taught), if it does not try to inculcate one set of 'beliefs', may instead present a smorgasbord of different ones to choose from, reducing religion to a 'subjective' personal choice between apparently random alternatives of equal value.[4] In reaction (see 2.b), there is also a dominant set

---

3   Goodwyn (2016) p. 14.
4   I discuss this issue, and alternative approaches to Religious Education, in Ellis (1997).

What is an Archetype?

of assumptions amongst academics in the social sciences that religion is entirely social in function, united by beliefs that are largely unconscious. This reductive view goes back to the early sociologist Durkheim, and is typified in contemporary thought by Jonathan Haidt, who insists that even individual religious experiences are reducible to 'the hive switch' – a social regulatory mechanism that leads people to prioritize group interests.[5] The basic error in both these (superficially opposed) views of religion is not to recognize any distinction between absolutized belief and provisional judgement, and to assume that many of the features of absolutization are those of religion in general – in the process ignoring the potential integrative impact of religious practice in both individual and social experience.

Yet against this we nevertheless have a growing interest in religion as practice, often understood as 'spirituality' with an ambivalent relationship to established religion. This interest tends to focus on alternative traditions to the dominant religion in a particular context: so that, to a Westerner, Buddhism is 'spiritual' but boring old Christianity is 'religious'; to an Asian, however, Buddhism may well be 'religious' and Christianity alive with the beckoning spirit. Religion as practice may be found most easily in alternative traditions, or re-discovered in ancient ones, but it is also still present to some degree even in the belief-orientated traditions we may have rejected in early life.

A function is fulfilled through a practice. To take a simple comparison, defecation is a basic human function, that can be fulfilled by the practice of regular visits to the toilet. Defecation is a function, but not a diachronic schematic function. The 'container' is a schematic function: that is, a human communicative need that is fulfilled through the development of associative patterns in the human brain and nervous system, enabling us to understand and use various words and other symbols that we can associate with that schema. But a container is not a diachronic schematic function, and we do not need a container practice to develop it. A diachronic schematic function, helping us to maintain our awareness of a function over a period of time, gains its meaning from action and modification rather than only from passive significance. I can appreciate the *significance* of the hero merely by understanding his story by means of

---

5   Haidt (2012) ch. 10; Haidt (2007).

a schema, but to fulfil the *function* of heroism I have to behave in a heroic way to some degree, and this requires continued effort *over time*. Continued and regular effort over time is what I here mean by *practice*.

Practice in religion can take a wide variety of forms, but all of them help to build up a set of developing complex associations with the archetypes, so as to maintain our awareness of the hero, shadow, anima/animus, and God functions over time. Ninian Smart's seven dimensions of religion (ritual, ethical, narrative, experiential, doctrinal, social, and material)[6] offer a helpful phenomenal checklist to help analyse how much religions can be geared towards these practical ends. Ritual and narrative remind us of the archetypes through stories and repeated actions that symbolize them and re-enact them. The material dimension may also reinforce these associations in buildings and works of art. The experiential dimension (e.g. prayer and meditation) may change our mental states so as to enable more receptivity. The ethical and doctrinal give us intellectual reminders of our values and commitments. The social dimension creates a group with expectations that constantly help us recall the archetypes. Section 5 in this book will explore in more detail how the archetypes can be found and practically integrated in some key example religious traditions.

However, what many people still think of as 'religion', i.e. projected religion, often lacks practice in this sense. Such religion gives priority to doctrine, interpreted absolutely, and makes the other dimensions subsidiary to it. 'Ethics' will generally consist in obedience to (or more often failure of obedience to) revealed moral rules. There may be ritual actions, but there is no creative reflection on these ritual actions of the kind that is needed to make them part of a practice. The experiential dimension may either become perfunctory (at one extreme) or hysterical (at the other). Narrative is rigidly interpreted as confirmation of doctrine, and the social dimension becomes a group with rigid boundaries and fixed expectations of conformity. The belief continually reinforces itself instead of developing or adapting to new conditions, so that when a new condition does arise (either in the individual or in the community), it is likely to be interpreted as a threat.

---

6   Smart (1968).

In the next section, I will say more about the relationship between this tendency and the perspectives that can be offered by a variety of other approaches: systems theory, bias theory, cognitive linguistics, neuroscience, and the politics of power structures. All of these can help us to form a composite picture of what it means to project the archetypes, and thus to rigidify religion as absolute 'belief'.

However, it is religion as practice that inspires. It inspires, most basically, by giving us regular reminders of what we could be as more integrated beings. It gives us emotionally-fuelled reinforcements of what we might think of as 'our better selves': our more perseverant selves, our less polarized and hateful selves, our more balanced selves (not solely masculine or feminine), and our more open, integrated, and complete selves. Not only does it confront us with highly meaningful symbols, but it links those symbols and their significance together over time, constantly enriching their significance for us, and in the process boosting our commitment to revisiting them and keeping ourselves on track. It can do this particularly through the recurrent features of ritual and symbolic narrative which express the archetypes in psychologically resonant ways.[7] It thus interacts with, rather than conflicting with, the arts, the sciences, philosophy, politics, and other religious and cultural traditions. Whatever our differences with others, our *practice* offers the possibility of re-framing the issues and resolving them, whilst absolute beliefs tend only to confirm us in the same frameworks and the same conflicting assumptions.

These two tendencies in religion, that I will refer to as *dogmatic religion* and *practical religion*, are not always easily separable in practice. We may think we can identify groups that clearly fall into either camp (perhaps the liberal Quakers at one end, and the Islamic State group on the other), but we are also likely to find elements of rigidity in those who practise practical religion, as well as unexpected elements of flexibility in the most repressive groups. James Ault's research into fundamentalism provides some remarkable examples of the latter – for instance, that those who strongly believe that 'God hates divorce' are nevertheless willing to allow it in certain cases.[8] Groups that are overwhelmingly dogmatic would cease to attract adherents without some degree of fulfilment of archetypal

---

7   Goodwyn (2016) pp. 36–8.
8   Ault (2004) p. 196.

functions: for example, by providing a disciplined environment in which the hero archetype can be fulfilled in the short term. This distinction between two types of religion, then, is not a basis for clearly categorizing religious groups, but rather a distinction between different ways in which any religion can function.

This way of understanding religion as operating in two different ways obviously combines descriptive and prescriptive features. On the one hand, an attempt to describe how most religions actually operate most of the time would categorize religion as mainly dogmatic, reinforcing particular social and psychological habits through defensive belief. This is the basis of much sociological discussion of religion, which follows Durkheim by reducing religion to its social role. On the other hand, an analysis of the function played by religion *over time* can show its adaptive features much more clearly. For example, those who appeal to Jesus today as a merely reactionary figure, reinforcing and rationalizing a set of social norms set by a believing group, nevertheless continue to transmit a complex set of stories about him that can be interpreted in much more challenging ways. The most reactionary religion thus preserves the seeds of its own cultural renewal, and the longer the time-scale in which we consider it, the more likely we are to encounter religion in its balancing, practical function. Description and prescription can thus be integrated in diachronic function: it is how religion *is* if we set the bounds of what *is* with sufficient inclusivity, although from the narrower bounds of a particular situation it may seem more like the prescription of an ideal. Again, we will see more of this complexity exemplified in section 5.

1.h. Archetypes, Tradition, and Modernity

Blind impatience is equally evident in the fruit section. Our ancestors might have delighted in the occasional handful of berries found on the underside of a bush in late summer, viewing it as a sign of the unexpected munificence of a divine creator, but we became modern when we gave up on awaiting sporadic gifts from above and sought to render any pleasing sensation immediately and repeatedly available.
Alain de Botton, The Pleasures and Sorrows of Work

One feature of archetypes that Jung clearly identified is that our typical relationship with them has changed. In Jung's account, modern culture has made us more conscious of the present (in the sense of the culture of the general time we live in), but at the expense of a necessary link with the unconscious:

> The man whom we can with justice call 'modern' is solitary. He is so of necessity and at all times, for every step towards a fuller consciousness of the present removes him further from the original 'participation mystique' with the mass of men – from submersion in a common unconsciousness. Every step forward means an act of tearing himself loose from that all-embracing, pristine unconsciousness which claims the bulk of mankind almost entirely.[1]

As I've already argued, what Jung conceptualized as the unconscious can be more economically and phenomenally understood as the diachronic function in human experience. This function is distinctive of the archetypes rather than other kinds of meaningful schema. If we understand Jung in this way, he is here helping us to identify a key feature of modernity in relation to the archetypes, even though the idea that this is solely about moving away from the 'collective unconscious' is not particularly helpful. Rather we are moving away from the archetypes' diachronic functions. Modernity does not lead us to lose the archetypes altogether, nor to wholly begin or end our tendency to project them. However, our understanding of the archetypal functions has passed from one form of limitation to another.

Both tradition and modernity are usually thought of as determinate features of cultures or of historical periods. However, we need to understand the terms more flexibly than this. They are contingent and approximate features of cultural periods, but more precisely they are features of judgement. Each of them involves the

---

1   Jung (1933) p. 227.

domination of some values applied to judgement and the exclusion of others. These values have been empirically identified in the work of Jonathan Haidt. His socio-psychological research has distinguished tradition, authority, and purity as types of values typically applied by conservatives in modern societies who still maintain some of the values of traditional society. Three further values – care, justice, and freedom – are usually adopted by modern conservatives together with the traditional values. However, modern progressives tend to adopt care, justice, and freedom exclusively (at least in the political realm), and reject tradition, authority, and purity as unacceptable.[2] This does not imply that moderns have abandoned values of tradition, authority, and purity entirely, but that they are increasingly less ready to recognize them explicitly or make them the basis of political judgement. Progressives (or 'liberals' in the American sense) thus tend to explicitly adopt fully 'modern' values, whilst conservatives are part modern, part traditional. The further you go back in time, the more traditional conservatives become.

Why is the rejection of traditional authority such a key feature of modernity? We can probably immediately understand that it is associated with the rise and the acceptance of science, in which empirical justification replaces dogma. Individualism, tolerance, democracy, and human rights are also features of modern socio-political organization that enable individuals to challenge authoritative dogmas on the basis of their experience. However, the thorough adoption of this post-traditional stance also requires the achievement of a stage of psychological maturity in which judgements are made on the basis of rationalized criteria rather than social loyalties. This stage of psychological maturity is theorized by developmental psychologist Robert Kegan, building on the earlier work of Piaget and extending it into empirical investigation of adult development, calling it stage 4.[3] The shift in values that constitutes 'modernity' thus involves a complex mixture of individual development, cultural norms, and political influences. It is not whole societies that are 'modern', but rather those within them who have adopted an additional level of complexity in their judgements. This new complexity is usually due to education and/or professional development that provides cultural transmission of these post-traditional values, when individuals

---

2 Haidt (2012) Part 2.
3 Kegan (1982).

What is an Archetype?   51

are ready and able to utilize them. This additional complexity is also often correlated with generally more 'liberal' (or less 'conservative') social and political attitudes, as is increasingly illustrated in political science by the degree of correlation between college education and voting left of centre.[4]

A shift in our relationship to archetypes is typical of modernity in this complex sense. We have not entirely given up on archetypes in their traditional mythic and religious forms, but we have changed our relationship with them so that either they are no longer governed by traditional authority at all, or the acceptance of that authority is seen as a matter of individual choice. In the process, as Jung recognized, we have often lost that sense of 'participation mystique' – that direct and confident engagement with the archetypes – that we can envy in those that are still embedded in tradition. When we have that traditional engagement, we take authority, loyalty, and purity in relation to archetypal symbols for granted as basic values. When we lose it, the values of care, justice, and freedom become relatively more important to us, and we are thus only likely to adopt archetypal symbols that we can interpret in terms of these values.

However, as we need all these types of values for embodied engagement with the conditions around us, we should not idealize that traditional standpoint any more than we should idealize its modern transformation.[5] Rather, the limitations of both standpoints can be overcome in what I describe as the 'third phase'.

The distinctive features of three phases in relation to archetypes can be defined in terms of the three constituent parts of my definition of archetypes as *diachronic schematic functions.* In traditional contexts, archetypes are treated as *diachronic but not schematic*, whereas in modern contexts, they are treated as *schematic but not diachronic.* In the third phase, however, archetypes can be treated as *both* diachronic and schematic.

In the traditional phase, archetypal functions are diachronic but not schematic, because their importance for us is recognized as transcending the beliefs and desires that we may have, either

---

4   For instance, in the UK 2019 general election, 68% of people with degrees voted for left of centre parties, but only 37% of people with only GCSE level education or below. https://yougov.co.uk/topics/politics/articles-reports/2019/12/17/how-britain-voted-2019-general-election (accessed 2020).

5   To do so is an example of the 'pre/trans fallacy' identified by Wilber (2000) pp. 120, 244.

individually or collectively, at present. However, that transcendence is not treated as schematic because it is identified with symbols from a particular context, with particular metaphors taken as definitive of the diachronic function. Thus, for instance, in medieval Christian mysticism, we see a quest to overcome the limitations of the sinful individual through prayerful identification with the archetypes as the eternal God, the eternal heroic Christ, and the eternal anima as Mary the Virgin. The eternal shadow also definitively takes the form of Satan, who is greater than individual sin. In this way, the diachronic function of archetypes, by which individuals are constantly reminded of longer-term perspectives, does operate. Some mystics, such as Meister Eckhart and Hildegard of Bingen, even began to dismantle the projection of the archetype by identifying it with themselves, and by developing forms of agnosticism.[6]

Nevertheless, this engagement with the archetypes was not in any sense recognized as schematic, because it was taken to reside in the symbols themselves, which were taken to directly represent a 'truth'. As long as people continue to cling, explicitly or implicitly, to this representationalist view of meaning, they are not in a position to understand or accept the ways that quite different symbols can express the same function in different cultural circumstances. Although a recognition of universality in religious functions was available to some people in ancient times, it was quite rare in the medieval period, and continues to be a minority position today. In the Crusades, for instance, it was obviously the standard Christian position that 'the infidel' (i.e. Muslims) should be fought, because their religion was considered *different* to that of Christians – even though they worshipped God. The schematic relationship between different symbols fulfilling the same function did not generally figure in people's awareness: only the symbol itself, and its value, did so. This tendency went along with the unquestionable exclusivity of the Christian group. Individual assumptions could be questioned in relation to the norms of that group, but the group norms could not be questioned in relation to other group norms.

This basis of judgement can be contrasted with the modern one, in which the similarities between human functions are much more widely recognized. Although very few people maintain an explicit understanding of schemas, a more general recognition of human

---

6   See Ellis (2018) 7.b for more details.

similarity is much more widespread, and is enshrined in the acceptance of universal human rights. Jung is only one of the modern influences who have helped to spread the concept of religious universalism (found for example in many New Age, Buddhist, Hindu, Bahai, Unitarian Christian, and other groups). Even though not everyone is a universalist, nearly everyone except a politically extreme minority accepts the principle of tolerance – which again involves an implicit recognition that other people's symbols may function for them to some extent something like yours do for you.

Not only have religious archetypes increasingly been treated in implicitly schematic ways, but 'secular' archetypes have also simultaneously developed in modernity, of a kind that are much more explicitly symbolic. Nature, Reason, Truth, Rationality, and Humanity are just a few common examples of concepts that have achieved substantial importance as sources of value and inspiration in modernity, even being graphically symbolized or personified in 'secular' settings such as civic statuary. However, these archetypal forms have universality as their point of departure, and are readily recognized as 'symbolic' universals rather than as projected representations. They are thus at least implicitly schematic. These archetypal forms will be discussed more fully in section 6.

Whether the modern relationship to the archetypes is 'religious' or 'secular', however, it tends to lack the diachronic power of the pre-modern. That is not necessarily because we don't intellectually understand the archetypes as needing to motivate us over time, but rather because of the constant danger of doubt that arises when they are overwhelmingly still understood in projected ways. In terms of the foundational values identified by Haidt, justice (which makes us think of our own view as equal in worth to others) and freedom (which makes us want to be free of authority from others) lead us to question previously unquestionable authority, loyalty, and purity values, and sometimes even reject them entirely. If I am a modern who 'believes' in God, for instance, I may strive to pray every day and be constantly inspired by him, but I also nevertheless have to maintain a constant effort to hold 'my faith' in ways that the pre-moderns did not have to do. If I lose this 'faith', perhaps even temporarily, I also lose the archetypal function.

The whole idea of religion as a 'belief', so typical of modernity, can only be premised on the archetypes being objects separate to ourselves, rather than simply aspects of our experience. This is hardly surprising when a schematic function whose symbolization works directly in experience is turned into an abstract and infinite entity beyond experience. It is also due to an implicit misunderstanding of ourselves as solely egos, and anything that challenges our immediate ego as necessarily beyond ourselves. Even if I do succeed in 'believing' in such a 'God', the thing I end up believing in becomes alienated from its archetypal function (becoming merely a tool of power, for instance). In traditional society there was often no need to 'believe' in order to relate to the archetypes, because the alternative modern values did not disengage us from the archetypes in the first place. As, for instance, Karen Armstrong argues,[7] literal belief is a peculiarly modern phenomenon.

	Traditional view	Modernity	The third phase
Psychological stage (Piaget/ Kegan)	3 – esteem dependent on social approval	4 – judgements dependent on rationalized framework	5 – Recognizing rationalized frameworks as provisional
Emphasized foundational values (Haidt)	Authority, loyalty, purity	Care, justice, freedom	Balanced practical use of all values
Diachronic aspect of archetypes	Archetypes able to function over time when not projected	Projection often prevents archetypes functioning over time	Archetypes function over time because not projected
Schematic aspect of archetypes	Archetypes solely identified with limited cultural range of symbols	Archetypes more often identified as universal	Archetypes recognized as universal and symbols as provisional

Figure 3. Table of relationships between archetypal functions, values, and psychological stages in different phases (by the author).

Although this loss of diachronic significance is most evident in the case of God, we can also trace it in the case of the other archetypes. The power of the anima to inspire a man to develop his feminine qualities is effectively lost when it is projected onto an 'ideal partner', who is in danger of being lost at every turn through cognitive dissonance. I may believe that I have found her, but have to put constant effort into not noticing her imperfection (an effort that the pre-moderns might have put into maintaining the transcendence of a divine feminine figure). When I do allow the imperfection to be

7   Armstrong (2010).

recognized, the archetypal function is lost. Similarly the power of the shadow is only maintained in a fragile fashion, even if I focus it on a hated group or leader rather than Satan, as is the hero even when focused on a real leader. My belief in these archetypal projections is in inverse ratio to my actual confidence in the archetypal function. The more the archetype is actually succeeding in inspiring me, the less I need to go through a fragile and factitious creation of 'belief'.

The shift between pre-modernity and modernity, then, does not amount to an overall integration of archetypes, only a shift between different kinds of asymmetry (or different kinds of projection). In the pre-modern period, integration of archetypes is possible within the terms of a particular cultural group, but the positive archetypes are projected within the terms of the group and the shadow is projected beyond it. In the modern period, integration of archetypes is possible beyond the group to some extent, but archetypes are increasingly projected on the rationalized individual when they have achieved that level of psychological development. Emerging from a group that worships projected heroes, we think ourselves heroes, and heroically adopt 'beliefs' to fit the universe to our wishes. Emerging from a group that worships the projected anima or animus, we project it onto other individuals. Emerging from a group that rejects the shadow in other groups, we project it onto any other individuals that thwart our wishes, rather than accepting them as an inevitable part of the world. Emerging from a group that worships a projected God, we implicitly think ourselves gods instead, and start to believe in the inevitable progress of human beings.

It is only in the third phase that both types of projection can potentially be overcome: that is, that we realize our responsibility both for the projected archetypes of ourselves as individuals and those of our society. 'The third phase' is simply a label for a set of possibilities that may or may not happen or even be possible, but that depend on the intersection of psychological development, critical awareness and positive appreciation of archetypes. The further detailed discussion of both projection and integration to be found in sections 2 and 3 will be needed before we can fully consider the conditions for the third phase.

1.i. Evidence and Testability

Traditional scientific method has always been at the very best, 20-20 hindsight. It's good for seeing where you've been. It's good for testing the truth of what you think you know, but it can't tell you where you ought to go.

Robert M. Pirsig

So far I have been trying to present the overall form of my theory of archetypes without much discussion of its relationship to evidence. That does not mean that it does not have one, but the issues are complex and will need unpacking. We need to clarify in what sense archetypal theory is actually in need of evidence, as well as what we might be trying to evidence, and what the purpose and limitation of that evidence might be.

The most important initial point is that archetypal theory works predominantly on the basis of intuitive appeal. By 'intuition' here, I mean the implicit recognition of a set of conditions over time, without the need for explicit matching of theory with evidence of the kind that occurs in formal science. The matching of a new situation with a pattern already established in associative memory can occur without this explicit process.[1] This kind of implicit recognition has itself been psychologically investigated, and shown to be an effective method of understanding conditions that are subject to a limited number of variables with relatively rapid feedback. Daniel Kahneman compares the intuitive judgements of an experienced firefighter, who can recognize the signs that a burning building is about to collapse, with the ineffective intuitions of even experienced stockbrokers, whose judgement in predicting the complex factors affecting stock changes prove no better than random.[2]

In our individual experience of archetypal functions, I would argue that the variables affecting symbolic forms that remind us to maintain our long-term intentions are relatively limited. If they were not, it would not be possible to identify a limited number of archetypal functions. The factors that actually lead us to maintain our long-term intentions are much more varied, but that does not prevent a manageable range of factors providing the *archetypal contribution* to the fulfilment of those intentions. The archetypes thus

---

1   Myers (2002).
2   Kahneman (2011) pp. 234–44.

have an intuitive appeal for us because they can readily match our experience of a manageable range of archetypal functions. Anyone who has ever fallen in love has a sense of the anima/animus function. Anyone who has ever enjoyed a heroic story has a sense of the heroic function. And so on.

However, the feedback time is long, so we are only capable of learning about the effects of archetypes through challenging reflection about them based on long-term experience. We are thus highly dependent on traditions, whereby those with more experience are able to pass on the fruits of their intuitive reflection to others, to make us aware of the importance of the archetypes. This helps to explain the adaptive value of religious tradition in the past.

Traditionally, then, people have adopted a relationship to the archetypes implicitly through religion, on the basis of intuition supplemented by traditional authority. However, because of the diachronic function of archetypes, the rise of scientific demands for evidence has made engagement with the archetypes much more dependent on acceptance of that authority. The scientific demand for evidence tends to have a limited diachronic tolerance: if we can't demonstrate the value of archetypes in the short-term, they are liable to dismissal on evidential grounds.

The intuitive appeal of archetypes helps to explain the popularity of Jung's theories about them, even though they are in many ways unclear. However, Jung also created an unhelpful diversion through his attempts to give his theories scientific credentials through analytic psychology. Here he was only able to supply anecdotal evidence of the efficacy of psychotherapeutic approaches, which may or may not have required archetypal theory as a condition. Rather than comparing that theory with alternatives, or testing its implementation against controls, he could only apply his theory indirectly in a context that was heavily subject to confirmation bias. There is a huge gap between the intuitive acceptability of his theories and their relationship to formal scientific evidence.

Does this matter? To some extent, it makes no difference to the personal application of archetypes as a source of inspiration, if you have adopted them on an entirely intuitive basis. However, it has great drawbacks when it comes to the integration of those archetypes as a practice. Those who are not prepared to apply critical criteria to evaluating the function of archetypes are likely to remain stuck in a pre-modern relationship to them – i.e. one that is dependent on socially sanctioned projections, and is unable to question those projections when they are reinforced at a social level. For such people, there is no critical boundary to the beliefs that may be adopted along with archetypal associations – which can often be seen in the more naïve Jungian circles today. For example, an appreciation of the archetypal importance of astrological symbols may uncritically segue into a belief in astrological predictions: the former may have archetypal value, but the latter is charlatanry. Criticality is crucial if we are to be able to challenge projections of archetypes that are widely shared (indeed institutionalized and enculturated) in a group, and scientific method provides a crucial tool of criticality where empirical claims are concerned.

I want to suggest that analytic psychology as a therapeutic practice offers very limited potential for testing the theory of archetypes, but there are much better potential ways of testing it scientifically. Clarity about what is being tested is crucial. I suggest that my formulation of archetypes as diachronic schematic functions is much more potentially testable than Jung's account of archetypes as forms in the collective unconscious.

To test schematic functions, we need to ascertain whether these schemas operate consistently through a similarity of functions across a variety of people. To test diachronic schematic functions, we need to ascertain whether the stimulus of archetypal symbols that function within that schema (i.e. practical religion) has a causal role in helping people maintain long-term intentions. The first of these types of testing is an essential prelude to the second, because it is needed to establish the consistency between the symbols that fall within the schematic function. Ideally, the same subjects would be used for both types of test, to ensure a consistency between the people who showed a schematic consistency and the people who showed a diachronic function for that schematic consistency. Ideally, too, both of these stages of the test would have controls.

A variety of evidence does already exist, not in a form that completely fulfils these requirements, but perhaps sufficient to increase confidence that such tests may be worth doing, and that any practical difficulties they raise can be overcome. For the first stage of the putative test, this evidence comes from the empirical evidence supporting prototype theory, whilst for the second, it comes from lifetime psychological studies and (to a lesser extent) studies of the psychological effects of religion.

There is already much evidence to support schematic functions based on prototype effects, of the kind originally researched by Eleanor Rosch and applied by George Lakoff.[3] Prototype effects, discovered through psycho-linguistic research, indicate that people's concepts of any general category (e.g. *bird*) are typically filled, not by an abstract list of defining features that provide criteria for membership of the category, but by a culturally specific prototype drawn from the more familiar and concrete (basic level) category below it (e.g. *robin*). This prototype fulfils the *function* of the wider category whilst maintaining an essential associative relationship with the narrower one.[4] Thus if you ask a British person for their image of a bird, for instance, they are likely to suggest a robin rather than a penguin. The prototype has a *metonymic* relationship with the category whose function it takes (the part standing for the whole), so the robin stands functionally for birds in general. This offers evidence that our ability to generalize is based on the functional relationship between the objects we are generalizing about, not on an abstract representation of the contents of a particular category.[5]

The relationship between a schema and its symbols, then, is likely to be a prototypical relationship in which we can only relate to schemas via symbols in a metonymic relationship with them. We can confirm the operation of the schemas, however, by observing the ways in which symbolic prototypes give access to a more general categorization. This allows us to understand members of the same category as fulfilling the same function. In practice we relate to penguins as birds because we have understood the category 'bird' through the generalization of robins, not because we have started off with an abstract understanding of birds that we then apply to both robins and penguins.

Although Lakoff does not discuss archetypal symbols, his interpretation of Rosch's research does indicate the form that future research into their schematic function could take. That form is the identification of prototypical symbols that metonymically maintain the schematic function of archetypes by helping us to intuitively relate to other such symbols. A simple example of this, if we use the shadow archetype, might be the use of Satan for someone with

---

3   Lakoff (1987) pp. 58-135.
4   Functions appear to be in the list of possible sources of prototypes in Gabora, Rosch and Aerts (2008).
5   Lakoff (2007).

a Christian background unlocking the functioning of a symbol with the same archetypal function in another culture, such as Mara in Buddhism. This might be tested, for instance, by systematically comparing the speed and readiness with which the meaning of unfamiliar archetypal symbols associated with the same schema are identified as relating to the same meaning, compared with other symbols that are not associated with the same archetypal schema. Would a Christian ignorant of Buddhism, reminded of Satan and then introduced to Mara, recognize the meaning of Mara more quickly than the meaning of, say, a bodhisattva?

Evidence of the operation of *diachronic* schematic functions is obviously more difficult to develop, because the longer the period of time over which evidence is judged, the greater the number of variables. In addition, researching the role of archetypes over a person's lifetime obviously creates a lot of practical difficulties. Nevertheless, research projects into the basis of effective maturation over a lifetime have been attempted, and George E. Vaillant discusses three of these.[6] He synthesizes their results within a broadly psychoanalytic framework that distinguishes immature ego-defences (e.g. displacement or passive aggression), intermediate ones (e.g. displacement, repression), and mature, integrative ones (e.g. sublimation, anticipation).[7] In his analysis of the elements of maturation found in these samples, there is a striking recognition that religious 'belief' may simultaneously involve self-deception and enable a shift to mature defences, with sacred places and ritual especially noted as aspects of religion that may support maturation.[8]

Future research in this area will need to grasp the nettle of religion's contradictory effects much more firmly in order to separate the effects of dogmatic from practical religion, and test my hypothesis that their effects on ego-defences are quite different (indeed, opposite). However, given that some religious groups stress the dogmatic elements of religion far more than others, it should not be impossible to separate out groups of subjects who have been predominantly influenced by projected as opposed to integrated archetypes, and to assess the comparative degree of correlation these respectively exhibit with some measure of personal integration or maturation (whether this is based on Vaillant's accounts of mature

6   Vaillant (1993) ch. 5.
7   Ibid. ch. 2.
8   Ibid. pp. 337–41.

ego-defence, or on more recent attempts to assess wisdom, such as the work of Igor Grossmann[9]). Although it would be impossible to use controls in such research, the two groups could to some extent offer contrasting controls for each other.

Another possible line of empirical research would be to focus instead on symbols that are frequently experienced as archetypal in a particular cultural context – for example, responses to images of God, Jesus, Mary, and Satan in a Catholic context. To assess the diachronic effects of such symbols, researchers could elicit qualitative responses, perhaps in conjunction with some quantitative measures of embodied responses (such as changes in pulse) to these symbols at different times over a period. This could help to establish to what extent these symbols are associated with integrative processes, again using either Vaillant's or Grossmann's, or perhaps other measures of diachronically integrative processes, as well as to what extent these associations are consistent. I am not aware of any such research ever to have been undertaken, and it would have the limitation of assuming consistency in the schematic function of symbols within a particular religious group: but such consistency may operate to a fair degree.

I am not a trained empirical psychologist, so can only offer here some indications as to what kind of research might in future be possible to support or challenge my thesis that archetypes are diachronic schematic functions, and that practical religion integrates those functions. I offer these primarily to show that such tests are possible, though they will only ever offer a degree of support or challenge rather than definitive conclusions. The supposed antipathy of religion and science could in this way be substantially reconciled, although only on the basis of practical religious effects being clearly differentiated from the absolutizations of dogmatic religion.

---

9   Grossmann (2017).

2. The Projection of Archetypes

2.a. The Projection Process

In the object which he contemplates ... man becomes acquainted with himself.
            Ludwig Feuerbach, *The Essence of Christianity*

We have already seen how the potential for both projection and integration is central to the nature of archetypes, and that distinguishing between those two relationships with archetypes creates a crucial condition for the functional success of religion. In this section I will be exploring in much more detail what occurs when an archetypal projection takes place, and why this is also the key to understanding what has gone wrong in religion. In the process, I will also be linking the concept of archetype to areas that have been insufficiently explored in relation to it: to critical metaphysics, to cognitive psychology, to cognitive linguistics, to systems theory, to politics, and to ethics.

Projection occurs when the archetypal function operates in an individual to create a meaningful symbol, but that symbol is assumed to be the only relevant feature of a complex object with which it is associated. The process of a meaningful archetypal symbol being created in the first place must not itself be confused with projection, because it is not dependent on the reality or unreality of any particular object. Archetypal meaning arises from the operation of the diachronic schematic function *in the individual's experience in relation to the symbolic object as it appears*, not just from the symbolic object itself as the key to some supposed essential reality. However, the projecting individual assumes that the object *does* have this essential feature, and that this connection to a supposed reality is the only relevant feature of the object. Further investigation, however, would show it to be far more complex than this and to have many aspects and many potential meanings revealed in different conditions. For example, a man projecting the anima onto his female lover assumes that she essentially *means* the unrecognized feminine qualities that he finds so attractive beyond himself. All other complexity in the character of his lover is neglected. Whilst he projects, he is incapable of recognizing her as a person with many other attributes, including masculine ones and unattractive ones, and may ignore or deny any evidence of these.

I say 'symbolic object', because the projection of the archetype could be onto a person, an inanimate object, or just a symbol, including words and/or texts. In dogmatic religion, projection is often onto a scripture. Scriptures are not only complex in themselves, but also part of a complex system of meaning that requires the involvement of their readers or auditors to give them meaning. Traditional revelatory interpretations of scripture, however, assume a direct link between meaning and reality regardless of the embodied interpreter. This is a projection because it entirely fails to take into account the complexity and variability of the interpretation process.

Projection as I have defined it is equivalent to *absolutization*, because it involves the assumption that there is only one correct interpretation of a symbolic object, and that its complexity should be completely ignored. Projection thus also has other features of absolutization that I have discussed more fully elsewhere. In a forthcoming book I will discuss 23 interdependent features of absolutization,[1] but for the moment will select four. These include:

- an absence of incrementality (the qualities attributed to the object are not a matter of degree, but either total or zero)[2]
- a confirmation bias (only features confirming the projection are sought)
- the substitution of 'fast thinking' to avoid the expenditure of more energy than would be required to become aware of other aspects of the object, the projection becoming part of an interconnected web of mutually reinforcing beliefs
- the reinforcement of the projection by group associations and repression of challenges.[3]

This definition of projection does differ from that used by Jung, in ways that have practical implications. In Jung's account, what is most definitive about projection is that the qualities attributed to the object come from the subject. Hence his definition of projection

---

1 Ellis (2022).
2 Ellis (2015a) 2.g.
3 Ibid. 3.d.

is 'the transveying of a subjective process into an object'.[4] It seems to form no part of his definition of projection to recognize its absolutization – i.e. that the other features creating the complexity of the object are repressed. For this reason, there is an ambivalence about Jung's view of projection, since to a large extent it is an inevitable aspect of human perception and understanding. It can hardly be differentiated from what Karl Popper called 'the theory-ladenness of perception'[5] – i.e. the recognition that any perceptions whatsoever we may use to understand features of the world are subject to our selection and interpretation.

Because of its inevitability, Jung thus sees projection as positive up to a point:

> It is the natural and given thing for unconscious contents to be projected.... Thus every normal person of our time, who is not reflective beyond the average, is bound to his environment by a whole system of projections.... So long as the libido can use these projections as agreeable and convenient bridges to the world, they will alleviate life in a positive way. But as soon as the libido wants to strike out on another path, and for this purpose begins running back along the previous bridges of projection, they will work as the greatest hindrances it is possible to imagine, for they effectively prevent any real detachment from the former object.[6]

The problem with this way of understanding projection is a lack of clarity about its practical implications. If projection is understood in a way that is to a large extent unavoidable, its identification does not help us to see a practical working-point in our relationship to the archetypes. Instead, Jung apparently waits for other indications that a projection is unhelpful before taking this practical indication of how to respond. Those indications may well be medical ones based on the therapeutic paradigm he comes from – one that is insufficiently generalizable to wider human experience. In effect, Jung has adopted a descriptive, avowedly neutral definition of a term that is often in fact used prescriptively (even by him), but without making clear the basis of that prescription.[7] In my account, on the other hand, projection can provide an important basis for understanding how moral prescription can itself be justified (see 2.h below). This way of understanding projection may also help to explain some of

4   Jung (1946) p. 582.
5   Popper (1972) p. 71.
6   Jung (1960) §507.
7   See Papadopoulos (2006) p. 17, and Ellis (2020) ch. 12 for a fuller account of Jung's explicitly moral perspective.

Jung's apparent over-tolerance towards some projective beliefs, such as his attitude to astrology mentioned in 1.i above.

His account of projection fails to identify precisely and universally enough what is wrong with it, because it is not the origin of the assumed beliefs about the person (or object) that is important, but their absolutization. The fact that a belief about an object is constructed on the basis of my own coherent assumptions is not in itself significant, because such beliefs may possibly be accurate, or at least not inaccurate enough to cause any problems. 'Projection' of this kind is just a basic element of the conditions of organic life. The problems arise when the qualities that have come from my own assumptions become practically relevant to my response to the object, and I fail to revise my understanding of it in the face of new information. For example, on meeting a new person I am very likely to respond to them on the basis of the immediate, but approximate, signs of what they are like, such as their gender, social position, education, emotional state etc., as indicated by features like appearance, language, and body language. In all of these cases, it is my assumptions about the relationship between certain categories of person and certain kinds of expected behaviour or attitude that will format my responses to them. This is all 'projection' in Jung's sense, but it will only become 'projection' in my sense when I start to make further judgements about them that shut off any challenge to these initial, provisional assumptions. For example, supposing I am standing at a bus stop next to a man who speaks in an uneducated way, and he unexpectedly starts talking to me about Proust: but I assume that his knowledge of this complex author is superficial or fake and cut off the conversation.

Projection of this kind, applied to a person, is equivalent to an *ad hominem* fallacy. When a person holds a belief, but we draw premature conclusions about the acceptability of that belief (either to accept or dismiss it) based entirely on who holds it, this is widely recognized as fallacious. For instance, an unqualified person disagreeing with an expert on their subject of expertise may well carry less *prima facie* credibility than the expert. An *ad hominem* occurs, though, when they are assumed by the expert or her audience to be *necessarily* wrong (not just as a matter of probability). It should be the evidence that decides us rather than just who says it, even if the probabilities guide us in how much attention to pay.

Similarly, when we make judgements about the nature of another person, it should not be our prejudices about them as a whole that form the basis of our judgement. Rather we need to form beliefs about their separate features that are constantly open to revision, even if in practice our quick intuitive assessments determine whether we start to pay attention to them in the crowd. It is the lack of openness to alternative evidence to modify our initial view that makes projection a matter of prejudice (see 2.e).

Furthermore, it is only if we understand projection in this way that we can make better sense of the value of archetypes, and thus of the ways that value can be interfered with by projection. If the value of an archetype is to provide a diachronic source of inspiration, but projection attempts to rigidify that source of inspiration by excluding alternative ways of understanding its relationship to an object, it is evident that it only takes a shift in conditions for that fixed source of inspiration to cease fulfilling its function. For example, those who enter into a relationship with the God archetype may initially do so with great joy, but when an attempt is made to maintain that joy by fixing it into a series of abstract beliefs about a projected supernatural being, the changing conditions of mental states are likely to rapidly make it ineffective as a source of inspiration. A person who was initially moved by their religious experience to embrace a new range of conditions (in their own character and capabilities, in their social relationships, in their ideas and beliefs about the world), may then rapidly become much more rigid, clinging to the security of a group and its beliefs and reacting to challenges in ineffectual stereotyped ways. By contrast, an account of projection that focuses only on its origins in the subject offers no differentiation between archetypes as fixed or flexible sources of inspiration.

Jung's account of projection encourages a fatalistic response because it is inevitable, which is an assumption I want to challenge. Projection in Jung's sense does seem to be unavoidable, because it is an aspect of the basic epistemological conditions of human experience. In my account of projection, however, we cannot know whether or not it can be completely overcome. The kind of progress we can make to overcome it (which I will be discussing in section 3) is experiential and thus probably partial, but in every case it consists in avoiding the absolutization of the projected belief, not in changing the basic epistemological conditions of human experience.

In the remainder of this section I will be exploring a number of other helpful aspects of this account of projection, synthesizing a variety of viewpoints. However, before this, it is necessary to consider the opposite of projection.

2.b. Reactive Projection

A man of clear ideas errs grievously if he imagines that whatever is seen confusedly does not exist: it belongs to him, when he meets with such a thing, to dispel the mist, and fix the outline of the vague form which is looming through it.

John Stuart Mill, *Essay on Bentham*

Opposed to positive projection there is a polarized over-reaction, consisting in an absolute denial of any truth whatsoever in the projection. Jung clearly recognizes this phenomenon:

Something that strikes me about the object may very well be a real property of that object. But the more subjective and emotional this impression is, the more likely it is that the property will be a projection.[1]

Projection, then, must not be confused with falsehood. We cannot know that a projected property is false any more than we can know that it is true. Yet the rejection of objects of projection as false in reaction to recognizing the projection is common, due to the widespread human tendency to confuse uncertainty with falsehood.[2]

I have sought in vain for a Jungian term for this polarized over-reaction to projection. There are two terms that might conceivably be confused with it, but on closer inspection have quite a different meaning. One is *counter-projection*, which refers to the way in which a person who is projected upon by someone else may project back on the projector (common, for instance, in sexual relationships).[3] Another is *introjection*, which Jung describes as the assimilation of an object into the subject (rather than vice-versa), in a way that seems equally deluded, and practically indistinguishable, from that of projection.[4] Both of these are opposites to projection in different senses, but neither of them identifies the over-reaction. Nor could this phenomenon be called 'negative projection' without a great danger of confusion with projection of the shadow. I am thus obliged to fall back on a coinage: I will call it *reactive projection*.

Reactive projection is a widespread feature of both religion and anti-religion. When we recognize the complexity in the object onto which we have projected the archetype, indicating the inadequacy

1   Jung (1960) §519.
2   See Ellis (2012) 1.h.
3   Jung (1960) §519.
4   Jung (1946) pp. 566-7.

The Projection of Archetypes 69

of the projection, we do not just reject the projection, but reject an idea of the object itself. We thus project again, but this time we project the *absence* of the archetype onto the object. Iconoclasm gives a good example of this. The iconoclast smashes the idol because it is believed to be 'false', i.e. it does not represent God, in reaction to an assumed belief that the idol *is* God. This fails to recognize that by smashing the idol, the iconoclast actually perpetuates the rejected assumption of idolatry that finite images can represent the infinite, the denial of God being just as infinite in its implications as the affirmation.[5] The idol *does* symbolize the God function to a degree, but does not perfectly *represent* it. From that, though, it does not follow that the God function is absent from our experience of the idol.

Rejecting the object does not remove the archetypal function. If you were previously projecting the archetype in one way (such as onto an idol), but you then reject that way, the function ensures that you will then start to project it in another way, as long as you fail to integrate it. In the case of puritanical iconoclasm, as found in both early Protestantism and many forms of Islam, projection onto the image is often replaced by projection onto words of a text that are taken to represent the will of God. Similarly, the rejection of a hero whose flaws have been discovered may then signal a transfer of projection onto the critic who found the flaw, or onto an alternative hero who can defeat the rejected one in the struggle. In the process, the previous objects of positive archetypes become the object of shadow projection. Dramatic conversions (such as that of St Paul in Acts 9) indicate not an overcoming of projection, but a flip between objects of projection, and/or between a positive and a negative archetype in relation to the same object.

Though it can be traced to some extent in the religious changes throughout history, reactive projection is a particular feature of modern responses to archetypes. As noted above in 1.h, my thesis is that modernity has maintained archetypal functions but largely in a less effective schematic, not diachronic, form. This can be directly linked to the modern anti-religious tendency to treat diachronic functions as though they were synchronic, not understanding that they require the recognition of a perspective beyond our current identifications and values to be adequately understood and appreciated. If interpreted from an entirely synchronic perspective,

---

5   See Ellis (2018) 3.c.

religious archetypes appear as (at best) worthless speculative diversions, or (at worst, when insisted upon by traditions) as power-based dogmas with no further justification than their inherited traditional form. The hero then becomes a merely amusing story, the anima/animus merely an elaborated sexual function, the shadow and God merely 'myths' (which comes to mean falsehoods). In all these cases, the function of the symbols is only appreciated in the present context, where they may appear to have trivial functions such as 'consolation', 'social bonding', or 'amusement', but are not appreciated as having any importance for psychological development, embodied confidence, sense of meaning over time, or ability to adapt to new conditions. Where these functions were previously projected onto supernatural entities, the secular modern has reactively projected their *absence* onto religious symbols, and to some extent developed secular expressions of the same archetypes (truth, rationality, democracy etc.) to take their place. However, these secular archetypes (discussed in section 6) also have the same limitation: of being predominantly interpreted synchronically rather than diachronically.

Reactive projection of archetypes as absent is primarily responsible for a sense of *meaninglessness* around them, so that secularists no longer experience the value of religious symbols directly, but just treat them as abstractions. The theoretical positions that follow, such as atheism (meaning the *denial* of the existence of God), seem to be rationalizations of that denial of meaning, as conceptual belief is used to substitute for the absence of full archetypal function. This does not necessarily imply that the meaningfulness of the archetypal functions may not instead be found elsewhere, even in religion. Atheists may still find meaning in the atmosphere of a church, and those who deny the value of heroic myth may still find themselves drawn into heroic stories. Social, political, artistic or other symbols may also take the place of religious or mythic ones, but it is doubtful whether they will always offer the same degree of function. That is because they are less systemically developed in all the religious dimensions recognized by Smart (discussed in 1.g) and thus offer less diachronic reinforcement of the function. For instance, an atheist may find God meaningless but be inspired by altruistic fund-raising for charity. This activity has some narrative and a strong social and moral dimension, but probably lacks the material, experiential, and ritual dimensions.

Even-handedness is vital in discussing reactive projection and its effects. It is a form of projection, but no better or worse than any other. Its interference in archetypal function is thus variable, like that of direct projection. Because the projection of archetypes does not in itself create meaning or inspiration, we should not assume that the projection of their absence necessarily removes it, still less that beliefs (such as atheism) that are associated with reactive projection are themselves necessarily the cause of ethical inadequacy, or of any other alleged effect. Theists and atheists do not necessarily have better or worse beliefs than each other. Nevertheless, the projection of meaninglessness onto archetypal symbols has a contributory effect as part of a complex system, especially when those archetypal symbols are part of a tradition that has been socially important to the individual concerned. When we assume that any of the archetypes are 'just delusive', we are losing something of importance.

2.c. Projection as Metaphysical Belief

Don't try to remake the world in your image. That was God's mistake.
Marty Rubin

The term 'metaphysics' is often a matter of confusion for non-philosophers, and of dispute by philosophers, but here I take it to mean beliefs about ultimate states of affairs: how things 'really' or 'essentially' are. Metaphysical claims might include ones about the nature of matter, the self, God, the universe as a whole, ultimate causality, time and space, the good, beauty or many other things. Importantly, they might also include *negative* claims about what is not ultimately true about these things. In any case, the metaphysical needs to be distinguished from the phenomenal: it is not concerned with what we experience, but with what is claimed to lie behind what we experience. Nor should the metaphysical be confused with the merely linguistic or analytic: clarifying the meaning and implications of the claims we make is not the same as making claims about how things 'really are'.

A set of arguments known as sceptical arguments, available in various forms in both Greek and Indian thought since around 500 BCE, make it clear that no metaphysical claim can be justified (as I have detailed elsewhere).[1] Our senses, understanding, and standpoint are limited and formatted by prior expectation and culture. We have no final way of distinguishing deluded beliefs from 'true' ones beyond probability based on the weight of previous experience, supported by provisionality of judgement. Any justification given for a belief is subject to an infinite regression of questionable prior assumptions. Squirm as philosophers might, our beliefs are ineluctably uncertain. Metaphysical beliefs, however, consisting of attempts to freeze or delve behind experience, could only ever be justified by some source of certainty – of a kind that we cannot conceivably justify. They are also not inevitable. The alternative to metaphysical belief is not the opposite metaphysical belief, nor a more refined and complex metaphysical belief, but *provisional* belief justified by experience.[2]

Projection, as I have defined it, is equivalent to metaphysical belief, because both consist in absolutization of our view of an

---

1   See Ellis (2012) 1.a.
2   Ellis (2015a) section 2.

object (or person). When you believe in metaphysical claims about an object, you claim that it has a certain essential nature regardless of your varied (actual or potential) experiences of it. For example, to claim that the universe is designed, or that all men are rapists, or that your true self or soul is immortal, would all be both metaphysical claims and projections, because in each case one partial characterization is imposed on an object and taken to be entirely true of it. The complexity of the object, and the uncertainty of our relationship to it (because we are also part of a complex system) is ignored when such claims are made. The same would be the case for the definite negation of any metaphysical statement (as opposed to the mere recognition of uncertainty about it). General statements about what we can't know (such as this one) are not self-contradictory as long as they are not negations – merely recognitions of uncertainty.

Projection of the archetypes is metaphysical belief, because the archetypal function in our experience is taken to be essentially or really present in an object, regardless of the range of experience we have of that object. So, if your view of a heroic leader is explicitly or implicitly that he is always *essentially* heroic (whether or not he has become supernatural or legendary, like, say, Hercules) and you do not accept information about his weaknesses, then you have a metaphysical view of the hero. The abstract beliefs that may accompany the absolutization, such as ones about supernatural status, essence, magical abilities, immortality, or timelessness, are possible indicators of this metaphysical status but are not essential to it. It is enough to have an absolutized view of the projected hero, and to ignore her complexity, for her to be treated metaphysically. For the hero to be otherwise, there would need to be some provisionality about your view of him, to allow him to turn out differently.

It is important to recognize these features as those of the projected archetype, rather than of the archetype itself or of the symbols that express it. Hercules may be a hero, and part of his *meaning* may include the status of being semi-divine and having magical abilities, without being an object of belief. Metaphysical belief starts as soon as one explicitly or implicitly affirms a proposition that these essential features are part of a reality. Until that point, one can have a strong relationship with archetypal symbols without 'believing' in them, as we typically do with the characters in novels and films.

My thesis is that all archetypal projection is also metaphysical belief, as well as that all metaphysical belief (by embodied humans) is archetypal projection. The chief arguments for this are functional, namely that both metaphysical belief and archetypal projection operate identically by repressing alternative options and preventing us from recognizing complexity. Their functional identity has been obscured by over-specialization and domain dependence, simply by people being used to discussing them in different ways in different contexts (philosophy and Jungian psychology). It has also been maintained by continually making distinctions that are reinforced by group ways of talking in different contexts, but that fail to identify any functional difference: for example, distinctions between reason and emotion, in supervenience relationships between different levels of study, or between 'religious' and other spheres. These mechanisms for maintaining absolutized and polarized boundaries between objects of discussion that are functionally identical are themselves metaphysical, and I have analysed them in detail elsewhere.[3] The case for this identification of metaphysics with projection will be strengthened during the next few chapters, as we see the synthetic relationships between metaphysical belief, archetypal projection, denial of embodiment, left-hemisphere dominance, bias, reinforcing feedback, power, and evil. Each piece of this synthetic jigsaw becomes more evidently part of a larger picture, the more of the remaining pieces we fit together.

To see all metaphysical beliefs as archetypal projections, it is necessary to be able to categorize them all in terms of the four archetypal functions. Since metaphysical beliefs held by people are all motivated, and our direct reactions to the objects of projection spill over onto background objects, this is not difficult. Four different aspects of projection can be identified in relation to the four archetypal functions:

1. The heroic function creates *goal-oriented projection*, as we assume the world to be a particular way in accordance with the conditions that help us to conceptualize our goals, and also assume that the goals are supremely valuable. For example, to fit your business ambitions, you may believe that business ultimately helps even the poorest in society, regardless of the 'selfishness' of our motives, by Adam Smith's 'invisible hand'.
2. The shadow function creates *negative projection*, as we assume the world to be a particular way in accordance with our

[3] Ellis (2015a) sections 3 and 4.

rejection. For example, if you are a white person with a fear of black people, this may lead you to believe that black and white people can be very clearly distinguished genetically through the 'one drop rule'. The shadow function can also create *reactive projections* against projections of the other archetypes (see 2.b), so that when our heroes turn out to have weaknesses, we start to demonize them.

3. The anima/animus function creates *appropriative projection*, as we assume the world to be consistent with our wish to make the attractive a part of ourselves: for example, you may believe that fate brought you and your partner together as destined 'soul mates'.
4. The God function creates *transcendence projection,* as we assume there to be metaphysical entities, forces, or 'truths' in accordance with our vision of potential beyond the current state of things, and that the world is consistent with these entities and their activity. For example, we might believe that the Bible contains communication from God as a supernatural entity.

Although we may be used to considering beliefs in isolation from each other, they are systemically related rather than isolated. Each metaphysical belief needs assumed consistency within a certain zone in order to be defended from potential counter-evidence, and it will create that consistency through projection. For the narrowly ambitious, every person or object becomes a potential instrument or obstruction to the fulfilment of the ambition, just as for the lover, the world seems to reflect the idealized features of the beloved.

The different kinds of projection related to the different archetypal functions are not determining of specific metaphysical beliefs formulated in a particular way, but rather of the motivations for holding those beliefs in relation to others. Thus, a shadow projection does not necessarily require that you believe in the supernatural existence of Satan. Instead, it is likely to make you adjust your other previous beliefs to include a fixed belief about something negative, such as your boss's total unreasonableness. Nor do such beliefs necessarily have to be formalized, explicit, or permanent to be metaphysical: I might demonize my boss only for a few minutes and unreflectively, but nevertheless during that time I have an absolute negative belief (a 'truth') about him.

Our motivated metaphysical beliefs contribute towards an attempt to fulfil the archetypal functions, by assuming a consistent set of conditions that can support the need behind the function over time. The more consistent a set of conditions is, after all, the more it seems likely to maintain itself, so it is not surprising that we convince ourselves that the conditions we need are 'true'. What exactly it is that is 'true' (or 'false') can vary between different forms of metaphysical belief. I have analysed these elsewhere:[4] they include beliefs about absolutized sources, the subject (including agency), objects (including persons, abstract concepts, and causal processes), values, spatial and temporal boundaries, times (past, present or future), and meaning. Any of these types of metaphysical belief can be related to both specific biases (see 2.f) and specific philosophical forms.

4   Ibid.

2.d. Projection as the Denial of Embodiment

So long as we keep to the body and our soul is contaminated with this imperfection, there is no chance of our ever attaining satisfactorily to our object, which we assert to be Truth.
Plato, *Phaedo* 66b (trans. Tredennick)

The denial of embodiment can only be understood in relation to an experience of embodiment. Mindfulness practice is probably the best context in which to experience embodiment as fully as possible. In order to avoid trains of obsessive anxiety or craving, in mindfulness practice we allow ourselves to experience more fully what it is like to have a body, to enter into its proprioceptive awareness and relax its tensions. In a state of mindful awareness we also encounter the embodied basis of meaning, and realize how obsessive states narrow this meaning just as they tense the body. Whenever distraction arises, too, we can readily see that projection is occurring. As we are immersed in a distraction, each time, we assume that it is the whole story, and the wider awareness fails us that we would need to recognize our part in creating that story. The wider story ceases to be meaningful to us for a short while. Each time we return to wider awareness, however, we can again experience the body as a vehicle for liberating awareness and meaning.

Embodied meaning theory (often known confusingly as 'cognitive linguistics') has already been mentioned as the basis for an understanding of meaning as dependent on schemas and metaphors, thus constitutive of the meaning of archetypes (1.c and d). Its account of meaning is basically associative, dependent on accretions of links in the brain and nervous system. This has the huge advantage of being compatible both with a phenomenological approach to bodily experience, and with a neuroscientific understanding of the brain. On the other side, however, lies the entrenched representationalist tradition, which sees meaning as solely cognitive and truth-dependent, with 'emotive meaning' demoted to a separate and inferior status. It is representationalism that is the assumed basis of metaphysical belief, and that depends on the denial of embodiment.

Representationalism denies embodiment by adopting a view of meaning that is detached from bodily experience. A representationalist account of the meaning of a term (for instance, the truth-dependent theory of meaning) tends to regard propositions as the units of meaning, and the criterion of meaning as the matching of what a proposition represents with an understanding of when it would be true or false.[1] This has the effect of reducing meaning to a conceptual picture judged solely by an abstract matching process with hypothetical 'truths'. It approaches meaning in a top-down fashion, not taking into account the way in which 'truths' as we may understand them have to be built up as propositions. These propositions depend in turn on conceptual models grounded in metaphor and schema. Our experience is that we cannot understand a proposition *until* we link it metaphorically and schematically to our existing web of associations (think of failing to grasp a new idea until it is explained through an analogy). However, representationalism insists that our *experience* of meaning is irrelevant to its purely conceptual construction of it. 'Truth', that fragile construction topping a pyramid of underlying semantic conditions, is instead alleged to support the whole edifice at its base, in an upending of everything suggested by both the scientific and the experiential evidence.

Representationalism denies embodiment because it insists on a disembodied account of meaning. Such a denial must also be a projection, because it involves assuming that 'true' properties of an object must be present, either in the world or in our symbols for it, regardless of the process by which our ideas about it were developed. Regardless of the complex process by which an individual builds up a sense of the meaning of symbols and applies them to objects in experience, the meaning is assumed to be present, actually or potentially, *in the objects*. As a projection, this is the ultimate defensive move, the projection that entrenches projection in general, by insisting that everything we say is about things out there must be potentially true or false. Once we have understood meaning itself in terms of projection, all other interdependent projections are potentially strengthened.

We do not need to hold any explicit theory of meaning, or to hold a representationalist view intellectually, for this to occur, only to implicitly assume the topsy-turvy requirement for conceptuality to determine meaning. All that is required for this topsy-turvy requirement to implicitly operate is projection itself. By assuming the truth is 'out there', whether actually or hypothetically, we assume that our

---

1   See much more detailed account in Ellis (2013b) section 3.

words are capable of lining up with reality and thus that properties of our own symbolizing process exist beyond it. Projection is functionally equivalent to implicit representationalism, which is also equivalent to implicit metaphysical belief or absolutization, which is functionally equivalent to the denial of embodiment, because all of these processes only operate with the others. For instance, if I project the shadow onto my boss, I assume that she *is* evil, and that the meaning of 'she is evil' comes from a state of affairs in the world. At the same time I block off my embodied experience of empathy.

This projection is *projection of an archetype*, insofar as it accords with any of the four kinds of archetypal projection listed in the last chapter: goal-oriented, negative, appropriative, or transcendent. As explained there, any of these types of archetypal projection involve the assumption that the world must be a certain way so that we can reach our goals, avoid threats, appropriate the attractive, or grasp potential. All these functions being diachronic, they require us to format the world as fixed in a particular represented way over time. In order to make that assumption, we must simultaneously assume that our symbols for those archetypes get their meaning from a relationship to their reality. They can only be assumed to be true on the basis of an assumption that their symbols are capable of representing truth.

As we turn any of these archetypes into projected 'truths', we simultaneously lose the sense of the range of meaning in our bodies. For example, an appropriative projection of someone with whom we have fallen in love is physically exciting, but at the same time as being suffused by that excitement, we cease to be aware of our more subtle competing feelings: perhaps a sense of unease about the idealized person or a sense of our own fallibility. A negative projection focuses us even more narrowly on an object of hatred, that again cuts us off from awareness of the wider meaning of the hated person or object, with its correlations in our embodied experience in a sense of compassion that we repress. Again, meditation practice can help us to become more aware of the ways that we distract ourselves from more open underlying feelings when we are obsessively focused on an object of craving, hatred, idealization, or worship. It is awareness of our bodies that can help us to reconnect with those wider feelings.

This relationship of projection to the denial of embodiment, and conversely of integration with re-connection to embodiment, also reveals much about the relationship of religious experience to the meaningfulness of the un-projected archetypes. Religious experience can be understood in terms of 'flow' states, of *jhana* experience (temporary integration), and in terms of de-automatization (in which we open up new neural pathways), but any of these ways of seeing it involve greater embodied awareness (see 4.f). We become aware of the fuller meaningfulness of symbols as we connect them with new areas of our brain and nervous system, which are in turn connected with wider awareness of our body and emotional state. Such religious experiences may often be immediately projected, as a matter of cultural habit, but can hardly be intrinsically projected while they are actually happening: instead the experience gets processed into a 'belief' subsequently, as new energy is recruited to our group's dogmatic system of belief by appropriating these new sources of meaning to it. Religious dogma feeds on the energy of religious experience, just as representationalism feeds on that of embodied meaning. In each case a merely conceptual formulation takes itself to be prior, when it actually depends on a pyramid of more basic meaning conditions.

I will say more in section 5 about the ways that religious experience has been interpreted in specific religious traditions so as to obscure its basis in embodiment. Recognizing that basis in embodiment, and maintaining a critical perspective on the Platonic metaphysical assumptions that obscure it, forms a crucial part of the process of redirecting our understanding of each tradition away from projection and towards practical religion that can integrate the archetypes.

2.e. Projection as Left-Hemisphere Over-Dominance

Nature gave us the dichotomy when she split the brain. Working out what it means is not in itself to dichotomise: it only becomes so in the hands of those who interpret the results with Cartesian rigidity.
　　　　　　　　　Iain McGilchrist, The Master and His Emissary

The inclusion of a neuroscientific perspective in a book of this kind tends to raise two kinds of polarized reactions. On the one hand, there is a section of the population for whom any mention of the brain is assumed to be necessarily reductive. On the other, there are those with some knowledge of neuroscience for whom no inclusion of it in a synthetic perspective will ever be precise enough. My response to both extremes is the same. For me neuroscience offers a valuable *addition* to what we could already work out phenomenally from our own experience. If there ever appears to be a contradiction between the 'internal' perspective of having a mind, and the 'external' perspective of examining a brain, then we have cause to think again, using each perspective to check the other. When they corroborate each other, though, we can have reasonable confidence in the general picture that emerges. In that case it is also no offence to describe processes in the brain in non-specialized, broad-brush terms. The brain is complex, but so is everything else, and if we are to see the brain's complexity in relation to the complexity of everything else, we need to be able to use broad-brush, but provisional, ways of discussing it. The only effective alternative to that would be to confine discussion of the brain to a specialized focus where it would never be put in a wider context. I am happy to correct any inaccuracies in my use of neuroscience, but necessary approximations must not be confused with inaccuracies.

In the light of these caveats, then, I wish to put forward one central neuroscientific thesis: that projection is generally associated with the over-dominance of the processes that occur in the pre-frontal cortex of the brain's left hemisphere. That description may in some ways be an over-simplification, because we cannot simply assign all brain functions neatly to brain areas. However, there is plenty of evidence both from MRI (magnetic resonance imaging) of the brain, and from 'split-brain' effects when the left and right hemispheres of the brain are divided (or one of them is disabled), to support this general thesis.[1] It must be noted that we are not just

---

1　　McGilchrist (2009) ch. 2 (who gives a wide range of further references).

talking about left-brain *dominance*, which is normal, but left-brain *over-dominance*. Beyond a certain point, the dominance of the processes of this part of the brain excludes or eclipses that of others to a delusive extent, so that it absolutizes its own view and takes it to be true of the world, thus excluding any potentially challenging new information. It also needs to be noted that the language of left/right hemispheres is a shorthand for 'the hemisphere that performs the function that is performed in that hemisphere in the majority of individuals', since in some individuals those functions are reversed.

The key figure who in recent years has synthesized scientific findings on brain lateralization (left/right hemisphere division) and drawn out their implications for human thought is Iain McGilchrist. McGilchrist's key point is about the deluded tendency towards self-sufficiency of the mind in which the left hemisphere, especially the left pre-frontal cortex, is over-dominant. He does not over-simplify the distinctions between left and right hemisphere operations (for instance, it should not be presented as a contrast between 'reason' and 'emotion'). Nor should it be assumed that any given brain process does not in fact involve the interdependent operation of many areas of the brain, or that these processes are not surprisingly flexible in their location. Rather McGilchrist notes the *specialization* of the left hemisphere, the pre-frontal cortex of which combines goal-orientation and linguistic representation in close relationship.[2] A specialization is not an inflexible usage, but it nevertheless has a big effect, because we are always likely to follow ease of use by using the more effective parts of the brain that are best adapted for a given function. The hemispheres are effectively joined by the corpus callosum, but one of the main functions of this bridge is to allow each hemisphere to inhibit the other.[3]

Due to the over-dominance of the left hemisphere, our representations of the world are strengthened. The self-sufficiency of our reasonings about those representations, and our bias towards the confirmation of our beliefs, all thus become quickly apparent. These tendencies are likely to form closed loops with motivations of anxiety or craving coming from the amygdala and striatum further towards the base of the brain. However, given the self-sufficiency of the left pre-frontal cortex, these closed loops are likely to be

---

2   Ibid. pp. 113–15.
3   Ibid. pp. 17–19; Cook (1984).

reinforced rather than challenged by the motivated 'rationality' of the left hemisphere.[4]

By contrast, it is adequate and active connection with information from beyond these loops of confirmation bias that can help us change our beliefs in the light of new evidence. This comes from the brain's right hemisphere, which is connected with the senses, with emotional awareness, and with the basis of metaphorical meaning that can help us shift to new models of understanding.[5] The awareness of the right hemisphere is alive and flexible where that of the left is dead – tending towards the literal, the mechanical, and the calculating. The right hemisphere is thus predominantly the source of meaning in the ways identified by embodied meaning theory, but the left has a strong tendency to think of meaning in its own representationalist terms (i.e. as a set of purely cognitive equivalences).

It is thus evident that brain lateralization provides us with a clear understanding of the neurological basis of projection. A projection is a set of beliefs about an experienced object in the world that are taken to be 'real', and are thus clearly a construction of the left pre-frontal cortex. As long as the left hemisphere remains over-dominant, a set of motivating loops will lock us into that set of beliefs about the object, and we will continue to see it only in the projective way. However, sufficient openness to the wider experience mediated by the right hemisphere is required to challenge or overcome projection.

The differences between the two hemispheres' processing of time are also crucial for understanding the difference between projected and integrated archetypes. The left hemisphere has difficulty discriminating the experience of the process of time passing, but greater facility in time measurement and other concepts applied to time.[6] This leads to Zeno's Paradox, in which it seems 'rational' from a left-hemisphere standpoint that time and space are infinitely divisible, and so that an arrow will never reach its target, and Achilles racing with a tortoise at ten times the latter's speed will never pass it (**figure 4**). It is only the addition of the right-hemisphere perspective that provides the experience of time passing, and thus the common sense understanding that arrows do reach their targets, just as other objects pass through time and space.[7]

4   McGilchrist (2009) ch. 6; Depue and Morone-Strupinsky (2005) pp. 327–8.
5   McGilchrist (2009) ch. 5.
6   Ibid. pp. 75–7; Buchtel et al. (1978); Bertoloni et al. (1978).
7   McGilchrist (2009) pp. 137–40.

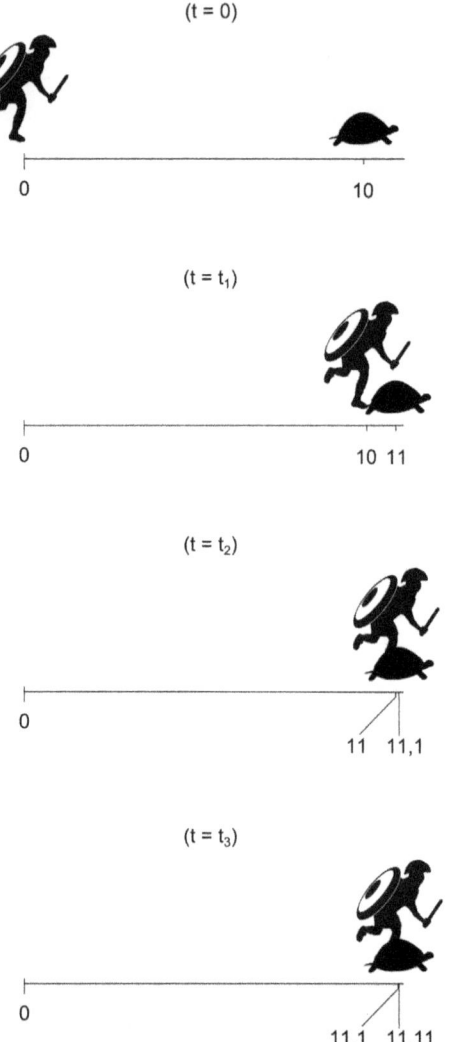

Figure 4. Diagram of Zeno's paradox of Achilles and the tortoise, by Daniele Pugliese (Wikimedia Commons).
Creative Commons Attribution Share-Alike 3.0 Unported license.

The diachronic nature of the archetypal functions is thus what makes them difficult to access from a left-hemisphere point of view. Rather than recognizing that archetypal functions are developed over time, an over-dominant left-hemisphere perspective may lead us to insist either that they 'do not exist' (just as the continuity of space and time 'does not exist'), or that they 'do exist', but in a form that is extra-temporal and thus 'supernatural'. Split-brain patients with injuries to the right hemisphere, when confronted with an experience that they cannot explain without its accustomed specialized activity, simply confabulate.[8] The projection of archetypes can thus be seen similarly as an assumption that an archetypal function that operates over time is absolutely present or not present at any one given time.

This results in the literalistic reduction of archetypal forms, the most obvious example of which is the eternality of God. The theological debate about what God's eternality means, and whether he operates within or beyond time, is evidently a product of our difficulty in reconciling the perspective of one of our hemispheres to the other. The other archetypal functions, however, have also been turned into extra-temporal ideals whose 'existence' can then be affirmed or denied: devils and demons, goddesses, apotheosized heroes, demigods, messiahs, Mahdis, and Buddhas amongst them. All of these can be integrated as archetypal symbols through their embodied and integrable meaning as metaphorical expressions of archetypal schemas, engaged through the right hemisphere. However, their projection as supernatural entities requires a left-hemisphere focus only on their dead literal meaning as a concept.

---

8   Ibid. p. 81; Drake and Bingham (1985).

2.f. Projection as Bias

If one harbours anywhere in one's mind a nationalistic loyalty or hatred, certain facts, though in a sense known to be true, are inadmissible.
George Orwell

Bias is now a well-established feature of cognitive psychology, supported by a wealth of empirical evidence about the ways we deceive ourselves. Although something like 200 or so separate biases have been identified and labelled, these are all inter-related phenomena that often imply each other to form patterns of delusion. Perhaps the most basic biases are confirmation bias,[1] attribute substitution,[2] belief bias,[3] and the belief disconfirmation paradigm.[4] Put together these respectively identify ways that we tend to focus on confirmations of what we already believe (ignoring contrary indications), substitute easier processes for more difficult ones, avoid reasoning that challenges our beliefs, and repress cognitive dissonance.[5] These four biases together create a cyclic process by which our assumptions are absolutized and projected. Any one of them potentially provides an explanation of the process of projection. This is based on economy of effort in some circumstances that, made habitual, is then disadvantageous in others. Confirmation bias, for instance, enables us to check a situation much more quickly and easily than we could do with more openness to new possibilities. Attribute substitution also saves energy: we use less glucose in the brain when we substitute an easier problem for a harder one.[6]

All other biases can also be understood in these terms. I have analysed these in detail elsewhere.[7] Biases absolutize sources, objects, values, subjects, agency, boundaries, time, and meaning – often in combining and overlapping ways. Whatever it is that we have beliefs about, whether positive or negative, can be judged in ways that avoid the examination of alternatives so as to save effort. Of course, we also save effort by using the parts of our brains to do it with that have developed to do it most economically: which will

1   Wason (1960).
2   Kahneman (2011) pp. 97–104.
3   Evans, Barston, and Pollard (1983).
4   Festinger, Riecken, and Schachter (1956).
5   Ellis (2015a) 3.d.
6   Kahneman (2011) ch. 2.
7   Ellis (2015a) section 3.

imply the use of the left hemisphere to confirm our existing beliefs in preference over the investigation of new ones using the right.

For example, the bias known as sunk costs fallacy prevents us from recognizing the need to abandon a project that we have put lots of time and effort into.[8] Rather than understanding the wider conditions of the failure of the project and that we will not achieve our goals through it, we continue to *project* success onto the project. A correlative negative of reactive projection is also possible in response to this fallacy, whereby on becoming aware of it we overcompensate and start to project failure prematurely onto projects that might well still succeed. This is obviously a goal-oriented type of projection, in which we see the whole world in terms that can fulfil our goals, and thus a projection of the hero archetype. Deluded heroes are especially prone to the sunk costs fallacy, pursuing a hopeless and fruitless quest, or 'flogging a dead horse'.

To take another example, in the actor-observer bias, we tend to minimize our own responsibility for negative outcomes of our actions by viewing them as situational, due to the surrounding conditions rather than our own judgements.[9] When our own actions have positive effects, though, we are keen to claim the credit for them (self-serving bias),[10] and when others' actions lead to negative effects, we tend to blame them and hold them responsible (known by psychologists, strangely, as the 'fundamental attribution error'). This is obviously either a goal-oriented projection or a negative projection, products of the projected hero or shadow archetypes. Where we ourselves are concerned, we again assume that the world is such as to make our goal-fulfilment possible (unless we overcompensate and start to believe it is intrinsically against us). Where others are concerned (at least when we do not identify with them), we project the shadow by seeing the surrounding conditions as though they were controlled by their malign designs rather than proceeding independently or unpredictably.

Other biases, such as the halo effect, reflect appropriative projection. Here we find a person attractive in one respect (for example, physical beauty), and assume that they have positive features in every other respect,[11] thus making them a more consistently fitting

8   Kahneman (2011) p. 343.
9   Jones and Nisbett (1971).
10 Campbell and Sedikides (1999).
11 Dion, Berscheid, and Walster (1972).

object for our positive projection. Just as any of the other archetypes can be developed into the God archetype, so can almost any bias also be developed into a projection of transcendence, merely by being turned into a totalizing projection seeing design, power, or goodness in the conditions of the universe as a whole. The sunk costs fallacy would become a transcendent projection, for example, if we believed that all our projects were fated to eventually succeed according to the designs of God or of the universe. Responsibility biases could become transcendent projections as soon as we adopt a belief that God wills all events through us, or that all events are fated. The halo effect could become transcendent when we start to apotheosize the idealized person, believing her beauty to be a manifestation of divine beauty in the universe as a whole.

In the same way, it is possible to go through all the biases identified by cognitive psychology analysing them as archetypal projections. This is of course not the way in which cognitive psychologists are accustomed to discussing them. This is not only due to overspecialization in which concepts from different areas of enquiry are not related to each other, though this must contribute. The prevailing discourse about biases has tended to focus, not on their practical effects, but on their evolutionary explanation. By being seen as evolved for a purpose in early human evolution, biases have also tended to have their ethical power neutralized. Rather than being seen as bad tendencies that we should try to overcome, biases are readily excused as unavoidable genetic hangovers from early human history. I will discuss the question of ethics further in 2.i below. However, I suggest that recognizing projection as an ethical issue is interdependent with recognizing bias as an ethical issue. In both cases it depends on us adopting a psychologically-adequate understanding of ethics as integration, rather than the binary assumption that ethics is either merely some kind of social regulatory function, or a matter of transcendent and dogmatic claims.

I do not pretend to know, nor am I concerned with, whether bias is entirely innate, or if so how and why it developed. We do not need to know how or why bias developed to recognize and work with how it functions now. Central to its practical function now is not its origin, but its relationship to absolutization as a response (which is merely another way of describing its relationship to projection). A bias *continues* to occur, in circumstances where we might possibly correct it, because we continue to assume that the way we are thinking about things under the influence of the bias is the whole story. We are not sufficiently aware of other options to make provisionality possible, but remain dominated by our goal, our rejection, our appropriation, or our transcendent view in a way that skews our whole sense of 'reality'. In some circumstances, we may also flip into reactive projection, in which we assume that total rejection of the bias is also the whole story, so that we assume there is no truth at all to our view of the projected object. Whatever the causes of bias, then, the general pattern of how we need to respond to it lies in the cultivation of awareness of alternative options, in between unreflective awareness of the bias and reactive rejection of it.[12]

The same case can be made about the fallacies discussed in philosophy and critical thinking as about biases. Fallacies are conventionally thought of as mistakes in reasoning or abrogations of rationality, but when we focus on the psychological conditions that lead to people failing to change their thinking when caught up in them, they are functionally equivalent to biases. The false dichotomy between 'reason' and 'emotion' is of no help here, because (although some attention to reasoning may help up to a point) avoiding fallacious reasoning cannot be wholly separated from 'emotion'.[13]

Fallacies, too, then, can be functionally analysed as absolutizations and projections. For example, the *ad hominem* fallacy consists of an attempt to defeat (or sometimes to uncritically accept) another person's argument by appealing to beliefs about how they are as people. The problem with this fallacy does not lie in an absolute distinction between the justification of an argument and the nature of the person making it, but rather in the absoluteness of the identification of an argument with a person. It is neither the case that the justification is totally independent of the person, nor that it is totally dependent, but rather that a complex (and usually *largely* independent) relationship between them is simplified so that alternatives that would require extra effort to consider are ruled out. If you accept someone else's *ad hominem* argument without any thought about the alternatives, you have adopted the same (usually goal-oriented and/or negative) projection as them.

Particularly common fallacies in our treatment of archetypes are, in addition to *ad hominem*, straw man (where we attribute a position

---

12   For a fuller argument on these lines see Ellis (2015b).
13   Ellis (2015a) 7.j.

to someone that they wouldn't accept), false dichotomy, appeal to authority, *tu quoque* (where hypocrisy is negatively absolutized), and single cause fallacy. A shadow projection, for example, could readily involve all of these. We would attack a hated person's arguments because of who they are, misrepresent their beliefs, treat them as a wholly separate negative thing with no positive features, appeal to other people's blame or condemnation as wholly legitimating our own, use any hypocrisy to discredit them, and assume them to be the sole cause of any negative events associated with them. Fallacy phenomena can help us to identify closely how projection works, and yet for some reason fallacy is hardly ever discussed in relation to projection.

2.g. Projection as Reinforcing Feedback

Watch out! If you see feedback loops everywhere, you're already in danger of becoming a systems thinker! Instead of seeing only how A causes B, you'll begin to wonder how B may also influence A – and how A might reinforce or reverse itself…. When someone tells you that population growth causes poverty, you'll ask yourself how poverty may cause population growth.

Donella Meadows, *Thinking in Systems*, pp. 33–4

A further perspective from which to understand the phenomenon of projection is that of systems theory. The mind-body is a complex system within which smaller complex systems are embedded, and which is in turn embedded within wider ecosystems, social systems, and meaning systems. None of these systems has absolute boundaries, but each consists in sets of interactive processes that maintain a certain degree of stability. These processes consist of two different sorts of feedback loops that either maintain or change the patterns of interaction in the face of new outward conditions. The two sorts of feedback loops can be described as positive and negative, closed and open, or reinforcing and balancing. After using these other forms of terminology for feedback loops in previous publications, I have now settled on Donella Meadows' usage of 'reinforcing' and 'balancing' as the clearest labels to use for them.[1] A further potential source of confusion is the fact that the term 'archetype' is used in the context of systems theory in a quite different sense (meaning a pattern of behaviour in a system): this is obviously distinct from the way I am using the term in this book.

Reinforcing feedback is defensive in nature, attempting to maintain an existing system in its current form. For example, a plant may respond to insecurity in its environment by reproducing more (creating more insecurity in its environment through competition), or a jealous lover may alienate her beloved by demands for energy and attention, creating a spiral of interdependent alienation and jealousy. Reinforcing feedback tends to lead to multiplicative, snowballing effects. Balancing feedback, on the other hand, adjusts the relationship between one system and its surrounding, interdependent systems back into the direction of greater stability, by incorporating new information. A thermostat does this in a simple way,

---

1   Meadows (2008) pp. 25–34.

by responding to feedback about temperature changes in a house with adjustments in the heat created, so as to maintain a constant temperature. In organisms such as human beings, reinforcing and balancing feedback loops can be seen as ways that we adjust or fail to adjust our implicit beliefs in response to new information that we either use or ignore (**figure 5**).

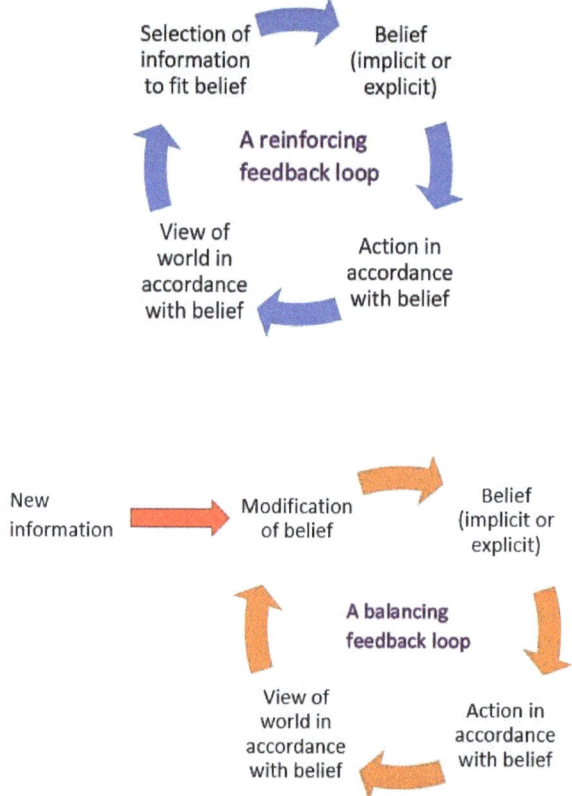

Figure 5. Reinforcing and balancing feedback loops (diagram by the author).

Systems theorists have generally discussed the cognitive dimension of systems in terms of 'knowledge',[2] but I think this is inadequate. Meaning and belief are feedback responses to our environment that can have a reinforcing or balancing effect. Knowledge, on the other hand, is a representationalist construction implying a

---

2   E.g. see Maturana and Varela (1987); Capra and Luisi (2014).

correspondence between beliefs and 'reality' that is quite foreign to a systems perspective. The representationalist habit of thinking of 'knowledge' as the starting point of justified belief seems to have carried over unnecessarily. The reinforcing or balancing effects of meaning and belief, however, offer a helpful perspective both on archetypes in general and on their projection.

Firstly, archetypal functions in general can be seen as balancing feedback functions. As discussed in 2.e above, the limitation of our dominant left pre-frontal cortex in experiencing the process of time creates a difficulty for us in developing sustainable habits and institutions (ones that can deal with a range of conditions, not just the ones we identify with at present). We tend to identify with a particular time, whether past, present, or future, and ignore or discount other times, resulting in a wide range of temporally based cognitive biases such as procrastination, sunk costs fallacy, survivorship bias, and neomania.[3] In compensation for this, a variety of human traditions have developed, including religious ones. As Nassim Nicholas Taleb puts this, 'religion exists to enforce tail risk management over generations'.[4] These traditions provide constant archetypal reminders of the importance of longer-term goals, threats, relationships, and potentials which help us to adjust our assumptions, our beliefs, and our actions and avoid multiplicative destabilizing effects.

In systems theory, however, reinforcing and balancing effects often build on one another. A process that initially balances can later overshoot and thus also create reinforcing effects. On the other hand, a generally reinforcing effect can develop balancing features to mitigate its worst effects. So it is with religious archetypes, which may have developed to have a balancing function, but then instead started to be used primarily in a reinforcing function. The balancing function of the archetypes consists largely of meaning – that is, of patterns of association between symbols and experiences – providing us with a greater sense of the meaningfulness of a diachronic perspective. However, in the transition to the modern era discussed in 1.h, 'religion' has come to be associated primarily with beliefs about projected archetypes that were possibly schematic but not diachronic. As a result the archetypes expressed in religion began instead to have a predominantly reinforcing function.

3   Ellis (2015a) 3.j.
4   Taleb (2018) p. 217.

Projection can readily be seen to have a reinforcing function, because it is the means by which an organism maintains its view of the world in defiance of potentially conflicting information. For example, a person who projects the shadow onto another, interpreting complex information about them as a threat, is maintaining a construction of the world as threat, and thus contributing to a proliferating cyclic response of gearing himself against that threat and seeking out further threats. By projecting, we reinforce the tendency to project further in the same way, and also encourage those we project onto to counter-project, feeding the same assumptions further by making them self-fulfilling.

The reinforcing feedback function of projected archetypes can also be seen in the dogmatic and absolutist nature of beliefs about them. Whilst a provisional belief can be reconsidered in the light of new evidence, a dogmatic belief can only be justified because of circular reasoning or false dichotomizing about the alternatives. These involve confirmation bias: the only justifications they offer are likely to involve appeals to authority without any alternative sources, or appeals to the negative features of one opposed alternative without other alternatives, or appeals to an emotion associated with the dogma without consideration of other ways we might feel. For example, dogmatic moral beliefs might be supported by selective appeal to the Bible, which will be entirely attributed to the authority of God, without any consideration for alternative ways of interpreting that source or its meaning. This justification will also be contrasted with only one caricatured, opposite, alternative that will be seen as a threat: for example 'atheism'. Confirmation bias tends to reinforce reliance on limited sources of justification and the ruling out of alternatives, again reinforcing this characteristic in the future.

Projection also creates reinforcing feedback through opposition, because it is the source of conflict.[5] Negative projection (of the shadow) creates conflict by simplifying a complex object into an object of rejection, whose utterances and actions are thus likely to be interpreted as in conflict with the projector. Positive projection, on the other hand, creates exclusivity (and thus conflicts) out of competitiveness in fulfilling the same goals, appropriating the same person's attention, or receiving an idealized person's favour. Conflict creates a cycle of further conflict, as others react in opposition to a

5   Zimmer (1955).

projection with counter-projection, or become allies with those on either side of a conflict through shared group membership.

A conflict may also be internal through a mechanism of repression. By projecting, we repress those aspects of our own psyche that are not projecting: for example, if we project the shadow by regarding someone as hateful, we repress our compassion for them. Repression then creates further reinforcing feedback, because continuing energy is required to maintain this repression that can no longer be given to other priorities – and one result of this can be psychosomatic disease. Such repression can be distinguished from temporary suppression, or an aware non-expression as opposed to unaware inhibition.[6]

There are thus a variety of ways in which archetypal projection produces a cycle of reinforcing feedback, in the process also inducing reinforcing feedback processes in other systems. Conflict, repression, dogmatism, and habitual reaction have negative effects on the whole human organism through stress. This in turn impacts the whole of human society through ongoing negative changes in culture, politics, economics, intellectual life, impact on the environment, and deterioration of relationships. In the next chapter I will trace the specifically socio-political impacts of this, and in 2.i the wider question of its moral valuation.

---

6   King and Emmons (1990).

2.h. Projection as Power

> *The ideas of the ruling class are in every epoch the ruling ideas.... The class which has the means of material production at its disposal, has control at the same time over the means of mental production, so that thereby, generally speaking, the ideas of those who lack the means of mental production are subject to it.*
> Karl Marx and Frederick Engels, *The German Ideology*
> (trans. Lough)

The projection of archetypes has huge socio-political implications, because it is an easy shortcut to power. Absolutization enables an instrumental mode in our relationships with others, which motivates domination, subordination, and group membership, in absolute forms that are not open to scrutiny. These range from the divine right of kings to workplace bullying. By the same means, it enables absolutized ideology, from state religions to Marxism. The archetypal projections are easily identifiable in exploitative political behaviour, by politicians who themselves may also be in the grip of archetypal projections. The exploitation of religious archetypes in politics is thus hardly surprising, and indeed scarcely separable from its exploitation in religious organizations.

Projection provides a basis of power because the absolute nature of projection makes it impossible to question (because alternatives apart from mere negation have been ruled out by the framing – see 2.c). Projection of the God archetype thus provides unquestionable authority. Projection of the hero archetype provides unquestionable belief in the hero's goals and his effort and sincerity in striving for them. Projection of the anima/animus creates a bonded relationship, even if it is dysfunctional. Projection of the shadow provides power through the allegedly shared threat of the common enemy. As long as we are unable to look behind the simplicity of our projections to identify a more complex picture, there is no possibility of questioning these forms of power when we are exposed to their influence. Although none of them offers a total determinant to our judgements, the result of them conflicting with each other is often entrenched conflict rather than a consideration of different options beyond the projections.

The instrumentality of these projections lies in the left-hemisphere dominant nature of the illusion (as discussed above in 2.e), the left hemisphere viewing others as objects to be manipulated or obstacles to be avoided, rather than live persons like ourselves.[1] Viewing others as live persons introduces a potential complexity to our response to them, which may make it much more intuitive (rather than calculating) or allow our thinking to engage in alternative interpretations of them. Very often, though, our intuitive responses seem subordinated to hierarchical ones, in which we either try to exploit others, or to subordinate ourselves to a more powerful person in the hope of receiving favour. Our thinking then becomes dominated by appeals to authority rather than attempts to weigh up whatever has been claimed, whether those appeals are to others' authority or to our own.

This relationship of domination or subordination operates not only in relation to other individuals, but in relation to groups as a whole. A series of identifiable group biases (groupthink, ingroup bias, social proof, and false consensus) show our tendency to bypass reflectiveness in groups, and allow the desire for group conformity to take over.[2] In accordance with prototype theory (discussed in 1.i), however, our projected view of the group is not one of all its members as an abstract mass, but of a prototypical member who fulfils the role of the group. This effect is stronger the more sharply defined the group is (for example, how clear its boundaries are and how justifiable generalizations are about its members). This can be readily seen in our relationships with clearly defined groups such as national groups, occupational groups, class groups, or kinship groups. Our archetypal projections onto groups are thus actually projections onto prototypical constructions of those groups, and these in turn allow us to be dominated by the group. These projections may often be onto the leaders of well-defined and hierarchized groups, or onto authoritative members who represent the wider group in other ways (e.g. localized leaders). Such projections are not inevitable. As social beings, we need the affirmation of groups, but that need can be fulfilled either in these absolutizing ways or in more open, complex, immediate relationships.

Groups can be readily seen as the objects of all four types of archetypal projection. Religious or political groups who offer a strong idealistic potentiality (such as monastics) may especially be recipients of the transcendence projection. Heroic groups attracting

---

1   McGilchrist (2009) pp. 54–6.
2   Ellis (2015a) 3.e.

goal-oriented projection will especially be ones that we are bound to in a joint effort, such as a close-knit work team. Appropriative projection may apply to groups of unattainable others (such as bathing maidens), or to romanticized other cultures (such as in the past or in the orient). Negative projection of course applies to demonized groups, such as enemies in war ('The Hun') or scapegoated immigrants.

Absolutized ideology is normally spread and maintained by a group and is the price of group membership.[3] Judgements which determine membership of, or rejection from, a group have been shown to be expressed more abstractly than those that do not.[4] We submit to the group's authority, and get a quick access to its support, by accepting its beliefs, which will be of an absolute kind so as to be placed beyond challenge. This is the main way that metaphysical beliefs are propagated. These ideologies can obviously also incorporate formalizations of projected archetypes, such as theological doctrines about God or racist claims about demonized ethnic groups.

The political exploitation of religion is thus scarcely surprising. A system that may have served most helpfully to provide humans with balancing feedback to compensate for their 'bounded rationality' has also been dangerously open to abuse by political leaders and groups from the beginning. It has compensated for the limitations of immediate consequential thinking by the introduction of general principles, and supported traditional authorities that maintained the values of groups over generations. However, those principles could very easily be interpreted so as to prioritize the interests of ruling classes. Obvious examples include the use of Hinduism to support the rigidly hierarchized Indian *varna* (four class) system,[5] and the co-option of Christianity for political ends by Constantine and his successors.[6] At one and the same time, religion could then provide its adherents with meaning and inspiration, whilst being a tool for their exploitation. The projection of archetypes is crucial for understanding both how that vein of cognitive dissonance running through religion has occurred, and also how it can be alleviated.

3   Ibid. 1.f.
4   Maass et al. (1989).
5   See Olivelle (2004).
6   See Kee (1982).

The Projection of Archetypes

The key Western figure who has contributed to our awareness of the exploitation of religion as a tool of political power is Marx. However, with the possible exception of some subtle modern interpretations, Marxism offers reactive projection rather than a way out of the effects of projection. Religion as a tool of class oppression is removed, in the classic Marxist analysis, by the atheism that accompanies the dictatorship of the proletariat.[7] The proletariat is thus obviously the object of a goal-oriented projection, identified with absolutely as the hero that will defeat the monster of capitalism along with its accompanying religious lackeys. The Marxian vision of the Communist Society at the end of history provides another type of projection, this time of the realization of ultimate potential of the kind we find in a transcendence projection.[8] Rather than an adequate account of the processes that would be required to move us gradually towards the resolution of class conflicts, Marx gave us metaphysical beliefs embedded in theories that are only superficially empirical.[9] At the same time, his reliance on these archetypes offers a further indication of how central they are to human aspiration.

---

7 'Economic and Political Manuscripts': Marx (1977) p. 108.
8 McLellan (1971) pp. 239 ff.
9 See Popper (1962) chs. 18–21.

2.i. Projection as Evil

The demonic is the elevation of something conditional to unconditional significance.

Paul Tillich, *Systematic Theology*

Modern discussion about ethics is marked by the prevalence of a false dichotomy between absolutism and relativism. If we don't follow the unreflective popular use of 'good' and 'evil' to justify our own or our group's preferences, we may try to avoid using them at all, or use them only descriptively to refer to 'relative' beliefs ('x people believe that y is evil' rather than any discussion of whether it actually is so). In this chapter I will draw on my more detailed discussions of ethics elsewhere[1] to offer a perspective that avoids this dichotomy, and that readily interlocks with the foregoing theory of archetypes and their projection.

The key point from which this begins is that ethics *does not* have to be justified metaphysically, nor is it reducible to a mere method of social control. Instead, it is rooted in our experience, and can be justified through an understanding of projection and integration. However, moral experience more readily tells us about evil than about good. It is easier to justify reversing the usual course of moral justification of making deductions downwards from a source of goodness, and instead to identify sources of evil *in our experience*, the avoidance of which will then offer an indirect understanding of good. The values that we identify as *good* from our own experience are likely to be very limited by our unavoidable confirmation bias, but *evil* is identifiable from experience diachronically, each time we find a wider perspective to contrast with a previous absolutized projection.

Evil in human experience is not a quality that can be applied to a whole person or a whole group. So we cannot possibly justify 'Hitler was evil' type claims: Hitler was complex. Instead, it can be identified with the quality of absolutization or projection itself. As Sartre expressed it, 'Evil is the systematic substitution of the abstract for the concrete.'[2] Not even the content of our beliefs is evil, but *the way they are held* can be evil, when they are taken to be the whole story and to exclude other options.

---

1 Ellis (2012) section 7.
2 Sartre (1963) p. 263.

In seeing evil in this way, I argue that we are helpfully fulfilling the shadow function rather than projecting it. There is nothing wrong with wishing to avoid threats, because some people, things, and conditions do pose a threat to us, and our embodied experience is unavoidably one in which we will react to potential threats with an activated amygdala and a burst of cortisol to mobilize our bodies against that threat.[3] We should not deny that there are such threats. To do so would be an overreaction against our tendency to unhelpfully project them. Some of these threats are also not just threats to us as individuals, but more profound and long-term threats – for example to our group, to human society, to the world's ecosystems, or to anything else that we can identify with more widely. Some of these threats also come from people's judgements (which can be absolutized) rather than unchangeable non-human forces. Our challenge is thus not to stop believing in evil, but rather to identify it appropriately. As we do so, we will cease to rely on reinforcing feedback loops in our way of thinking about the threat, even though those loops continue at the organic level to maintain our existence. What's most important is not to give up thinking about evil, but not to think about it in an evil way.

The evil that we discover each time we move from a narrow projection to a wider recognition beyond projection is not a 'relative' evil in the sense of being equal in value to every other 'subjective' identification of evil. Identifying absolutization (for instance in my boss's judgement, or in my reaction to it) is not just a matter of preferences. Nor is it an absolute evil guaranteed by supernatural beliefs. Rather it is an incremental move forward in the direction of good that arises from identifying an evil to be avoided. Our beliefs about it need to be provisional rather than absolute, but nevertheless they are the best available basis of judgement in a given set of circumstances.

It is this process of recognition of evil that provides a point of leverage, and thus enables us to define evil in an entirely practical way. There is no practical benefit in defining projection in general as evil, given that much projection is not reflected upon, nor compared with the possibility of integrating the archetypes. That would not be likely to enable better judgement that avoids that evil. So, for instance, unreflecting traditional 'belief' in God is probably not

---

3   Mobbs et al. (2009).

helpfully identified as evil. Instead, evil should only be identified at points of leverage where its identification as such in our own experience can help us to avoid it. Thinking diachronically, we need to be able to identify the threat posed by absolutization and projection to our long-term ability to meet needs in a variety of conditions. For instance, it might be at the point where a traditional believer starts to notice the effects of her community's dogmas about God. The idea that the effects of this dogma are the very opposite of what she has believed (evil rather than good) might then start to be fruitful. The use of the shadow function is appropriate for this – not in a projection of evil without awareness, but in an aware recognition of what is genuinely evil. Far from being an example of demonizing, such a use of the concept of evil will help us recognize that demonizing is itself evil, along with avoidable positive forms of projection.

One major justification for seeing evil in terms of projection and absolutization lies in the meaning of evil as it is identifiable in our cultural constructions of it. Human figures that we construct as representing evil consistently show extreme over-dominant left-hemisphere features,[4] and these are also features of projection. We can trace depictions of all the four types of archetypal projection in the way that symbols of the shadow are depicted, for example in figures like Satan, J.R.R. Tolkien's Sauron, or J.K. Rowling's Voldemort. Such figures tend to project transcendence on themselves, making them obsessed with power: Satan's rebellion against God symbolizes this (**figure 6**). They are excessively goal-oriented, typically being obsessed with world domination, revenge, or some other malevolent aim that they will achieve at all costs. Thus they are heroic, but only in a projected way that lacks insight into the limitations of their obsessive goals, or proportionality in their approach to achieving them. They are totally instrumental and manipulative in the use of others as tools for their purposes, lacking any capacity for genuine relationships that recognize others as living persons, indicating appropriative projection in relationships. Cruelty is also the result of a narrow focus on ideas about someone rather than a response to them as a whole. Shadow figures also tend to project the shadow in their turn, assuming their own limited perspectives in others. In Tolkien's *Lord of the Rings*, as in many other similar narratives, this blindness to any wider motives than their own is

---

4   Ellis (2015a) 3.n.

the weakness of figures of evil. If someone else possesses a tool of power, a figure of evil assumes that it will be necessarily used in the narrow pursuit of power: 'That we should seek to destroy the Ring itself has not yet entered into his darkest dream.'[5]

Figure 6. Satan's rebellion: Michael casts out rebel angels, illustration by Gustave Doré for John Milton's *Paradise Lost* (1866).
Public Domain picture.

It thus seems that evil is intuitively associated with projection, just as it is associated with falsehood in general. Such falsehood is not necessarily a matter of deliberate or manipulative lying, but rather of maintaining a basic construction of the world in which one's own projections are all there is. These constructions do not only consist of beliefs about the world and about others' characters, but also of the emotions associated with those beliefs. False emotion has been associated with left-hemisphere control,[6] in which emotion

5   Tolkien (1954) book 3 ch. 6.
6   Gazzaniga and Smylie (1990).

becomes narrowly goal-oriented rather than a spontaneous expression of an embodied state. The evil laugh, in which a constructed idea of mirth substitutes for the spontaneous version, is perhaps the most striking manifestation of such false emotion. The villain with the evil laugh not only lives in an entirely projected world of narrowed assumptions, but sees no higher possibility in which things could be otherwise.

We sense evil in such figures because we have a response to threat that recognizes projection as a long-term source of it, whether that projection occurs in others or in ourselves. Very often, however, our response to this intuition about projection is to wholly misunderstand its value, and to project it in turn onto figures of evil that we take to 'exist' or 'not to exist' as such. We have also taken evil to be a rebellion against an easily definable good, and thus counter-dependent on our metaphysical constructions of a universe run by a good God or a natural order: however, my thesis is that these metaphysical constructions are themselves evil projections. In order to find good, we need to be able to move beyond projections of good as well as those of evil, substituting balancing feedback loops for reinforcing ones by opening our minds to new information.

St Augustine's influential definition of evil as the privation of good[7] has dominated Western thinking on the subject for many centuries, but this is a theoretical approach that needs to be completely up-ended. It is only by coincidence that there has been some degree of accuracy in our traditional conception of evil as an absence of the projected features of a divine absolute, because the negative rejection of one absolute is another absolute, and both are applicable (at best) only in certain specific conditions. Belief in Satan as a supernatural entity is evil because it is metaphysical, just as belief in God is. However, our conception of good needs to change entirely, to one based on agnosticism about absolute claims and thus avoidance of projection of all kinds. This puts us not in a sphere of closely-defined divine rules, but rather in a sphere of openness in which there are many possible ways to be good, and in which optionality rather than conformity is recognized as the direction in which an embodied human can move towards a sustainable and harmonious relationship with itself, its fellows, and its environment. It is that sphere of openness to which I turn next.

7   Augustine (1945) 11.9.

3. The Integration of Archetypes

3.a. The Middle Way and the Integration Process

The high-blazing flame is the middle way, whose luminous course runs between the human and the divine.
    Carl Jung, *The Red Book,* Liber Secundus 43

It's now time to turn to the more positive process by which the projection of archetypes can be overcome. Integration enables archetypal functions to be fulfilled and religion to operate practically. In that process, too, many other things will occur: moral development towards good, movement out of power mode, the use of balancing rather than reinforcing feedback loops, the weakening of bias, the more effective working of the right hemisphere with the left, and the avoidance of metaphysics. However, there will be no need to go over all these different ways of describing what is occurring at every point, because the main emphasis for understanding the integration process needs to be practical – namely, understanding what kinds of actions can *help* it to occur. I will thus be organizing the next four chapters in terms of different kinds of practices. Before launching into these, though, we need an overview of the nature of integration, and also of the Middle Way.

Integration is the process by which projection is overcome, not by reaching some delusion-free 'reality', but by dialectically reducing the conflicts that produce projection. Every projection is comprehensible as a conflict of some kind, whether understood at a social or a psychological level. For example, a projection of the shadow is a conflict between a threat response and our sense of compassion towards another person, whilst a projection of the God archetype is a conflict between a strong sense of open potential and a realistic recognition of the ways that potential remains unfulfilled in practice.

Integration does not *necessarily* dissolve these conflicts, but they can nevertheless be lessened by the application of awareness to re-frame the assumptions on which they are based. In the dialectical structure that characterizes integration, thesis and antithesis (conflicting desires with attendant beliefs) are placed in a wider context in which synthesis is possible, because the assumptions about the entities that create the conflict become questionable. New options are opened up that allow a better adaptation to conditions than the previous framing allowed. To the extent that previously clashing energies are united, new energy also becomes available for more integrated goals. There is a 'peace dividend', not just in the economies of areas that have resolved previous conflict, such as Northern Ireland, but also for individuals who can devote their lives to something more productive than hatred.

Although Jung did use the term 'integration', that of 'individuation' is more common in his work. He is also more likely to articulate the process in terms of the resolution of conflicts over a lifetime than in terms of a particular process of resolution seen in a more restricted time frame. However, both the long-term and short-term frames offer instances of integration, which can occur at different scales. Sometimes conflicts are apparently so deeply rooted that a lifetime's patient engagement with them may seem inadequate. At other times, however, a false assumption (say, that ambiguity is due to deception) creates an entirely unnecessary conflict just within a given practical situation.

Immediate conflicts usually combine a psychological and social dimension. For example, a politician may avoid the addressing of an issue by the use of an *ad hominem* diversion (see 2.f), attacking a person rather than addressing the relevant issue. There, the conflict occurs within the politician psychologically (against his awareness of, and potential sympathy with, the opponent's perspective) as well as socio-politically. This conflict can be resolved in that particular situation by that individual becoming aware of a bigger picture. That means that both sides in the conflict need to be united in dealing with problems rather than trying to beat each other, and that it is recognized that *ad hominem* argument (or any other displacement) will not facilitate this process. This creates the conditions for healing the division at a socio-political level simultaneously with that at a psychological level. So integration is not only about individual development, but can also consist in the refinement of group perspectives.

The two mules pictures (**figure 7**) illustrate the process of integration through dialectic. The two mules are in fruitless conflict only because of the way they are framing a particular situation. They

The Integration of Archetypes

both want to eat hay, but the hay is in two piles, and it only occurs to them to eat one pile each at a time. Because they are tied together, this desire is impossible to fulfil, and each blocks the other from fulfilling it. To fulfil their needs, the mules need to be forced by frustration to re-frame the situation, which they do at a moment of greater awareness. In this re-framing, their previously separate views are synthesized, so that they can work together. Interestingly, too, the resolution involves a shift from a synchronic to a diachronic perspective. A situation of conflict at one time is resolvable when it is considered over time, so long as the mules co-operate in eating both types of hay.

Figure 7. The two mules, based on a traditional fable and originally used on a pacifist poster created by the Society of Friends (Quakers) with the caption 'co-operation is better than conflict'.
Public Domain picture.

This diachronic element of the integration process shows the ways in which the practical use of archetypes can directly aid integration. In the third picture, where the mules are straining against each other, you could see them as caught up in a projection of the goal-oriented function, each seeing themselves as acting heroically within their small set of parameters. The mules do not lose this goal-orientation after their moment of realization, but just find more integrated ways to apply it over time. You could also interpret the mules as overcoming a shadow projection, as they cease to interpret each other as a threat, and as engaging at a very basic level with the

God archetype, as they develop a new potential which will also help them and possibly others to act more wisely in the future.

To make integration occur requires judgement that is open to alternatives at a given moment, thus avoiding absolutization. Whether alternatives are available to us depends on both active judgement and prior conditions, in a mysteriously complex combination that could never be reduced to either 'freewill' or 'determinism'. In some respects, we can take responsibility for our judgement, and make a difference by trying to make it open rather than closed whenever the conditions allow. In other respects, we are nevertheless subject to conditions that have both created the context of our judgement, and made some kinds of judgement both easier and more probable than others. We can only ever engage in an integration process by taking both conditions and responsibility into account together. In the process we avoid both the projection of the goal-oriented function onto an absolute idea of ourselves, or a reactive projection that completely denies the link between goals and effort.

Much of the effort we can make, however, is long-term, and thus cannot occur without a diachronic motive, sustained over time. Any of the types of practice I will discuss in the next three chapters occurs over time rather than only at one time. Given that its effect is to set up new associations, allowing potential new channels in our brains and nervous systems, it is far more effective if repeated so as to strengthen and consolidate neural links. The repetition of a practice at intervals, however, has to be motivated, which is where archetypal forms can provide vital support.

The long-term maintenance of practice is one aspect of integration – one that can be associated with virtue ethics, the active cultivation of a better habitual character. However, long-term cultivation also equally requires good judgements to be made at each moment. If our practice was solely long-term, it would be impossible to change our judgements, but the resources we bring to bear at any given moment, to ensure balancing rather than reinforcing feedback loops in judgement, do also matter, even if it is impossible to say exactly how much in any given case. The principle of balanced judgement, avoiding both positive and negative absolutes, is the Middle Way.

The Middle Way does not offer any moral or consequential certainty, but it does offer an approach to identifying error. We can judge that projection is error because it blocks us from self-correction or provisionality in relation to what we are encountering. The Middle

Way is simply the space between a naïve projection and a reactive response to that projection (e.g. between a belief in my total freewill and the complete denial of my responsibility). This offers a way of avoiding error in an embodied and experienced situation, where error is understood in terms of the limitations of our assumptions at one moment (as they can be understood from a wider diachronic perspective). The Middle Way must not be mistaken for a 'truth' or as metaphysical 'knowledge' about the universe. Rather it is a way of judging effectively in an acknowledged position of uncertainty.

Elsewhere I have offered an analysis of the Middle Way in terms of five principles.[1] These are scepticism, provisionality, incrementality, agnosticism, and integration. The last of these, integration, has already been discussed in this chapter, Scepticism is the basic recognition of uncertainty that follows from our position of embodiment. Sceptical arguments establish the absence of the sources of certainty we would require to justify metaphysical belief of any kind, whether positive or negative. The implication of scepticism, however, is not one of justified negative belief, but rather *provisionality* in all our beliefs, whether they are positive or negative.[2] A provisional belief is one in which alternatives are available to us apart from an absolute belief or its mere negation, and we are therefore able to make integrative judgements that avoid projection and absolutization.

Avoiding absolute beliefs also implies the principle of *incrementality*: namely that our judgements should be a matter of degree, except when they have to be focused in binary terms as a basis of action.[3] Incrementality is a powerful tool for overcoming projection, because our projections consist in the mere assumption that a particular person is (or is not) wholly positive or negative in a particular respect in relation to our needs. Whenever we can use reflection to penetrate behind that binary assumption, re-framing an absolute into a quality that is a matter of degree helps us to put it into a form that can be integrated. Whilst absolutes remain opposed to each other, a variety of incremental qualities can be compatible with each other side by side. For instance, when we stop projecting the hero as someone who is unequivocally committed to the goal at all costs, we start to see the hero as someone with a variety of goals,

---

1 Ellis (2019) pp. 35–7, 102–34; Ellis (forthcoming, 2023).
2 Ellis (2015c); Ellis (2012) section 1; Ellis (2019) pp. 135–40.
3 Ellis (2012) 1.d; Ellis (2019) pp. 117–20.

and indeed a variety of qualities, some of which work in favour of achieving the goal and some against. The achievement of a given goal becomes a matter of probability, and its value something to be weighed up in a wider context.

Agnosticism is also a crucial element of the Middle Way in relation to metaphysical beliefs, whether positive or negative. Given that these beliefs are entrenched in their opposition to each other, and that ideologies and groups are often set up entirely in their terms, considerable determination is required to avoid the magnetic pull of absolutization and its projections.[4] Far from the stereotype of indecisiveness, then, agnosticism is a decisive refusal to be sucked into binary absolutes wherever they are found. These binary absolutes often simply take the form of the affirmation versus the rejection of a metaphysical claim (as with theism versus atheism), but can also take the form of ideologies appealing to rival absolutes to the exclusion of all third options. Examples of the latter would include freewill versus determinism excluding realistic responsibility, or a political reliance on justice or freedom as political values to the exclusion of all others (implying absolute socialism or absolute libertarianism).[5] Other principles of the Middle Way, such as provisionality and integration, may be very difficult to develop in some circumstances without a prior critical perspective on dual absolutes that is also balanced (not just a rejection of one absolute in favour of the opposite). Without this, the absolute perspectives of a dominant group may constantly undermine all attempts at integrative progress.

This has been of necessity a brief exposition of the Middle Way, because although an important part of the perspective of this book, it is not its main explicit focus. My other writings are available for more detailed discussion and justification of these principles. My hope is that in this book, much of the architecture of the Middle Way can emerge from the discussion of archetypes and their projection and integration, without any need to give the concept too much explicit prominence. However, for a further development and wider view of the perspective of this book, I think the concept of the Middle Way is practically indispensable.

---

4   Ellis (2019) pp. 121–8.
5   See Ellis (2015a) 4.h for more on the Middle Way in relation to political values.

3.b. Integration and Mindfulness

The glass of juice has a very stable base. But your sitting is not so sure. Those tiny bits of pulp only have to follow the laws of nature to fall gently to the bottom of the glass. But your thoughts obey no such law. To the contrary, they buzz feverishly, like a swarm of bees.... [Nevertheless], we can do what the apple juice does, and more. We can be at peace, not only whilst sitting, but also whilst walking and working.

Thich Nhat Hanh, *The Sun My Heart*

For the habitual development of integrated rather than projected responses to the objects we meet, it is awareness that makes the crucial difference. It is awareness that allows us, in a specific moment of judgement, to distinguish a projected form from assumed 'truth', and consider other possible ways of seeing it. There is a well-established tradition of the practical cultivation of that awareness, which is the practice of mindfulness. Mindfulness consists in the relaxation of reinforcing loops in our emotional response to whatever we encounter, so as to prevent the over-dominance of particular limited ideas in it. As the constant reinforcement of a closed emotional state is reduced, greater openness becomes possible. Opening of the emotional state is totally inseparable from opening of the cognitive state.

Mindfulness is an embodied state – namely one based in, and developing out of, awareness of the body. Anyone who has ever tried mindfulness meditation (**figure 8**) will recognize that the starting point is sufficient relaxation of the body whilst mental alertness is maintained. Body-based practices such as yoga can help to produce such relaxation and body awareness, or it can be directly cultivated in the course of meditation through, for instance, body-scanning and awareness of the breathing process. Unsurprisingly, then, mindfulness also connects us to the roots of our experience of meaning in bodily states. That is why meditation can be used to make us more aware of emotional states that would otherwise take us by surprise, or it can allow new creative ideas to arise. Integrated responses that overcome projection become more likely when we have access to a wider range of meaning in this way.

Figure 8. Meditator, photo by Mokoti Tonn on Unsplash.

The relationship between this embodied awareness and the archetypes is crucial, because the schematic and diachronic nature of the archetypal functions depends on our ability to pay attention to wider possibilities of meaning beyond an immediate sensation and its most obvious symbol. The more mindful we can be, the better we can create the conditions for linking any particular symbol to its underlying schema, and thus recognize alternative symbols that fulfil that schematic function rather than absolutizing only one. The more mindful we can be, too, the more we can recall archetypal symbols that were important to us in the past, and continue to relate them to the present so that they inspire continuing open decision-making. Some Buddhist accounts of mindfulness already distinguish between these two aspects, both of which are involved in the cultivation of mindfulness: *sati* is mindfulness at one particular time, which can thus give wider attention to a situation and its potential meaning, whilst *sampajana* refers to mindfulness as recall over a period of time (see 1.e), allowing archetypal symbols to re-inspire us.

The avoidant aspect of the cultivation of mindfulness is what is sometimes referred to as the 'soothing system'[1] – namely the ability to avoid reinforcing feedback loops of a kind that would otherwise *disrupt* our attention by bringing it back continually to a narrowly obsessive point. Neurologically, the fuel for such reinforcing loops comes from the 'reptilian' part of the back of the brain, particularly the amygdala and the striatum, that can rapidly put us on high alert for immediate threats and opportunities, thus overriding all other kinds of awareness. This motivation may form a loop with the left pre-frontal cortex, by which absolutized beliefs remain stuck, because the same motivations that maintain them keep recurring, and the beliefs according to which we interpret our environment keep reproducing the same motivations. For example, we remain addicted because of our dominant belief that the object of addiction can satisfy us, or we remain anxious because we continue to over-interpret minor or remote threats disproportionately. Mindfulness can help us to *soothe* such cycles by relaxing the body enough to allow alternatives to emerge in our awareness. This seems to work partly by developing the connectivity of the orbitofrontal cortex of the brain, allowing more flexible consideration of the relationship between stimuli and experience.[2]

The ways that this 'soothing system' can operate over time are reflected in neuroscientific findings as to the development of the hippocampus in practised meditators. As Fox et al. note in a review article on the neuroscientific evidence about the effects of mindfulness practice,

> *The hippocampus appears to be critical for contextualised emotional learning, i.e. facilitating emotional responses that take into account the current context, as opposed to a single salient cue. Diminished hippocampal functioning, for instance, is associated with inappropriate expression of stress…. Recent research suggests that the reactivation of memories puts them again into a labile state*

---

1 Gilbert (2009) pp. 23–30; Depue and Morone-Strupinsky (2005).
2 Fox et al. (2014) p. 63,

requiring reconsolidation by the hippocampus…. One function of reconsolidation may be to integrate new information with older memory traces. Many meditative practices place a strong emphasis on re-evaluating past behavioural patterns and default emotional reactions to events. Differences in hippocampus, then, may play a role both in seeing past experiences in a new light, and allowing greater flexibility in present behaviour.[3]

The 'single salient cue' is of course exactly what dominates in projection, but mindfulness practice appears to set that cue in a wider diachronic context by developing the connectivity of the hippocampus.

Such techniques as MBSR (mindfulness-based stress relief) can help us to relieve stress or pain, not by anaesthetizing it, but by putting it in a wider context.[4] In effect, it prevents us from absolutizing (or projecting the shadow onto) a source of pain or stress. The loop of anxiety, or of longing for relief, that exacerbates the stressful effects of pain can then be reduced. In this way, mindfulness can help us to integrate projections of a kind that arise very directly in our experience. Not only is an unnecessarily negative reaction to pain a projection of the shadow, but a contextualization of pain is an integration of the shadow.

Mindfulness directs the attention in relation to concentration, suspending the default mode network[5] and activating the task-positive network. These are both connected sets of associated areas in the brain that become respectively dominant when we are, or are not, focusing on a specific task. However, the default mode network (which includes the hippocampus) is not inactive or irrelevant in our experience of attention and judgement, but rather seems to be shaped by mindfulness practice into denser connectivity, allowing a wider scope of potential for the task-positive network.[6]

Neuroscientific evidence also suggests that mindfulness helps to create stronger inter-hemispheric connectivity, by strengthening the connections in the corpus callosum that links the two hemispheres (particularly those linking the pre-frontal regions of each hemisphere).[7] This reinforces the idea that absolutization and projection are neurally associated with over-dominance of the left

3   Ibid. p. 64.
4   Kabat-Zinn (2013).
5   Garrison et al. (2015).
6   Prakash et al. (2013).
7   Fox et al. (2014) p. 64.

hemisphere, repressing the activity of the right. This can, however, be corrected to some extent by strengthening the links between the hemispheres, to allow scope for more two-way influence.

As one would expect if mindfulness helps us to overcome projection, it also helps us to overcome bias (as discussed in 2.f above). Recent research in this area shows this relationship through the example of the impact of mindfulness on prejudiced responses against people.[8] If negative bias is an automatic shortcut for the avoidance of a threat, we should expect it to involve a rapid shadow projection. This can be avoided, however, by relaxing the loop of anxiety that gives rise to it, not so as to prevent us responding to all possible threats, but so as to place our judgement about those possible threats in a wider context. Similarly with positive biases, our immediate attraction to another, our attachment to a goal, or our awe in the face of transcendence may occur rapidly as a projected shortcut that can also be seen as a bias (for instance, the halo effect or the hedonic treadmill). Mindfulness helps us to put these positive assumptions into context by providing more possible awareness of alternatives. For instance, a leader's striking charisma may also have an edge of fragility that we are only likely to become aware of through a broader attention to their character beyond our initial positive impression.

Mindfulness by itself is not an infallible solution to bias (indeed, all solutions are fallible), but it provides the first possibility, together with two other types of contextualization discussed in the next two chapters. Extension of attention at one moment may be of little value in avoiding bias without both imagination and critical thinking to accompany it, and the reliance on mindfulness as a panacea for all problems can easily become a further projection, turning a helpful method into an absolute one – and a projection of the hero archetype.

One of the current debates on mindfulness is over the question of whether it is a 'religious' or 'secular' practice. I hope the treatment in this book helps to put the assumptions that accompany this rather futile debate into a wider context. For those who identify 'religion' with supernaturalist projections, it should be evident that mindfulness helps to challenge those projections (though again, whether it is used to do so depends on its relationship to other practices). On

---

8   Lueke and Gibson (2014 and 2016).

the other hand, to use mindfulness to enhance religious practice is not 'secular', in the sense of non-religious, but rather a direct application of the practical dimension of religion as it has developed over millennia. To see mindfulness as a contributory, but not sufficient, technique for archetypal integration should be a way of avoiding the unnecessary conflicts created by the whole way this discussion is framed.

3.c. Integration and the Arts

A man should hear a little music, read a little poetry, and see a fine picture every day of his life, in order that worldly cares may not obliterate the sense of the beautiful which God has implanted in the human soul.
                                                          Johann Wolfgang von Goethe

Although mindfulness is a key area of practice for integration of our *immediate* emotional state in relation to our objects of attention, there is also another, equally important and interdependent, area of practice. This involves the integration of the symbols (both linguistic and non-linguistic) that we can draw upon when we imagine possibilities and form beliefs. Symbols are needed, as we have seen, to represent archetypal functions, and our capacity to use archetypes in practical religion is thus limited by our available symbols. Awareness that different symbols can be used to represent the same function through schemas and metaphors (as explored in 1.c and d) is also one of the helpful ways that we can avoid projection. That awareness breaks the one-to-one relationship between symbol and represented reality assumed when we absolutize. Awareness that symbols vary over time also helps us to avoid projection of our current preferred symbols (usually associated with particular beliefs) as the only acceptable ones.

The *integration of meaning* is a term I use for the overcoming of *fragmentation* (not strictly conflict) between meaningful symbols available to us.[1] This fragmentation is distinguishable from the conflict inherent in our struggle with an immediate source of distraction on the one hand, or on a cognitive dissonance in our beliefs on the other. Rather it consists in the symbols available to us in one state being unavailable in another, so that we are unable to 'understand' the alternative state. This failure to *understand* is likely to be due to a complex mixture of cognitive limitations and limited emotional engagement, in widely varying proportions, from struggling to apply a basic course in Japanese to a conversation in Japan, to trying to connect with an alienated adolescent son. We are most accustomed to not being able to 'understand' other people, rather than not being able to understand ourselves, but actually the two are inseparable, since the image of others as we interact with them is

---

1   Ellis (2013b) sections 2 (fragmentation of meaning) and 5 (integration of meaning).

part of our own psyches, and our own conflicts of meaning are often projected onto others. The integration of meaning, and its opposite, the fragmentation of meaning, can be understood both at a psychological and at a socio-political level simultaneously.

When we integrate meaning, then, we connect previously separated symbols, in a way that allows us both to recognize previously strange symbols cognitively *and* to engage with them emotionally. At one end of the spectrum, learning a foreign language is a process of predominantly cognitive integration, but still only possible because of our emotional access to the other. At the other, understanding someone against whom we have some kind of emotional barrier is not a matter of learning new words, but of broadening our sense of that person as a whole so as to integrate the projected shadow that blocks our ability to connect with them. In the latter case we still have to 'learn a new language' as we recognize new and different kinds of meaning, including the meaning of our own responses to them. Whether predominantly cognitive or predominantly emotive, both processes can be interpreted in terms of the integration of archetypal functions, whether overcoming our anima/animus projection to engage with the exotic, or overcoming our shadow projection towards those we reject in some way. Whenever these barriers are removed there are also both kinds of integration of meaning, increasing our capacity for relating new symbols to our embodied experience.

New meaning connections of this kind are crucial both in the arts and in education. In the arts, we are able to extend and integrate our available symbols through the use of the imagination. In education, new meaning is developed as we become able to use new concepts, and gain the capacity to understand new areas (this is far more important than 'knowledge' as the goal of education!). The moment of meaning-integration can be readily recognized by anyone who has struggled to understand a new concept, and then, perhaps prompted by a skilful teacher, connected it by means of a metaphor. The metaphor may quite suddenly allow us to 'get it' – just as we suddenly 'get' a complex work of art, or a person whose perspective we have been struggling to understand. At that point the metaphor connects to the schema, so that concepts are no longer meaningless abstractions, but rather become connected to our bodily capacity for meaning. At the same time, an archetypal projection is often overcome, as we schematically understand our meanings as having a variety of symbols, and can no longer absolutize the claims we have constructed out of them. For instance, we may stop absolutizing the authority of a teacher as we realize that they are just talking about something from their point of view that we can also access through our own experience.

This integration of meaning can also be understood in neurological terms as the associative linking of synapses – a tiny new development in the trillions of synaptic links in the brain. The more these links are made, through the connection of experiences and symbols, the stronger they become: as Donald Hebb famously wrote, 'What fires together, wires together.'[2] At times these associative links are also pruned to remove what remains unused, ensuring that the strongest links remain the ones that are most helpful to us.[3] The capacity of the human brain to develop complex meaning-connections is nevertheless astonishingly immense, and in practice it seems that we cannot have too much meaning – only meaning that needs reshaping from time to time.

It is meaning, rather than belief, that is primarily responsible for offering us alternative options beyond projection. By way of analogy, we could say that though mindfulness provides the strength of momentary illumination that can give us the sense of what is in our interior room, it is meaning that determines the size of that room and what is available in it. The third type of integration – of belief, which will be discussed in the next chapter – then enables us to take the tools and the materials in the room and make something with them. Before we can work, though, we need the tools to be at hand and we need to be able to see them. If we only have one kind of tool, we are likely to restrict ourselves to one kind of job, but if we have a variety of tools, we can greatly expand our potential creativity.

The integration of meaning applied to others also provides a practicable Middle Way for interpretation of the tradition of emphasizing love and compassion in both Christianity and Mahayana Buddhism. Compassion *is* the integration of meaning applied to our understanding of others, at least if it is to avoid being treated as another projected abstract concept. When we merely assent to the idea that we should love our neighbours, this is likely to remain an abstract belief, but if we find more of our neighbours meaningful

---

2   Hebb (1949).
3   Chechik, Meilijson, and Ruppin (1998).

and overcome our projections onto them, we are far more likely to actually extend our feelings of love towards them. That is why meditation practices that work to extend compassion using the imagination (such as the Buddhist *metta-bhavana* or cultivation of loving-kindness) can be seen as exercises in developing the practical integration of meaning.

Engagement with the arts, whether as creators or appreciators, is, however, the most widespread way of integrating meaning.[4] If we are sufficiently receptive to a work of art that introduces or reinforces new symbols, merely contemplating it may help us. Contemplation of this kind is in any case an active process, whether that involves reading a novel, looking at a painting, watching a play, or listening to music. Merely being in the presence of the work of art is unlikely to integrate meaning unless we actively engage with it in this way, and some works of art are more likely than others to do so (though I lack space to discuss that here). *Creating* a work of art, however, is likely to be even more profoundly integrative, as we reflect on our experience and find new forms of metaphorical expression for that experience. In the process we widen the metaphors associated with a particular schema, potentially also offering that new connection to others. Our neural associations become richer, and in the process so do our options.

The larger a work of art, the more diachronic elements are introduced in our relationship to it, and thus the more it can serve integrative archetypal functions. A 'larger' work of art may take more time – perhaps many years – to create, and thus develop a sustained vision synthesizing various elements in its creator. Even for its appreciators (listeners, readers, or viewers), however, sustained works of art are unparalleled in the impression they make because they can so much integrate archetypal functions. In a developed and complex novel, for instance, we keep forming and re-forming new associative connections in relation to the characters, and thus have the opportunity to gradually refine and integrate our view of them from whatever projections we may have begun with. Similar considerations apply to films, plays, or other narrative art forms. In music, the symbols are not linguistic, but bypass linguistic systems so as to integrate meaning directly by association with our embodied experience over time – the rhythm of our pulse, the melody of

---

4   See Ellis (2013b) section 6 for a fuller account.

voice-tones, and varying speed of our bodily movements.[5] Musical patterns can operate as symbols by developing strong associations, but they can also have a directly aesthetic effect and thus aid mindfulness. Visual symbols can also powerfully extend our meaning through painting, sculpture, or any other visual art. Revisiting those same pictures can build up visual associations that likewise maintain our inspiration over time.

It is thus almost impossible to distinguish between the integration of meaning through the arts in a general sense, and the integration of archetypes through the use of the arts in practical religion. The arts in general may integrate a range of meanings that are not specifically archetypal in function (i.e., that are not schematic and diachronic), but my guess is that the vast majority of works of art are archetypal (and thus 'religious') in some sense and to some degree. Novels, for instance, have a high potential to help integrate the hero, anima/animus, and shadow archetypes, as long as they offer us new insights into characters that are likely to express these archetypes, rather than merely reinforcing our projections. In general, 'literary' novels seem more likely to do this, while popular romances seem very likely to merely reinforce anima/animus projections rather than integrate them. This is only a matter of probability, because it depends on the reader in each case exactly how the characters function archetypally.

In exceptional works of art, we may even encounter the God and Middle Way archetypal functions in ways that help us to integrate them. This is more likely to occur through development of one of the other three archetypes so as to connect with a wider sense of open potential, rather than explicit discussions or depictions of a projected God. For example, when a hero has to go through a profound moral re-examination, revising both the conception of her goal and of the evil she is overcoming, she expands into a new zone of potential in her own experience. The German tradition of the *Bildungsroman* is one that often offers this kind of process, beginning with Goethe's *Wilhelm Meister's Apprenticeship*.[6] When the hero moves back from that glimpse of potential to engage with the ordinary conditions that make it possible, we also begin to get the Middle Way function (see 4.g).

5   See Johnson (2007) ch. 11.
6   Goethe (2011).

Figure 9. *Ecstasy of St Francis* by Stefano di Giovanno (Sassetta) (1392–1450), Bernson Collection, Settignano. Photographer unknown (Wikimedia Commons).
Public Domain picture.

One of the key reasons for the decline of religion in the modern world since the 18th century is thus revealed. Most of the archetypal functions that were once carried by the use of archetypes within religious traditions have now been taken over by the 'secular' arts. These archetypal functions that are so vital to human development are thus now predominantly seen as nothing much to do with religion at all. Fortunately, many of the explicitly religious arts of the past are preserved so that it is still possible to begin to enter their world and experience how religious archetypes *function* in it. In a short walk through London's National Gallery, for instance, one can move from early Renaissance religious images like Sassetta's *Ecstasy of St Francis* (**figure 9**), to the 19th-century 'secular' art of Turner, Renoir (e.g. **figure 14**, below), or Monet in another. Are the latter any less about God than the former? Not in any sense that really matters. Not in any sense that makes a practical difference to the inspiration we can get from these works of art.

The problem is not one of whether the archetypes will continue to support human potential: the archetypes will be part of human experience however crudely we misunderstand them. It is rather that in our completely unnecessary attachment to abstract distinctions of 'belief', we have broken the continuity of the ways that archetypes are expressed and integrated through the arts. The obvious practical solution lies in greater categorical flexibility: namely that 'religion' should be recognized more widely as embracing all the arts in its functions, and simultaneously that the implicitly religious dimension of 'secular' arts should be recognized. What matters most of all, however, is that we continue to practise the arts, and to recognize them as a valuable dimension of practice that expands our options in every context, rather than only treating them as a diversion or embellishment of some kind.

3.d. Critical Universalism

Truth is uniform and narrow.... But error is constantly diversified; it has no reality, but is the pure and simple creation of the mind that creates it. In this field, the soul has room enough to expand herself, to display all her boundless faculties....
Benjamin Franklin, *Report on Animal Magnetism*

After our immediate states of attention and the associative networks of meaning we can draw on, the third level of conditions affecting our integration is that of judgement and belief. In judgement, a particular set of conditions comes into contact with our mind/brain and the associative resources it has available. We respond in more or less pre-determined ways, depending on the rigidity of the associations available to us in response to that situation. A pattern of responses to specific kinds of conditions, whether or not this is made explicit through verbal formulations, is a belief, and we cannot avoid dependence on our beliefs to some extent when we make our judgements. However, those judgements can be refined through the cultivation of more options that enable us to respond in different possible ways in unpredictably varied conditions. That optionality depends firstly on our immediate attention and on the meaning available to us. Secondly, though, it depends on critical awareness of the strengths and weaknesses of different possible beliefs about a situation and of different possible criteria we could apply to it. By considering different beliefs in comparison with each other, drawing on as wide a range of meaning to construct new beliefs as possible, we can judge in more adequate ways.[1]

Projection, or absolutization, is the central source of interference with that judgement process, leading us to react to it in ways that are already pre-formatted by other situations. Recognizing and avoiding absolutization is thus a central aspect of integrative practice, prior to the recognition of specific information from our environment. Absolutization is a matter of both 'facts' and 'values', as it can create rigid assumptions both about what we are experiencing and about the criteria we should use to judge it and respond to it. Once we are past absolutization, of course, there is still a weighing-up process to be gone through. However, we can be confident that we will apply whatever resources we have available to that weighing-up, without

1 See Ellis (2015a) section 2 for a fuller account.

prejudice, only if we can first avoid absolutization. It may be that we never succeed in completely avoiding absolutization, but we can reduce it.

'Critical thinking' is a general term for the process of considering our beliefs with awareness of their potential strengths and weaknesses in relation to alternative beliefs, rather than absolutizing them by assuming that some beliefs are necessarily correct and others incorrect. Simply by not assuming that beliefs are absolutely true or false, we cross a crucial boundary of awareness.

As I have been arguing throughout this book, the process of absolutization that can be avoided by critical thinking can be equally well described as a projection of archetypes. This is most obvious when it is beliefs about a person that we are absolutizing, but even beliefs about, say, a theory of chemistry can be seen as an aspect of the background beliefs for an archetypal function, through either a goal-oriented projection or a transcendence projection (see 2.c above). I may assume that the elements always act in a particular way because it fits my goals to do so, or because I believe that this is how 'nature' ultimately is. In the process I displace my awareness of how best to actually reach my goals, or of how to be inspired by symbols that represent potential breakthroughs.

Our beliefs cannot be entirely turned into 'facts' that are completely separated from our motives for holding them, and if we take embodied meaning seriously, we have to recognize that a degree of objectivity (which is also inversely a degree of 'subjectivity') is a feature of our whole response to stimuli, not of a set of abstract representations. Critical thinking about our archetypal projections is thus a feature, not only of philosophy and religious thought, but also of both effective scientific thinking and effective everyday thinking. It is equally a requirement in all these contexts.

To recognize this point fully, it is important to get away from the entrenched idea that critical thinking is just a matter of 'rationality'. Concepts of rationality vary, but they all involve some kind of association between effective judgement and the reasoning process – the reasoning process being the drawing of conclusions from premises according to a logical relationship of implication between them. There are indeed logical laws that are correct within their own closed system of assumptions, as is also the case with the rules of mathematics. However, the use of these logical laws has virtually nothing to do with the practical question of to what extent we make justifiable judgements. The belief that objective judgement is a matter of 'logic' can be readily attributed to another kind of projection of the transcendence function, as I shall argue more fully in 6.e. The value of critically analysing arguments lies not in detecting 'valid' implications from 'sound' premises (or their absence), but in becoming aware of our assumptions so that we can *avoid* the projection of 'true' or 'false' beliefs implicitly as well as explicitly. The fallacies that we can avoid through critical thinking are not formal ones of faulty logic (formally speaking, helpful judgements are often logically invalid and unhelpful ones valid), but informal ones that can be more readily analysed as breaches of the necessary conditions of trust for potential agreement within discussion.[2] Of course, it is possible to re-define 'rationality' in ways entirely distinct from 'reason', but this proceeding carries such a danger of the re-appropriation of objectivity by 'logic', that to me it seems preferable to start again with entirely fresh conceptions of what incrementally justified judgement looks like.

Projection involves just as much reasoning, and just as valid reasoning, as any other way of thinking. If one begins with the assumption that the world is full of truths and falsehoods that can be represented by language, then one will apply that assumption by deducing (for instance) the 'truth' that one person is one's enemy, another one's true love, and a third the messiah. There is nothing wrong with that deduction relative to the assumptions it is based on, and indeed critical thinking skill is often exerted merely to make our accounts of projections more consistent.[3] However, those consistent accounts will still remain in conflict with other accounts to which they are absolutely opposed. We need our critical thinking to be combined with an aspiration to universality to be able to overcome projection, either at individual or social level.

Critical universalism requires the combination of a critical perspective with the schematic and diachronic perspective offered by the archetypal functions. Our criticality requires us to note the limitations of each assumption, but not in order to leave us in a set of relativist assumptions in which no one given judgement is better than another. Instead, the archetypes can offer us a positive source of inspiration for the value of recognizing two things: firstly that

2   Walton (1987) pp. 19–20; Ellis (2015a) 3.c.
3   The 'intelligence trap': see de Bono (1994); Robson (2019).

our symbols are schematically, not representationally meaningful; and secondly that their meaning accrues over time. Universalism is often unnecessarily associated with absolutization, but a critical perspective can maintain provisionality about all our universal values and prevent them becoming absolute. So 'universalism' here refers to a belief not that we know what is universally true, but that we can maintain values that engage with all conditions by developing the meaningfulness of the archetypes.

If critical thinking skills are always needed to balance the inspiration we can get from the archetypes, then, we need to consider critical thinking as a practice that can be cultivated, as much a necessary part of integration as meditative and arts practices. The resistance that many may have to this is likely to be due to the association they may have between critical thinking and formal education. In general, the critical thinking of those with higher levels of formal education tends to be better developed than those with less. However, systematic and explicit teaching of critical thinking skills in formal education is still the exception rather than the rule, and levels of critical thinking skill amongst the public are still far too low (look at any popular media for evidence of this). I hope that will change in future, but at present, formal education is not very much more likely to give people a foundation in critical thinking in most countries than it is likely to give a foundation in mindfulness. It is our responsibility to learn basic critical thinking, if we have not been taught it, and, I would argue, the responsibility of *religion* to help support people in developing those skills, to help them engage with the archetypes appropriately. Critical thinking skills, like most other skills, can also be continually refined, so that even if our education has given us some of those skills, we can still improve them.

Generic critical thinking skills are teachable and learnable, just like any other such skills.[4] The prime effort goes into developing the habit of *applying* critical awareness of various kinds, primarily to questioning our assumptions, and to understanding a wide range of factors that can limit the justification of those assumptions. A teacher can aid a student's awareness of those factors in various contexts, but it is then the responsibility of the student to continue applying that awareness and extending it to every new potential context.

4   Halpern (1993).

The term 'critical feeling', coined by Rolf Reber,[5] is just as applicable here, though less widely used, as 'critical thinking', since every thought is also a feeling and every feeling is also a potential thought. If, however, we experience our thoughts primarily as feelings, we may need to interrogate them as feelings. That is likely to mean first an emotional recognition that we have a particular feeling, followed by a contextualization in which we recognize that the feeling depends on certain assumptions, which are in turn linked to aspects of our embodied situation. This process is obviously closely interlinked with the types of practice discussed in the previous two chapters, working with attention and imagination respectively.

My analysis of the skills of critical thinking divides them into six areas:

- **Assumptions** are the foundational issue of critical thinking. Whenever we make a judgement it is on the basis of assumptions, and we cannot address the limitations of these if we are not first made aware of them through constant practice in identifying them. The most important assumptions are immediate and contextual (for example, the assumption that the reason someone's coat is missing is because they've gone out), but others are a matter of background (for example, that when I tell you there's a bear behind you, it's not a toy). Background assumptions can be just as vital as any other, but they are less often in question.
- **Argument structure** is the way in which assumptions are combined and conclusions drawn from them in a process of reasoning. Traditionally seen as 'informal logic', this aspect of critical thinking is useful not because it enables us to produce perfectly 'valid' arguments, but because it helps us to understand, firstly our assumptions, and secondly the *limitations* in the extent to which assumptions can justify conclusions, in any given argument. We can thus avoid projection both of our own assumptions and those of others. Awareness of argument structure comes from practice in analysing arguments in the language we habitually put them in, not from symbolic logic.
- **Interpretation** is a vital area of awareness in our understanding of others, the skill lying in recognizing that our first projection is not necessarily 'the true meaning' of what we see, hear,

---

5   Reber (2016).

or read. Instead, even the most precisely formulated statements are vague and ambiguous to some degree. We need to tolerate that vagueness and ambiguity rather than insisting on false precision, and take responsibility for our interpretations by making them provisional. This, again, is a skill that can be developed and practised, for instance by reading texts and deliberately considering both the variety of possible interpretation, and the *practical* (not just scholarly or traditional) justifications we may have for adopting one interpretation rather than another.

- **Contexts** are a vital aspect of many arguments, because no argument works only in abstraction. Instead, particular kinds of principle are more likely to be applied in different contexts dependent on the goals of communicating and reasoning in those contexts: for instance, the goals in scientific, religious, and artistic contexts are likely to differ. We need to cultivate awareness of those contexts, not to follow rigid rules about what sorts of assumptions are appropriate in a given context, but rather to question and adapt such rules whilst maintaining a sense of the distinctive value of this particular form of discourse. This area of practice requires us to keep crossing cultural or disciplinary lines and become *aware* of the context we are working in by comparing it to others, when we may have previously taken it for granted.
- **Fallacies and biases** can be a matter of helpful practice, because they consist in recognizable patterns of thinking that work against the integration of judgements. These have already been discussed in 2.f, where I argued that both fallacies and biases are projections. The skill of working with fallacies and biases is that of recognizing when they are taking place, and then working to change the conditions that block awareness of the bias in the context where it arises. For example, *procrastination* involves a bias in our judgements that projects the fulfilment of goals (the hero archetype) into the future. We can work with procrastination in practice through critical awareness of its limitations, and reflection on our own tendency towards it and its emotional triggers.[6]

---

6   Pychyl (2019).

- **Credibility** is a process of awareness brought to the assumptions we make about our sources of information. As such it can be a crucial element in avoiding projection, where we absolutize someone else's claims because they symbolize a goal, relationship, threat, or potential that we find valuable. Credibility analysis, using criteria like reputation, ability to observe, vested interest, expertise, bias, and corroboration, can provide a ready way of recognizing that a source of information only has a certain incremental degree of justification rather than a totality, and thus weighing it appropriately with other possible sources of information. Again, we can only do this more effectively through repeated practice in different contexts.

In all of these areas of critical thinking skill, there are explicit concepts that can be used to deliberately cultivate the skills. This is far more effective than leaving it to chance as to whether we absorb the skills implicitly through study of a particular discipline. Overcoming dependence on only one particular domain where we are most likely to apply these skills is also crucial. As in language learning, for instance, this continuing application in new contexts may be initiated in a classroom, but after that its effectiveness depends entirely on how much an individual has made it into a practice.

Most discussions of both archetypes and religion give far too little weight to this area of working with them: but archetypes are not just a matter of intuitions, they are also a matter of concepts and judgements. Practical religion of a kind that actually helps us to change our lives, in accordance with the schematic and diachronic inspiration offered by the archetypes, thus needs to emphasize these skills as much as the other types of practice. Of course, any survey of the actual practice of religion in the vast majority of instances is more likely to show that critical thinking skills are sidelined, if not actively discouraged, because of their potential to disrupt 'faith' (i.e. absolute belief). To consider how and why religious traditions should support critical thinking, a contextual understanding of the wider way we can work with such traditions is needed.

3.e. Working with Traditions

A culture of awakening cannot exist independently of the specific social, religious, artistic, and ethnic cultures in which it is embedded. It emerges out of creative interactions with these cultures without either rejecting or being absorbed by them.
　　　　　　　　　　　Stephen Batchelor, *Buddhism without Beliefs*

Our relationship with traditions is perhaps the most crucial practical question that will continually confront us in any attempt to integrate the archetypes. On the one hand, traditions are our source of archetypal symbols, giving them immense power, because they guard the wellspring of the satisfaction of our distinctive human needs. On the other, that power is continually used in the service of shortcut absolutizations based on projection of archetypes, thus blocking our capacity to integrate them. In modern conditions we may at least have the potential option (though probably only if we have a helpful cultural background, and have developed enough personal confidence) to control our relationship with traditions to a much greater extent than was available to the pre-moderns. But how should we use those options? How should we best navigate this endless social dilemma?

Before I attempt to answer this question, some characterization of what I mean by 'tradition' may be helpful. Traditions are group-identities continuing over time, meaning that they consist in shared social institutions and rituals in which archetypal symbols are made available to individuals to aid their adaptation to conditions. When institutions and their rituals are analysed it is easy to identify the four functions in them: for example, the heroic function in coming of age rituals, the reinforcement of relationship (anima/animus function) in marriage, the avoidance of threat in propitiatory rituals, and the transcendence function in Christian worship – as well as in the whole structure of the church. Rituals are given their meaning for the participants not only because of the symbols used in them, but also because of the way that a weight of tradition maintains that significance. A 'weight of tradition' consists in many reinforcing feedback loops of confirmation, as each successive person publicly re-uses the same symbols for the same purposes. It is hard to understand quite how meaningful ritual may be even for a specific individual in someone else's tradition, because its meaning is so dependent on reinforcing loops of confirmation over a lifetime of experience of the tradition of symbolic interpretation in that group. Is it at all surprising, given this, that so many individuals just assume that the symbol *is* the function – that worshipping 'God' is the only way to channel awareness of open potential, for instance?

We may think of such traditions primarily as 'religious', but in the modern context, traditions have become much more differentiated than this. They may pass on the archetypes in other 'non-religious' ways, taking the form of political, artistic, or other social traditions. The civic tradition of investing a mayor enables communal goals to be met by a leader who is given the power to pursue them. The artistic tradition of painting nudes provides us with an aesthetic and symbolic connection to the other that compensates for the barriers created by the necessary formality associated with clothes-wearing. The social tradition of charitable fund-raising helps to limit the threat created by the less fortunate if they were left unsupported, helps to maintain a wider solidarity of relationships in society, and perhaps even helps us to realize new potentials at a communal level. Once-religious functions have become distributed much more widely through society, but they are no less dependent on tradition for that.

The process by which these traditions are passed on is part of a complex system – one that continually patches and re-patches itself in response to new conditions. Many of the patches may have been added to meet long-defunct past conditions that now seem extremely unlikely. We may struggle to understand any justification for, say, dietary laws in Orthodox Judaism, or the requirement for Black Rod to assist in the opening of the UK Parliament. The fact that we do not immediately understand the justification for a tradition, though, does not mean that it lacks value. That value quite often consists in providing a symbol for a diachronic function that will only become potentially more evident over a period of time in which new and perhaps unexpected types of events occur. Those who do not yet understand the value of marriage, for instance, have probably not yet experienced the advantages of formalizing our relationship to the sexual other to help us integrate it. Those who do not understand the value of the political institutions of government have probably not lived without them.

However, that reflection on the value of traditions should not justify an unreflective conservatism. Traditions become dogmatic, not because they maintain customs whose justification has become mysterious, but because they defend traditions regardless of the current reasons for changing them. There is no magic, simple answer to the question of whether radical reformers or conservatives are right in any tradition, but there are ways of judging the issues that weigh up the value of tradition with more or less awareness of the full range of options. Utilitarian reasoning, of the kind that is willing to destroy traditional practices for the sake of a perceived greater good, is more likely to be right when it considers the full weight of the value of traditional symbols, rituals, and institutions in their organically developed system, and persists despite that awareness. It is more likely to be wrong when tradition is instantly dismissed as valueless. Traditional conservatism, on the other hand, is much more likely to be wrong when it finds any alteration to the tradition to be unthinkable, as opposed to when it gives the benefits of reform full weight but prefers tradition nevertheless. The narrow option in each case consists in reinforcing feedback loops of projection, believing that the value of an archetypal symbol in itself, at one point, will be sufficient. The wider option allows new options from the other side to enter our consideration and sustainably modify our pattern of judgement, whatever it may be, in the direction of improvement.

To open up our options in this way when we judge the products of tradition, the three levels of practice discussed so far are all needed. We need sufficient awareness and immediate attention to take everything into account, sufficient sense of the meaning of the symbols we are dealing with, and the application of critical thinking to detect fallacious shortcuts in both traditional and anti-traditional thinking. These are all individual qualities, but nor can we entirely stand apart from the group. Rather we also need to encourage the group to share and spread these qualities. Traditions can potentially become preservers of integrating archetypal symbols as well as projected ones, but the tradition in that case needs to also work in all three of the areas of practice: supporting mindfulness, supporting education in meaning, and developing channels for critical thinking to be applied to a tradition.

If traditions are complex systems, we need to start thinking of them neither as inviolable, nor as too easily modified. A complex system that never changed would not adapt to new conditions – and this applies to socially-based traditions as much as to individuals (who are also complex systems). On the other hand, any attempt to change a complex system instantaneously is bound to fail – for all change in systems involves gradual modification over time (the principle of incrementality), whether that modification is relatively faster or slower. Any change to a system also needs to consider its functions in the long term rather than only in the short term, which effectively means that we need to value and cultivate the archetypes in order to be able to think in a balanced way about how to modify traditions. A decision about a tradition is thus not just a utilitarian calculation, because if we are trying to integrate the archetypal symbols preserved and passed on by traditions, we will already be investing in other sorts of value (the kinds that preserve our inspiration over time) beyond that of the goals we can clearly articulate and weigh up in the framework of our current set of assumptions.

Let me return to the questions with which I began this chapter, then. These are questions about how individuals can navigate the dilemmas created by traditions. These are very big dilemmas for many modern individuals, who feel more or less alienated from the archetype-bearing traditions of their background. One obvious illustration of this is the rapid decline of church-going in the nominally Christian communities of Europe. Some find (or create) alternative traditions, for instance of art or spirituality, to provide a medium for the archetypes, but the majority continue to seek the archetypes in a disconnected, deracinated way: for instance in films, television, video gaming, or popular fiction. Far from finding ways of working with their ancestral traditions, these people often effectively have no tradition to work with. As discussed in 1.h, this tends to mean that although they are more likely to perceive the archetypes schematically, they have no relationship with their diachronic function. They have no inspiration over time.

Traditions are not monoliths, and we do not have to accept their dogmas to work with them. Nor are we necessarily confined to the ancestral traditions we happen to inherit, in a world where a plurality is available to us. However, at the same time, maintaining a relationship with traditions as a source of meaning is vital. Without some kind of continuity of tradition, there is almost no chance of practical religion providing the kind of diachronic framing we need to fulfil the archetypal functions by returning to them – and thus fulfil the key advantages of the human state. That continuity may in some cases consist only of an appreciation of symbols and their power that we can regularly access, not in any endorsement of beliefs in that tradition. For instance, an art gallery may be a more powerful place to encounter Christian symbols than a church. Nevertheless, if we have no tradition, we have no source of symbols to express the archetypal function over time. This will not prevent us projecting the archetypes in the way we may blame 'religion', but it may well deprive us of the opportunity of integrating them.

How we engage in a tradition without accepting its dogmas is an issue that requires many small balancing judgements, not one big instruction. There is probably no aspect of tradition that we could not participate in with an epoché – a sense of provisionality – except perhaps the recitation of creeds, or any other public statements that it is almost impossible not to interpret metaphysically. Everything else in religious and other traditions, though – worship, rites of passage, stories, communal solidarity, shared religious experience, artistic activity – all of these can usually be interpreted in ways that acknowledge their archetypal meaning but do not involve acceptance of absolute claims. To do so consistently against the grain of those around you, however, is very difficult. It becomes much easier in a religious group (such as, for instance, the Quakers) with a wide range of tolerance in religious interpretation. More religious institutions are needed that explicitly acknowledge the non-absolute nature of the archetypes, and encourage integrative practices in support of depth and consistency in that interpretation. This in turn may require leadership from highly integrated individuals.

If we focus on the functional elements of any religious or other traditional activity, this can always support integration of the archetypes, regardless of the context and how other people are interpreting it. The specific symbols used are contingent, so their absolutization is entirely inappropriate, but we can still see how the symbol is being used to express the archetypal function. If others adopt a perspective that is limited in time, by taking no account of changing mental states or other conditions, this too is contingent. It is quite possible for two worshippers to look at the same religious image in the same ritual, and for one to have a merely projective experience whilst the other has an integrative one. We need to be realistic about the extreme difficulties most people will have in reaching this point, if they have not developed sufficient confident individuality. Nevertheless it is possible, and it may be that it is only through an increasing number of each traditional group relating to it in this way that a tradition as a whole can be turned in a more thoroughly practical and integrative direction.

4. Categorization of Archetypes

4.a. The Basis of Archetypal Categorization

On pragmatistic principles, if the hypothesis of God works satisfactorily in the widest sense of the word, it is true. Now whatever its residual difficulties may be, experience shows that it certainly does work, and that the problem is to build it out and determine it so that it will combine satisfactorily with all the other working truths.[1]
William James, *Pragmatism and Religion*

If we understand archetypes in a strictly functional way, how does this affect our understanding of how archetypes are divided up or categorized? I have already suggested that archetypes are diachronic schematic functions, and that there are four of these functions: the heroic, the shadow, the anima/animus, and the God function. Readers with a background in Jungian archetypes may have been surprised by my restriction of archetypes into these four functions, given that Jungians frequently describe a much wider range of archetypes than this, but my argument is that other archetypes can be most helpfully categorized within these four functions. In this section of the book, I will offer a fuller explanation and justification of this approach.

The four archetypal functions emerge from the combination of three functional axes: attraction/repulsion, self/other, and projection/integration. Although humans have a wide variety of needs at different levels, my thesis is that these three axes define the most basic and universal functions. In order not just to survive, but also to relate, and to develop more fulfilling lives as individuals, we need to select some things positively and reject other things (attraction/repulsion). We also need to maintain a sense of the boundaries of our concern and protection (self/other). If we are to develop sustainably in the longer term, we also need to be able to distinguish between integration and projection.

---

1   This quotation conveys the spirit of a pragmatic approach to archetypes, but its inclusion should not be interpreted as an endorsement of the pragmatist definition of truth.

The axis of attraction and repulsion is the most basic and immediate one, On the one hand this arises from our need to sustain ourselves in various respects using resources around us that attract us. On the other hand it comes from the need to avoid threats, in which we become a resource for some other creature, through repulsion. The most basic needs served by attraction and repulsion are those of food, reproduction, and self-preservation, but we are not only attracted by food and sex. At a more subtle level, for instance, we could be attracted by someone who can offer wisdom, or by a place of tranquillity in which we can reflect. Repulsion may come immediately from a predator wanting to eat us, but more subtly it may be a reaction to someone who threatens to take a little too much of our time, or to ideas that we disagree with because of reflection on their negative long-term effects. A whole hierarchy of needs can be served by attractions and repulsions at various levels.

The archetypal functions created by this axis differentiate the shadow on the one hand from the three positive archetypal functions (heroic, anima/animus, and God) on the other. As already discussed in section 1, not all of these basic functions are archetypal, but the diachronic and schematic symbolization of these functions is archetypal. We thus have no need to appeal to the 'supernatural', the 'rational', or the 'unconscious' to differentiate distinctively human archetypal functions from basic animal ones. Rather the archetypal functions are a diachronic and schematic expression of that basic function for many humans.

The second axis is that of self and other. This refers not just to what is part of one body or another, but what we *identify with* and thus seek to protect, whether it is part of our own bodies or not. Obviously, we do usually identify with and seek to protect our bodies, but we tend to do the same for children, lovers, or others who are close to us. Beyond that, we may identify with objects as possessions, or with groups – even with nations. We may not know where the line will be drawn of what we would make an effort to protect, until it is threatened in some way and we have to test it in practice. The 'self' referred to here is not the 'Self' as the word was used by Jung (which was equivalent to the God archetype), but closer to the 'ego' as the term is used in analytic psychology.

On one side of this axis is the heroic function. The hero and his goals are also our goals, and engaging in a heroic narrative consists in identifying with those goals. On the other, however, is the anima/animus and the God function. These are generally other, even though we are attracted to them. Of course, the more we are attracted to them, the more we will try to possess them, either by relationship or by conceptual belief. Our wish to relate or to transcend may thus quickly be reduced to a heroic function, in which we try to achieve the goal of possession – marriage or heaven, for instance. As long as we maintain some sense of uncertainty and humility about the other, though, it will also maintain at least some of its otherness, and that otherness will not be entirely reduced to possession.

The shadow can fall either side of the self-other axis. Quite often we will be repulsed by what we regard as other, because its otherness makes it easier to project negative qualities onto it. However, we can also be repulsed by aspects of ourselves. Someone in a state of inner conflict, such as an addict, is likely to encounter a shadow version of themselves that they identify with but also reject. We can thus talk of both the self-shadow and the other-shadow.

The third axis lies between our experience of projection and integration. We experience projection entirely by contrast with integration, because we only become aware of past delusions and limiting assumptions over time after the arising of wider awareness. That wider awareness includes both a previous narrower state and a later broader state, but the earlier narrower state will not have reliably predicted the later broader state (such is the nature of left-hemisphere dominance – see 2.e). Nevertheless, we can hardly conclude from this that states of narrower awareness have no inkling at all of wider or more integrated ones, even if they only appear as fleeting thoughts or lurking anxieties. They are, after all, products of the same mind/brain, and there will probably have been broader awareness in the past as well as the future. Although our awareness of the potential for more integrated states is often either marginalized or projected, it is part of our experience. It consists not in an abstract idea of greater integration, but rather an intuitive sense of it, a *gestalt* that is irreducible to current conceptual identifications. The awareness of potential that we get from this needs to be contrasted with our degree of awareness of projection of evil, already discussed in 2.i.

On one side of this axis is the God function, and on the other the shadow, together with the relatively unintegrated versions of the heroic and anima/animus function. However, the hero can also be experienced in relatively integrated forms that guide us towards a recognition of the God function, as in the figures of Christ, the Buddha, or Muhammad. The anima/animus function may also take on the features of feminine goddesses or masculine gods that primarily help us to engage with the potential qualities that they symbolize. Even our spouse may be described colloquially as our 'better half'. This axis, like the others, is thus a matter of degree.

It needs to be emphasized that although the experience of integration itself has a function (that of reminding us of integrative potential), and that function is likely to be symbolized, that experience is also subject to interpretation that is likely to be dictated by contextual assumptions rather than just by the experience itself. If the pressure from the surrounding culture is towards the projection of God, a symbol of integration itself can very quickly be projected. On the other side, an experience of recognizing our degree of projection (a highly negative experience) can also be interpreted in an integrative context and thus used to support integration, so that it's no longer 'losing our faith', but rather just another stage in an integrative process. We always need to separate the nature of the experience from the interpretation it later receives.

There is a common temptation to reduce the integration-projection axis to the attraction-repulsion one, that is to assume that our glimpses of integration are just a form of attraction (for example, that a man's connection with a feminine figure is 'just sexual'). This is not always the case, and there are intuitive as well as reflective ways of recognizing this. The experience of awe, in which a sense of integration is linked with one of fear, is one indication that at some level we appreciate that our immediate sense of attraction needs to be subjected to a longer-term process. The more rationalized version of this is the idea that some desires are 'rational' because they will serve us in the longer term, whilst others are 'irrational'. Although that distinction may confuse a complex integration process with mere reasoning, it does at least attempt to capture the distinction between an immediate desire and a long-term desire.

If we put these three axes (**figure 10**) together, we find that although they leave us with many ambiguities, each of the four major archetypes can be defined reasonably clearly in relation to at least one of the axes. The shadow can be defined basically as that which is repulsive to us, or, in the context of a more refined experience, what is projective. The hero can be defined as what we identify with the self. The anima/us can be defined as what we identify as other even though we are attracted to it. The God archetype can be defined as a symbolization of integration experiences.

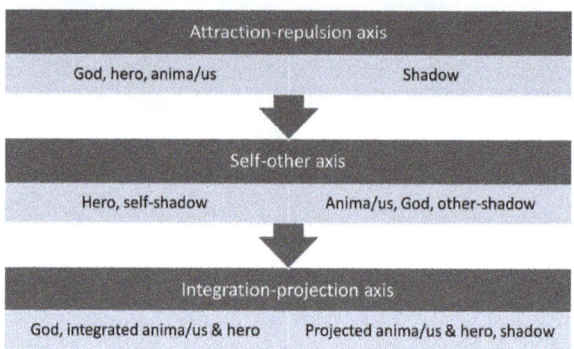

Figure 10. The three axes creating archetypal categorization (diagram by the author).

The great advantage of this way of classifying archetypes is that it focuses on their *functions* and differentiates only according to function. As the archetypal functions are schematic, it also avoids the confusion of schemas with symbols derived from those schemas. A number of other commonly claimed archetypes, such as the mother, the father, the child, the trickster, the magician, the crone etc. are specific symbols fulfilling one of these four functions rather than functional schemas, and thus treating them as separate archetypes tends to have the effect of diverting attention to the surface features of the symbol and/or the other causes of that symbol arising in a particular personal or cultural imagination. It does not help us to identify what makes that symbol archetypal, and especially does not help us to *work with* that archetype.

A practical response to an archetype requires a basis of moral differentiation through projection or integration, and in order to identify these readily, we need to understand what function is being projected or integrated. A function is projected when it is no longer sustainably fulfilled by the expression of the archetype. If, however, we judge only on the basis of the phenomenal or other causal relationships of the *symbol*, we will have no clear idea how that symbolic expression may or may not be fulfilling its aims better or worse. For example, if we interpret the anima/animus function only in terms of the mother where it is expressed in that form, we will only be considering the specific issues of maternal relationship, rather than understanding a mother figure as potentially representing a wider set of issues in engaging with the other. Without a wider functional criterion to apply, our judgement in relation to it will then be more likely one of uncritical acceptance or rejection according to our specific expectations of the role of the mother, rather than critical evaluation that puts that role in a wider context.

In the ensuing chapters of this section I will be exploring a number of different examples that underline this point. To do this I will need to explore more fully how each of the four different functional archetypes can have very different symbolic expressions, and yet how these different symbolic expressions can fulfil the same basic functions. The next chapter considers the general features of archetypal variation, with the following four focusing on each of the four archetypes in turn.

4.b. Variations of the Four Archetypes

The causal point of view tends by its very nature towards uniformity of meaning, that is, towards a fixed significance of symbols. The final point of view, on the other hand, perceives in the altered dream-image the expression of an altered psychological situation. It recognizes no fixed meaning of symbols.

Carl Jung, *General Aspects of Dream Psychology* §471

Jung himself refused to say how many archetypes there were. Popular writing on the subject tends to multiply the numbers. Scott Jeffrey, for instance, lists 325 archetypes, but defines an archetype simply as 'a pattern of behaviour'.[1] It is hard to see what use the concept is for us if it is interpreted in such a vague and general way. Erik D. Goodwyn, on the other hand, tries to ground archetypes on basic neural responses.[2] For instance, if the snake is associated with seeking and fear systems in the brain, we are 'hardwired' to react to snakes and thus also have a strong 'archetypal' connection with them. Snakes are thus one of many 'animal spirits' which are one category of archetype. Goodwyn's approach can be embedded in embodied schemas, and it attempts to reconcile neurological evidence with Jung, but it is strangely distanced from the practical function of archetypes, whether in culture, religion, or therapy. We could classify an indeterminate number of 'archetypes' on the basis of neurological responses correlated with cultural symbols, dream imagery and so forth, but this classification would not help us to identify different ways of working with them.

The large number of archetypes identified by modern Jungians, then, should in my view be seen as variants on the four functional archetypes rather than a basis for classifying them. A functional basis needs to be used because that best helps us to overcome projection and integrate our responses. When a functional basis is contrasted with the large number of popular variants, however, this then raises the question of on what other basis the latter vary. There seem to be two potential ways in which they vary: firstly in symbolic form, and secondly in specific brain events.

The symbolic form is incidental to the function, as the same symbolic form can serve several different functions. The snake (**figure 11**) can be a symbol of threat and thus serve the shadow function,

1   https://scottjeffrey.com/archetypes-list/ (accessed 2019).
2   Goodwyn (2012).

but it can also symbolize otherness and the insights of the other. Consistent with a long tradition of mythology, Jung encountered the snake in his *Red Book* visions as his 'soul'[3] – effectively the integrating anima, the seeming other that is also part of you, and engaging with which can enable a process of integration. We cannot categorize the 'snake' as an archetype in itself, because it can serve quite different functions, and we would need to respond to an encounter with a snake symbol in a way that worked with that function, not just with the form of the symbol. A shadow-snake, representing a projected threat, would need to be examined to try to distinguish genuine threat from delusion. An anima-snake, however, needs instead to be examined in terms of projections of otherness, to try to distinguish what is genuinely other from what is self. With a God-snake, similarly, we would need to try to distinguish what was genuinely an experience of potential integration from externalized projection of that potential.

Figure 11. Snake (Asian cobra), photo by David Clode on Unsplash.

3 Jung (2009) Liber Secundus 172 ff.

These variations of the meaning of forms are what makes dream interpretation so difficult. You cannot just apply an allegorical key to the dream whereby one particular form in the dream 'means' a particular other form in 'real life'.[4] Instead, you need to understand enough of the context to try to judge how the form functions in that context. The dream may be warning you of projections or offering potential integrations, but if you focus instead on the form you may well be distracted from the function. To a lesser extent, the same point applies to myth, fantasy, or any other manifestations of what Freud and Jung called the unconscious. It is possible to not only become over-obsessed with the symbols themselves, but to focus so much on the causes and origins of the symbols that one pays little attention to the role they are playing. This seems to have happened a good deal to Jung himself in many of his later writings, in which he gets lost in the details of antiquarian research into the origin of symbols, and the reader looks in vain for further insights into how they operate.

A second type of variant lies in the different kinds of brain events that may accompany a particular archetypal function. We do not need to be able to describe those brain events precisely to recognize that they are associative in nature: namely that they consist in neural connections that are either being newly made or re-used. Neural links enable us to associate symbols with experiences, and the re-activation of neural links between symbolic forms encountered in experience and associated schematic meaning, repeated at intervals over time, forms the basis of archetypal function. Nevertheless, the brain may have many different ways of fulfilling that function. One such variation, already discussed in 2.e, is between a 'dead' metaphor turned into a mere concept through the dominance of left-hemisphere activity, and a 'live' metaphor still connected to wider experience. As explained there, metaphors need to be dead to provide a basis for projection. Brain events can thus provide a way of differentiating between projected and integrated archetypal symbols as different variations on the same archetypal function.

However, the brain events that correlate with a particular archetypal function could also vary in all kinds of other ways, some of them associated with profoundly important processes in human life. The status of the mother image is a strong example of this,

---

4   Jung (1960) §471.

discussed by Jung as the basis of an archetype, and given a neurobiological basis by Goodwyn:

> The mother 'image' appears to comprise a particular class of subjective feelings rather than specific imagery – all likely correlated with highly conserved deep brain activity involving oxytocin, AVP, opioid, and likely many other systems yet to be identified. As we have seen, female recognition systems already exist within the perceptual/conceptual system and are likely present from a very early age. What makes these images mothers, then, are that they are female images imbued with the intense feelings of the mother bond.[5]

Neither the distinctive and vital brain activity associated with the mother, however, nor the intense feelings that may accompany that activity, make the mother an archetype in its own right. To make the mother an archetype in the terms of this book, it would need to have a distinctive diachronic function of its own, rather than just a participation in one or more of the four archetypal functions. That function seems most likely to be an anima/animus function, which is neither essentially based on sex nor perhaps even necessarily dependent on the release of oxytocin or other specific hormones. The mother is other, the first other encountered by the infant, and our functionally oriented work with the mother thus seems likely to consist of differentiating other from projected self, just as it would be with a more directly sexual symbol. Alternatively, however, mother images may also operate as hero, shadow, or God functions.

In some cases, there may be a substantial correlation between archetypal function and brain events that are identifiable either by location, by complex combinations of locations, or by chemical processes. However, such correlations will still be contingent, and there will always be the possibility of the brain (a highly adaptable organ) producing similar functions by new means. Variations in function and in corresponding experience, however, can provide the basis of further analysis of variations within a particular archetypal function, just as the variation of symbolic forms can do.

The following chapters will look in more detail at the four functional archetypes, including some of the variations that may be associated with each of them. In each case, focusing on the function of the archetype rather than either the symbolic form or the brain events may require some deep re-assessment of the archetype concerned. Archetypes like the mother, that were previously

---

5   Goodwyn (2012) p. 102.

considered to be separate, may need to be reclassified. Our understanding of the boundaries of what may or may not indicate the operation of the archetype may also need to be reconsidered – especially the common confusion of the anima/animus function with essentialized gender. Reconsidering the archetypes with a focus on their function, however, can make a big difference to how we treat them in practice, and may help to resolve needless disputes between those who have adopted absolutized positions regarding the nature of particular archetypes.

4.c. The Hero and the Ego

The hero of a fairy tale achieves a domestic, microcosmic triumph, and the hero of myth a world-historical, macrocosmic triumph. Whereas the former – the youngest or despised child who becomes the master of extraordinary powers – prevails over his personal oppressors, the latter brings back from his adventures the means for the regeneration of society as a whole.

Joseph Campbell, *The Hero with a Thousand Faces*

The heroic function is a basic response to an unavoidable feature of being a human being: having an ego. The ego consists in a set of identifications, not only with ourselves as we conceive them, but also with other people, groups, objects, beliefs, or 'facts' as we represent them. The ego links desire to implicit belief.[1] We identify with things because we want them a certain way, whether we want that way to be part of ourselves or part of the other. Even what we fear and reject (the shadow) we identify with being a certain way for our purposes.

The link between how we understand our desires and our beliefs about the world can be made in the brain. Linguistic representation and tool-using are closely related, and both are focused in adjacent areas of the left pre-frontal cortex.[2] We represent what we manipulate in some sense (whether directly or as essential background), so as to fulfil our goals. Development of the ego and its representational language is the first step towards maintaining our goals over time, as we can represent our goals, the surrounding conditions, and our plans for fulfilling those goals using representational language. Imagine a group of early hominids making plans for hunting: they are better able to co-ordinate their activities by using descriptions not only of the goal, but also the surrounding environment and the co-ordinated actions that will achieve the goal. Such hunts were depicted in cave art (**figure 12**). It's not only a failure of drive, but also the surrounding conditions turning out differently, that could stop the hunt succeeding. It's likely that the first heroes were those foremost in the hunt, who dealt the death-blow to the animal and were thus represented as models for the effective fulfilment of human goals.

1   See Ellis (2012) 6.a for a fuller account.
2   McGilchrist (2009) p. 111.

Figure 12. Cave painting of hunt from Cueva Manos, Santa Cruz, Argentina. Photo by Mariano Cecowski (Wikimedia Commons). Creative Commons Attribution Share-Alike 3.0 Unported license.

However, that egoistic representation, although it provided the first stage in enabling our goals, also proved a stumbling-block. Again, imagine a group of early hunters. However, this time the environment or the behaviour of the prey has changed, but the hunters are still attached to the representations they have of the correct and heroic way to hunt. Now the hero becomes the hunter who recognizes that the established story is not the whole story, and that new conditions require new options. The tendency for the egoistic representation to become fixed through a habit of left-hemisphere over-dominance needs to be challenged, but can only be challenged through greater awareness of the relationship of different ideas and representations over time, with more involvement of the right hemisphere, as well as enough psychological stability not to be caught up in reinforcing loops of obsession or anxiety linked to the old model. To achieve the goal in a longer-term, more sustainable way that meets a variety of different conditions, then, the story of the hero needs to be not simply one of following old models, but of challenging and going beyond them, then of persuading the rest of the tribe of the value of the innovations.

Perhaps the best-known writer on heroic myth across cultures, Joseph Campbell, analyses the hero archetype in exactly this basic way:

> *The standard path of the mythological adventure of the hero is a magnification of the formula... separation – initiation – return.... Prometheus ascended to the heavens, stole fire from the gods, and descended. Jason sailed through the Clashing Rocks into a sea of marvels, circumvented the dragon that guarded the Golden Fleece, and returned with the fleece and the power to wrest his rightful throne from a usurper.*[3]

The hero's 'initiation' consists in a challenge in which he engages new options, in the process perhaps radically re-framing his view of the world and questioning old beliefs. The return of the hero, however, marks a dialectical process in which the group accepts the hero's innovations, incorporating the new understanding into a wider development for the group alongside the older traditions. It is not simply a question of the hero winning by fulfilling his goals, because, to a human as a social animal, the fulfilment of those goals is not sufficiently meaningful without social recognition and acceptance. On being re-accepted, the hero takes his place with the succession of past heroes in the tradition of his society. That outward process is also paralleled by an inward one in the mind of the hero, who must struggle to overcome both outward difficulties and doubts about his goals, only to have those difficulties reconciled with the basic values he has adopted from his society.

Sometimes the hero is very clearly an innovator, as when we make explorers, inventors, or thinkers into heroes. At other times the innovation may consist in leading his group in risky resistance to another group, as we find with the martial hero. The quest in legend may alternatively be an entirely symbolic representation of the hero's inner struggle, as in Campbell's example of Jason and the Golden Fleece. What these heroes have in common is not the nature of their goals, but a universality of function in which egoistic identification needs to be made more adequate by greater awareness over time.

To meet challenging new conditions, at any stage the hero may need to be 'reborn' or 'initiated': both ways of conveying the need to re-frame. In the process, the hero may need to reconsider the nature of the goals that he has been so set on. So the hero does not pursue fixed goals by any means: rather the goal itself may need adjusting as he realizes that his previous understanding of what he was seeking has been inadequate. He may also need to focus on the process

---

[3] Campbell (2008) p. 23.

rather than the goal – again as a way of re-framing what it means to attain the goal. The hero's previous view of the goal may well turn out to have been a projection that he needs to integrate, but the ability to do so makes him more, not less, of a hero. For example, in one of the heroic narratives that most influenced me as a child, J.R.R. Tolkien's *Lord of the Rings*, Frodo Baggins, setting out with the goal of destroying the ring, finds as he gets closer to that goal that he can only focus on the process, and on the final brink that he is unable to fulfil the goal as originally conceived.[4] He is obliged to re-frame the goal as one that is finally fulfilled by the intervention of others, rather than simply as one of his own willed actions. In the process, however, he becomes more, not less, of a hero.

The problem of goal-seeking behaviour being undermined by the delusions that accompany it is also encapsulated in the psychological understanding of the hedonic paradox.[5] When we finally achieve the pleasure or fulfilment that we have been striving towards, the experience of that success usually proves to be quite different from the beliefs and identifications that led us to keep striving for it. For example, the energetic business executive who has been amassing money for her retirement finds herself bored and frustrated when she actually retires. The test of our heroism in pursuing our goals, then, is not just our commitment to them, but also our ability to re-evaluate them by returning to a more basic embodied experience as the basis for re-assessing our values.

The shock of having to re-frame our limited identifications can even be represented by an act of killing. Jung had a vision, described in his *Red Book*, in which he lay in wait for the hero Siegfried:

> *As he came around the bend ahead of us, we fired at the same time and he fell slain. Thereupon I turned to flee, and a terrible rain swept down. But after this, I went through a torment unto death and I felt certain that I must kill myself, if I could not solve the riddle of the murder of the hero.*[6]

The hero now becomes Jung's view of what it means to be a hero, which includes the strong identification with heroic goals. To fulfil the quest in a deeper sense, however, the whole idea of what it means to be a hero in relation to those fixed goals must be re-considered, and thus symbolically the hero himself must be

---

4   Tolkien (1954) book 6 ch. 3.
5   Fujita and Diener (2005).
6   Jung (2009) Liber Primus iv (v).

destroyed. Ironically, Jung's near-suicidal feelings of conflict on killing the hero are themselves a heroic initiation into the next level of heroism. It is only our identifications at a specific time that need to be sacrificed, but it certainly doesn't feel like that.

This sacrificial motif is of course also a religious one, particularly represented by the crucifixion of Christ (discussed further in 5.h below). Christ is the hero that is apparently killed, but is then unexpectedly resurrected, symbolizing the extension of the hero archetype into a diachronic awareness. We believe that the goal is entirely lost because we identified with it only in a specific form, but it appears 'reborn', along with the hero himself, when he is re-framed in a new form. In the going forth and the discovery of the Middle Way, the Buddha also goes through two similar processes of heroic loss and re-framing (see 5.b below).

However, egoistic projection of the goal may sometimes only be challenged by a reactive projection that sees the ego, not as symbolically, but as actually or finally, destroyed. There is thus a paradoxical type of hero (an ascetic sage) who is said to have destroyed the ego completely – even though we can only appreciate his achievements through the use of our egos. This kind of model results from an assumption of disembodiment, in which the interdependence of the mind with the body is ignored, and it is believed that some kind of 'non-physical' Platonic soul can provide the basis for continued 'existence' while we destroy the ego completely. Since the ego is interdependent with the body, however, and the desire to destroy the ego is itself egoistic, this is an obviously contradictory view based on metaphysical projections. The integration of the ego is not the destruction of the ego, but rather its stretching into something more adequate. The hero may be symbolically destroyed, but does not literally destroy himself.

Given that the hero may need to completely revolutionize all our assumptions in order to 'succeed' in his quest, it is also not surprising that another variant form of the hero is the trickster – the hero who breaks the rules.[7] Odysseus provides a positive heroic form of this, but in other circumstances the trickster may also become shadowy, as we are not sure whose side he is on – as in the case of Loki in Norse mythology.

---

7   Jung (1959a) §456 ff.

The hero may alternatively be a magician: someone who tries to use magic as a shortcut to achieve his goals. 'Magic' may just mean the belief that similarity (e.g. pushing pins into a model of your enemy) or contagion (e.g. casting spells over nail clippings) provide absolute causal laws that can help to bypass complexity and uncertainty in our model of conditions.[8] On the other hand, working beyond this view of magic as projection, the magician-hero may need engagement with that complexity and uncertainty as the basis of her model of magic. Again, one of Jung's visionary encounters in the *Red Book* provides a strong example: when Jung first meets Philemon, he has too many preconceptions about him as a 'magician', and has to deeply reconsider what a 'magician' is.[9]

Our conception of the hero in the West has also varied substantially during the last hundred years or so from overwhelming symbolism as an elite male, to greater symbolism of the female hero and/or the non-elite hero. As long as we maintain the distinction between hero as function and the specific symbols we are using, this should not even be surprising. Though I don't have space to do justice to the topic, it's important to bear in mind that the goals and obstacles of the hero may also be found in humble or domestic settings (e.g. in Ibsen's *A Doll's House*) or focus on connection rather than individuation (e.g. in the Chipko movement).

Whether we identify the hero with another person (male or female), with an entirely symbolic form, with ourselves, or with a group, makes no difference to the basis of the function in egoistic identification, and the stretching of that identification over time to make that function archetypal. In doing this, as we shall see, the hero interacts with the other archetypal functions profoundly.

---

8   Frazer (1922) §3.1.
9   Jung (2009) Liber Secundus 139 ff.

4.d. The Anima/Animus, Sex, and Specialization

Wasn't that the door just now? My God, someone is standing there! Am I seeing straight? – a slim girl, pale as death, standing at the door?
Carl Jung, *The Red Book*

It will probably come as a surprise to Jungians, when I state that in my view the anima/animus has no necessary relationship to sex, sexual difference, or gender. Jung, after all, presents these two corresponding archetypes entirely in terms of essentialized sexual difference: the anima is the innate and essential feminine for a man, and the animus is the innate and essential masculine for a woman. Jung even identifies these, in his later work, with the qualities of *eros* and *logos*.[1] A biological basis for them can also be readily found. As Erik Goodwyn puts it, 'both men and women have innate "fertile, high-quality female" detection systems'[2] and they also both have '"dominant or investing male" recognition circuits'.[3] To deny that the archetypes are about sex is not to deny that sex and sexual difference are very important to us. What it is to deny is that sexual difference is definitive of the *function* of the anima/animus archetype.

For the earlier Jung, at least, that function is *compensation*. In his own experience, Jung identified the anima as his 'soul', which counterbalanced his own mature masculinity by tending to take the form of a young female. He notes, however, that other kinds of counterbalancing are also possible, such as between dominance and subservience, or cleverness and simplicity.[4] The sexually compensating form is common but contingent, not definitive of the nature of the archetype itself. The archetype itself helps to complete the self by ensuring positive engagement with the *other* over time. The *other* may be a sexual other, or it may be some other sort of other.

Gender essentialism in discussing the anima/animus is also projective, like any other sort of essentialism. If we do not begin by recognizing the complexity of any membership of a class by an individual, a description of them as necessarily having particular qualities by their membership of that class is likely to leave us attributing those qualities where they do not fit. Such is Jung's attribution of *eros*, not to the feminine, but to females, and likewise of *logos*, not

---

1   Jung (1959b) ch. 3.
2   Goodwyn (2012) p. 90.
3   Ibid. p. 98.
4   Jung (2009) Liber Primus iii (r).

just as a masculine quality, but a male one. Non-binary understandings of human sexuality have become much better known and accepted since Jung's time, whether we are discussing homosexuality, trans-sexuality, or any other non-binary sexual identification. Our understanding of the anima/animus needs to be as adequate for the LGBTQ community as for anyone else.[5]

Instead of focusing exclusively on sex, then, we need to situate the anima/animus archetype within a wider practical situation. That practical situation is one in which we need to relate positively to others who have contrasting qualities to our own. The archetypal relationship may thus not just be that of a lover or spouse, but also a mother, father, or child – all of these established Jungian archetypes. Relating to these different people positively may well have mutual benefit, but in the longer-term can also provide a basis for developing some degree of those contrasting qualities in ourselves.

This raises the practical problem that in any kind of relationship between people with contrasting qualities, specialization is likely to emerge as people 'play to their strengths', as we see in the division of labour between men and women in traditional societies. In the long-term, however, this can also be a maladaptation of relationship, just as too narrow a focus on certain means or ends can be a maladaptation of goal-orientation. For instance, a man dependent on his wife to care for his children suddenly finds that he has to discover completely new qualities in himself if his wife dies and he becomes a single father. Similarly, if we are over-dependent on our economic relationship with technically trained experts to fix our machines, we will be unable to carry on using the machines for long if we lose access to these experts. Instead, then, we will need to internalize what we have learnt in the context of these relationships in order to develop some of those qualities for ourselves and become more resilient.

Jung tends to focus on the sexually charged aspects of this over-specialization, in the process mistaking the part for the whole:

> *You seek the feminine in women and the masculine in men. And thus there are only men and women. But where are people? You, man, should not seek the feminine in women, but seek and recognise it in yourself, as you possess it from the beginning. It pleases you, however, to play at manliness, because it travels on a*

---

5 A similar criticism of Jung has been made by feminist commentators such as Wehr (1988) ch. 1.

well-worn track. You, woman, should not seek the masculine in men, but assume the masculine in yourself, since you possess it from the beginning.[6]

Where, indeed, are people? 'People' are relatively integrated, and sexual conflicts arising from over-specialization are part of what they have to integrate. However, there are many other such conflicts in every sphere of life, wherever relationship and specialization occur. Up to a point, specialization is of social value, but beyond that point, its negative effects on the integration of the individual start to overtake that social value, and thus also to affect society negatively. Our assumptions about our relationships and their attendant specializations become fixed ones where both ourselves and others are concerned. It is by breaking down those assumptions, not by abandoning the relationships themselves, that we work towards becoming 'people' rather than merely, say, engineers, socialists, Catholics, women, or Germans.

To use our relationships as a basis of learning is at least as deeply embodied in us as specialization ever has been. After all, as children we continually learn from adults, who are models for imitation. The psychological mechanism of bonding between mother and child, to begin with, creates the kind of secure context where this process can begin to take place. The operation of mirror neurons also provides us with a basic capacity not just to imitate others and fall into a pattern of sympathy with them, but also to learn from them and thus to change ourselves. Such learning, however, requires recursion. We are much more likely to develop ourselves by learning from others if we keep repeating the process over a period of time. This is the most basic reason why the anima/animus needs to be a diachronic schematic function, not just a set of innate responses.

To repeat our learning from others, some distancing from the relationship itself may actually be required. Although we may be inspired by the full embodied presence of the other, we can also be overwhelmed so that the specialization in the relationship is reinforced rather than weakened. To cultivate the qualities of the other in ourselves, we need a combination of direct embodied inspiration and more distanced independence. Every competent teacher is familiar with this, and recognizes that they are not only a catalyst, but also a barrier to the learning of the student, who needs to learn and practise independently away from the teacher increasingly as

6   Jung (2009) p. 263.

they develop. When the student is far from the teacher, though, a mental image of the teacher provides a transitional reminder of the values that form that relationship. In the same way, people in committed monogamous relationships need time apart rather than to spend all their time together, for them to continue to develop as individuals, but to be sufficiently reminded of one another to develop each others' qualities to a greater extent whenever they are required in a different environment.

The use of anima/animus archetypes in religion has potentially served this function through the last few millennia of human history, the most obvious of these being female images used in patriarchal societies. However, it is obviously difficult to differentiate how far this archetypal function has historically been used for genuine integrative development, how far it may simply reflect projection, and how far it may show limited projection that is either diachronic or schematic without the other (see 1.h). An image of the Virgin Mary in Christian tradition, for instance, may operate both for men and for women as a reminder of compassionate and receptive qualities they lack. This may be reinforced by aesthetic features in the image, such as the deep blue derived from lapis lazuli traditionally used for the Virgin's robes **(figure 13)**. However, she may also be projected as an independent supernatural force that can solve our problems for us if pleaded with through intercessory prayer. We may be impressed by her in a way that is not regular enough to make a practical difference, or we may use her as the basis of a claim to exclusivism unrelated to the archetype – for example by reacting to claimed sacrilege. There are no guarantees that any given evocation of the archetype will be integrative.

If we are to try to distinguish those occasions when the archetypal function may operate helpfully, though, I think it's important firstly to recognize what a wide range of possible symbols may work in this way, and secondly to recognize that they may do so either aesthetically or symbolically. The wide range of possible symbols means that the anima/animus function cannot be confined to our responses to either masculine or feminine symbols, regardless of whether we are ourselves male or female (or both or neither). As a mature heterosexual male myself, I recognize that I'm particularly strongly affected by images or evocations of young fertile females: but I'm also affected by glimpses of the other in males, in animals, and even in inanimate symbolic forms such as alluring landscapes, stars, or artworks.

Figure 13. Virgin Mary and angels from the *Wilton Diptych*, unknown artist, England, circa 1395-9. National Gallery London. Photo by Sailko (Wikimedia Commons).
Creative Commons Attribution 3.0 Unported license.

As explained above, our potentially integrative response to the other is primarily one of *relationship*, so it's also necessary here to make a distinction between our responses to a symbolic person, and our aesthetic responses, which may extend beyond persons. Our capacity to have integrative responses to people depends on brain processes that create *gestalt* recognition of humanity and of animation, based in the right hemisphere's temporal region.[7] We

---

7   McGilchrist (2009) pp. 55-6.

enter into relationship as soon as we have this sort of response, as opposed to the objectification that occurs when we regard a person or animal instrumentally as prey, or when we focus only on body parts as opposed to bodily wholes. It is in the context of such relationships that we learn from others through *mimesis,* living imitation with variation, as opposed to exact, decontextualized, mechanical copying.

An integrative response to a symbolic other, then, is most likely to occur when we recapitulate that relationship in some sense, whether strongly or mildly, and whether in the company of an actual person or only reminded of them. Our *diachronic* renewal of that relationship to the symbolic other is what most enables the archetype to have an integrative effect. For example, a devout male Catholic, on again seeing an image of Virgin Mary in church, again feels a connection with her qualities and thus regains the potential to adopt them through the strengthening of those synaptic links. This renewal of a relationship, however, is likely to be far less effective if it is not also schematic. If the Catholic man walks out of church and shortly afterwards meets a highly compassionate Muslim woman whom he reacts to negatively because of her religious group, his failure to recognize the archetype in different contexts is also actively undermining its effectiveness.

However, I want to suggest that there is also another kind of response to the other which is not dependent on these instinctual responses to the human. Our aesthetic responses to beauty can also provide the opportunity to learn from the other, but this time far less directly. Instead of enabling learning experiences directly in relationship, aesthetic responses create a temporary mental state of greater openness in which we can become more receptive. This may well operate through the stimulus of the task-positive network in the brain, possibly then developing into 'flow' states in which we become positively engaged in an object, and mindful states in which that focus of attention is securely attached to bodily awareness. Such states do not necessarily depend on particular objects, and can be cultivated through meditation. We can appreciate that aesthetic state in itself, but we may also identify it with the archetype through association. For example, the Catholic man may experience the renewal of a sense of peace and self-acceptance triggered by seeing an image of the Virgin Mary, perhaps particularly by the blue lapis lazuli traditionally used for her robes. Aesthetic integration may both be triggered by symbols, and in turn facilitate our response to symbols by helping us to focus our attention on them.

The strongest and most sublime responses to the archetype of the other, then, are likely to combine both the personal response in relationship and the aesthetic response. This helps to explain some of the power of works of art that simultaneously remind us of our relationship with the other, and also trigger a greater aesthetic openness in response either to the beauty of the person depicted, or perhaps to the background they are placed in. There are many possible examples, both 'religious' and 'secular', but one that springs to mind is Renoir's painting 'The Skiff' (*La Yole*), in which two female figures are depicted in a small boat on a most wonderfully luminous river on a summer day (**figure 14**). The femininity of the figures does make a difference to the whole, but only in combination with the intense beauty of the whole setting. This is an example of a work of art that is not formally 'religious', but actually far more effective in the religious function of integrating the archetypes than many formally religious works. If our archetypal responses become genuinely schematic rather than dependent only on traditional contexts and associations, we should be able to recognize Renoir's painting as every bit as 'religious' as a Raphael Madonna.

Figure 14. The Skiff (*La Yole*) by Auguste Renoir (1841–1919), National Gallery London. Photo by Jean-Pierre Dalbera, Fondation Vuitton (Wikimedia Commons).
Creative Commons Attribution 2.0 Generic license.

Our ways of working with the anima/animus archetype need to take into account the paradox of possession that tends to accompany it. Our likely response to an attraction to the other is to egoistically appropriate it by making it self. When this is a person of the opposite sex, our response may be to want to have sex with them, and to permanently possess them by marrying them. If it is a picture, we want to take photos of it, put them on our wall and show them to friends. If it is an exotic place or culture that triggers our fascination with the other, we appropriate it by having the experience through travel. However, when we marry the man or woman who is such an object of attraction, we may find that they become less attractive as they become more familiar. Similarly, the stunning artwork that we put on our wall gets ignored after a while, and tourism can spoil the otherness of the place that we find so attractive by making it just like home. There is a delicate balancing involved in maintaining our relationship with otherness without fully appropriating it: maintaining some independence from a spouse, renewing our mental states for appreciating otherness through mindfulness practice, and avoiding contributing to processes that wreck the environments on which the other depends.

Traditional religious responses often only crudely approximate to this delicate balance, because they assume a projected form of the archetype rather than an integrative one. The religious sanctification of marriage can be seen as an institutional response that tries to maintain our diachronic relationship with the archetype through a committed relationship with one person. If marriage is seen as a relationship with God as well as with another individual, the ways in which we can engage with our overall potential for integration through our engagement with the other is emphasized. In the context of modernity, however, our commitment to religious marriage has been eroded, because we increasingly recognize that the archetype can be fulfilled in other places apart from in a sacralized relationship with one person. That may be correct in some respects but not others, for in some ways a commitment to work on one relationship may be by far the most effective means of making our relationship with the anima/animus diachronic.

Another potentially crude response to the anima/animus is that of religious celibacy, which often seems to be based on a reactive projection, assuming that because sex often leads to projection onto the other, therefore we can avoid that projection by avoiding sex altogether. In some cases, withdrawal from the sexual other may help us to sublimate sexual drives, but there's also now evidence that this does not always happen, and that celibacy may just have the effect of creating a dangerous idealization of the other free of intimate relationships with it. This can be particularly linked to widespread sexual abuse committed by celibates in the Roman Catholic Church. Successful celibacy requires a delicate balance in a wider context of Middle Way practice, so that sexual drives are not simply repressed, but only suppressed so that they can be sublimated.[8] It is much harder to cultivate that balance in a context of dogmatic rather than practical religion, where counter-evidence on the negative effects of celibacy is likely to be dismissed if it conflicts with authoritative teachings.

Overall, then, religion needs to encourage relationships with others that engage our fascination so that we can learn over a period of time, but recognize these relationships as dynamic and as the responsibility of each individual. Support for particular relationships that are judged to be integratively helpful, then, needs to be balanced by an avoidance of idealization of those relationships. The same goes for our relationships with the symbolic images of others, or even with the impersonal other. That the other is separate from us gives it an uncertainty that always needs to be respected rather than projected on, even whilst we recognize its power over us.

---

8   In the context of Buddhism, Sangharakshita (1983) discusses the distinction between 'neurotic' and 'non-neurotic' celibacy.

4.e. The Shadow, Death, and Suffering

Which way I fly is hell; myself am hell;
And in the lowest deep a lower deep,
Still threat'ning to devour me, opens wide,
To which the hell I suffer seems a heaven.
  John Milton, *Paradise Lost*

Much has already been said on the shadow in 2.i above. There I argued that the shadow involves a recognition of evil that is helpful if integrated rather than projected, as with the other archetypes. I also argued that evil consists in projection (or absolutization) at the point of judgement. We often have an intuitive sense that evil is projective, reflected in the personal features we habitually regard as evil (such as cruelty, deception, and egomania), but fail to recognize that much of what we have habitually regarded as 'good' also comes under that category, because of the assumption that evil is a privation of good rather than good an avoidance of evil, as well as metaphysical assumptions about the nature of good. We thus often fail to recognize the shadow when it would be most helpful to do so, mixed in with the 'good' around us, and at the same time project the shadow onto persons or objects that at best partially reflect it.

Our projection of the shadow is most basically associated with death and suffering, because these are a genuine threat. Given our embodied situation, the avoidance of suffering is our most basic value, justifying the whole operation of our threat system, the flow of cortisol shutting down other functions and putting us in an emergency mode in response to threats.[1] However, our perception of difficulty in controlling that threat system, and its tendency to be set off in circumstances when it is unhelpful, can also create a reactive projection in which death and suffering are regarded as good, and only our response to them problematic. This is reflected in philosophical approaches as diverse as the theistic belief that God created death and suffering (so they must be ultimately good), the ascetic belief that deliberately undergoing suffering is meritorious, and the Nietzschean belief that suffering will at least toughen us up if it fails to kill us. Even death is embraced by martyrs as good, when placed within an ideological justification.

---

1 Mobbs et al. (2009).

All of these counter-projective beliefs are false substitutes for the integration of the shadow function, substituting an easier belief for a harder and more complex one. The integration of the shadow requires us, not to justify suffering and death, nor to over-generalize about their positive value, but rather to differentiate more carefully between genuine threats and false threats by applying awareness over time. We do not distinguish genuine threats by denying that there are any threats, nor do we avoid false threats by over-generalizing about which things are threats. There is no substitute for critical discrimination in the light of experience. Scientific investigation, both physiological and psychological, has added hugely to our ability to differentiate between genuine and false threats, but this ability always needs to be applied at an individual level to be helpful. Recognition of the shadow archetype can provide us with a kind of negative inspiration: namely, an awareness of the possibility of threats which has sufficient emotional power to keep motivating us to counteract them over time. This negative inspiration is embedded in a wider context of positive inspiration by its relation to the other archetypes.

Differentiation between threats we can avoid and those we cannot is expressed in the religious context of the Serenity Prayer written by Reinhold Niebuhr:[2]

> *God, grant me the serenity to accept the things I cannot change,*
> *Courage to change the things I can,*
> *And wisdom to know the difference.*

Death and suffering are obviously, on the whole, things we cannot change. However, we may be able to influence how soon they occur, how intense suffering is, and whether suffering has positive as well as negative further effects. The ways in which suffering can be unnecessarily multiplied by not 'knowing the difference' is also reflected in the Buddha's parable of the second arrow, in which a suffering person 'feels two feelings – a bodily one and a mental one' which are compared to two arrows striking a person one after the other.[3] The first arrow, which is unavoidable, merely reflects the conditions of our embodied lives, but the second, consisting of the reinforcing feedback loops of our psychological response to suffering, can be allayed, for instance by the practice of mindfulness. The

---

2   Niebuhr's authorship is attested by Shapiro (2014).
3   *Samyutta Nikaya* 36.6: Bodhi (2000) p. 1264. See also Ellis (2019) pp. 113 ff.

wisdom to know the difference, and thus also when and how to try to avoid the second arrow, however, depends on our capacity to put our awareness of the basic threat (the first arrow) into a framework that is both diachronic and schematic. We can recognize that death and suffering are of a universal type, not uniquely threatening, and the degree of threat can be compared with threats at other times in the light of understanding of causes and consequences. The practice of integrating the shadow as a feature of practical religion can help us to 'know the difference' as opposed to either the direct projection or the reactive projection of the threat.

Niebuhr's use of the term 'know' in the prayer, however, reflects a widespread tendency to understand our differentiation of that difference in primarily cognitive terms, when it is not merely maintaining an abstract belief about the difference that is sufficient to grant us the serenity and courage we need, but rather having sufficient and timely reminders of it with a sufficient emotional impact. Niebuhr prays to God, not Satan, for such awareness, showing the way in which it is only by placing awareness of the shadow in the context of our whole integrative potential that we can integrate the shadow. Satan and his associates are a necessary aspect of religion, but they are not the object of worship – with good reason.

The apparent paradox of the shadow is that we tend to see it as chaotic, because of the way it threatens our own construction of order. However, it consists not in disorder but in the attachment to unchallenged order that disrupts our ability to differentiate between those threats we can change and those we can't. Projection, after all, consists in the imposition of a fixed order by an over-dominant left hemisphere, on a context that is uncertain. Uncertainty is not chaos, but we often interpret it as such just because it lies outside our projection of order. So, rather than lying in the apparent chaos outside our fortress of order, the shadow needs to be understood more as cast by the walls of the fortress.

Religious responses to the shadow often confuse our intuition of the evil of projection (with its recognition of egomania, cruelty etc. as evil) with the idea that a rejection of order is evil, because we are unaware of our own fortress. The Judaeo-Christian story of the Fall of Lucifer, rejecting divine order, reflects this, but Milton's tendency (in his epic poem *Paradise Lost*) to depict the supposed shadow (Satan) as heroic also reflects the inadequacies of this story **(figure 15)**. If the engaging process of integration only occurs to 'evil' characters it is a sign that our conception of good is too static. Rejection of order is not itself evil, but can indeed be a rejection of evil. This mistake seems to result from beginning with a prior projection of God as an orderly force for good, and deducing from this that evil must be a disorderly rejection of that good. Other mythologies have alternatively either recognized good and evil as coeval (Zoroastrianism and Manichaeism), or even evil as the predominant force (Gnosticism), but they have nevertheless projected evil as an external power.

Figure 15. Milton's heroic Satan, illustration by Gustave Doré for John Milton's *Paradise Lost* (1866).
Public Domain picture.

The different variants of the shadow that can emerge symbolically reflect the range of meaning that it has, from death and suffering through to absolutization of human judgement. For instance, in Western tradition, the figure of Death (often with a black cloak and a scythe) has a shadow role. The Four Horsemen of the Apocalypse from Revelations 6:1–8 (War, Pestilence, Famine, and Death) reflect a range of representations of the shadow as 'the things I cannot change'. However, the villain of most novels and films is likely to reflect the personal evil of absolutization. The link between these variants can be readily illustrated by the figure of Mara in Buddhist mythology, whose name means 'Death', but who is personified in the Buddha's life story as working against the Buddha's spiritual progress through fear and temptation.[4]

Other variants of the shadow can be categorized in terms of the shadow-self or the shadow-other. Although most commonly our rejection of the shadow implies that we also see it as separate from us, it is also possible to identify it with ourselves, particularly as a symptom of profound inner conflict of a kind that may also be understood in terms of mental illness. We may hate ourselves sufficiently to create disassociation and multiple personality disorder, or repress ourselves through asceticism that regards our shadow-self as not the true self. The possibility of the shadow-self is one of the indications that the self-other axis should not be conflated with the attraction-repulsion axis (see 4.a above), as we can perceive something as self without identifying with it, just as we can perceive something as other whilst identifying with it.

Not only the symbols we employ, but also the mind/brain events may vary so as to create variants on the shadow. There are different forms of negative emotion that seem to have adapted for different circumstances, such as anger, hatred, envy, and disgust, and these emotions then often influence the symbols of evil that we use. Anger, as an explosive rejection of an obstacle, is likely to be conveyed with metaphors of fire and energy. Hatred, as long-term negativity against an object, is likely to be associated with calculations of long-term harm and be associated with devils, demons, or unpredictably or unmanageably dangerous animals (Buddhist tradition uses a snake). Envy is likely to be associated with the largely positive features that we are envious of, but with one crucial disabling flaw that dramatically turns our admiration into resentment, making cunning, strength, or power into threats. Disgust is associated mainly with objects that might cause disease and where distancing ourselves is more important than combat: 'vermin', insects, deformity, and other people's bodily excretions. Satan and other devils are often depicted with reptilian or insect-like features reflecting disgust, for example in Hieronymous Bosch's depictions of Hell (**figure 16**).

---

4   Ellis (2019) pp. 38-1.

Figure 16. Hell, detail from *Hell and the Flood* by Hieronymous Bosch (1450–1516), Museum Boijmans, Rotterdam.
Photographer unknown.
Public Domain picture.

Further forms of the shadow may come from its relationships with the other archetypes. The shadow of the hero is the villain or anti-hero. The shadow of the other may be a demonization of the opposite sex and of other opposing qualities (such as age or appearance) – resulting, for instance, in the witch-accusations against women in medieval and early modern European culture. The shadow of God may be not just a devil but a Manichaean counter-God.

Whatever form the shadow takes, however, it is the temporal isolation of our rejection that makes it the object of an unacknowledged projection. If we are able to respond to the shadow more schematically, we may begin to link together different variants and recognize their similarity of function. If we are able to respond to the shadow more diachronically, we may also be able to maintain integrative practice that helps us to see each manifestation of it in a wider context. That does not mean defusing all threats, but being able to distinguish the degree of genuineness of the threat.

If we become better able to distinguish real threats, it then may become easier to identify when suffering or even death form part of a balancing feedback loop in a system. We take the nasty medicine to cure the disease, have the tooth extracted, or even recognize death itself as an aspect of renewal, clearing the way for new life. In this way, what we previously regarded as the shadow becomes integrated with positive functions. If we did not recognize and accept the shadow to begin with, however, this process of renewal would be impossible, because we cannot integrate the pain without first recognizing that it is painful. I will have more to say about this process in the final chapter of this section.

4.f. God and Religious Experience

> *Then felt I like some watcher of the skies*
> *When a new planet swims into his ken;*
> *Or like stout Cortez when with eagle eyes*
> *He star'd at the Pacific – and all his men*
> *Look'd at each other with a wild surmise –*
> *Silent, upon a peak in Darien.*
> John Keats, 'On First Looking into
> Chapman's Homer'

We must come to the God archetype (what Jung called the 'Self') last amongst the archetypes, because its understanding is so dependent on that of the other three. The integration of any of the other three archetypes can lead us to develop our relationship with the God archetype, whilst the projection of the God archetype is also often associated with projection of the other three archetypes. Considered in its own right, though, the God archetype is hugely prone to metaphysical idealization that has constantly undermined its function in human experience. That idealization has also divided the concept of 'God' from many other concepts (such as those of enlightenment, nature, truth, or humanity) that may serve the same archetypal function, creating false dichotomies both between different religions and between 'religion' and 'secularity'.

It must also be reiterated that the God archetype is a *function*, and thus our identification of it with any particular symbol is contingent. The use of the term 'God' as a label for that function is merely a convenient one, that seems to me to maximize the functional connections in Western culture. Once we enter into the meaning of the term 'God' with any degree of sympathy, it seems to offer the nearest symbol for the meaning we need to convey here – that is, of potentialities stretching far beyond our immediate understanding. However, there are lots of reasonable objections to the selection of that label (and to 'his' gender). I do not find such objections decisive, because we have to call it something, and there are other objections to other labels. Please interpret all uses of the 'God' label in this book as contingent and functional, and by all means substitute your own. Enlightenment, the Self, nature, reality, truth, the good, the logos, even Niebuhr's 'ultimate concern' can easily take the place of the word 'God', *provided* that it is noted that these concepts can just as easily be projected and absolutized as God can. There is no shortcut route out of God projection just by changing the word we use.

The God archetype can arise from the hero archetype, because as we integrate the heroic function we are obliged to increasingly engage with unknown potential. As discussed in 4.c, the difficulty in achieving our goals over time may lead us to reconsider both the nature of those goals and how they are achieved. In addition, a re-framing of our egoistic identifications may require us to go through a heroic rebirth. The more we expand our conception of our goals, the more we also integrate ourselves in relation to them, overcoming conflicts between different imagined ends and means through a dialectical process. The more we integrate our pursuit of goals, the more we gradually shift from the hero archetype to the God archetype. It is thus not surprising if the greatest religious heroes are identified with God or gods, from Hercules to Christ. The Buddha, on the other hand, fulfils the same function by reaching the furthest point of human potential as the goal of his quest, even if he is not technically divine (**figure 17**). Our projected assumptions about God can also get stuck with the idea of God as the ultimate hero – an agent beyond us who possesses the superpowers necessary to dispel all difficulties.

The God archetype can also arise via the anima/animus archetype, as we progressively move from appropriating the other to engaging with it and learning from it. As we engage in dialectic with the other, its significance gradually changes from 'otherness' to a wider potential that is neither self nor other. The practical significance of the soul, which Jung understands as his anima, reflects this, along with the religious associations between the soul and God. The belief that God is wholly other reflects this way for the archetype to arise, whilst its interrelationship with the hero can be reflected in triangular relationships between self, other, and God, as in the Christian tradition of the incarnation in which Mary (the anima) bears the infant Jesus (the hero) who is also God.

The God archetype can also arise in response to the shadow. As we saw in the Serenity Prayer in the previous chapter, God is invoked to cope with difficulty. He is even sometimes invoked to defeat enemies. The functional relationship between God and the shadow thus lies in our response to extreme events outside the norm. These events not only produce suffering and death beyond the range of our normal expectations, but also require us to engage with potential that we were unaware of before that point. Although our heroic projection onto God may be to imagine him as being able to magically remove our suffering, it is the access to new resources in our own experience that is more crucial to the God function in these new situations.

Figure 17. The Buddha, Gandhara sculpture. Photographer unknown.
Public Domain picture.

However we come to engage with it, the God archetype is a term for a schematic and diachronic access to *experiences* of potential, marked by openness in contrast to previous closedness. Such experiences can vary greatly in intensity and in the degree of openness experienced. At one end are experiences of what Csikszentmihályi called 'flow': a focusing of attention and a sustained capturing of intrinsic motivation which may contrast with previously scattered or distracted states of attention.[1] Such states begin to unify our energies and thus offer a new sense of potential and enjoyment. Csikszentmihályi comments on the way that these states help us to develop towards greater complexity, and also how they require a balancing of the right sort of stimulus to be maintained, neither overwhelming nor understimulating. A step up from flow, however, are mindful states, up to and including *jhana*, the state of meditative absorption described in Buddhist sources and accessible to regular meditators. Mindful states differ from flow states in being more strongly grounded in bodily awareness and relaxation, thus allowing a more profound (though still temporary) unification of energies and even ecstatic emotions. At the far end of this spectrum are the most profound religious experiences, involving the stimulation of the limbic system to dramatically intensify our experience, particularly the temporal lobe. Stimulation of the temporal lobe results in a sense of unification in time and space.[2] This seems to happen, for instance, in near-death experiences, where the neural system goes into overdrive in response to a profound threat to the whole organism.[3] Near-death experiences are often life-changing encounters with both God and the shadow.

Such experiences are not necessarily solely individual, but may be shared by a group. Shared religious experience, such as that of the children of Medjugorje who shared a vision of the Virgin Mary, has been recorded.[4] The potential we experience in such experience may also not only be individual potential, but that of a wider group. Nevertheless, group religious experience needs to be carefully separated from group hysteria, which allows the group to override individual experience as opposed to individual experiences being shared in solidarity.[5] In such states of group hysteria, conformity to the group is the foremost motivation, and cognitive dissonance commits the group to beliefs that cannot be questioned by individuals. This can be found, for instance, in the 'Toronto Blessing' – a Christian charismatic movement developing from the 1990s. Here people showed signs of dramatic emotional release, such as uncontrolled laughing or physical jerking, in a group context pumped

1   Csikszentmihályi (1990).
2   Ramachandran and Blakeslee (1998).
3   French (2005).
4   Soldo (2016).
5   E.g. Robin (1981).

up by rhythmic music and miraculous testimonies,[6] but not of any greater reflective awareness that would allow them to sustainably contextualize that emotion.

Although a basic criterion that we need to apply to experiences of God is that they be *integrative*, beyond this we cannot identify God only with one type of experience. Rather the God function consists in a set of associations between experiences of new openness or potentiality and the meaning that they enable people to access.

Whatever one's degree of spiritual experience, whether mild or profound, the diachronic re-enactment of that experience enables us to be re-inspired even when we cannot access it directly. The experiences may well have both a symbolic and an aesthetic dimension (see 4.d above), both accessing meaning through association and providing experience of beauty, and when we recall them diachronically there is likely to be a complex mixture of symbolic association and aesthetic experience. However, what we can be clear about is that God is not simply a representational sign, and that re-inspiration by the God archetype is not dependent on how we conceptualize that archetype, nor on beliefs about it. Practical beliefs may well be necessary, such as the belief that it is good to expose oneself to archetypal symbols on a regular basis, but these are not absolute beliefs about the archetype itself, rather provisional beliefs about the ways that we should work with it.

The Jungian tradition has noted different ways in which the God archetype can be symbolized in individual experience. These can be both personal and impersonal. The wise old man image that is the basis of most Western depictions of God in art can be matched amongst personal images by a wise old woman, or by heroic and goddess images. Impersonal images particularly include the mandala, which Jung recognized as a universal symbol of integration, occurring not only in Buddhist tradition (**figure 18**) but also spontaneously in dream imagery, city layouts, gardens, and many other contexts where divisions of a circle suggest the unification of different elements.[7]

What seems distinctive about the kinds of concepts and symbols that can represent the God function is their infinity: they lack boundaries, are 'open-ended' in some sense, or show a capacity to

---

6   Poloma (2003).
7   Jung (1959a) §627 ff.; Ellis (2020) ch. 5.

absorb different influences to an unknown extent. The theological definition of God as infinite, eternal, omnipotent, and omniscient captures this most formally, as long we interpret it *from our perspective* rather than from a 'God's eye view'. From our experiential perspective as finite creatures, limited in time, space, power, and understanding by our embodiment, infinity is just an absence of the limits we would normally expect. An experience of vast potentiality, beyond our limited identifications and concepts so far, feels infinite just because it is open, and because we have no way of understanding where its boundaries might be. However, the theological tradition insists on treating infinity as a representational concept that projects ourselves into God's own position. We *define* (the irony!) God as *infinite*, in the process actually making him finite by giving him clear conceptual boundaries that substitute for the experiential absence of such boundaries. As usual, we thus substitute a simple problem for a complex one so that we can pretend to have control over it. The Church cannot control the universe, but instead it can substitute control over concepts that supposedly encompass it.

Figure 18. Green Tara mandala, Ladakh. Photo by Christopher Michel (Wikimedia Commons).
Creative Commons Attribution 2.0 Generic License.

Terms like 'truth' or 'reality' can be treated in exactly the same way. In our more philosophically reflective moments, we may at least implicitly concede the sceptical case that we have no 'knowledge' of truth or reality, the reason for this being their infinite scope. Even the 'truth' about a small object, such as a pen or a mug, is inaccessible to me, because I cannot penetrate to what it 'really is' – I just have lots of sensory interactions with it giving me different phenomenal impressions. So it is not just God who is infinite. The sense of awe or wonder that we might feel when encountering God can also be applied to even the most everyday objects. Nevertheless, the development of well-justified conceptual beliefs about objects tends to lead us into the assumption that we 'know' the 'truth' about them. The substitution of 'secular' symbols or concepts for 'religious' ones does nothing either to make infinity more tractable, or to remove our tendency to project 'knowledge' onto mere conceptual belief.

However, there is also a long history within religions of warnings about the projection of the God archetype, each one an attempt to reform dogmatic religion back into practical religion. The early Israelite rejection of idolatry can be seen as the first recognizable attempt to warn against the reduction of the infinite into a finite form. At that time, in a society where few people would have been literate, the most likely way of trying to confine the infinite into the finite would have been visual – the making of 'graven images' that would become objects of worship in the place of an unpictured God, whose infinity could thus have continued to have been recalled (see 5.f for more on this point). The parallel in Buddhist tradition is the doctrine of emptiness, with its insistence that no phenomenal object should be taken to have essential features (see 5.c). Enlightenment and its perspective were recognized as unrepresentable from an early stage.

The problem in all these traditions has remained the substitution of conceptual projections for archetypal symbols, even if visual ones were avoided. As literacy has spread, those projections seem to have become more, not less, deeply entrenched in religion. For the early Israelites, words were the lever of universality and objectivity over images that were specific to the context. To help people experience God, you had to impose rules that took them away from images and made them depend on words instead. However, the representationalist delusion that words do, or even can, conceptually represent 'truths' is implicit even in the early Israelite rules, and still present in the attitudes of those who believe in the possibility of scientific 'law' that entirely encapsulates the behaviour of conditions in a verbal formulation. The God function has been projected in words that are believed to be revelatory and to have ultimate authority, whether the revelation was allegedly received through religious experience or through scientific observation. The inspirational function of the God archetype was thus also profoundly misunderstood as a source of 'truths', whether these were transmitted through exceptional experience, authoritative individuals, or 'nature'. In each case our claims are not necessarily 'untrue', but nevertheless they are projected, because they are accompanied by the assumption that we have fully understood the message.

The projection of God is also accompanied by a loss of experienced responsibility. As long as we encounter a potentiality to act differently from our previous default patterns, we are capable of taking moral responsibility and thus stretching our moral practice.[8] When we identify our moral responsibility with obedience to an external figure, however, we simultaneously make it dangerous to consider alternative courses of action, or to take responsibility for those alternatives for ourselves. When we worship that figure, there may remain some diachronic function (see 1.h above), but the lack of schematic understanding still grossly undermines the moral function of the archetype, by making morality a matter of diachronic obedience to certain limited representations. Instead of promoting creative exploration beyond our current assumptions, projection of our potential leads us to confine it within a particular dominant model.

'Worshipping God' in archetypal terms is any activity that connects us to inspiring potential by symbolically or aesthetically re-enacting that experience of potential.[9] As Patrick McNamara strikingly puts this,

> *Performance of religious rituals will periodically activate a number of possible Selves, including an ideal Self. The chronically activated ideal Self is then in a position to contribute to self-regulation by providing a standard by which to evaluate progress towards a goal and resolution of internal and social conflicts.*[10]

---

8   See Ellis (2012) 7.b.
9   See Ellis (2018) 8.a.
10 McNamara (2009) p. 25.

The church-goer may do this to some extent despite their projection of the archetype, but others may find that inspiration far more effectively in green environments, in creating or appreciating art, by engaging with others, in solitary meditation, or in scientific research. However we do it, the crucial point is to recall that God is a practice that puts us in touch with an experience. Shortcut conceptual substitutes simply will not do where God is concerned.

4.g. The Middle Way Archetype

These two extremes should not be followed by one who has gone forth into homelessness. What two? The pursuit of sensual happiness in sensual pleasures...and the pursuit of self-mortification.... Without veering towards either of these extremes, the Tathagata [Buddha] has awakened to the middle way....
      The Buddha (*Samyutta Nikaya* 56.11.421, trans. Bodhi)

So far, I have discussed four functional archetypes, each of which has innumerable variants. Can I be sure that there are only four? Obviously not. If there are any further archetypes, however, I argue that they should be distinguished as diachronic schematic functions, not on the basis either of variations of symbol, or of brain/mental state. I do have one other further archetype to suggest on these lines, which I think it is helpful to distinguish, and which plays an important part in religion. Its function, however, is only comprehensible in relation to the four archetypal functions already described, and whether it is a full fifth archetype may be somewhat debatable. This is the Middle Way archetype.

The Middle Way archetype has the diachronic and schematic function of reminding us of the way, i.e. the method by which we develop integration. Whilst God inspires us with a glimpse of the potential for integration achieved, the hero with the effort needed to achieve integration, the anima/animus with the relationships we will need to develop integration, and the shadow with the perils of projection, the Middle Way inspires us with the need to maintain a balanced awareness of starting points in relation to goals. We can neither assume that there is no goal of value to us, nor that the goal can take us over and save us for itself. A gradual process of constant provisional judgement is needed to move from projective states to more integrated states. *This process itself* is what we need archetypal reminders of more than anything else.

It may well be argued that the other four archetypes, especially the God archetype, can already fulfil this function of reminding and inspiring us on the way. Symbols of the goal can undoubtedly fulfil the function of symbolizing the way to the goal, but the question is how well they do so. As long as the symbols that inspire us on the way are associated primarily, through the weight of cultural interpretation, with its completion, a further mental reflection or adjustment is required to recognize moral and spiritual life as being just as much about the starting point as the end point. Our left-brain over-dominance gives us a bias towards the absolute that means we need all the help we can get to make us shift towards a more effective emphasis on process, balance, and context, to navigation rather than racing, and to reflection rather than seizing. By using and developing the Middle Way as a distinctive function, we may be able to do this.

A variety of symbols, both personal and impersonal, can fulfil that distinctive function. The strongest ones tend to explicitly symbolize some kind of ambiguity, marginality, balancing, or process, even though these features can also be implicitly understood in symbols that more directly symbolize the other archetypes. The Middle Way itself is an image: a metaphor of a path between opposed alternatives.[1] Mandalas also offer a complex balancing between different kinds of extreme rather than only a binary balancing. A tree, such as the Tree of Life, can symbolize the Middle Way as a process, with its roots in conditions but growing towards a goal.[2] Christ fulfils the requirement for a personal symbol of the Middle Way because of his ambiguous nature – both fully human and fully divine, provided that ambiguity is emphasized rather than sidelined.[3] The Buddha is also an obvious candidate for a personal symbol of the Middle Way, but whether he functions as such depends on whether enlightenment as a final state is emphasized, or the dialectical process by which he made progress towards it.[4]

Symbols more commonly associated with the hero, anima/animus, and shadow, may also at times function as Middle Way symbols. This comes not only from the function being increasingly integrated, but more importantly from that process of integration itself being turned into a symbol, so that our degree of direct experience of the integration process can be diachronically connected to practical inspiration. The hero effectively finds the Middle Way as his efforts become more integrated, with those efforts becoming balanced – not merely the wilful pursuit of a goal but also awareness of the balanced states of mind needed to make helpful judgements about it. The anima/animus finds the Middle Way as we engage

1 See Ellis (2019) pp. 100-1.
2 See Ellis (2020) ch. 5.
3 See Ellis (2018) pp. 134 ff.; Ellis (2020) ch. 4.
4 See Ellis (2019) pp. 221-4.

with the ambiguity of being both self and other – a self moving into other territory who can't be totally identified either with a fixed self or with a fixed other. Androgyny or androgynous figures can sometimes fulfil this function, and Jung discusses the hermaphrodite as a symbol of the creative union of opposites.[5] The shadow fulfils the Middle Way function as we recognize the complexity behind it, symbolically converting the enemy into a friend: Christ's descent into hell is an example of this kind of symbolism.[6]

Just as I suggested with the other archetypes, the Middle Way archetype may vary with brain/mental state as well as with symbol, provided the same function is preserved. I do think that the recollection of the Middle Way is consistently associated with one aspect of mental states – namely the presence of optionality, or the ability to consider alternatives to a claim beyond its bare negation. However, this optionality could appear to widely varying degrees in different circumstances, and at different levels of awareness, meaning that other aspects of brain/mental states at the moment of recollection can be very varied. The presence of optionality means that any Middle Way function in the mind-brain is likely to be a more complex version of the variety of states corresponding to the other archetypal functions: namely a more complex goal, relationship, threat, or transcendence orientation.

In the most extreme cases of mental states that are lost in projection, such as those of a drug addict, there may still be moments of optionality in which the Middle Way function can operate, in which it is realized that there can be some progress towards alternative states without denial of one's current state. In the most deluded states, such alternatives are only conceived as a mere negation of the current absolutizations. Awareness of an alternative potential may take the form of any of the four main archetypes (particularly the God archetype, as used functionally in the 12 steps of Alcoholics Anonymous[7]). However, awareness of alternative potential *that is sufficiently linked to awareness of one's current state to enable some kind of practice* involves the Middle Way function. Without the Middle Way function, there remains a danger that a brief experience of alternative potential will only result in an idealization, and a process of

---

5   Jung (1959a) §292-7.
6   Jung (1958) §149.
7   See Ellis and Sheath (2016).

'flipping' between idealized fantasy and despair about one's current state.

At the other end of the spectrum, there will be those for whom the Middle Way function is sufficiently part of a habitual embodied reflection to become a reliably frequent source of inspiration. We do not need such reflections constantly, but we do need them at moments of judgement, so as to be able to consider alternatives that will help us develop our responses beyond whatever binary absolutes have become entrenched in the situation. The more we become aware of the Middle Way as an implicit possibility, the more those options are likely to become an entrenched part of our neural associations. In this case, the entrenchment is not merely one that limits the possible responses, but one that enables further new associations to be formed.

To function as an active reminder of the Middle Way, then, a Middle Way symbol needs to *combine* the kind of evocation of a more integrated state that is used for the God function, in tension with a basic dissatisfaction that is grounded in an adequate awareness of the actual situation. It may do this through ambiguity, by managing to combine the two kinds of awareness simultaneously. It may work through marginality, in the sense of evoking schematic experience of the borderline between two zones (those zones often being associated closely with different framing assumptions). It may schematically evoke an experience of process or movement, or one of balancing combined with forward movement.

The most direct version of the Middle Way, then, is obviously that suggested by the term itself. However, some of the alternative types of schemas may have stronger affective power for many. The story of the Buddha's early life symbolizes the Middle Way as a process in which two alternative absolutes (the Palace and the Forest, associated with self-indulgence and self-mortification respectively) are avoided, holding in tension both dissatisfaction with the starting point in the Palace (from which the Buddha-to-be 'went forth' – **figure 19**) and avoidance of idealization represented by the religious teachers and ascetics in the Forest (**figure 20**, also see 5.b).[8]

---

8   Also see Ellis (2019) section 1.

Figure 19. Buddha leaving his family to 'go forth', fresco from a temple in Sarnath, India. Photo by Ajay Tallam (Flickr).
Creative Commons Attribution Share-Alike 2.0 Generic license.

Figure 20. Buddha leaving the ascetics, fresco from a monastery in Laos. Photo by Sacca (Wikimedia Commons).

Categorization of Archetypes 183

Christ, on the other hand, symbolizes the Middle Way through ambiguity, combining the divine and the human in a way that (in the Nicene Creed formula that he is *wholly divine* and *wholly human*) requires the Middle Way in its functional application in human appreciation. In Andrea del Sarto's representation of the Holy Family, for instance (**figure 21**), the divine is simultaneously suggested by the way that the infant Jesus holds the world, whilst his humanity is still obvious from the fact that he is a vulnerable child. The Christian who is moved by Christ cannot suddenly become divine, nor can he just be human in the normal sense. At the very least, then, there is a dissatisfaction with the human state that is held in tension with a vision of the divine one.

Figure 21. *Holy Family* by Andrea del Sarto (1486–1530), Metropolitan Museum of Art, New York. Photographer unknown.
Public Domain picture.

It must be stressed in both of these religious examples of Middle Way symbols that their capacity to function as such depends entirely on their context, and on whether this is one of dogmatic or practical religion. As with the other archetypes, what makes them Middle Way symbols is neither the form of the symbol nor the entire brain/mental state that accompanies it, but whether or not that symbol functions as a Middle Way symbol. In many cases Middle Way symbols are appropriated to the God archetype, or in some cases to the hero archetype, and lose their function. Nevertheless, it would be surprising if Middle Way functions had not emerged at least to some extent in those societies where practical religion had developed. The symbols that are used for it are then adaptations of the cultural symbols that come to hand.

Like the other archetypes, too, the Middle Way archetype can be projected. What may start as a genuine sense of connection with both the starting point and goals of the way can rapidly become a matter of merely conceptual belief, over-simplifying the complex dialectical process involved in treading the path. The symbols associated with the Middle Way then start to mean the conceptual shortcut rather than the process. This occurs in metaphysical accounts of the Middle Way, such as those offered by many Buddhist schools, by Christian Christology, and by scholastic Aristotelianism that turns the 'golden mean' into a cosmological truth. A recent unfortunate example of this is offered by Lou Marinoff's book *The Middle Way*, which presents the Middle Way as a metaphysical absolute almost from start to finish.[9] The idea of the path may continue to be represented, but it is then no longer a path of constantly renewed judgement: rather it is an idealized path of heroism towards the God archetype.

Just as the integration of the hero, anima/animus, and shadow function start to engage us with the God archetype, integration of the God archetype starts to engage us with the Middle Way. Glimpses of integrated potential cannot be either schematically understood or diachronically sustained if they are not grounded in practice. It is our awareness of our bodies, the surrounding conditions, and our limitations that enables us to challenge idealizations of the God archetype that only express our experience in particular limited conditions. At the other extreme, understanding of conditions without

---

9   Marinoff (2007).

Categorization of Archetypes

sufficient schematic and diachronic engagement with the implicit God archetype will leave us unmotivated.

The Middle Way is thus (as I have argued much elsewhere), the clearest and strongest expression of the good as we can engage with it as embodied beings. Unlike the projected God archetype, it has the potential to unite different religious traditions, and to unite 'religion' with 'secularism'. It does this, not by making vague dogmatic claims about ultimate unity, but rather by inspiring and enabling a critical, experiential process whereby the absolutizations that create these divisions can be questioned and disassembled.

5. Archetypes in Religious Traditions

5.a. Ethnic and Universal Religion

> *Paul stood up before the Council of the Areopagus and began: 'Men of Athens, I see that in everything that concerns religion you are uncommonly scrupulous. As I was going round looking at the objects of your worship, I noticed among other things an altar bearing the inscription "To an Unknown God". What you worship but do not know – this is what I now proclaim.'*
>
> Acts 17:22-23 (Revised English Bible)

In this section of the book I intend to examine some selected examples of the four (or five) archetypes in the context of various religious traditions. One of the dangers of my exposition so far is that it gives an impression of archetypal functions that might be taken in some ways as abstract, static, and decontextualized, when actually concrete context and process are crucial to the ways that archetypes operate in religious traditions. We can only consider this more fully by going into a little more detail as to how religious traditions have treated some specific archetypal forms. Since religious traditions themselves are interrelated, complex, and contiguous, it is also helpful to show that some of the ways they have developed new religious forms are themselves due to tensions in the archetypal functions that these religions serve. If, as I am arguing, the archetypal functions can explain the positive point of religion for humans, but nevertheless the continued gravitational pull of projection has often distracted from that purpose, it is hardly surprising to find that the development of crucial new religious ideas throughout the history of religion can be readily explained by the need to renew the archetypal functions.

One of the most common ways of classifying religious traditions is as 'ethnic' or 'universal': an 'ethnic' religion being one that is primarily an aspect of the identity for a particular ethnic group, whilst a universal religion is one that is equally open to all ethnic groups. This distinction is, of course, not a neat one, but rather a matter of qualities on a spectrum. Judaism and Hinduism, for instance, may be largely ethnic religions, but both have adopted some marked universal features, and may in some circumstances accept converts from other ethnic groups. The three great universal religions – Buddhism, Christianity, and Islam – are also prone to becoming more or less 'ethnicized' when they become closely associated with a particular ethnic identity: as is the case with Greek Orthodox Christianity, or Newari Buddhism in Nepal.

As I have described the archetypal functions as *universal* ones (see 1.b), does this imply a universal model of religion in general, in accordance more with that of the big three than with the more ethnic traditions? Not necessarily. The universality of the archetypes is schematic, not symbolic, as I have argued throughout. One of the features that distinguishes one religious tradition from another, however, is the prevalence of specific identifiable symbols throughout that tradition (for example, Christ in Christianity and Buddha in Buddhism). Universal religions try to make the archetypal functions available to all in a particular symbolic form, in the process failing to recognize that their meaning in human experience is schematic. If the religion is varied and tolerant, there may be a wide range of interpretations and specific forms associated with one basic symbol (such as black, white, and Chinese Christs), but nevertheless the symbol is often seen as having certain defining formal features: for instance, God must be infinite, and must not be confused with finite things. The universality of symbol in a universal religion may or may not aid acceptance of the more important schematic universality that helps people to overcome unnecessary conflicts over symbols. In many cases, a coherence of doctrine merely adds to attachment to certain conceptual symbols and propositional beliefs about them, preventing rather than supporting schematic understanding. It is not merely a matter of everyone worshipping the right 'universal' (and conceptually defined) God.

Ethnic religions, on the other hand, may often accept the limitations of their symbols to a particular group. Jews, for instance, do not generally expect Gentiles to adopt Jewish beliefs and practices. In some cases that may make them better able to implicitly acknowledge the schematic nature of their meaning by recognizing that there can be different symbols with the same value for different groups. Of course, in other cases this ethnic restriction merely results in parochial exclusivity in which there is no recognition at all of alternative symbols for the archetypes. Even where there is a recognition of alternative symbols, this may be accompanied by relativism in which all such values are assumed to be equal, and thus the value of integration over time cannot be recognized.

Ethnic and universal religions thus tend to have slightly different strengths and weaknesses in recognizing and using the archetypes. Whilst universal religions have developed new symbols for the God archetype, and have developed Middle Way archetypes of a kind that might be less likely in an ethnic religion, they have also projected those archetypal symbols in ways that are more rigid because of their links to a highly systematized conceptual theology or philosophy. In ethnic religions, such highly systematized conceptual absolutizations are less likely, but nevertheless, the limitations of the culture with which the ethnic religion is associated can be easily rationalized, either chauvinistically or relativistically.

Some of these differences will be reflected in the discussion of specific religions in the remainder of this section. This will begin with Buddhism, the complex archetypal nature of the Buddha, and the even more complex Mahayana Buddhist ramifications of that archetype. It is to Buddhism, above all, that we can turn for instantiations of practical rather than dogmatic religion, even though the tradition as a whole also offers substantial dogmas.

Although Buddhism originated in a context that we could call 'early Hinduism', it was actually a substantial influence on the subsequent development of Hinduism as an ethnic religion with many universal features. At first glance Hindu monism may seem highly compatible with a recognition of the archetypes as schemas rather than symbols, but, as we will see, the limitations that tend to accompany ethnic religions also limit this recognition in practice. In China, by contrast, the God archetype takes the form of various types of Nature symbols. I think it is crucial here to recognize the underlying similarities in archetypal usage, despite the great cultural differences with most of the rest of the world's traditions.

I will then move on to the Abrahamic religions, beginning with the role of Yahweh in the Hebrew Bible. The contradictions between ethnic and universal features, and of dogmatic and practical elements, are extremely striking here, but provide a stimulus for much subsequent religious development. Another major influence on Christianity and Islam is Graeco-Roman religion and philosophy, which, like Hinduism, come tantalizingly close to recognizing the archetypes as schemas. The role of Christ, as well as other archetypes in Christianity and in Christian mysticism, depends on a creative synthesis of these two very different expressions of the archetypes found in Greek and Hebrew traditions.

Islam then gives a powerful new expression to the universal urge reflected by Christianity, but one that is also heavily dependent on specific projected symbols that take a conceptual rather than visual form. Although Islam as a tradition may seem highly resistant to archetypal treatment, I will here at least try to sketch out the archetypal roles of Allah as the fiercely undivided God, and of Muhammad as the heroic prophet. Finally, I will return to Judaism to consider the Kabbalah, a medieval Jewish mystical tradition with a highly sophisticated archetypal symbology. This will once again show the margins of ethnic and universal religions to be perhaps more creative places than their centres.

5.b. The Buddha

The danger of duality, against which the Buddha warned his followers, does not lie in oppositional thinking itself. Rather, it lies in how we use such thinking to reinforce and justify our egoism, cravings, fears and hatreds.

Stephen Batchelor, *After Buddhism*

'The Buddha' refers primarily to the historical (or legendary) individual, Siddhartha Gautama, whose deeds and words are recorded in the Pali Canon. However, secondarily it also refers to an image that is very clearly symbolic, the representation of enlightenment in the form of Buddha figures in a huge variety of styles across the Buddhist world. In verbal form that symbolic representation also occurs as a universal figure, largely separated from his supposed historical Indian background, preaching in the Mahayana Sutras. It is widely recognized that not all symbols of the Buddha are intended as representations of Gautama, especially in Mahayana Buddhism. Rather they are symbolic of a human potential, and thus quite obviously archetypal. However, I want to argue that the 'historical' Buddha, too, is archetypal. This chapter concentrates on that 'historical' Buddha of the Pali Canon, also discussed in *The Buddha's Middle Way*.[1] Consideration of the universal Buddha of the Mahayana follows in the next chapter.

To see that the Buddha of the Pali Canon is archetypal, we only need to focus on his function *for us*, rather than on traditional or historical claims about his status. As with most religious figures, we can identify that function with that of the God archetype (which we could just as easily call the 'Buddha archetype', the 'Nature archetype', or any of a number of other terms). The Buddha represents our own potential in human form: in the words of one Buddhist liturgy, 'The Buddha was a man, as we are men.... What the Buddha attained, we too can attain.'[2] Traditionally, that potential is understood in the discontinuous terms of gaining enlightenment – but it can also have a significance to us that is much more continuous and incremental, namely the capacity to develop from where we are now, and to carry on developing.

---

1 Ellis (2019).
2 FWBO (1990) p. 34. A gender-neutral alternative is also suggested.

The story of the historical Buddha, as has often been remarked by Jungians,[3] also offers a heroic narrative. In his early life, Siddhartha Gautama is born a prince in the highly protected environment of a palace, but finally comes to question the assumptions of that environment, 'going forth' into the forest. In the forest, he is taught by religious teachers, but these do not give him the final answers he seeks, and he then tries ascetic practices, but these also do not lead to enlightenment. He then finds the Middle Way that is said to lead him to enlightenment. He thus sets out in pursuit of a goal, encounters difficulties along the way, overcomes those difficulties with perseverance, and finally achieves his object. In the process, as in all cases of an increasingly integrated heroic function (see 4.c), the nature of the goal and the way it is attained both change as the hero gradually gains better understanding of it.

In addition to the heroic and God functions in accounts of the Buddha, however, there is the paradigm case of the Middle Way archetype. As discussed in 4.g above, the Middle Way archetype inspires us with a combined recognition of the potential for integration (which incorporates the function of the God archetype) with the current conditions. Instead of merely presenting us with an ideal, the Middle Way archetype reminds us that there is a gradual and ambiguous process involved in moving from current conditions into the direction of the ideal, and foregrounds that *process* as a more adequate version of the ideal in the embodied circumstances of human life. We can find inspiration for this archetypal function in the Buddha's discovery of the Middle Way, symbolized for instance by his acceptance of food (**figure 22**).

The Buddha's discovery of the Middle Way operates as a particularly powerful symbol for the Middle Way function, because it incorporates both a dialectical process and a return to embodiment. The dialectical process consists in the Buddha's 'going forth' from the Palace, followed by his countervailing recognition of the limitations of the Forest and rediscovery of some valuable elements of his time in the Palace (when he remembers his experience under the rose-apple tree in his youth[4]). He thus fully accepts the assumptions of neither of the two opposing contexts, and re-frames the terms of his options, but nevertheless adopts some of the most helpful aspects of both of the avoided extremes.

3   E.g. Campbell (2008) pp. 46–8.
4   *Majjhima Nikaya* 36.31: Ñanamoli and Bodhi (1995) p. 340.

192　　　*Archetypes in Religion and Beyond*

Figure 22. The Buddha accepts food to end his asceticism: roundel from carved ivory tusk by unknown Indian artist (early 20th century), National Museum, New Delhi. Photo by Nomu420 (Wikimedia Commons).
Creative Commons Attribution Share-Alike 3.0 Unported license.

The Buddha's returning memory of his experience under the rose-apple tree is also crucial to the recognition of embodiment involved in his discovery of the Middle Way. This positive experience was one of *jhana* – of meditative absorption that needs to be developed through bodily awareness and acceptance. The Buddha marks this acceptance of the conditions of the body by taking food, in the process giving up the absolutized ascetic belief that one can defy the basic conditions created by the body.[5] Accepting the conditions of the body also implies the recognition of uncertainty and

---

5　　*Majjhima Nikaya* 36.33: Ñanamoli and Bodhi (1995) p. 340.

the avoidance of projection with its deluded certainty maintained by absolutized opposing groups. The distance between the Middle Way and the absolutizing, projecting group is symbolized by the story of the five fellow ascetics abandoning him in disgust when he decides to take food.

If the crucial elements of the Middle Way archetype as a schema are repeated reconnection with the experience of greater integration *together with* awareness of current state, there are a variety of embodied schemas associated with that experience. The Middle Way as a metaphor in the context of the Buddha and his teaching has two of these: the embodied experiences of walking a path and of balance.[6] Both of these experiences need to be held in tension together to appreciate the Buddha's Middle Way. There is always some kind of movement 'forward' (though transposed from space into time) as we make judgements at different points on the path, but the Middle Way is not just any such path. There is also always an element of balance, which means avoiding absolute options on both sides, although not all judgements that involve a balance are necessarily Middle Way judgements (the recognition and avoidance of opposing absolutes is crucial). The path metaphor holds together an awareness of our current state with an awareness of a future goal, but the balancing metaphor ensures that the future goal is one that takes our current state sufficiently into account rather than simply idealizing an alternative.

In the context of the Buddhist tradition, the balancing of the Buddha's Middle Way is not typically presented as simply one between opposing absolutes, but rather as the path between 'eternalism' and 'nihilism'. These two alternatives identify opposing absolutes that were important in the Buddha's time, but in my view they do not offer adequate descriptions of the extremes to be avoided in other times and places, the specifics of the Buddha's time having been mistaken for the basis of a universal account. My arguments for this position are explained much more fully elsewhere.[7]

The Buddha's Middle Way is also typically presented in Buddhist tradition as the way to nirvana (enlightenment, or awakening), with nirvana being not merely the God archetype as a source of inspiration, but also constitutive of the Middle Way, with the Middle Way

---

6   Ellis (2019) 3.b.
7   Ibid 4.b and c.

defined in terms that require dogmatic beliefs about nirvana to be accepted. Depictions of the Buddha's enlightenment may include depictions of some of the qualities that helped him in the process of reaching it, as in the confidence that emanates from Kawanabe Kyosai's picture, but at the same time the formal trappings of enlightenment, such as the halo, are also seen as crucially validating the Buddha's status (**figure 23**). This emphasis on the enlightened status may fatally undermine the addressing of present conditions in the Middle Way, and turn the operation of the Middle Way archetype into another version of the God projection. The Middle Way cannot be the path to a destination that is conceptually pre-defined and at the same time avoid absolutes on both sides, as beliefs about the destination become a new absolute.

Figure 23. Face detail from Buddha Shakyamuni by Kawanabe Kyosai (1831–89), Musee Guimet, Paris. Photo by Jean-Pierre Dalbera (Wikimedia Commons).
Creative Commons Attribution 2.0 Generic.

The Buddha's Middle Way is potentially a powerful archetypal symbol that has inspired people across Asia, and more recently in the West, to engage in practical religion. The Buddha's formulation of the Noble Eightfold Path follows up that inspiration with instruction in a range of integrative approaches, especially mindfulness and some aspects of criticality in wisdom, all of which has helped to create a living tradition of practical religion in Buddhism in which technique is combined with archetypal inspiration. However, it is also important not to idealize the Buddhist tradition, but rather to examine it closely and critically for those dogmatic elements that interfere with its practical functions. The ossification of the Middle Way in the form in which it was described in the Buddha's time is one of these dogmatic elements.

The projection of the God archetype, however, is perhaps the more obvious indication of the development of dogma in Buddhism. The attribution of a discontinuous (and thus absolute) state of enlightenment to the Buddha means that his words are often then given absolute authority. Rather than a source of inspiration for integrative practice including critical practice, then, at this point the Buddha's advice becomes rigidified and gradually loses its relevance in a range of contexts. The rigidification of the Middle Way is thus interdependent with the projection of the God archetype, and thus the absolute interpretation of doctrines such as those of conditionality, karma, and rebirth, or ethical precepts. The words attributed to the Buddha offer a rich resource of both inspiration and instruction, but only if they are constantly interpreted in ways that prioritize practice, and critically anticipate dogmatic interference in their practical standpoint.

5.c. Mahayana Symbology

The virtuous one has asked why I have no servants; well, all demons and heretics are my servants. Why? Because demons like the state of birth and death which the bodhisattva does not reject, whereas heretics delight in false views in the midst of which the bodhisattva remains unmoved.

Vimalakirti Nirdesha Sutra ch. 5 (trans. Luk)

With the development of the Mahayana schools of Buddhism, beginning in India from around 500 years after the Buddha, the symbology becomes much more complex, with a multitude of Buddhas, bodhisattvas, and other symbolic figures sharing or extending the archetypal significance of the 'historical' Buddha (now known as Shakyamuni). These varied figures are found to some extent throughout Mahayana Buddhism – in the Himalaya, China, Japan, and Korea – but reach their greatest efflorescence in the tremendously rich complexity of Tibetan Buddhist iconography.

Though there may be a variety of historical causes for all this symbolic development, there are two major effects of it that impact on the archetypal role of these figures. One is a relatively high degree of awareness that archetypal figures are formed in human minds (even if this awareness is not formulated in exactly the same terms as modern psychology). This gives a potential boost to practical religion with its challenge to projection, even whilst dogmatic elements also continue. Another is the more direct addressing of the archetypal functions that were not so much expressed in the Buddha figure, particularly the anima and the shadow.

One reason for increased awareness that archetypal figures emerge from human minds comes from the development of visualization practices in which archetypal figures are deliberately created and dissolved in the mind's eye. They may be built up from a blue sky, and eventually fade away back into that blue sky. These kinds of practices existed in earlier Buddhism as visualizations of the Buddha Shakyamuni, but developed in some Mahayana traditions as *sadhana* practices for the development of a deeply embodied faith response to a particular figure. This figure may have been selected in relation to the specific temperament of the person doing the visualization, so as to address their strengths or weaknesses most effectively, and given to them specifically in an initiation. For example, someone who is either lacking in feelings of compassion, or who is especially receptive to them, may be set a practice of visualizing a figure of compassion by their teacher, such as the compassionate red Buddha Amitabha, the Bodhisattva Avalokiteshvara (**figure 24**), whose thousand arms reach down to aid the multitude, or the female 'essence' of compassion, Tara. The iconographic and descriptive traditions of these figures are often represented as emerging from the experience of meditators, rather than the meditators always merely visualizing forms that have been defined by the icons.[1]

Figure 24. Thousand-armed Avalokiteshvara by unknown artist (traditional Tibetan image), Art Gallery of New South Wales, Sydney. Photo by Google Cultural Institute (Wikimedia Commons).
Public Domain picture.

1   Vessantara (1993) pp. 33–4.

The recognition that these forms emerge from human minds is also aided by the concept of emptiness (*shunyata*) in the perfection of wisdom literature (*prajñaparamita*), formalized by the philosophy of the Madhyamaka school. Madhyamaka philosophy uses sceptical argument to stress the uncertainty of both positive and negative claims, and that they lack *svabhava* (self-existence, i.e. ultimate metaphysical existence). Instead, all phenomena have a conditional status, dependent on other phenomena.[2] When this argument is applied to archetypal experience, whether in the context of visualization meditation or that of ritual, the result is obviously a strong disincentive against projection. Mahayana practitioners may thus often accept that the figures they meditate upon and venerate do not have supernatural or *a priori* 'existence', although that also does *not* imply that they do not 'exist': rather, their operation is dependent on the practice that gives rise to them.[3]

If the Madhyamaka interpretation of the Mahayana offered a completely adequate archetypal account of human inspiration, there would be little need to write this book, for its standpoint would already be well established as an option. Unfortunately, however, it has many limitations. Whilst employing balanced sceptical argument to identify the extremes that we need to avoid on the Middle Way, it also relies on revelatory appeals to special insight to delineate what the Middle Way positively means in experience. It continues to rely only on philosophical critiques of the absolutes, rather than clearly identifying their psychological correlates in projection and absolutization, or offering any concept of provisionality of judgement (see 2.c and 3.a) that could help identify the Middle Way as part of everyday experience. Nagarjuna's influential doctrine of 'two truths' instead leaves us with a total discontinuity between the 'ultimate' perspective offered by sceptical argument and the 'conventional' perspective of ordinary human judgement, so that any Buddhist judgement that fails to take into account its own provisionality can be readily rationalized in an *ad hoc* fashion because it is 'conventional'.

Thus, although a strong practical tradition exists in Mahayana Buddhism, enabling some impressive individual practitioners to engage deeply with the archetypes as sources of meaning and

2   Nagarjuna (1995).
3   Govinda (1969) p. 104.

inspiration whilst largely avoiding projection, there are also other competing tendencies in that tradition that encourage projection. With an understanding of the Middle Way that is dependent on appeals to the ultimate authority of the perspective of enlightenment as a revelatory state, the God archetype is often projected, either on the symbolic figures themselves, or perhaps more often on the guru – the spiritual teacher who introduces the disciple to these special revelatory states. The projection of the God archetype onto Mahayana deities begins with explanations of them as representing 'ultimate reality',[4] and continues with practices that seem to require a literal interpretation of their role, for instance the belief in the reincarnation of lamas who are also believed to be bodhisattvas in Tibetan Buddhism.[5] The Dalai Lama could only be an incarnation of Avalokiteshvara if Avalokiteshvara is assumed to be something rather more than a phenomenon of practice. The projection of the same absolute status onto the guru can only be justified by the assumption that the guru is the sole source of initiation into discontinuous insight, being the Buddha's representative in the present. The guru's commands must then be obeyed, and critical thinking about them suspended, even if he commands pointless tasks such as the successive building and demolition of towers,[6] or appears to be breaking important moral precepts. The application of these assumptions has recently given rise to a whole set of sexual abuse allegations against gurus across Buddhist groups in the West,[7] all of whom have adopted this uncritical tradition towards the guru in dependence on the absolutization of enlightenment.

However, even whilst the Mahayana's success in helping practitioners of the Middle Way avoid projection is mixed and limited, it can offer further achievements in extending its archetypal symbology in ways that allow the whole range of archetypal functions to be effectively fulfilled by those who do manage to make use of its traditions without projection. Although early Buddhism, as discussed in the previous chapter, could offer a focus for both the God and hero archetypes in Shakyamuni Buddha, the anima and

4   E.g. Govinda (1969) p. 130.
5   E.g. ibid. pp. 111-25.
6   Tsang Nyön Heruka (1995) p. 67 (including note).
7   See http://beyondthetemple.com/tibetan-buddhist-teachers-accused-of-abuse/ (accessed 2020).

the shadow remained uncatered-for. As the female perspective long remained very marginal in the tradition, so did the animus: but it could also be argued that Shakyamuni Buddha could fulfil the animus function for women. It is thus female figures who particularly represent the anima/animus in Mahayana Buddhism: Tara the embodiment of compassion, Prajñaparamita the bodhisattva representing wisdom, Kuan Yin or Kannon, the female variant of Avakokiteshvara found in China and Japan, various female consorts of symbolic Buddhas, and the dakinis and yoginis of the Tibetan Vajrayana. In many cases, meditating on these figures has helped masculine practitioners integrate their feminine aspect more completely.

Mahayana Buddhism is also distinctive in the ways that it has symbolized the shadow as an aspect of enlightenment, recognizing that the integration of the shadow is an important aspect of the path symbolized by enlightened figures. In this it is in some contrast to the strong tendency to separate shadow figures and present them in absolute opposition to the God archetype that we find in Christianity and the other Abrahamic religions (discussed further in 5.i below). It is also in some contrast to the depiction of Mara in early Buddhism, as the evil figure who frustrates the Buddha's quest and represents the forces of unenlightenment. In Tibetan Vajrayana Buddhism, particularly, we find *dharmapalas* or 'wrathful deities' depicted who also have 'peaceful' forms. Avalokiteshvara, the bodhisattva of compassion, is also Mahakala ('The Black One') **(figure 25)**, and Manjushri, the bodhisattva of wisdom, is also Yamantaka ('Ender of Death'). Such 'wrathful deities' are guards protecting against threat, and are acknowledged to form part of the total range of symbolic enlightenment.[8] Even better, positive figures such as Padmasambhava ambiguously combine shadow features with their positive features: Padmasambhava has a 'fierce smile' and is ornamented by skulls and severed heads[9] **(figure 26)**. The idea that the shadow needs to be acknowledged and integrated, rather than merely rejected and destroyed, thus plays a healthy part in the Mahayana symbology.

---

8   Vessantara (1993) ch. 24.
9   Ibid. pp. 243–51.

Archetypes in Religious Traditions 201

Figure 25. Mahakala by unknown artist (15th-century Tibetan image), Philadelphia Museum of Art. Photo by Google Cultural Institute (Wikimedia Commons).
Public Domain picture.

The widespread use of mandalas in Mahayana Buddhism also helps practitioners to constantly place archetypal forms in a wider context of integration. A mandala is a circular diagram in which different elements are shown in relation to each other as part of a symbolization of integration (see **figure 18** above). That which is placed in the centre of the mandala most closely symbolizes the central values that will produce integration, whilst as one moves towards the edge one finds elements that are more partial, but are still being placed in a context in which they are shown to have both integrating qualities and other qualities that need to be integrated.

In short, then, mandalas express the God archetype.[10] Of course, this archetype becomes projected when mandalas are glossed unhelpfully as depictions of 'reality', but their very form encourages us to become aware of dynamic relationships between elements rather than absolute claims.

Figure 26. Padmasambhava image at Tsozong Gongba Monastery, Eastern Tibet, unknown sculptor. Photo by Kosi Grammatikoff (Wikimedia Commons).
Public Domain picture.

Perhaps the most interesting development of the use of mandalas in the Mahayana tradition combines it with the Buddha symbol to form the Five Buddha Mandala. Here the red, green, blue, and yellow Buddhas on the edge of the mandala symbolize contrasting relative qualities, all of which need to be integrated in the wider, long-term context. For example, the qualities of the Red Buddha Amitabha are those of compassion, the Yellow Buddha Ratnasambhava of generosity, the Blue Buddha Akshobhya unflinching 'mirror like'

10   Jung (1959a) § 627 ff.

wisdom, and the Green Buddha Amoghasiddhi practical judgement. These are united in the features of the White Buddha at the centre.[11] This dynamic element, acknowledging our starting point as well as our ideals, makes the Five Buddha Mandala potentially an important symbol for the Middle Way archetype rather than only the God archetype.[12]

For the richness and potential archetypal value of its symbolic development, then, Mahayana Buddhism is evidently unsurpassed anywhere else in the world's religious traditions. However, we should not allow these undoubtedly significant achievements to lead us to idealize Mahayana Buddhism, or to lose sight of the need for continued critical awareness in the way its traditions are utilized and interpreted.

---

11   Vessantara (1993) part 2. For an illustration see Ellis (2020) p. 98.
12   See Ellis (2015a) 5.a.

5.d. Hinduism: The Great Appropriation

This earth is honey for all beings, and all beings are honey for this earth. That radiant, immortal person who indwells this earth, and, in the case of the [human] self, that radiant immortal person who consists of the body, is indeed that very Self: this is the Immortal, this Brahman, this the All.

Brihadaranyaka Upanishad 2.5 (trans. Zaehner)

Hinduism is an ethnic religion that has been profoundly challenged by a universal one that emerged in its midst. That has led to it adopting many of the archetypal features and techniques of Buddhism, its challenger, but it has also fought back, appropriating the Buddhist Middle Way and turning it into a tool of power through projection to a much greater extent even than Buddhism itself has done.

Despite the tradition of six competing philosophical schools, the Hindu tradition's most characteristic philosophical stance is monism: the claim that 'all is one', whether God, the universe, or the self. This is influenced primarily by the Advaita Vedanta philosophy,[1] summarized in the *'Tat tvam asi'* ('Thou art that') of the *Chandogya Upanishad*,[2] meaning that the self is the universe and the universe is Brahman. On the surface, this suggests a recognition that both God and the 'truth' of the universe are archetypal, because resolution of one's own conflicts is also union with God. However, this relationship between self and God is constantly presented as a metaphysical truth rather than a process of judgement, which means that it can readily be made into the basis of authority claims (as can the other types of philosophical position in Hindu tradition). Rather than only being a development through individual and social experience, the union of God with the self is a matter revealed to the sages, whose status in Hindu tradition also depends on their acceptance of the authority of the Vedas (the original source of the hierarchical and ritualistic elements in Hinduism).

There is an important difference, then, between on the one hand recognizing that individual integration systemically resembles, and potentially contributes to, socio-political integration, and on the other asserting the identity of the two in order to 'privatize' individual integration and disempower the individual from socio-political change. The archetypes in Hinduism can undoubtedly be used to

1 The extent of its influence is testified to e.g. by Deutsch (1996).
2 *Chandogya Upanishad* 6.8 and subsequent verses: Zaehner (1966) p. 109.

inspire individual integration and thus have a practical element, but the authority claims that the tradition appeals to allow its monism to become a tool of dogma for socio-political purposes. This can be seen particularly in the message of what is often taken to be the central inspirational text of Hinduism, the *Bhagavad Gita*.

The *Bhagavad Gita* is one episode excerpted from the vast heroic epic of the *Mahabharata*, which tells of a long dynastic struggle between two sets of cousins. In many ways this struggle shows the fruitlessness of limited goal-driven versions of heroism appealing to honour, which only create conflict, and it ends with the renunciation of worldly ends by the victors.[3] In some ways the hero archetype is thus integrated in the epic as a whole. However, in the *Bhagavad Gita*, the integration of the hero archetype is blocked by an appeal to dogma from a supposed divine representative. In the midst of the battlefield of Kurukshetra, Arjuna is struck by conscience at the thought of killing his relatives, but his charioteer, Krishna (said to be an avatar of Vishnu, and thus divine), is depicted as urging on him that his *dharma*, or moral duty, is his specific caste duty as a warrior, namely to fight.[4] This is further justified through an appropriation of the idea of integration for specific socio-political ends, as Krishna argues that the *yoga-yukta* (a person integrated by spiritual exercise) must act in the world, but renounce his own will to that of Brahman.[5]

The *Bhagavad Gita* has long been a source of inspiration for Hindus, because in some ways it does offer a path of integration, some degree of integration of the hero archetype, and some elements of the Middle Way archetype. Arjuna, the hero in the field of battle, is given a wider context in which his understanding of the goals of the battle is broadened and made compatible with his own specific situation. Hindu practitioners can thus be inspired not only by the symbolization of an ideal, but by its effective linking with the starting-point of individual experience and the path of practice of the individual through *yoga* (i.e. integrative practice in a broad sense). However, the goals of this practice (namely the God archetype) are also projected in the socio-political terms required by the caste system, which remains an unquestionable feature of the context, and defines the development of the individual within specific

3   Ganguli and Roy (2018).
4   *Bhagavad Gita* 2: 31–7 and 18: 41–8: Zaehner (1969) pp. 137–9 and 393–5.
5   Ibid., chs. 2 and 3.

socio-political tracks. Given that it probably dates from the 4th century BCE, shortly after the time of the Buddha, it is easy to read the *Bhagavad Gita* as a Brahminic appropriation of the Buddha's Middle Way. The individual is encouraged to treat the archetypes in an integrative fashion, but only within the terms of a wider projection that maintains the supreme power of Brahmins at the ritualistic apex of the caste hierarchy.

The other major heroic narrative in Hinduism, the *Ramayana*, offers similar limitations on the integration of the hero, even though in this case the main hero, Rama, is said to be an avatar of Vishnu and thus divine. Rama follows an extreme of duty by going into exile for 14 years so as to fulfil a promise made by his father. When in exile, his wife Sita is abducted by the demon Ravana. He is only able to rescue her from Ravana's clutches on the island of Lanka with the help of Hanuman, the monkey god. Hanuman may represent the need for integration with one's animal nature. At the end, too, Rama rejects the rescued Sita, assuming that she must be impure, and her purity has to be proven to him by fire: but this hardly does much to change his binary assumptions about the female other. In most other respects the *Ramayana* is just a conventional heroic narrative in which the hero defeats evil to fulfil his goal, without having to change his view of that goal or how it is achieved. Like the *Bhagavad Gita*, the *Ramayana* may inspire, but only within the bounds of a highly conventionalized Hindu ethics that restrains and limits much of the potential opened up by Buddhism.

However, a whole branch of Hinduism (Shaktism) does develop the cult of the anima in ways that have surely helped many generations of Hindus to maintain a sense of the inspiring power of the other in the feminine. Devi, the Goddess, takes a great variety of forms, including Durga, Kali, Manasa the snake goddess, and Shitala the goddess of smallpox. Often Devi is a divine mother, but sometimes also a fearsome feminine version of the shadow. Shaktism also connects with Shaivism (the worship of Shiva) in the concept of Shakti as the yogic male god's consort, her energies needing to be integrated with the masculine in a symbolic sexual union **(figure 27)**. In the Tantric developments of Hinduism, shared with Mahayana Buddhism, counter-balancing engagement with the other may even go so far as (regulated and initiated) ritual involving things normally forbidden in orthodox Hinduism: alcohol, meat, fish, and sexual intercourse. The Tantric way can be seen as a relic of

Buddhism that has escaped Brahmanical control, as it is open to all without distinction of caste or sex.[6]

Figure 27. Shiva-Shakti on Nandi, unknown Indian sculptor. Reproduced by kind permission of Lotus Sculpture, Oceanside, California.

The meaning of the Shakti as the anima in Hindu Tantrism also extends to directly embodied meaning as it can be encountered in meditative or other yogic practice, with the awakening of the kundalini energies being directly related to the Shakti within. As Klostermaier explains:

Shakti is supposed to lie dormant, coiled up like a snake at the base of the spine: through yoga in the Tantric sense she is awakened and sent through the six Tantras or nerve centers up through the spinal cord into the thousand-petalled lotus, situated above the base of the nose, where Shakti meets with Shiva.[7]

6   Klostermaier (1994) pp. 283–6; Bharati (1966) ch. 9.
7   Ibid. p. 287.

A whole symbolic physiology accompanies this, constantly identifying the body, the world, and the divine in ways that can be ritually played out as well as experienced inwardly in meditative practice. As long as we interpret this symbolic physiology archetypally instead of in terms of belief, it can provide us with a richly embodied inspiration for integrating the anima function. The *other* is after all not merely something we experience externally in sexual or other exotic forms, but something we can also find within our bodies in the form of unexpected sources of energy with a similar allure. That energy is something primarily experienced rising in the spine is something that can be directly encountered even through relatively basic meditation. The integrative process is then to make these energies part of our more habitual awareness. In some ways, indeed, when we fall in love with someone outside ourselves, we are also falling in love with the arising of our own embodied energies that that person stimulates. To treat that symbolized 'other' as a new form of 'scientific' information about the body (in the form of beliefs about the chakras, for instance) is projection, but to accept its archetypal power is merely to credit its functioning in our own experience.

The figure of Shiva as destroyer, as well as the fearsome female figures such as Kali and Durga, also show some attempts to integrate the shadow in Hinduism. Shiva is associated with asceticism, yoga, energy, and freedom. As a dancing figure (Nataraja) he tramples on a dwarf or demon representing ignorance (**figure 28**). In union with Shakti, and in the symbols of *lingam* and *yoni*, he connects the energy of sexuality with both creative and destructive power. Rather than rejecting the shadow here, then, we are constantly reminded to put it in a larger context in which some degree of destruction may be a side effect of freedom and creativity.

The vast and complex Hindu tradition thus offers a range of possible paths for integrating all the major archetypes, within an overall context in which it is basically accepted that there are different inspirational paths for different individuals to address different starting conditions. The basic perception in Hinduism that all archetypal forms are aspects of God can also be productive of the integration of symbols of the divine with both individual experience and social ritual. However, the overall treatment of the archetypes in Hinduism is limited in its pragmatic value by the great appropriation in which Brahminic power has shaped and limited a whole civilization's engagement with the archetypes. Appropriation can be used for helpful purposes, but the grand appropriation by which all is included in one archetypal vision in Hinduism has had a purpose that maintains fixed social power for an elite, accompanied by the dogmatic projection that the universe must be of such a nature as to constantly maintain that social power. To this day the Hindu tradition is still invoked to justify the violent repression of Dalits and others judged to be 'low caste'.[8] However seductive Hindu tradition might seem as an interpretation of the integrative insights that primarily began with the Buddha, the role of the caste system continues to cast a very long shadow over that tradition.

Figure 28. Shiva Nataraja (Lord of the Dance), unknown sculptor, Tamil Nadu, Chola dynasty, Los Angeles County Museum of Art. Photo by the museum.
Public Domain picture.

8   https://thediplomat.com/2016/05/india-violence-against-dalits-on-the-rise/ (accessed 2020).

5.e. The Archetype of Nature in China

The Master said, 'Who can go out without using the door? Why, then, does no one follow this way?'
Confucius, Analects 6.17 (trans. Lau)

Chinese religion is for the most part not differentiable into separate religious traditions, apart from those like Buddhism or Christianity that have been imported, or various 'salvationist' groups. Instead, a variety of folk deities and a tradition of ancestor worship tend to serve the overall function of the God archetype through veneration of an underlying natural order. 'Nature' in the West may often be seen as a 'secular' concept (see 6.a below), but it has often offered an impersonal focus for the God function even in the 'Natural Law' tradition of the Catholic church, as well as in the concept of an underlying order (*dharma* or *ṛta*) in India. As in other parts of the world, that archetypal concept can serve a helpful function of inspiration over time – or it can be projected and appropriated.

Natural order in Chinese thinking is interlinked with ritual that both reflects and maintains it. It is often understood in terms of the balance of *yin* and *yang*, feminine and masculine principles that are in turn differing manifestations of *qi* (energy or matter) shaping the universe. The natural order, which completely integrates what modern Western thought would think of as fact and value, is also known as *Dao* (or *Tao*, the 'way' or 'principle'), as the 'mandate of heaven' (*tian*), as *li* (inherent order), and as *bao ying* (moral reciprocity in the universe). It is served by the development of personal virtue, as in Confucius's ideal of the 'gentleman' (*chun tzu*), who contributes to social order through personal integration.

The balancing of *yin* and *yang* in the *Dao* should not be confused with the Middle Way, as it is a description of a balance said to operate in the world rather than the path in human judgement. Formally speaking, in the Daoist tradition, the path is the *De* (or *Te*), and generally emphasizes intuitive acceptance of the natural order of things (*wu wei*). In *wu wei* the concepts of 'inaction' and of an adapted economy of energy are ambiguously combined,[1] so that at some points it seems to offer a projected God archetype of fate, but at others potentially a more integrated Middle Way archetype. That ambiguity is found in the variety of interpretations in the Chinese tradition,

---

1   Slingerland (2007).

with contemplative Daoism suggesting a more passive relationship with the *Dao*, whereas the Neo-Confucian tradition applies *wu wei* to the political realm.

Everything depends on whether the concept of nature is primarily a prompt for awareness of our uncertainty in relation to a wider system, or on the other hand the basis of appeal for a false certainty that is then used as a tool of power. That the former interpretation forms an important part of the Chinese tradition can be seen in many texts, for example in these two extracts from the *Analects* of Confucius:

> *There were four things the Master refused to have anything to do with: he refused to entertain conjectures or insist on certainty; he refused to be inflexible or to be egotistical.*[2]

> *The Master said, 'Do I possess knowledge? No, I do not. A rustic put a question to me and my mind was a complete blank. I kept hammering at the two sides of the question until I got everything out of it.'*[3]

This recognition of uncertainty can be related to the ways in which the Neo-Confucian understanding of *li* and *qi* can be interpreted as offering a systems theory rather than a metaphysics, as Jeremy Lent has recently argued.[4] The natural order expressed in neo-Confucian thought as *li*, he says, has the stability of an organic system, despite the changes that continually take place in the energy and matter that sustain that system: he compares *li* to a candle flame and *qi* to the molecules of matter or energy feeding that flame. *Li* has also been compared to the flow of water, or to the grains in wood.[5] However, it is quite possible to project absolute features onto a changing 'natural' system of this kind, and to use it as a basis of appeal. For instance, the appeal to 'order and stability' forms a basic part of the 'Asian values' appealed to by defenders of political repression both in modern China and other Chinese-influenced countries.[6]

Arguments for the superiority of the Chinese concept of nature over dominant Western religious forms, like those of Jeremy Lent,[7]

2   Confucius (trans. Lau) 1979, 9.4.
3   Ibid. 9.8.
4   Lent (2017) ch. 14.
5   Watts (2011).
6   E.g. https://www.nytimes.com/1998/04/10/opinion/IHT-what-are-asian-valuesa-justification-for-repression.html (accessed 2019).
7   Lent (2017) pp. 300–3.

depend on a claim about the construction of values in Chinese culture over Western culture that would need a lot of psychological and sociological evidence (of a kind he does not offer) to show how the philosophical and religious concepts have actually been habitually interpreted in practical judgement. Lent contrasts the tolerant Chinese Admiral Zheng with the genocidal Christopher Columbus in their very different responses to strange peoples: but there are so many different possible conditions at work here, and so much danger of confirmation bias, that we cannot simply ascribe the contrast only to the formal philosophies found in each culture. In the absence of adequate evidence, there is no particular reason to assume that one particular cultural way of conceptualizing the God function is inherently better at avoiding its projection than another. The God function can always be projected, whatever form it takes, whether that results in the Spanish slaughter of native Americans or the Chinese repression of Tibet, and we should not allow our greater cultural familiarity with certain projections of the God function to lead us into idealizing one over another. What matters is not the symbolic form taken by the archetype (whether it is personal or impersonal, 'natural' or 'supernatural'), but whether sufficient awareness is developed to prevent projection from occurring. That awareness may or may not be aided by many surrounding cultural factors that help to determine how archetypes are interpreted – not merely the formal philosophical commitments. Many of these surrounding cultural factors were discussed in section 1: embodied schemas, traditions of integrative practice versus dogmatic habits in religion, and the impact of modernity are surely major ones.

As in other cultures, there are, of course, also important symbols of the other three archetypes in Chinese religious culture, and these may all contribute towards helping people engage with the God archetype as nature. These include legendary heroes that may help to provide inspiration to engage with the path of enlightenment, often through the martial arts tradition which channels goal-directed energy towards integration. They also include goddesses, which offer a corrective emphasis on *yin* as opposed to *yang* when engaging with the path. The shadow tends to take forms that warn of human obsessions and vices.

The legendary heroes of Chinese culture include military leaders from the three kingdoms era such as Zhuge Liang and Guan Yu. These heroes were idealized in the 14th-century *Romance of the Three*

Kingdoms[8] and have since been adopted and widely worshipped in Buddhist and Daoist traditions as well as Chinese folk religion. In Chinese Buddhism Guan Yu has been co-opted into the God archetype by becoming a *Dharmapala* (protector of the teaching) and being identified with the bodhisattva Sangharama.

Perhaps more familiar to western audiences is the hero Xuanzang ('Tripitaka') from the Chinese story *Journey to the West*, translated into English and later televized as *Monkey*.[9] In this episodic, magical adventure, a Chinese monk journeys to Vulture's Peak in India to receive the scriptures from the Buddha, in the belief that these will help to reform China from the evils it has fallen into. What challenges the limited conceptions of the quest here, however, is comedy. When Xuanzang and his companions finally reach the Vulture's Peak, they are fobbed off by the Buddha's attendants with blank scrolls that only outwardly resemble scriptures, and it is only by accident that they discover this and then go back to get the 'real' ones.[10] There's a rich suggestion here that despite the effort taken to retrieve them, the exact words of the scriptures may not have quite the value placed on them.

There are several goddesses in Chinese mythology, but perhaps the most influential focus for the anima/animus function is Xi Wangmu. As Max Dashu describes her,

> *She lives in the Kunlun mountains in the far west, at the margin of heaven and earth. In a garden hidden by high clouds, her peaches of immortality grow on a colossal Tree, only ripening once every 3000 years. The Tree is a cosmic axis that connects heaven and earth, a ladder travelled by spirits and shamans.*[11]

The Tree of Life, connecting heaven and earth, is a potent symbol of the Middle Way found in a variety of cultural settings, including the book of Genesis and Norse mythology. It has its roots in human conditions but branches into heaven, thus relating to our embodied experience of growth and relating our experience of the God archetype to the conditions of ordinary life.[12] The idea of immortality is also a (potentially projected) symbol of diachronic meaning, moving beyond the limitations of our concern with a particular

---

8   Luo Guanzhong (2014).
9   Wu Cheng'en (1942).
10 Ibid. ch. 99.
11 Dashu (2017).
12 See Ellis (2018) 4.d for a more detailed account.

time. To be conducted into the strangeness of the immortal realm, however, we need someone who is both enticingly strange and comfortingly familiar: 'wangmu' apparently means 'grandmother' as well as 'sovereign mother'.[13]

Figure 29. Xi Wangmu (Queen Mother of the West), unknown artist, China, Ming dynasty. Photo by King Muh (Wikimedia Commons).
Creative Commons Attribution Share-alike 4.0 International license.

Xi Wangmu is a shaman, making her a guide to unknown regions of the psyche. Shamans often take the form of animal spirit guides, and hers is the form of a tigress, adding to the encounter with the other not only through sex but animality. Alternatively, she may be

---

13   Dashu (2017).

depicted riding a tiger **(figure 29)**. Her mountain, Kunlun, is said to be inhabited by thousands of strange animal spirit guides.[14] She is said to have taught the Daoist sages,[15] but to have had an untamed femininity, confronting men with uncompromisingly seductive *yin*. Patriarchal attempts to tame her by giving her a male consort were rejected by popular tradition.[16] Overall, then, the symbolic place of Xi Wangmu in Chinese mythology offers a rich example both of the role of the anima in offering inspiration for an integration process, and also of the ways that such a figure can be potentially projected and appropriated by making her subject to a structure of power.

Finally, the depiction of the shadow in Chinese tradition is marked by the absence of a central figure of evil corresponding to Satan. However, the Buddhist concept of Mara as the forces of unenlightenment is imported into China as Mo, and combined with *gui* ('ghost') to form *mogui* or *mogwai*: disruptive spirits or demons. The heroes in *Journey to the West* have to encounter and overcome a number of these. What seems most striking about them is that they tend to mark human characteristics caught in repetitive reinforcing feedback loops rather than an active supernatural malevolence. In some ways, then, these shadow figures already seem partly on the way to becoming integrated, because although we may fear them unnecessarily and even project them, they are already easily recognized as states we may fall into ourselves, rather than as wholly other. For example, vengeful ghosts (*yuan gui*) have been subject to an injustice when they were alive, whilst hungry ghosts (*e gui*) are addicted and constantly craving.

However, it would be rather surprising if Chinese religion had no representations of the shadow beyond ghosts, particularly as the shadow has a habit of emerging when we least expect it to do so. Richard von Glahn gives us an example of this in his study of the cult of Wutong:

> *In the late Ming dynasty (sixteenth to seventeenth centuries), Wutong emerged as the dominant cult figure in Jiangnan, the economic and cultural heartland of China, in the form of a god who governs the dispensation of wealth. The most remarkable feature of Wutong's incarnation as a god of wealth was the deity's diabolical character. Wutong was perceived neither as a culture hero nor as a reification of normal human qualities, but rather as an embodiment of humanity's*

---

14 Cahill (1993) pp. 51 ff.
15 Ibid. pp. 14-15.
16 Dashu (2017).

> *basest vices, greed and lust, an actively maleficent demon that preyed on the weak and vulnerable.*[17]

A god of wealth, it seems, turns into a demon of wealth precisely because the drawbacks of wealth are insufficiently acknowledged. If one looks at the rhetoric of the modern Chinese state with its ready demonization of foreign powers, 'splittists', and dissidents, it also seems likely that it is insufficient acknowledgement of the shadow (as a basis of critical thinking) that is problematic rather than its positive symbolization in Chinese culture. Symbolizing the shadow, and recognizing that symbolization, is one of the basic conditions for avoiding its projection. If you do not symbolize the shadow, perhaps due to an over-emphasis on the projected orderliness of nature, then symbols will nevertheless emerge.

---

17 Von Glahn (2004) p. 17.

5.f. Yahweh, Idolatry, and Literacy

Moses went up [Mount Sinai] with Aaron, Nadab, and Abihu, and seventy of the elders of Israel, and they saw the God of Israel. Under his feet there was, as it were, a pavement of sapphire, clear blue as the very heavens; but the Lord did not stretch out his hand against the leaders of Israel.

Exodus 24:10 (Revised English Bible)

Thus occurs one of the most striking epiphanies of many in the Hebrew Bible. In ancient Israel, it seems that many people together experienced the God archetype collectively. The God archetype is a matter of awe: a mixture of admiration with fear, for Yahweh is dangerous. The extraordinariness of the vast potential they experienced cannot be communicated directly, it seems, but only through this glimpse of the pavement under God's feet. This sense of awe continues to inspire the Israelites in their committed pursuit of a whole way of life that they believe to have been given by Yahweh, maintained by rituals specific to their tribal identity, but enshrined in written law that must be strictly obeyed.

What is distinctive about the version of the God archetype found in the Hebrew Bible is its insistence on the singular dominance of God. This was not initially concerned with denying the *existence* of other gods (monotheism), but only with the practical goal of maintaining *commitment* to only one god (henotheism). That singularity is double-edged. On the one hand it maintains commitment to integrate perspectives in response to the glimpse of integration offered by religious experience. An expectation of unity boosts our motives for overcoming conflicts in motivation within the individual and group. However, on the other it also stimulates a state of over-dominance by the left hemisphere, insisting on the primacy of one conceptual explanation – with all the dependence on representationalism, reinforcing feedback, confirmation bias, and use of power that are often associated with this (see section 1). The emergence of Yahweh expresses both the 'God of the Right Hemisphere' and the 'God of the Left Hemisphere', as subsequently developed throughout the Abrahamic religions, and traced particularly in the work of William Blake by Roderick Tweedy.[1] Blake's picture of Moses receiving the commandments emphasizes their written form (**figure 30**).

1 Tweedy (2013).

Figure 30. *Moses Receiving the Law* by William Blake (1757–1827), Yale Center for British Art, New Haven, CT. Photo by Google Cultural Institute.
Public Domain picture.

The first two of the Ten Commandments reinforce both this singularity, and its implication – the forbidding of idolatry.

You must have no other god besides me.

You must not make a carved image for yourself, nor the likeness of anything in the heavens above, or on the earth below, or in the waters under the earth. You must not bow down to them in worship; for I, the Lord your God, am a jealous God, punishing the children for the sins of the parents to the third and fourth generation of those who reject me. But I keep faith with thousands, those who love me and keep my commandments.[2]

Here we have an astonishingly early recognition of the key functions of the God archetype. Firstly, that the God who genuinely functions as such is schematic, not to be identified with any specific symbols. Secondly, that maintaining constant recollection of that single schematic God has an important diachronic function, benefiting us (or avoiding suffering) over time. Often our attention is distracted here by the portrayal of God as a personal agent, rewarding and punishing: but this was the easiest way for the Israelites, in their context, to envisage the effects of maintaining or losing the God archetype (one which, as we have seen, was used impersonally in India and China). As in our interpretation of the Buddha's Middle Way, it is important to try to distinguish the universal from the contextual features of an influential past insight, rather than assuming that all the contextual features are universal.

In this case, the personality of a 'jealous' God is not the only contextual feature that might interfere with our understanding of the insights of a past engagement with the God archetype. Another important one is the emphasis on *visual* as opposed to *conceptual* representation. Here we need to bear in mind the immense cultural differences between the society of the ancient Israelites, in which the vast majority of people would have been illiterate and writing would have seemed to many like a form of magic, and modern developed societies in which the vast majority of people are at least functionally literate. This difference obviously dictates the form that projection of the God archetype is likely to take.

Pre-literate people who project are likely to assume that an image with a powerful meaning contains that meaning within itself, rather than the meaning residing in the mind-body of the viewer of the image. Literacy helps to provide a standpoint from which this assumption can be questioned, because of the extent to which it allows the abstract comparison of otherwise separated concrete

---

2   Exodus 20:3–5 (Revised English Bible).

cases.³ When Isaiah complains that a man can cut wood, and use half of it to burn fire whilst turning the other half into a god,⁴ the perception that both of these operations are done on the same substance of 'wood', and thus that they are contradictory, depends on the abstractions of literacy. It is this literate standpoint that enables the God of Moses to write the law on tablets of stone and expect it to be consistently obeyed in all the different cases generally defined by that law. However, to try to prevent projection amongst the pre-literate, one forbids them from creating the concrete visual images that they may then worship.

The literate are often just as unaware of the contradictions of their use of propositions formed out of words as the pre-literate are of the contradictions inherent in their materials. The absolutization of the literate takes the form of what Piagetian psychology calls 'thematization' – the positing of 'a referential core around which information concerning the referent is organised'.⁵ We thematize by associating the words in a linguistic proposition with the assumed representational meaning of the whole. This is a process that we first learn orally, and then have to laboriously practise once more in the process of learning to read and write, as we associate letters and then words with larger written structures,⁶ and thus develop to a greater extent through literacy. The written word also tends to be more decontextualized when compared to the spoken word, to adopt a register of authority, and to be delivered with more commitment by the writer, thus offering greater scope for cognitive dissonance when it is implicitly challenged.⁷

Just as Isaiah's wood-worker burns one piece of wood and makes a god out of another, the literate person applies a conceptual idea to form a proposition in one context that serves the archetypal functions, but then makes an (absolute) god of that proposition in another by assuming that it is always 'true'. Let us say that the proposition is 'Honour your father and your mother, so that you may enjoy long life in the land which the Lord your God is giving you.'⁸ Here a particular type of action is associated with diachronic value. Your

3   Huettig and Mishra (2014).
4   Isaiah 44:14–20 (Revised English Bible).
5   Perfetti and Goldman (1975).
6   Ferreiro (1985).
7   Fondacaro and Higgins (1985).
8   Exodus 20:12 (Revised English Bible).

father and mother provide valuable understanding based on experience, and your care for them also provides a basic social compact that is central to social ethics. A society in which fathers and mothers are honoured is likely to be more integrated. Yet your father and mother may also often be deluded, and may especially fail to understand new conditions as they advance into old age. Taking their instructions may create conflict as well as resolving it, and judgement is needed as to how far and when to honour them rather than politely ignore their wishes. God's commandment is subject to human interpretation, and as long as we accept our responsibility for that interpretation, we can avoid projecting the God archetype onto his supposed words. We can recall that the form we are using is only words, just as the idol is only wood.

The prohibition of idolatry in Exodus had a powerful effect on the subsequent development of the Abrahamic religions. Not only did it stimulate the ongoing struggle for the obedience of the Israelites, constantly tempted by the worship of images and constantly upbraided by prophets and reformers, as recorded in the remainder of the Hebrew Bible, but it also affected the religious development of both Christianity and Islam. There are periodic eruptions of iconoclasm in the Christian tradition, most recently in early Protestant puritanism. However, it had an even more powerful effect on Islam, where the oneness of God (*tawhid*) and the prohibition of idolatry (*shirk*) are closely related, and are discussed below in 5.k. It is only if we strip back the prohibition of idolatry to its basic archetypal function, however, that we can readily see that the vast majority of subsequent Abrahamic religion remains idolatrous, however strictly it may have prohibited the worship of visual images. For the literate, the idolatry of words remains a very much bigger problem, resulting in an understanding of religion as 'belief' in verbal formulae which prevents the fulfilment of archetypal functions through constant projection of those functions. As we will see, it is largely only mystical, or sometimes highly intellectualized 'liberal', forms of the Abrahamic religions that manage to escape this near-ubiquitous idolatry of words to any extent.

A third effect of the singularity of God is a tendency to focus on the God archetype to the exclusion of the other archetypes. In the most puritanical or iconoclastic versions of the Abrahamic religions we look in vain for expressions of the hero and the anima/animus, because these archetypes, far from being propaedeutic to the God archetype as they often are, are seen as distracting from God's singularity and encouraging idolatry. Even the shadow as Satan takes some time to develop as an archetypal figure in the Hebrew Bible, developing from the idea of an adversary or accuser who nevertheless serves God. He only becomes an adversary of God rather than a servant of God in the Second Temple period, probably under the influence of Zoroastrianism.

However, the Hebrew Bible does contain heroic, anima, and shadow figures that are often (though not always) the object of projection. Perhaps Moses himself is one of the first heroes who has to alter the conception of his quest as he goes along, first leading his people to freedom from slavery, but then unable to lead them to the Promised Land himself. Though many other heroes then do apparently conquer the Promised Land 'flowing with milk and honey' (for instance Joshua, Gideon, and Samson), in the larger story of the Hebrew Bible it turns out that conflicts with the idolatrous local inhabitants are not ended by that conquest, and that the larger quest is that of the Israelites for their own integration in relation to God. The assumption that the land itself is the final object of the quest is one that even some of the modern successors of the Israelites are very prone to – with resulting conflict.

For the anima/animus in the Hebrew Bible, we need look no further than the role of Eve ('the woman') in the story of the expulsion from Eden. The fascination and temptation of the other comes first in her yielding to the serpent's temptation, then in Adam's (the man's) yielding to her.

> *The woman looked at the tree: the fruit would be good to eat; it was pleasing to the eye and desirable for the knowledge it would give. So she took some and ate it; she also gave some to her husband, and he ate it.*[9]

The eating of the fruit is double-edged, as I have previously discussed elsewhere:[10] on the one hand it is an absolute choice marking the maturity of left-hemisphere dominance with its binary distinctions ('knowledge of good and evil'), but on the other it marks a development of human capacities that is not inevitably a state of conflict, but rather a context for potential integration. To engage with the attractive other in a way that expands our potential in unexpected, perhaps double-edged, ways, is central to the

9   Genesis 3:6 (Revised English Bible).
10 Ellis (2018) 4.c.

anima/animus function. So it is not simply a matter of Adam being seduced by Eve's temptation, but also of Eve too being seduced by something that turns out to be a source of growth as well as of pain. We can reduce that process to only a threat (meaning that we project the shadow into it), or only a seduction (meaning that we project only the anima/animus onto it), but the larger picture is that it is both, as well as marking a stage of ordinary embodied development profoundly affecting our relationships. The Abrahamic religions are divided between an Augustinian Christian tradition that often sees the story as a source of 'Original Sin', and the Jewish, Irenaean Christian, and Muslim traditions that avoid putting such a total construction on it, and are more open to the positive as well as negative aspects of the story.

The insistence on one God does provide a single focus for the God archetype, which the other archetypes then clearly have to be subject to. The hero serves the higher quest set by God, the anima brings us into a higher relationship with God, and the shadow serves God by preparing us for threats. However, none of these subsidiary archetypes provides particularly effective inspiration if the one God himself is projected, and thus becomes a contradictory personality rather than a symbol of integrative experience. The contradictory personality apparently then both creates evil and fights it, sadistically sets tasks that he knows we will fail, and contradicts his previous positions despite his omniscience. This God leaves the hero mired in the endless conflict of Canaan, punishes Eve for her innocent curiosity,[11] and sadistically lets Satan inflict torturous suffering on Job only in order to test his faith.[12] This other Yahweh that was also created in the Hebrew Bible, the God of the Left Hemisphere, is one of the most destructive concepts to be let loose on the world: an absolute basis of appeal to justify the most divisive, destructive, and short-termist human behaviour. At the same time as we can celebrate the archetypal God who appeared on Mount Sinai, we also need to bear in mind with constant critical awareness the evils of the God of power, projection, dissonance, and dogma who was born at the same time.

11 Genesis 3:16 (Revised English Bible).
12 Job 1:6–12 and 2:1–6 (Revised English Bible).

5.g. Graeco-Roman Tradition

The divine, being good, is not, as most people say, responsible for everything that happens to mankind, but only for a small part; for the good things in human life are far fewer than the evil, and whereas the good must be ascribed to heaven only, we must look elsewhere for the cause of evils.

Plato, *Republic* 2.378 (trans. Lee)

Before I move on from the Hebrew Bible to Christianity, it would be helpful to take a brief look at the archetypal background of the other main influence on Christianity and the development of Western culture in general – the Graeco-Roman world. That the Western arts and thought have continued to draw so much on 'classical' archetypal symbols in combination with Christianity tells us something about both the strengths and the limitations of how those symbols have functioned. On the whole their strength seems to be that of making the basic archetypes of hero, anima/animus, and shadow very readily accessible, but their weakness seems to be a lack of engagement with the God archetype. In this they display the features of ethnic religion, as discussed in 5.a above. They tend to avoid highly systematized absolute conceptions (these developed in Graeco-Roman philosophy, which they regarded as distinct from religion), but at the same time be subject to relativistic rationalizations that may limit the process of integration.

The power of Graeco-Roman mythology in its depiction of hero, anima/animus, and shadow is well known, so I shall be very brief in mentioning it. Whether we are discussing Hercules, Perseus, or Odysseus, complex heroic narratives abound. Heroes often do need to change the conception of their quests, with Troy won by guile rather than force[1] and Odysseus challenged at the homecoming where he might assume a return to comfort.[2] Sometimes, as in the case of Oedipus, the quest ends in tragedy and the revealing of delusions.[3] Sometimes heroes become gods. Tragedy, comedy, and complexity all help to refine the heroic archetype, but there is nevertheless still a question about whether Graeco-Roman heroes ever really embrace a universal perspective of the kind reached by the Buddha or Christ. Instead they continue to fight for the interests

1   Virgil (1991) book 2.
2   Homer (2003) *Odyssey* books 16–24.
3   *Oedipus the King* from Sophocles (1962).

of their group. The expressions of the hero archetype here lack universality because they are insufficiently linked to the God archetype.

Graeco-Roman mythology also has a whole array of goddesses representing different aspects of the feminine other from a male perspective: Aphrodite/Venus for sexuality, Ceres/Demeter for fertility, Hera/Juno for power and jealousy, Diana for virginity, Athena/Minerva for wisdom. *The Judgement of Paris*,[4] in which a man gets to choose between these aspects of the feminine, emphasizes human agency in engaging with different aspects of the other, and our responsibility for the way these choices shape us (**figure 31**). By idealizing the sexual, man creates competitiveness where he might have chosen helpful power or wisdom. However, again there is little evidence of this engagement with the other being integrated within the mythological narrative. Compared with Indian mythology, where sexuality is always in tension with the integrative demands of yoga, Greek mythology seems in some respects undeveloped. Arguably, the religious rites of tragedy as performed in ancient Greece compensated for this to some extent, by providing a wider sense of 'Dionysian' embodied meaningfulness in tension with the conceptualized 'Apollonian' (as argued by Nietzsche).[5]

Nor is the shadow neglected in Graeco-Roman mythology, even if there is no precise equivalent to Satan. The forces of evil are largely those of chaos, in opposition to the order imposed by civilized culture. These rarely have much personality, but they do have names, for instance Erebos (darkness), Typhaeus (storm), Kampe (destruction), Oizys (misery and woe), Akhos (pain and suffering), and Ate (blind folly). These forces intrude not so much personally, but by taking over the personalities of the gods from time to time. Ares/Mars is, predictably, a violent and unpleasant individual, Zeus/Jupiter is a serial rapist who killed his father Saturn, and the heroic epics are full of vengeful negative interventions by one god or goddess or another. The Greeks faced up to the shadow, but again there is little indication in the mythology of them putting it in the wider context that could be created by more engagement with the God archetype. Although Zeus has supreme power, he is a completely unapologetic patriarch where his own transgressions are concerned.

---

4 Homer (1987) *Iliad* 24: 25–30.
5 Nietzsche (2008).

Figure 31. *The Judgement of Paris* by Anton Mengs (1728–1779), The Hermitage, St Petersburg. Photo from Steffi Roettgen (2003) *Anton Raphael Mengs 1728–1779, vol. 2: Leben und Wirken* (Hirmer, Munich). Public Domain picture.

These limitations in Graeco-Roman mythology are also reflected in the religious practices that drew on that mythology. Such practices typically consisted in sacrificial ritual intended to propitiate or gain the favour of a god or goddess responsible for a particular area of life.[6] Although one of the strengths of the Roman Empire was its capacity for religious synthesis, adding new deities to the pantheon and recruiting local gods to the cause of wider order in the empire as a whole, this synthesis still lacked the universal perspective of contemporary China and India. It was not expected that conflicts between gods, or between cultures, would be reconciled, only that the strongest would win and subject the weaker. A tolerant but appropriative attitude to new gods was merely a method of increasing Roman strength.[7]

It is this limitation in Graeco-Roman engagement with the archetypes that may help to explain the rise of Greek philosophy in response. Philosophy asked critical questions that were challenging of the cultural group assumptions within which expressions of the archetypes continued to reside. In the very process of sceptical

6 Scheid (2012).
7 Turcan (2001).

questioning, the philosophers simultaneously created the possibility of a universal outlook. Some of these philosophers were careful to stay only at the critical level, and applied a Middle Way perspective by being critical of negative and relativistic assumptions as well as of positively absolute ones – notably the Pyrrhonian Sceptics, who probably also had contact with Indian thought.[8] Many others, however, created absolute concepts to represent the God archetype, whether they did so by *a priori* reasoning (Plato), by a projection on the concept of nature (the Stoics), or by materialist reductionism (the Epicureans).

In any of these cases, the integrative function of the concepts used needs to be distinguished from the metaphysical claims being made. It is quite possible to read Plato, for instance, in archetypal terms with 'the Good' that he rationally defends (see 6.b below) as primarily a source of inspiration for development in virtue. At the same time, however, his belief that 'the Good' can be justified as necessarily existent is a projection. The conflicts created by that projection can be readily seen in Plato's presentation of the trial and death of Socrates.[9] Instead of using his capacity for criticism as a continuing means for virtuous development, Socrates embraces martyrdom. The conflicts between Socrates and the Athenians are not resolved through practical dialectic, even though dialectic is in theory a central part of Plato's philosophy. Instead, Socrates embraces death through his dogmatic belief in the independence of the soul from the body.

Greek philosophy thus gives us access to a number of the 'secular' concepts with archetypal power that I will discuss in section 6. At its best it also supplements the limitations of Greek mythology and religion by providing a means of relating to the God archetype that can potentially be separated from projection. At its worst, it created a whole new means of projection of the God archetype: the Platonic absolute or 'Form' (*eidos*) known through reason. Although any absolutization can become deeply entrenched as we continue to interpret all new information in its terms, an absolute that is believed in due to 'reason' alone is perhaps especially intractable, and an intellectual elite continuing to believe in Platonic absolutes (whether theological, philosophical, or mathematical) has been

8   See Ellis (2019) pp. 244–6.
9   *Apology* and *Phaedo* from Plato (1993).

a major force for the continuation of absolutization in Western thought.[10]

However, Greek philosophy was only ever largely an elite occupation, because it required critical thinking as a starting point for engaging with the God archetype. It seems that the limitations of the ways that Graeco-Roman tradition helped a wider section of the population to engage with the God archetype may have been a major factor in the appeal of Christianity in the later Roman world. Unlike the Graeco-Roman tradition, Christianity offered a symbol of the God archetype that did not have to be accessed through critical thinking, but rather could be engaged with directly in relation to religious experience. It was nevertheless able to appropriate many features of Stoicism and Platonism to provide it with theological resources. Even more significantly, it offered a powerful symbol of the very dialectic, or process of the Middle Way, that Platonism had only offered in refined intellectual form: Christ.

---

10   See Ellis (2001b).

5.h. Christ

You can certainly leave Christianity but it does not leave you. Your liberation from it is delusion. Christ is the way. You can certainly run away, but then you are no longer on the way.

Carl Jung, The Red Book

The rapid spread of early Christianity through the Mediterranean world is one of the most astonishing historical events – perhaps only paralleled by the early spread of the two other great universal religions, Buddhism and Islam. In each case a complex mixture of historical conditions helped to facilitate it. However, my hypothesis is that the ways universal religions fulfilled previously neglected archetypal functions in their context must have made some contribution. In the case of Buddhism, as we have seen, the Middle Way provided a new synthesis between the God archetype and the other archetypal functions, that enabled practical progress towards universal goals. Though this new function was then appropriated in India by Brahminism, this was not before Buddhism had spread to many other parts of Asia. In the case of Islam, as we will see later, new access to the God archetype alone seems to have released a huge amount of energy. In the rapid rise of Christianity, however, I think we have both of these elements. Firstly, the single-minded focus on the God archetype developed in Jewish tradition suddenly became available to the whole Graeco-Roman world, where the God archetype had previously been confined to more abstract philosophical models. Secondly, Christianity offered a distinctive Middle Way function, allowing mediation between the divine and the human. The powerful new symbol was not just God, but Christ.

At one level, it could be argued that the Roman Empire was ripe for a more popular source of the God archetype, given that Graeco-Roman mythology lacks this, and its philosophy was insufficiently accessible for many. The ethnic nature of Judaism would always be a barrier to it spreading far in its older forms, but the new universal form that St Paul gave to Christianity, separating it from observance of the Jewish law, made it possible for it to spread among Gentiles across the Roman Empire.

Key to this spread are features of the God archetype, which demands a *consistent* application of ethics: a movement from particular goals, relationships, and avoidances towards universal ones. Early Christianity was unusual in its context in demanding care of the weak and including women and slaves in its fellowship, thus introducing new expectations of equality, care, and social justice that applied the same standards to everyone. It supported this with a spirituality that also demanded consistency – of prayer and ritual observance to one God alone. These ethical and spiritual features were brought together in the symbolism of the eucharist, which simultaneously united the community breaking bread together and inspired them with the symbolism of Christ.

At another level, Christ added a further dimension to early Christianity that evoked the Middle Way archetype through a selection of powerful symbols. The divine status of Christ connected him to the expectations of consistency and unity in outlook of the God archetype, but at the same time his human status gave him the status of a hero. In some ways the story of Christ is that of the refinement of a heroic quest for God's kingdom – but refinement to such an extent that the terms of the quest were completely transformed. Jesus's contemporaries were likely to understand his quest for the kingdom either in terms of political change or in terms of the fulfilment of rules. The crucifixion seemed to make all such fulfilment impossible: it was the failure of the hero. However, the resurrection then symbolically reawakened that quest in a new form, in the tradition of hero narratives that even go beyond death. That new form links the heroic attempt to transform ordinary conditions to the idealization of a total and consistent vision for human life – evoking the Middle Way archetype. This made it possible at least in some respects for Jesus's followers to be inspired to transform their practical conditions through determined action supported by the community.

The central symbols of the Christian tradition constantly draw on this archetypal function. The eucharist symbolically unites the humanity of Christ – his flesh and blood – with the reminder of his crucifixion and thus of the need to transform the quest and move from the hero to the God archetype.[1] Baptism (in its early total immersion form) also immerses the solid body in the liquid, schematically associating openness to the God archetype with bodily change.

Christ as an archetypal symbol needs to be distinguished from Jesus, the legendary individual. Christ is a specific symbol that fulfils

---

1 See Ellis (2018) 8.c.

the archetypal functions of hero, God, and Middle Way, whilst Jesus is an individual whose speeches and actions are recorded in the gospels. The archetypal function of Christ is entirely independent of all questions about either the historicity or the supposed metaphysical status of Jesus. However, the accounts of Jesus's speeches and actions in the gospels may help to contribute towards the archetypal inspiration. There are lots of potential examples of this, but I will briefly mention Jesus's ethics and his miracles.

Jesus's ethics as expressed in the Sermon on the Mount emphasize motive over outward observance in a way that helps to turn attention towards the integration of the individual in maintaining consistent motivations rather than merely presenting an appearance of morality to gain group approval. Many of Jesus's apparent moral injunctions are best not taken as instructions on how to act so much as pleas to adopt the universal perspective of the God archetype, rather than restricting one's moral practice to fulfilling relational norms or reaching group goals.

> *'You have heard what they were told, "Love your neighbour and hate your enemy." But what I tell you is this: Love your enemies and pray for your persecutors; only so can you be children of your heavenly Father, who causes the sun to shine on good and bad alike, and sends the rain on the innocent and the wicked. If you love only those who love you, what rewards can you expect? Even the tax-collectors do as much as that.... There must be no limit to your goodness, as your heavenly Father's goodness knows no bounds.'*[2]

Here, the idea of being a child of your heavenly Father seems to be a symbolic evocation of the God function, which demands of us that we look beyond our most immediate narrow assumptions, taking as wide a perspective as the sun and the rain. Of course, it is unrealistic to suggest, as a moral instruction, that there should be no limit to the goodness of a human being. Since humans are not divine, of course there is always a limit to their goodness. *Archetypally*, however, Jesus is suggesting that we use reminders of the heavenly Father's infinity to connect ourselves to a more open experience. It is that more open experience (i.e. of the God archetype) that can lead us to provisionality in judgement that potentially helps us to make better use of our human situation.

Jesus's miracles are another area in which archetypal accounts are often confused with historical ones, either to insist that the

---

2 Matthew 5:43–8 (Revised English Bible).

miracles offer 'proof' of Jesus's supernatural status as a support to 'belief', or to debunk such an insistence, either by reducing miracles to 'natural' events or by showing the accounts of 'supernatural' events to be unreliable. However, this whole way of framing the discussion imposes a false dichotomy on accounts of miracles that are instead important for their *meaning*, and the archetypal inspiration they can offer. For example, the Feeding of the Five Thousand (**figure 32**), like the instruction to love your enemy, challenges our normal assumptions about what will satisfy us, and forces us to juxtapose our normal expectations about food with the wider and more provisional perspective suggested by 'the food of eternal life'. Once again, here, the idea of eternality can function in our experience to draw attention to the diachronic aspects of archetypal inspiration.

> *'Amen, amen I say to you, it is not because you saw signs that you came looking for me, but because you ate bread and your hunger was satisfied. You should work, not for this perishable food, but for the food that lasts, the food of eternal life.'*[3]

The idea of satisfying hunger here is reminiscent of the embodied perspective reached in Buddha's Middle Way, as he accepted food to end his asceticism. The frequent denials that 'signs' are important (especially found in the gospel of John) also suggest that absolute interpretations on either side should be avoided.

Figure 32. *Miracle of the Bread and Fish* by Giovanni Lanfranco (1582–1647), National Gallery of Ireland, Dublin. Photographer unknown.
Public Domain picture.

3   John 6:26–7 (Revised English Bible).

However, it will also be obvious that by far the most common interpretation of this passage in Christian tradition, as of Jesus's moral instructions, as well as the crucifixion, resurrection, and all the other significant events in the gospel narrative, subsumes their archetypal value into a grand projection of what are taken to be the basics of Christian 'belief'. These commonly include that Jesus was (contradictorily) both fully divine and fully human, that the miracles are proofs of Jesus's divine status, that the significance of the crucifixion is to atone for original sin, that humans can be magically 'saved' merely by believing that Jesus has saved them from sin, that eternal life refers to a literal eternality either after death or after God's final judgement, and that Jesus's moral injunctions should somehow be followed as rules (even though they are 'counsels of perfection'). All such beliefs clearly avoid our basic responsibility for archetypal interpretation, and alienate it from our experience. The denial of such beliefs, which implicitly accepts the cognitive model through which believers interpret the stories, is no better, merely substituting a reactive projection for a naïve one.

There is a generally helpful Jungian tradition of interpreting Christ in symbolic terms, which make clear the universality of the psychological function of the Christ archetype, and thus puncture Christian claims of unique revelation. As Jung points out, 'the archetype of the redeemer-god and Original Man is age old',[4] having counterparts in both ancient Persia and India. The archetypal idea of Christ, Jung says, 'is a reflection of the individual's wholeness, i.e. of the Self, which is present in him as an unconscious image'.[5] He then goes on:

> *But since man knows himself only as an ego, and the self, as a totality, is indescribable and indistinguishable from a God-image, self-realization...amounts to God's incarnation. That is already expressed in the fact that Christ is the son of God. And because individuation is a heroic and often tragic task, the most difficult of all, it involves suffering, a passion of the ego: the ordinary, empirical man we once were is burdened with the fate of losing himself in a higher dimension and being robbed of his fancied freedom of will. He suffers, so to speak, from the violence done to him by the self.*[6]

---

4 Jung (1958) §202.
5 Ibid. §230.
6 Ibid. §233.

Edward Edinger, following up this line of interpretation, even sees the image of Christ as 'a vivid picture of the Self-oriented ego, i.e. the individuated ego which is conscious of being directed by the Self'.[7] All of this helps to show the ways in which the image's functional power inspires us by connecting us to a wider and more profound experience, but at the same time fails to indicate sufficiently how those functions actually operate in ordinary human experience. It also fails to differentiate the helpful from the unhelpful forms of interpretation of the Christ image clearly enough.

Few images have had such a huge impact on the world, given the cultural and political success of the European civilization that adopted Christianity, but few images have also been so hugely appropriated. Christ on the one hand is the idealized man of peace, a pacifist and anarchist, and on the other he is the ruler of the world, whose name has justified endless intolerance, power hierarchy, war, torture, physical abuse, sexual abuse, and economic exploitation of other cultures. It is not helpful to argue about whether or not 'religion' caused all these abuses. It is the *projection* of Christ, whereby he is reduced to an infinitely manipulatable concept to be 'believed' in, that abuses this archetypal power. To avoid it, Christians need, not to embrace their belief in the 'real' Christ even more fervently, but rather to clearly separate the power of the archetypal Christ from Christian 'belief'. As I have argued elsewhere,[8] an appreciation of the *meaning* of Christ is quite compatible with *faith* in Christ as an embodied response. *Faith*, as embodied confidence or trust in the value of an archetypal experience, is not necessarily the same as absolute belief, but the projection of Christ is, instead, a piece of verbal idolatry that needs to be clearly separated from that faith.

---

7 Edinger (1992) p. 146.
8 Ellis (2018) section 2.

5.i. Christian Mythology

The one you are looking for is the one who is looking.
St Francis of Assisi

Christian mythology, beyond the central stories of Christ, has three major sources: the Hebrew Bible, the remainder of the New Testament, and the many legendary saints in subsequent Christian history. There are also many medieval developments that go well beyond what is found in Biblical material, such as the story of the harrowing of hell between the crucifixion and resurrection. The interaction of theological illustration with the arts through most of Christian history has produced further imaginative developments of the mythology that may be readily accepted as fictional, but may still have a substantial archetypal impact – for instance Dante's *Divine Comedy* and Milton's *Paradise Lost*. 'Mythology' here does not exclude history: there are also quite well-authenticated historical accounts that have archetypal significance.

Where the core narrative of God and Christ focuses very much on the God archetype and provided new ways of engaging with it in a Graeco-Roman world that lacked them, many other areas of Christian mythology have provided inspiration through the other three archetypal functions – heroes, anima/animus figures, and shadow figures. These figures are often appropriations from earlier pagan mythology: for instance, St Brigid of Kildare is a legendary figure closely associated with a pagan goddess of the same name, and adopting many of the same features.[1] This appropriation has even been formalized as *interpretatio Christiana*.[2] However, when made part of the Christian mythology, these archetypal figures became potential conduits to the God archetype in ways they had not been before. Saintly heroes change their quest in the light of divine inspiration, anima figures may help to connect male devotees with divine love, and devilry may help Christians to identify genuine threats – even if, as often, these functions are also very frequently projected.

Christian heroes may range from Hebrew prophets and early Christian apostles to saintly martyrs, missionaries, churchmen, reformers, and mystics. The mystics are a particular case that I will

1 Berger (1985).
2 Eberlein (2006).

discuss in the next chapter. The others, however, are heroic because they overcome obstacles in their quest to fulfil what they see as God's will – whether that is overcoming idolatry, spreading the gospel, or leading the church into new policies. In the process, their initial beliefs are often challenged due to contact with inspiration from God, forcing a reassessment of their assumptions about their goals in the light of a wider awareness of some kind.

Often that inspiration takes the form of a conversion or commissioning experience in which the hero has to question his entire self-view. The Hebrew prophet Jonah goes through two challenges to his assumptions: firstly that he should not try to help the non-Israelite people of Nineveh, and then that the people of Nineveh should be forgiven for their sins. In the first case he changes his mind due to being cast overboard and swallowed by a fish, and in the second by watching a gourd wither and feeling sorry for it.[3] The most famous example of conversion is the experience of St Paul, in which he falls off his horse, hears the voice of Jesus, and is struck with temporary blindness, before dramatically changing his outlook from a persecutor of Christians to a Christian missionary[4] (**figure 33**). In the early 13th century, too, St Francis of Assisi moved on decisively from a life of war and self-indulgence when praying in the dilapidated church of San Damiano, when he heard the voice of Christ telling him to repair the church.[5] In this case the repair of the church also implied the repair of his soul.

However, the fact that Christian heroes offer models of growth in learning to engage with the God archetype in their own experience does not prevent them from going on to project the God archetype. This projection usually depends not only on the belief that God 'exists', but also that he is offering explicit revelations in the form of messages knowable by humans, and that these revelations then describe precisely how humans should act. These messages may be revealed through scripture or religious experience, or they may depend on the further metaphysical belief that God controls all the events in the universe, and thus that God's will can be interpreted from events. Due to such absolute beliefs, Christian heroes have often had an unconditional commitment to their group and its perceived goals, justifying them in the use of intolerance, violence,

3   Jonah 1–4 (Revised English Bible).
4   Acts 9:1–30 (Revised English Bible).
5   House (2000) pp. 63–5.

repression, and torture regardless of their nominal commitment to peace. Christians have rationalized figures such as Joshua as heroes, regardless of their obedience to God's command of the 'solemn ban' (now known as genocide), under which all the inhabitants of a captured city should be killed without mercy.[6] St Bernard of Clairvaux, despite his helpful mystical analysis of four increasingly refined degrees of love, also preached the Second Crusade.[7]

Figure 33. *The Conversion on the Way to Damascus* by Michelangelo Merisi da Caravaggio (1571–1610), Cerasi Chapel, Rome. Photographer unknown.
Public Domain picture.

---

6   Joshua 6–7 (Revised English Bible). For comparison of various commentarial rationalizations, see https://biblehub.com/commentaries/joshua/6-17.htm
7   Norwich (2012) p. 134.

One of the most difficult areas of projected Christian heroism is martyrdom. At first sight this may appear to be a development of the hero archetype, in which the quest of the hero engages with the totality of the God archetype by moving beyond the limitations of narrow self-interest and fear of death. However, such an interpretation depends on a projected standpoint of survival beyond death in which bodily experience is not appreciated as the basis of meaning, but rather an entirely abstract metaphysical belief in a transcendent cause is substituted. The value of martyrdom can only make sense in the terms of such metaphysical abstraction, for otherwise all values depend on meanings, which in turn depend on our living bodies. If martyrs were weighing one bodily value against another, we might imagine them concluding that their fully felt love for others (for instance) outweighed the value of their own lives, but typically the early Christian martyrs died instead for their *beliefs*. In the case of Christ, the symbolic value of the resurrection allows the value of the crucifixion to be understood in a wider context of balancing feedback (see 2.f), but in the cases of Christian martyrs such as Stephen,[8] Peter, Paul,[9] and many others, we appear to be confronted merely with an absolute justification for giving up one's life. To venerate a martyr *for that reason*, then, seems to involve a projection rather than an integration of the hero archetype.

The Christian relationship to the anima/animus (overwhelmingly the anima) is similarly fraught with difficulty. Christians through the ages have often been inspired to engage with more integrated states by female figures, particularly that of Mary the mother of Jesus. The Church's dogmas of the Dormition, Assumption, and Coronation of Mary (where she falls asleep rather than dies, and is brought up to heaven to be crowned) can be seen as ways of reflecting an archetypal path from the anima to the God archetype. By dwelling closely on the feminine qualities of Mary in prayer, meditation, and devotion, it might be thought, both men and women alike can help to develop feminine qualities in themselves that aid an increase in overall integration, and may help to create a glimpse of a much bigger potential. Renaissance pictures of the Annunciation (as exemplified on the cover of this book), with the angel appearing to Mary from the heights of awe-inspiring otherness, often show a

---

8   Acts 7:54–8:1 (Revised English Bible).
9   Tertullian (undated) ch. 36: https://www.ccel.org/ccel/schaff/anf03.v.iii.xxxvi.html (accessed 2019).

strong connection with this archetypal route, with the angel representing the God archetype and Mary our qualities of innocent, awestruck receptivity.

However, projections seem to have crept in almost immediately in the very way that the figure of Mary was understood. Mary is simultaneously both a virgin and a mother, and thus manages to combine the passive and self-contained aspects of femininity with the fertile and compassionate ones. What the image misses out, of course, is any attribution of active sexuality. The whore remains unintegrated with the virgin and the mother, presumably because of a male failure to accept any counterpart for their own sexuality in any archetypal female figure. As long as sexuality is excluded from the anima, one would expect that the sexuality of men who rely on it, too, would remain unintegrated. Instead, repressed sexuality in men is expressed in the equally repressed sexuality of a female image that avoids all stimulation of male sexuality. A denial of sexuality in general, stemming again from representationalism which fails to recognize the whole body as the basis of meaning, thus cannot be separated from the projection of the anima figure. When sexuality was denied in nuns (as 'brides of Christ') the converse phenomenon also seems to have operated, with women who repressed sexuality in themselves projecting the animus onto a supposedly sexless Jesus. Neuroscientific research has identified brain processes for such repression.[10]

The repression of sexuality in Christianity as a whole can be traced not only in the depiction of Mary as a virgin who miraculously remained 'intact' despite childbirth, but also in the idealization of female saints who died for their virginity, the celibacy of monastics and later of priests in Catholicism, the forbidding of contraception, masturbation, and homosexuality, and the development of misogyny from the projection of male difficulties in maintaining celibacy. All this is documented in detail by Uta Ranke-Heinemann in her brilliant critique of the Catholic repression of sexuality.[11] However, the repression of sexuality needs to be seen as just one indicator of the wider projection of meaning that we experience in the body onto an absolutized 'mind' with over-dominant left-hemisphere functions (see 2.d and e above). Ranke-Heinemann

---

10 Anderson et al. (2004); Hanslmayr et al. (2009).
11 Ranke-Heinemann (1991).

blames the anti-sexual tendencies in Christianity on Stoic and Gnostic influences,[12] but the Stoics in turn were influenced by the Platonic projection of the powers of integration onto *a priori* reason, making the goal of human beings the conquest of 'the passions' (which are understood in apposition to 'reason'). In its adoption of the elite God archetypes found in Graeco-Roman philosophy, early Christianity seems to have also taken on some of the projections found in that philosophy. These projections would not have been possible without the assumption of representationalism.

The shadow function in Christianity is primarily focused on Satan: a development of the 'adversary' figure, influenced by Zoroastrianism, that appears in Judaism after the Babylonian exile. Satan is not usually seen as wholly responsible for human sin, but both as a tempter and as the owner and torturer of damned souls following their judgement by God (either at the end of history or after death). It is important to distinguish these two roles. As a tempter (identified with the serpent in the Garden of Eden), rather than as governor of Hell, Satan merely symbolizes an aspect of human experience. Like the Buddhist Mara, he represents the sources of conflict in the human psyche, in which judgements that would help to maintain integration are diverted by obsessive, reinforcing states with a short-term focus. The seven deadly sins of Christianity – lust, gluttony, avarice, sloth, wrath, envy, and pride[13] – each represent genuine threats in the sense of reinforcing feedback loop states that are likely to impede our ability to respond to conditions. However, the helpful recognition of these states as threats is impeded by the projection of a cosmic scheme of punishment as the source of the threat, which prevents the recognition of that threat as an aspect of one's own mental states.

A further projective feature of the role of Satan is false dichotomy. Rather than sin and temptation being recognized as disruptions that are a matter of degree, Satan's role encourages us to regard anything he is associated with as wholly evil, whilst everything associated with God is wholly good. Although the Catholic church does offer a gradation between mortal sins and venial sins, and even mortal sins can be made less grave by ignorance, a dichotomous understanding of evil nevertheless encourages people to interpret it in

---

12   Ibid. pp. 9 ff.
13   Aquinas (1920) I-II 84.3: http://www.newadvent.org/summa/2084.htm#article4 (accessed 2019).

very inflexible ways. A strong example of this is Catholic teaching on masturbation, which is defined in the catechism as 'an intrinsically and gravely disordered action',[14] leading to a belief[15] that masturbation, an extremely widespread and normal human activity,[16] is a mortal sin.

The Christian concept of Satan, whilst theoretically able to help us fulfil the shadow function, has thus also produced a great deal of maladaptation. Christians have greatly overreacted to minor threats and underreacted to major ones. This is not just from turning the shadow into a personified symbol, but also of projecting that symbol as wholly distinct from the good and as possessing power in itself. Distracted from any consideration of the causes and the complexity of genuine threats, then, Christians have far too often made terrible decisions about them based only on rigid deontological thinking or on mere association with evil – for instance rationalizing slavery or domestic abuse whilst punishing children for masturbation. A more balanced recognition of the extent of these threats has arisen during the last few hundred years in the West from the development of scientific understanding of them, rather than being motivated by fear of the devil.

---

14   Catechism of the Catholic Church #2352, http://www.vatican.va/archive/ENG0015/__P85.HTM (accessed 2019).
15   E.g. https://www.mostholyfamilymonastery.com/catholicchurch/masturbation-mortal-sin (accessed 2019).
16   Das (2007).

5.j. Christian Mysticism

People who've had any genuine spiritual experience always know that they don't know. They are utterly humbled before mystery. They are in awe before the abyss of it all, in wonder at eternity and depth, and a Love, which is incomprehensible to the mind.

Richard Rohr

Before moving on from the Christian tradition, it is important to acknowledge another strand in that tradition that has often worked against the overwhelming projection issues noted in the last two chapters, and thus enabled Christian symbols to function more effectively as archetypes. That strand is the Christian mystical tradition. Though 'mysticism' is often misunderstood in ways that presuppose projection as the sole basis of religion, here I take it to refer to any tradition that puts a strong emphasis on religious experience. Though most mystics do not explicitly challenge dogmatic religion, this is generally because they have more important matters to concern themselves with, like genuine spiritual development. Implicitly, whenever the value of experience is emphasized, dogma immediately becomes far less important by contrast.

I have argued elsewhere that the Christian mystical tradition has a variety of approaches that may help to keep Christian absolutism at bay. These approaches are rarely all to be found in one individual mystic, but together they offer a composite approach to the Christian Middle Way. These approaches are an agnostic view of God, a positive view of the body, a cultivation of integrated states, an integrative understanding of the role of love and wisdom, an identification of God and Christ with the self, a practice of humility, and a nurturing of creativity.[1] I am not going to reproduce the whole of that argument here, but rather just to focus on some examples of the use of archetypes in the Christian mystical tradition. This might consist either of the ways that past mystics have related to archetypes, or of ways that mystics themselves have become archetypal figures.

It is the mystics that have come closest to engaging with God as an archetype as opposed to an assumed represented object, by recognizing the unknowability of God. The strand of Christian practice known as the *via negativa* (which could also be called Christian

---

1   Ellis (2018) 7.b.

agnosticism) goes back to Pseudo-Dionysius in the 5th or 6th century CE. Although Pseudo-Dionysius inconsistently thought we can know God's will but do not know God himself,[2] the crucial point is probably that for him a religious experience is understood as one of openness rather than as one of 'knowledge'. Our responsibility for beliefs about God is also implied by Meister Eckhart's writings in the 14th century. Eckhart writes about the incarnation of Christ in the soul, thus placing the significance of the historical event in the context of individual experience.[3]

The modern heirs to the *via negativa* are people like Thomas Merton and Richard Rohr in Catholicism, and also the radical edge of the Protestant tradition amongst Unitarians and Quakers. For Quakers, for instance, 'that of God in every one' is a source of judgement that precedes any kind of scriptural revelation, requiring a basic tolerance for a wide range of interpretations of God and his will, and a social identity based on an open shared contemplative practice rather than 'belief'. Of course, this does not guarantee that Quakers will not project the God archetype in some respects, such as believing that their experience tells them about a divine 'reality'. However, it does help to set up many of the basic conditions for an integrative relationship with the God archetype by allowing both its diachronic and schematic aspects to emerge in experience. Quakers typically 'wait on God', as do other mystics, allowing time for a variety of perspectives to emerge. Their tolerance of a variety of symbols for the archetype also allows its schematic nature to be recognized.

The mystics also made a contribution to the integration of the other archetypes by relating them more fully to experience rather than to projected forms, and often by questioning restrictive assumptions about them. In relation to the anima, St Bernard of Clairvaux in the 14th century laid much emphasis on Mary as an intermediary to God. Domenico Puligo depicted him seeing the Virgin Mary in a vision (**figure 34**). St Bernard compared Mary to an aqueduct from which the water from the fountain of God flows down to people.[4] He wrote of her as a necessary redeemer, suggesting that both men and women could only be redeemed by integration of feminine

2   Pseudo-Dionysius (1924) Caput V.
3   Eckhart (2009) e.g. Sermon 2.
4   'Sermon for the Nativity of the Blessed Virgin Mary' 6, from Bernard of Clairvaux (1997) pp. 39–40.

qualities: 'For if man fell on account of woman, surely he will rise on account of another woman.'[5] He also laid much more emphasis on Mary's humility than on her virginity,[6] perhaps enabling some avoidance of the projections associated with an obsession with repressed sexuality.

Figure 34. *The Vision of St Bernard* by Domenico Puligo (1492-1527), Walters Art Museum, Baltimore. Photographer unknown. Public Domain picture.

The engagement with the masculine other from the feminine side as a route to the God archetype is perhaps even more strongly marked by certain female mystics in the Christian tradition. St Teresa of Avila speaks of a process of progression from betrothal to marriage and union with Christ, often accompanied by ecstasy.[7] Although Teresa insists that this process is incorporeal, it seems

5 Bernard of Clairvaux (1989) p. 17.
6 Ibid. p. 9.
7 Teresa of Avila (2004) sixth and seventh mansions.

much more likely that she is in denial of the embodied basis of her sublimated sexuality. One does not need to resort to reductive Freudian explanations to recognize that her religious experience is *rooted* in a body that is sexual, but is nevertheless leading her into profound contact with the God archetype:

> So powerful is the effect of this [calling by God] upon the soul that it becomes consumed with desire, yet cannot think what to ask, so clearly conscious is it of the presence of its God. Now, if this is so, you will ask me what it desires or what causes it distress. What greater blessing can it wish for? I cannot say; I know that this distress seems to penetrate to its very bowels; and that, when He that has wounded it draws out the arrow, the bowels seem to come with it, so deeply does it feel this love. I have just been wondering if my God could be described as the fire in a lighted brazier, from which some spark will fly out and touch the soul, in such a way that it will be able to feel the burning heat of the fire; but, as the fire is not hot enough to burn it up, and the experience is very delectable, the soul continues to feel that pain and the mere touch suffices to produce that effect in it.[8]

Christian mystical engagements with the heroic and with the shadow are perhaps less obviously developed than with the anima/animus, but still present. The heroic aspect of Christian mysticism can be seen in the Christocentric emphasis of many mystics, who focus on identification with the suffering of Christ in order to break through to what they see as the higher perspective of God's love. Sometimes this may be very much focused on the story of Christ, or sometimes more focused on an individual process that parallels that of Christ. The latter type of mysticism was particularly boosted by St Francis's emphasis on contemplation of the incarnate Christ, and can also be exemplified by St John of the Cross's 'dark night of the soul'.[9] The shadow is also engaged with in mystical visions of the Devil, notably for instance in Hildegard of Bingen's *Scivias*.[10] Hildegard does depict the Devil as repulsive, but also vividly tries to place that repulsion in a wider context by helping us to understand the subtlety of the Devil's appeal at the same time. Much of this is conveyed through allegorical features of the vision that are subsequently explained: for instance, he is portrayed as being in a marketplace, showing the allure of consumer goods as a source of the reinforcing feedback loops of his evil.

8 Ibid. p. 129.
9 John of the Cross (2003).
10 Hildegard of Bingen (1990) 2.7 (p. 193).

It could well be argued that all of these mystical engagements with the archetypes are still strongly imbued with the projections that are common in the Christian tradition, particularly through the medieval and early modern periods that the mystics are most strongly associated with. Hildegard, for instance, still encourages us to see the Devil as something beyond ourselves. As noted in the previous chapter, too, St Bernard of Clairvaux's devotion to Mary does not prevent him from preaching the Second Crusade. Nevertheless, we find an overall context in the lives of the mystics that continually draws them away from this towards genuine archetypal practice. Those who seek archetypal inspiration from the Christian tradition can still find it in the mystics to this day, as long as they are read with an understanding of their context and critical awareness.

5.k. Islam: The Tawhid

Say: He is Allah, the One and Only;
Allah, the Eternal, Absolute;
He begetteth not, nor is He begotten;
And there is none like unto Him.
               Qur'an 112

The last of the three great universal religions to develop, and of the three today probably the most prone to literalist absolutism, Islam may seem at first sight to be unpromising territory for archetypal functions. However, the estimated 1.6 billion Muslims[1] in the world today are human beings, and do not lack the need for archetypal functions found in all other human beings. Like other complex religious traditions, Islam has developed informal ways of trying to address them, even in those contexts where the formal ideology is resolutely restricted to a thoroughly projected account of them. So, even in the most repressive fundamentalist forms of Islam, such as the currently influential Salafism, we should look out for the possibility of informal expressions of the archetypes that do not fit the official narrative. Islam also has an extremely rich and varied history, and a wide variety of interpretations in which we can look out for more archetypally adequate forms of the tradition.

The most central and defining doctrine of Islam is *tawhid*, the oneness and uniqueness of God. This is a re-statement and clarification of the first of the Ten Commandments of Exodus, re-asserted in the previously polytheistic context of 7th-century Arabia. As in the context of the early Israelites, the oneness of God introduces a new demand for consistency, and such consistency can only be achieved through integration. As Islam has developed over the centuries, that demand for consistency has become the most thorough-going in the world's religions, even if that demand has also often taken a projected form that interferes with the very conditions for integration that would enable it to be met.

Islam tries to develop the consistency of *tawhid* by working rigorously at three different levels: *islam* (obedience), *iman* (belief), and *ihsan* (inspiration). At the most superficial level, Islam only consists in obedience to what are believed to be the commands of *Allah*, but at the next level, the basis of these commands needs to be accepted

---

1   From a 2012 demographic study by the Pew Research Centre: https://www.pewforum.org/2012/12/18/global-religious-landscape-muslim (accessed 2019).

intellectually, and at the most crucial level of *ihsan* one's emotions also need to be transformed. Though it is easy to take the outer two of these three layers as ends in themselves, if we interpret Islam as charitably as possible these can be interpreted as attempts only to set up the conditions for the transformation of one's motives. The chief way of working on *ihsan* in traditional Islam is through the astonishing discipline, potentially for all Muslims, of praying five times a day (**figure 35**). These prayers (*salat*) always follow a prescribed pattern and timing, are preceded by ritual purification through washing, are reinforced by ritualized bodily movements and orientations, and are shared simultaneously with millions of other Muslims. Each prayer begins with the first *shahadah*, 'There is no god but God.'

Figure 35. Islamic prayer, photo by Rumman Amin on Unsplash.

As the term *Islam* itself means something like 'obedience', 'submission', or 'discipline', it is hardly surprising that this is the chief means of engaging with the God archetype. Religious experience is stressed only in the mystical Sufi tradition, and its individualism seems to make it a source of suspicion to mainstream Islam. However, by subjecting oneself to a constant discipline of opening up to God, with constant reminders of the unity of the view of God to be cultivated, it is implicitly believed that one can shape oneself into integration. Anyone who has practised a discipline of any kind will be aware that up to a point this works, as in some ways the direction of our attention only depends on constant reinforcement. In other respects, however, it flies in the face of the psychological evidence of the effects of repression and conflict. We, or our social environment, can force ourselves into certain habitual motives only up to a certain point, and beyond that point we can integrate our recalcitrantly conflicting motives only by sympathetically identifying them with awareness and placing them in a wider context.

Just as the First Commandment in Exodus seems to contain an insight about projection in its forbidding of idolatry, the Muslim stress on avoidance of the sin of *shirk* seems to follow through that insight rigorously.

> Shirk means 'to share, to be a partner, to make someone share in, to make someone a partner, to associate someone with someone else.' In the theological context, shirk means to give God partners and, by implication, worship them along with God or exclusive of God. The Koran employs the word in seventy-five verses.... [for example] 'Worship God, and do not associate any others with Him'. (4.36)[2]

The most central sin in Islam (often translated as 'idolatry' or 'polytheism') is thus to absolutize something that is not God, implicitly taking the finite as infinite, the imperfect as perfect, the contingent as necessary, and the impermanent as eternal. This is, of course, exactly what we do when we project the God archetype, assuming that something or someone in the world we perceive has the features of that archetype. Our attachment to these limited things as final is simultaneously the result of an unintegrated desire. To continue quoting from Murata and Chittick's excellent account of this topic, one of the worst forms of *shirk* is 'caprice':

---

2   Murata and Chittick (2000) p. 49.

> Remember that caprice is a god and that those who follow caprice are mushriks (associators of others with God). To follow one's own opinions and feelings, then, is a form of shirk. According to many authorities, it is a worse form of shirk than idol-worship, because idol-worship is clear and plain and therefore relatively easy to deal with and to cure. But the worship of caprice is hidden and found in people who appear outwardly to be very pious.[3]

One can thus hardly fault the basic Muslim diagnosis of the problem: we need the God archetype to inspire us to integrate our scattered motives over time. The God archetype is also schematic, not symbolic, so it is important not to confuse the God archetype with one symbol and its attendant motives and context. That diagnosis is in harmony with other such diagnoses across world cultures. That underlying insight has resulted in a fierce opposition to idolatry, even, in many forms of Islam, an avoidance of representational arts altogether. However, the limitation of the Muslim response to the human condition lies in an over-reliance on solutions to that problem that are repressive rather than integrative.

A repressive response – whether through holy war, killing of apostates, patriarchy, puritanism, or mere austerity – uses power to enforce one representational account of the truth over others. Of course it is not acknowledged that this repression is in conflict with *shirk*, even though it entirely fits the most common definition of *shirk*. A representational account that assumes God's authority in words associates or partners God with something else, to use the traditional Muslim language. It mistakes the finite for the infinite, the imperfect for the perfect, and so on. In terms of desires, it presents caprice as a fully integrated perspective, no matter that the voice of caprice has a long white beard and quotes the Qur'an. As I argued above in 5.f, the idolatry of words is a far bigger trap in a literate society than the possible idolatry of images. Nevertheless, such an idolatry of words seems to be implied in the second *shahadah* of Islam. After acknowledging that 'There is no god but God', the praying Muslim goes on to repeat, 'Muhammad is his prophet'. This is usually interpreted as meaning that Muhammad offers an absolute and final revelation from God: Muhammad is not just *a* prophet, but 'the seal of the prophets'.

Muhammad has a personal status as hero, which I will discuss in the next chapter. However, his impact on the understanding of

3 Ibid. p. 50.

the God archetype seems to consist mainly in the reduction of an ambiguous religious experience to a representational message. His earliest experience is described in the Qur'an as of 'one mighty in power, endued with wisdom' and appearing 'in stately form':[4] a highly ambiguous description that was probably only subsequently identified with the Angel Jibreel or with messages from God. His second vision is then described as near a lote-tree: 'Behold! The lote-tree was shrouded (in mystery unspeakable!)'[5] It seems likely that Muhammad encountered deeply inspiring visions, reflecting both his gathered energies and a breakthrough of awareness, as he gained a glimpse of his own more integrated potential in the solitude of the cave of Hira. After this experience, he was then encouraged both by his wife and by his Ebionite Christian cousin Waraqa to interpret it in revelatory terms as an absolute message from the one God,[6] and thus to interpret the words that came to him as absolute.

Commentators have pointed out the social function fulfilled by the monotheism in the environment in which early Islam developed. In early 7th-century Mecca, a previous reliance on nomadism amongst fiercely independent tribes was in the process of being altered by the impact of trade, which stimulated the breakdown of the tribal values in greater contact with other cultures.[7] In this context, in parallel to that of the succession of Christianity to Graeco-Roman culture, consistency and sustainability of values becomes increasingly important, and thus access to the God archetype becomes capable of inspiring more inclusive interpretations of justice and more rigorous legality, just as it did for the ancient Israelites. However, Islamic projection of that archetype as a source of verbal revelation beyond themselves simply followed the norms established in Judaism and Christianity.

Despite the intensity of its projection, Islam has provided a new and vigorous access to the God archetype for many millions of people since its inception. Its degree of sole reliance on the God archetype and strenuous rejection of the other archetypes, however, is exceptional. It is to the place of these in Islam that I will turn in the next chapter.

4   Qur'an 53:5-6: Ali (2000) p. 455.
5   Qur'an 53:16: ibid.
6   Ibn Ishaq (1955) p. 107.
7   Watt (1961) p. 46.

5.l. Islam: Jihad and the Satanic Verses

Mahound begs for peace. 'If we quarrel, there's no hope.' He tries to raise the discussion to the theological level. 'It is not suggested that Allah accept the three as his equals. Not even Lat. Only that they be given some sort of intermediary, lesser status.'
'Like devils,' Bilal bursts out.
'No,' Salman the Persian gets the point. 'Like archangels.'
Salman Rushdie, *The Satanic Verses* p. 107

The heroic function is well established in Islam, and was applied in its early spread by the sword. The concept that most encapsulates heroism, and is given religious sanction in Islamic thinking, is that of *jihad*, 'struggle'. Immediately associated by most Westerners with holy war and terrorism, jihad is indeed used in the sense of armed violent struggle in support of Islam (the 'lesser jihad' or 'external jihad'), but also in that of internal struggle against one's own sins or weaknesses (the 'greater jihad' or 'internal jihad').[1] Muhammad as hero can illustrate both of these forms of jihad, as he was a leader in war, fighting for Islam, but at the beginning also had to overcome his own crises of confidence in the value and implications of his religious experiences.[2]

What this dominant heroic concept fails to show on the whole, however, is the integrative development of the hero archetype. For the integrative hero, as we have seen, the nature of the quest changes along with the nature of the desire for its fulfilment and the nature of the hero's understanding of himself. In the case of Jesus, there is even a complete dramatic reversal from the failure of the quest to its reinstated fulfilment in radically different terms. In Islam, the nearest we come to this is martyrdom: but, as I argued in 5.i in the context of Christianity, martyrdom seems to absolutize the value of sacrificing one's life rather than encouraging any re-framing of the loss involved. Jihad requires the Muslim hero to overcome both his own vices and the enemy, but in both cases the method is repressive. There is no suggestion of dialectical engagement with the object of struggle so as to change one's conception of what one is doing. Instead one simply exerts will to overcome resistance. This is what in Buddhist terms would be called 'wilful effort' rather than 'balanced effort': the kind of effort that tries to eliminate

1   Bonner (2008).
2   Watt (1961) p. 15.

resistance, whether external or internal, rather than engaging with both kinds of conditions more effectively by separating the helpful from unhelpful elements in them. Muslim writers on jihad,[3] at pains to point out that it is not merely holy war, seem entirely unaware of the possibility that even the 'greater jihad' may be highly problematic in its effects.

To try to interpret the Islamic tradition with maximal charity, it is difficult to believe, in such a vast and rich tradition, that no Muslims at all have ever found their way into a more integrative perspective in their interpretation of heroic effort. One possible way into it may be found in the Sufi tradition, with its great emphasis on entering into a state of love and maintaining a passionate relationship with God: for instance in the lyrics of the Persian Al-Ansari. Another theological approach that may be fruitful for some Muslims consists in the balancing of the two qualities of *tanzih* (incompatibility of God with humans) and *tashbih* (the opposite compatibility), which are somewhat reminiscent of *yin* and *yang* in Chinese tradition. Whilst a *tanzih* approach is likely to lead to a highly assertive, masculine, and indeed repressive approach to imposing God's will, *tashbih* emphasizes God's mercy and love.[4] The unity of God of course implies that God must encompass both of these, also implying that humans need to integrate them. However, with the exception of the Sufi tradition, most Islamic practice seems to be overwhelmingly weighted towards *tanzih* in spite of this formulation.

However, Islam's tendency to relentlessly project the hero's quest is in some ways counterbalanced by a more integrative approach to the shadow than that adopted in Christianity. Islam does have a Satan figure, known as Iblis. However, Iblis is not a rebel against God, nor a direct adversary of God in the manner of Satan. Rather he is seen as merely distanced from God, and divided from him by a refusal to bow before Adam.[5] Like Satan, Iblis dwells in Hell and is a tempter of humanity, but he is obedient to God. This suggests that the shadow can be ultimately integrated, even though it is in conflict with human will. In one Sufi account, Iblis did not even fail to bow before Adam due to opposition to humans, but only to avoid the sin of *shirk*, because he would bow before nothing other than God.[6]

3 E.g., Fatoohi (2002); Noorani (2002).
4 Murata and Chittick (2000) pp. 170-7.
5 Qur'an 7:11: Ali (2000) p. 115.
6 Awn (1983) p. 104.

In some ways, then, it seems that Islamic attitudes to the shadow have been softened by the strength of their commitment to *tawhid*. A recognition of the ultimate importance of integration means that evil must be seen as ultimately as much a part of the integrated whole as anything else. However, to a lesser extent this is also the Christian position, and that has not prevented a great deal of projection of the shadow. Jihad (whether lesser or greater) always has to be directed against an enemy of some kind. For instance, modern shadow targets of demonization for fundamentalist Muslims (even those preaching in mosques) have included Israel, Christianity, the US, and 'the West' in general. That does not mean that these targets do not deserve criticism, but that shadow projection interferes with the ability to distinguish their helpful from unhelpful features.

It is the Muslim attitude to the anima/animus, however, that shows the strongest signs of repression. This is most clearly documented in the story of the 'Satanic verses'. The section of the Qur'an's early surah 53, immediately after the accounts of Muhammad's two earliest visions mentioned in the previous chapter, contains these lines:

> *Have ye seen Al-Lat and Al-Uzza,*
> *And another, the third goddess, Manat?*
> *What! For you the male sex, and for him, the female?*
> *Behold, such indeed would be a division most unfair!*
> *These are nothing but names which ye have devised – ye and your fathers – for which Allah has sent down no authority (whatever). They follow nothing but conjecture and what their own souls desire! – even though there has already come to them guidance from their Lord!*[7]

Al-Lat, Al-Uzza, and Manat are all goddesses of the pre-Islamic pantheon of Mecca. This verse in its current form is clearly a rejection of the worship of goddesses. However, the earlier form of this verse, recorded by several of Muhammad's biographers, goes differently:

> *Have ye seen Al-Lat and Al-Uzza,*
> *And another, the third goddess, Manat?*
> *These are the exalted gharaniq, whose intercession is to be hoped for.*[8]

'Gharaniq' literally means 'Numidean cranes', but is presumably a term of respect and praise for the goddesses. According to the

7   Qur'an 53:19–23: Ali (2000) p. 455.
8   Ibn Ishaq (1955) p. 165.

biographers, Muhammad first uttered this verse but then abrogated it as Satanic, substituting the ending that we now find in the Qur'an.

If the Satanic verses had remained, they would, of course, have been inconsistent with *tawhid*. However, the whole episode seems very revealing in regard to Islamic attitudes to the anima function. Whilst in Christianity the most common response to the worship of the feminine is to appropriate it, but make it subsidiary to God, in Islam it is very definitely to repress it. According to the verse, the goddesses are explicitly rejected as objects of worship, not because of *tawhid*, but because of their sex. It is also highly revealing of cognitive dissonance that this inconvenient story of Muhammad temporarily accepting a false verse from Satan made it into early biographies of Muhammad, but that its authenticity is now rejected by fundamentalist Muslim commentators. This suggests a conflict both in Muhammad himself, and in later Islam, about the repression of the feminine. Such repression is consistent with the overwhelming, but fragile, power of absolutized patriarchy throughout Islamic history.

There are of course some prominent female figures in Islam, particularly the Prophet's wives and daughters. However, these are generally celebrated only as models of subordinate femininity. The only woman to be mentioned in the Qur'an is Maryam (Mary) the mother of Jesus, the belief in whose virginity Muslims traditionally share with Christians.[9] However, unlike the Mary of Christianity, Maryam is not only sexless but powerless: there is no Assumption into heaven or Coronation of the Virgin. It is very difficult to see how dominant male Muslims can fulfil the anima function, if the entire symbology of their sexual other offers so little spiritual challenge to their existing assumptions and identifications. Instead, their accounts of the feminine reinforce a projection onto real women as sexless and powerless, which of course is then likely to be reinforced by the women themselves if they have had no access to alternative possible views of their role.

It can thus be concluded that, despite potentially challenging the projection of the God archetype in some respects through the insistence on *tawhid*, Islam is exceptionally weak amongst the world's religious traditions in actually supporting the fulfilment of the archetypal functions. One reason for this is that the other archetypes

---

9   Qur'an 19:20–22: Ali (2000) p. 247.

are either denied (the anima) or not developed in an integrative way (the hero and shadow), blocking many of the channels by which Muslims can engage with the God archetype. Another weakness, shared with the other Abrahamic traditions, is that the God archetype is so relentlessly projected. There is a strict framework of social ethics, but without archetypal functions that sufficiently engage and integrate human motivation in relation to a variety of symbols over time, that ethics is likely to remain fragile. For all Islam's rigour and vision, then, and despite the ways that some of its weaknesses have been mitigated in Sufism, the Muslim failure to engage the archetypes adequately remains one of the major religious sources of conflict in the modern world.

5.m. The Kabbalah

We only speak in a parabolic manner to satisfy the needs of comprehension, but a wise person will understand by himself that this does not reflect an actual representation of divine reality.
  Rabbi Isaac Luria (trans. Unterman)

For the final chapter in this section, I will return to the Jewish tradition. Beyond what I have already said about the impact of the Hebrew Bible (5.f), I am not going to attempt to assess the archetypal functions of that tradition as a whole, but merely to focus on one later aspect of it that is of particular interest. Following the postbiblical development of rabbinical Judaism, in a Jewish community in exile in medieval Europe, the mystical strand of Jewish tradition known as the kabbalah arose. Grounded in the ethnic identity of Jewish tradition, but also influenced by Graeco-Roman philosophy and having an outsider perspective on Christianity, the Jewish thinkers who produced the kabbalah were in a unique position to synthesize different elements of archetypal function into what became an extremely complex and subtle system of symbology. They appeared much more willing to experiment and think radically than their Christian peers, perhaps because they were under less pressure of orthodoxy, and because they also protected themselves from misunderstanding through esotericism.

Another advantage that Jewish mystics seem to have had over their Christian peers was a greater acceptance of the body. Rather than solely accepting any Platonic assumptions about the soul as wholly separate from the body, kabbalist tradition is also influenced by Aristotle, and speaks of the body-soul as having a life-principle (*neshamah*), personhood (*nefesh*), and spirit *(ruach)*:[1] but these show their value through the body rather than by separating from it. Kabbalistic tradition thus regards sex as potentially a holy or sanctifying activity rather something to be avoided as a matter of purity.[2]

Alongside this, there is a recognition that God is unknown and cannot be represented, shared with the *via negativa* of Christianity and reflected in the quotation from Luria at the head of this chapter. Kabbalists referred to God in himself as *Ein Sof*, the Infinite Godhead. If we put together this genuine avoidance of idolatry

---

[1] Genesis 2:7, Leviticus 17:11 (Revised English Bible); Scholem (1974) pp. 154-5.
[2] Unterman (2008) 171-2, quoting Isaac Luria and Jacob Tzemach.

with relative acceptance of the body, we have helpful conditions for an understanding to emerge of how God can inspire us *through* the embodied conditions and meanings of human life: in other words, for an implicit understanding of the archetypal function. This understanding was not entirely free of projection, as it was often accompanied by various forms of speculative belief (for example, about reincarnation and destiny), but it did provide a rich symbology with the potential to be highly integrative.

The kabbalistic understanding of God's inspiration through human life makes use of the concept of *Adam Kadmon* or primordial man, who is an emanation of *Ein Sof* preceding the creation of Adam in the Torah.[3] Adam Kadmon is described as a spiritual or essential level of human existence, which is then succeeded in the divine emanation by creation at the level of psyche or form, and then finally of physical matter.[4] This 'Jacob's ladder' between God and embodied human existence could be interpreted in a metaphysical or Platonic way, in which immateriality is confused with integration, but it can also be interpreted in terms of interdependent potentialities that are experienced through the God archetype. We experience the God archetype in our bodies, interdependent with potentialities that may emerge from them.

The function of the archetypes, to help us bridge the gap between divine perfection and actualized human experience, is then engaged by the symbology of the *sefirot* – ten interrelated qualities of human experience that are said to have counterparts at every level of God's emanation, from the organic through to the ideal.[5] These ten *sefirot* form a symbolic diagram of interconnected relationships (**figure 36**), also connecting into three triads. The diagram shows them as ranged vertically on a spectrum between God and humanity, as well as distinguished into a symbolic left-right-centre pattern that reveals further aspects of their relationships. This diagram is often called the 'Tree of Life', as it shows the growth of human experience from the embodied state of *malkhut* to the crown of *keter*. The ten points can also be superimposed on a human body representing Adam Kadmon.

---

3   Ibid. p. 9, quoting Luria.
4   Halevi (2009) pp. 35–9.
5   Ibid.

Archetypes in Religious Traditions

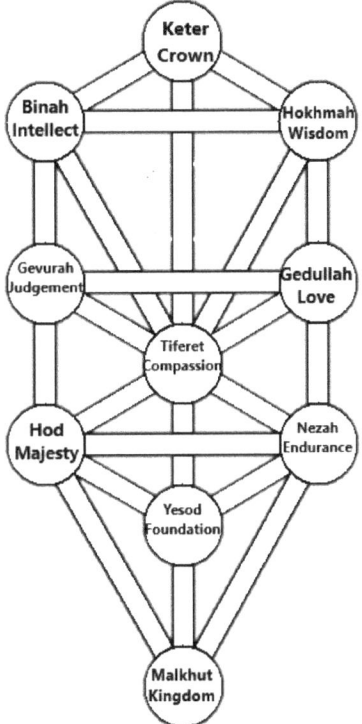

Figure 36. The *sefirot* (diagram by the author, adapted from traditional kabbalist diagrams).

There appears to be wide variety in the interpretation of the ten *sefirot* and their interrelationships, but I am going to offer an interpretation in harmony with my account of the archetypes in the remainder of this book. The aim of this is not to reveal the 'correct' interpretation so much as to show that such an interpretation is possible and can be chosen, consistently with our practical use of the archetypes. In the process I will be disagreeing with the traditional interpretation of 'masculine' and 'feminine' (or 'active' and 'passive' pillars).[6] Instead I want to suggest that the insights of the kabbalists are in some ways an expression of archetypal function, but that these functions have also sometimes been obscured by the tendency to interpret the *sefirot* metaphysically. Metaphysical accounts of the *sefirot* will tend to impose a superficial schema of explanation on them that is then taken to be all-explanatory, rather than a set of

6   Developed throughout Halevi (2009).

provisional symbolic relationships that can continue to be revised in the light of our increasing understanding of the human body and brain both from the inside and the outside.

A provisional but helpful interpretation of the ten *sefirot* might be to categorize them in terms of the three forming the left pillar (intellect, judgement, and majesty), balanced out by the three forming the right pillar (wisdom, love, and endurance). These qualities can be associated with the left and right brain hemispheres (see 2.e), with the left pillar qualities all requiring distinctions to be made and a particular representation to be maintained, whilst the right pillar qualities require the capacity of the right brain to be sensitive to new stimuli, to recognize others, and to synthesize over time. The middle *sefirot* can thus be associated with various aspects of the Middle Way: *malkhut* being the base conditions we need to recognize, *yesod* body awareness, *tiferet* provisional judgement with awareness, and *keter* the God archetype that can inspire us in the Middle Way.

The sefirot form three triads: (1) *keter* (crown), *binah* (intellect), and *hokhmah* (wisdom), (2) *gevurah* (judgement or power), *gedullah* (love), and *tiferet* (compassion or beauty), and (3) *hod* (majesty), *nezah* (endurance), and *yesod* (foundation). In each of these triads, there is a quality from each of the left and right pillars and a mediating quality. The relationship between the left and right is not entirely symmetrical in each case, but rather a mediating function is found by using the qualities of the right pillar to integrate those of the left. The topmost triad is concerned with analytic thought as opposed to synthetic wisdom, with the integrating 'crown' achieved by putting analytic thought in the wider context offered by wisdom. The second triad allows the integration of necessary judgement with our emotional responses to others and to our environment, forming *tiferet*, which is translated either as 'compassion', or as 'beauty'. The 'beauty' here can be understood as temporarily integrated mental states that develop from using emotional awareness to unite otherwise decontextualized judgements, seeing them in a wider positive context. The third and lowest triad unites the egoistic 'majesty' of *hod* through endurance over time, through the medium of the 'foundation' of body awareness.

Although the *sefirot* may seem to be primarily a symbolization of the God function and of the Middle Way, it is also possible to incorporate the hero and anima/animus functions into it. The left-brain related qualities of the left pillar are very much those of the heroic function, dependent on goals and their representation, whilst the right-brain related qualities of the right pillar involve engagement in relation to the other and are thus functions of the anima/animus archetype. Apart from giving an overall schematization of the Middle Way, then, the *sefirot* can also be interpreted as helping us to put two of the other archetypes in a wider integrative context.

For a kabbalistic understanding of the shadow, however, we have to look 'below' the *sefirot*. Here we can find further confirmation of an implicit understanding amongst the kabbalists of the limitations of the over-dominant left-hemisphere perspective. Perhaps the best-known scholar of the kabbalah, Gershom Scholem, writes

> *During the differentiation of...forces below the sefirot...evil became substantified as a separate manifestation. Hence the doctrine gradually developed which saw the source of evil in the superabundant growth of the power of judgement which was made possible by the substantification and separation of the quality of judgement from its customary union with the quality of lovingkindness. Pure judgement, untempered by any mitigating admixture, produced from within itself the sitra ahra ('the other side'), just as a vessel which is filled to overflowing spills its superfluous liquid on the ground. This sitra ahra, the domain of dark emanations and demonic powers, is henceforth no longer an organic part of the World of Holiness and the sefirot.*[7]

'Pure judgement, untampered by any mitigating admixture' is an insightful account of evil as I discussed it in 2.i: namely an account that recognizes the arising of evil in the absolutized human projection process, rather than itself projecting evil out onto some supernatural power. The fragility and discontinuity of that evil projection is also conveyed by the use of the term 'shell' (*kelippah*) to describe it in kabbalah.[8]

At the same time, the kabbalah recognizes the ways in which recognition of genuine threats is helpful to human beings. As one text puts this

> *The righteous...whose eyes only have a small light at the present time...have the light of their eyes strengthened by the shadow. This is true of weak eyes who are not able to see well when the light is strong and bright, and they need the shadow so that they should be able to see....*[9]

---

7   Scholem (1974) p. 123.
8   Unterman (2008) pp. 284 ff.
9   Unterman (2008) p. 247, quoting *Likkutei Moharan* 1:55:3.

I take this to mean that much of fruitful religious practice involves the recognition and avoidance of threats, including those in the form of absolutizations, even though this negative emphasis may seem relatively uninspiring compared to the positive archetypes.

This can only be a very brief survey of the highlights of a complex tradition that is also open to a wide variety of interpretation. As with the other traditions, some will doubtless be outraged at my setting aside the metaphysical interpretations of it that still dominate. However, amongst the Western and near Eastern religious traditions the kabbalah seems to me unrivalled in the subtlety of its psychology and thus in its integrative potential – in world religious traditions surpassed only by Buddhism. That subtlety is perhaps purchased at the expense of the limited accessibility of the archetypal symbols used, in what remains an esoteric or niche approach even in the context of Judaism.

6. Archetypal Function in 'Secular' Concepts

6.a. Nature

Knowing that Nature never did betray
The heart that loved her; 'tis her privilege,
Through all the years of this our life, to lead
From joy to joy: for she can so inform
The mind that is within us, so impress
With quietness and beauty, and so feed
With lofty thoughts, that neither evil tongues,
Rash judgments, nor the sneers of selfish men,
Nor greetings where no kindness is, nor all
The dreary intercourse of daily life,
Shall e'er prevail against us....

William Wordsworth,
'Lines Composed above Tintern Abbey'

In a society in which we seem overwhelmingly inclined to falsely separate the 'conceptual' from the 'symbolic', as well as the 'religious' from the 'secular', it seems important to include this final section pointing out the archetypal functions of concepts that people may often think of as 'secular'. That there is no clear dividing line can be seen in a number of respects. 'Secular' concepts have been turned into visual symbols as 'allegories' in artistic depictions (especially of 'truth', 'virtue', 'science' etc.) since the Renaissance. More importantly, concepts *play the same role* as visual symbols when they operate as archetypes, connecting to schemas that inspire us over time, and being likewise subject to projection.

The concepts I will be discussing are often assumed to be 'secular' merely because they do not necessarily imply belief in God or other supernatural entities. As we should already have seen from the discussion so far, this is an extremely narrow way of defining religion. It also neglects the fact that many of these concepts have been used in 'religious' contexts: Natural Law, Divine Truth, attempts to prove God's 'existence' through rationality, and ideals of virtue and health being pursued through 'religious' practice. That is why I am putting scare quotes around 'secular': a term whose usage here reflects widespread assumptions, but little justification. Like the concept of 'religion', I use it reluctantly, and only to try to engage to some extent with the existing discourse.

'Nature' is a complex and much abused term. It can refer to the totality of all conditions, or only those conditions that are not under human control: either including humans as part of 'nature' or excluding them. It can implicate the predictability of certain patterns of observed events ('Laws of Nature'), the belief that such predictable patterns can be observed and represented by humans ('naturalism'), or the belief that these patterns are necessarily good and form a model for human ethics ('Natural Law'). At the same time 'Nature' is an object of appeal for science focusing on supposed facts to the exclusion of values, and of what are taken to be underlying right metaphysical values. Also at the same time, it is taken to underlie actual human values and activities, and to threaten (or sometimes to reform) them as something separate from human artificiality. Was there ever a more confused and confusing term, meaning opposite things simultaneously? Was there ever a term so infinitely manipulable, so that it can be used to endorse anything from papal prohibitions of contraception, to precise observations of animals and plants, to intense aesthetic experience stimulated by landscape, and to the advertising of food preparations that happen not to contain certain 'artificial' chemicals?

If, however, we consider the *functions* of the conceptualization and symbolization of Nature, we can trace schemas and inspirations over time that are obviously archetypal in form. Schematically, 'Nature' may appear to be different from the anima/animus, the shadow, or God only because we are using a different symbol for the same function. We may identify otherness with other people, or we may identify it with the landscape of the Earth – when it becomes 'Mother Nature' or 'Gaia', but its function of representing the other for us is identical. We may identify the shadow as a Dark Lord or a hated person, or we may become afraid of 'Nature Red in Tooth and Claw', with its volcanic eruptions, drowning tsunamis, and poisonous spiders, but the function of response to threat is the same. We may respond to the totality of potential identified with a personal form beyond our current identifications, such as God, or as the totality of an endlessly growing, changing Earth of which we feel a part – but the function of responding to awareness of that potential is the same. Ruggero Rovan's sculpture of 'Nature' **(figure**

37) seems to combine the nurturing qualities of the attractive other with some aspects of Nature as shadow.

'Nature' can also continue to inspire us diachronically in any of these forms, often linked closely to our more basic embodied responses. There is evidence that immersion in green environments reduces stress,[1] and that playing in those green environments is highly beneficial to children.[2] When we look out at an open landscape, it may be that we respond with an openness of mind to match, perhaps because of an atavistic sense of the security of a savannah in which we could see any potential danger from a long way off.[3] These embodied responses become associated with 'Nature', even though they are actually responses not to 'Nature' as a whole, but to specific kinds of beneficial environments.

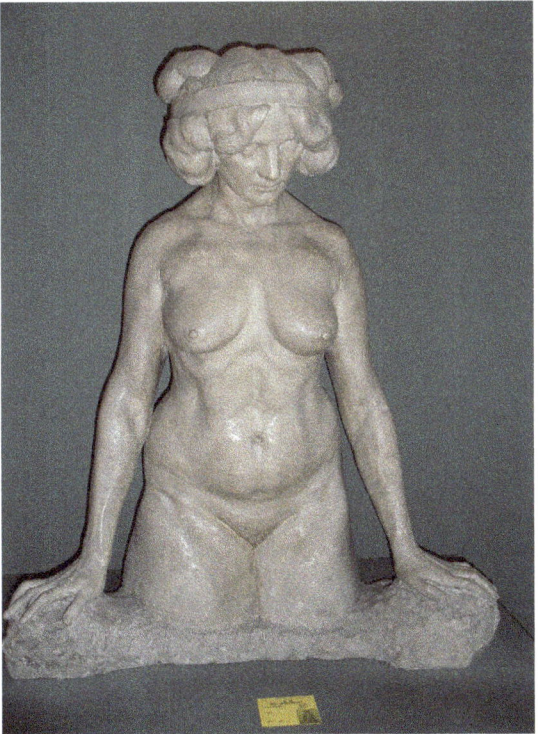

Figure 37. *Nature,* sculpture by Ruggero Rovan (1877–1965), Museo Rivoltella, Trieste. Photo by the author.

1   Berto (2014).
2   Kaarby (2004).
3   Appleton (1975).

Similar points can be made about our recognition of the importance of complex systemic relationships such as ecosystems. We may identify these with 'The Balance of Nature' – but actually systems may compete with each other and destroy each other, and what we identify with in that balance is the need to address certain conditions so as to maintain much valued features of the ecosystems we live in. The need to conserve mangrove swamps, coral reefs, or tigers, and even more general features such as biodiversity, is a need to maintain certain types of potential which are only found in complex systems. The world would be impoverished without these things, both because of their interdependence with many other things and processes (including ones that we rely on), and because without them we would lose archetypal features such as otherness and potential. To call them 'Nature' is thus one way of representing that archetypal relationship, whether to integrate with it or to project it.

Projections occur whenever we use that archetype as a shortcut, usually by reducing it to a limited conceptual form within a set of beliefs that can rationalize our exploitation. We may believe that it is 'natural' to behave in the particular exploitative ways our culture leads us to behave, for instance to raise animals for slaughter and eat their meat (whilst using disproportionate amounts of land, water, and energy to support them). We may believe that it is 'natural' to behave as a majority do rather than a minority (thus condemning homosexuality). We may believe that our scientific theory, because it is merely consistent with all the evidence so far (even though that is an infinitesimal amount of evidence in terms of the universe as a whole), is 'true' and 'a natural law', thus dismissing all alternative proposed theories that are inconsistent with it, and failing to investigate anomalies. Or we may believe that it is 'natural' to behave in counter-cultural and perhaps self-indulgent ways, such as being sexually promiscuous (if we have 'natural' sexual urges, why not act on them?), regardless of the damage this may do to others' long-term welfare. In all these cases, 'Nature' is no longer something that challenges our current assumptions through awareness of otherness and greater potential, but a conceptual form that is appealed to so that we can *restrict* the range of options we consider.

On the other hand, it is possible to integrate the Nature archetype very effectively by using the concept, the symbology, or even the aesthetics of Nature to synthesize disparate phenomena, much as the concept of a single God forces an ethical and legal synthesis. The concept of Nature can also help us to maintain inspiration over time by obliging us to consider possible 'natural' options that go beyond our previous 'artificial' limitations. The concept of nature as used in science may be used positively to provide a presumption of consistency in our understanding of phenomena that encourages us to continue to investigate their complexity. The symbology of nature as used in religions (particularly, but not only, paganism) can fulfil all the functions of the God archetype, with the additional assistance of all our embodied responses to the wider environment to help prompt our inspiration over time. For example, the pagan celebrations of seasonal changes in the 'Wheel of the Year' provide neo-pagans with a constant connection to the seasonal cycles as a perspective beyond more limited concerns.[4] The aesthetics of Nature, perhaps more than anything else, transforms a huge number of people's mental states on a daily basis, allowing the reduction of stress and thus the development of more mindful states in which we can pay attention to more potential options. The arts can also respond to and spread that aesthetic (for example, through landscape painting) in ways that not only reproduce it, but also give it symbolic power as a source of further inspiration.

---

4   Harvey (1994).

6.b. Goodness

> *For one who no longer thinks in terms of 'it is' and 'it is not', there can be no ontological basis for ethics.... Those who have entered the stream of the path...will recognise how each moral dilemma arises out of a unique blend of complex conditions.... They are willing to make what they consider to be an appropriate response, fully aware that they might get it wrong and make things worse.*
> Stephen Batchelor, *After Buddhism* pp. 86–7

'The Good' is an absolute concept that has shaped Western thinking since Plato, endlessly raising different versions of the dilemma between absolutism and relativism. Absolutists insist that goodness can only be defined in the terms set by the absolute concept, so that if we match that conceptual ideal, we are good, and if (almost inevitably) we are not, it becomes difficult to explain in what way we are not simply evil. For relativists, however, goodness can only be discussed in relation to limited contexts, and thus there are no grounds for general goodness. This conceptual double-bind continually conflicts with our experience that moral judgement can indeed be applied universally, and indeed that it *should* be. However, moral judgement in experience is a matter of degree, simultaneously both universal and contextual, fitting neither the mould of absolutism nor that of relativism.

There is a relatively simple solution to this set of philosophical contradictions if we start to understand goodness in terms of archetypal functions. According to this, moral ideas of all kinds are archetypal, i.e. diachronic schematic functions. We have moral ideas *not* to fulfil the will of a supernatural God, *nor* just to maintain social requirements, but rather to remind us of the possibility of more integration over time. At times when we might make a very narrow decision, not taking into account alternative perspectives – typically ones that are more long-term or broader in concern, ethical inspiration (or 'the voice of conscience') may remind us of those alternatives by symbolic means. As argued above in 2.i, it is easier to justify our beliefs about evil than about good on the basis of experience. However, that does not imply that we should have no conception of good at all: rather, that conception of good needs to be recognized as fulfilling an inspirational rather than justificatory function.

I am not suggesting that goodness is itself a distinct archetypal function: rather, that all the archetypes have an ethical function, and that the three positive archetypes give us different types of ethical ideal that can supply us with both inspiration and challenge. The three types of normative ethical theory – deontological, consequentialist, and virtue[1] – can be respectively related to the focus of each of the positive archetypal functions.

The God archetype tends to yield deontological (principle-based) commands based on the application of an idealized set of potentials. The moral commands of Jesus, such as 'love one another' are obvious examples of this, because they make no attempt to take our current limitations into account, but only set out an ideal in the form of an imperative. As mentioned in 5.h, these are 'counsels of perfection'. The great systematizer of deontological ethics, Kant, similarly used universalizability as the basis for distinguishing a right 'categorical' imperative: 'Act only according to that maxim by which you can at the same time will that it should become a universal law.'[2]

The anima/animus archetype tends to yield virtue ethics based on relationships with the other (primarily other humans). The conceptual descriptions of good states as virtues are diachronic ways of relating: patience, courage, wisdom, kindness. Each of these qualities can be contrasted with opposites that assume a particular desire at a particular time is the whole story: impatience, cowardice, ignorance, cruelty. The more we grow into these virtues, the more we integrate the other, adopting those features of others that are sustainable and address conditions.

The hero archetype tends to yield consequentialist ethical imperatives derived from a goal, with judgements about the good all subordinated to that goal. For example, the utilitarian goal of the greater good for the greater number subordinates other concerns (such as those given in deontological principles) and defines goodness in terms of what is calculated to achieve that goal. The more we take into account, both in the way we understand the goal and the way we seek to achieve it, the more integrated that hero archetype can be.

The very concept of integration as good can also be represented in the Middle Way archetype. This is sometimes represented in the moral sphere by symbolic presentations of goodness as balance. For

---

1   For more detailed discussion of the three ethical theories and their relationship, see Ellis (2012) section 7.
2   Kant (1995) §421.

example, Aristotle's golden mean,[3] whilst not exactly a presentation of the Middle Way in philosophical terms, can nevertheless offer inspiration for it symbolically by connecting us to the schemas of balance and progression that need to be activated to practise the Middle Way. Even the Buddha's Middle Way, apparently the most direct symbolization of the Middle Way archetype, needs careful philosophical interpretation, but regardless of that presents itself as a helpful archetype in the sense that it can remind us to judge using the Middle Way.

There is thus no single correct theory of normative ethics, but there are different forms of inspiration over time that can prompt us to behave in ways that are more in accordance with a vision of our potential, more closely related to an integrative course of development, more directed towards increasingly helpful goals, or at least avoidant of absolutes and seeking balance between their extremes. It is archetypal symbols that can help us to do this: in some cases these can be God or other religious figures. In others they may be fictional figures: think of the impact of Harry Potter as hero on the psyches of a whole generation of children. In others they may be actual people known to us who set a direct moral example, beginning with our parents, and the Freudian idea of the superego as internalized parental voice. Our inspirations may alternatively be more conceptual in form, in a few cases actually being a worked-out theory of ethics in which we are inspired by concepts of goodness that then motivate us. These differing inspirations may drive us in the direction of contradictory beliefs, for example the disagreement between deontological and consequentialist views of abortion. However, the more significant point for archetypal ethics is that we are thinking ethically and considering new possibilities for right action – not that we will manage to identify an *absolutely* right action. Rather than deducing our moral expectations from absolute formulae, we need to develop them from an adequately embodied account of the normative role of ethics in human life.

Rather than the fruitless quest for absolute ethics (often based on the mistaken belief that ethics must be intrinsically absolute), the much more practically relevant moral question is that of whether we are projecting the archetypes or integrating them. Rigid moral formulations need to be recognized as harmful because they are

---

3   Aristotle (1976) book 2.

projected. Rather than experiencing a sense of responsibility, and finding a helpful new channel for it through the moral function of the archetypes, projected moral beliefs lead us to pass that responsibility elsewhere.[4] If we have an absolute moral instruction from God, for instance, we have passed the responsibility for our moral judgement to him. If we are relativists who believe that morality is entirely contextual, and thus cannot be legitimately challenged from beyond a specific context, we pass responsibility to the determinism of context, failing to recognize our responsibility for choosing and defining that context over other possible ones we may have come into contact with. If we are rigid political ideologues, for example rabid nationalists, we have exempted ourselves from responsibility for other nations, and thus by implication for the long-term welfare of our own nation insofar as that is bound up with the welfare of other nations. It is projection, not the 'wrong' moral theory, that produces bad ethics in practice.

The integration of the archetypes, as already discussed in section 3, also implies the integration of the moral theories. If I start off with a strong sense of the hero archetype, for instance, but integrate it increasingly to modify my goal or method of achieving it so as to address conditions better, I simultaneously allow the perspectives of virtue and deontology to broaden my consequential calculations. If, on the other hand, I start with absolute rules derived from an ideal of the celestial kingdom, but gradually realize all the ways in which that kingdom can only be built by taking into account the real one on earth, then I am allowing virtue and consequentialism to begin to inform my deontology. Moral perspectives are in no way separate from archetypal ones, the actual application of moral ideals being entirely dependent on the operation of archetypes. In that way, the most justifiable moral judgement in a particular context becomes the one that draws most effectively on our potential sources of inspiration.

Goodness is a 'secular' type of archetypal concept only in the sense that it can be understood in a way that is entirely independent of religious traditions. Those religious believers who still assume that belief in God is the only genuine source of goodness are projecting the archetype onto religious sources. Goodness, however, is a

---

4   For more detailed discussion of responsibility, see Ellis (2012) 7.b; (2015a) 3.f and 4.c.

function with a schematic meaning that can appear in a wide range of symbols – 'religious' or 'secular'. Even if it was Plato who first gave it a 'secular' form that was worked out through 'reason' rather than being derived from a religious revelation, there are plenty of other 'secular' sources of inspiration for goodness over time: particularly, as we have seen, people, whether these people are historical or fictional.

6.c. Truth

Supposing truth to be a woman – what? Is the suspicion not well founded that all philosophers, when they have been dogmatists, have had little understanding of women? That the gruesome earnestness, the clumsy importunity with which they have hitherto been in the habit of approaching truth have been inept and improper means of winning a wench?
Friedrich Nietzsche, *Beyond Good and Evil* (trans. Tanner)

For many people, 'truth' stands for everything worth fighting for. The word demands attention to the world, to others, and indeed to our own inner states beyond our limited assumptions. It demands an *attitude* of objectivity, encompassing awareness of the limitations of our view. Unfortunately it is also closely associated with a near all-pervasive projection: i.e. the belief that our own beliefs, or even verbal statements to others, are 'true'. The converse of this is obviously that opposing statements or beliefs are 'false'. Sceptical arguments have been reminding us for millennia that such claims are unjustifiable, but such is the strength of the projection, that we tend to assume that such arguments undermine the archetype of the truth rather than only its projection. This has created widespread misinterpretation and misunderstanding of the implications of sceptical arguments, which only tell us about the equal uncertainty affecting all claims to the 'truth' or 'falsehood' of claims,[1] not anything about the value of the archetypal functions that can be symbolized by 'truth'. Separating truth the archetype from 'truth' in propositions can help unravel a great deal of confusion.

That truth is not a proposition, but a symbol, can be perhaps most directly recognized by considering visual depictions of truth in art. Truth as an 'allegorical' visual figure is usually female, sometimes naked (reflecting a lack of pretension), and always severe. Sometimes truth shows us a mirror in which we can see ourselves (**figure 38**). It is this reflective aspect of truth that is perhaps most important in its archetypal role: for we can only avoid projection by constantly bearing in mind our own contribution to, and responsibility for, the development of our beliefs. That responsibility is present by implication when we think of truth as a form of archetypal inspiration experienced through our bodies, but cannot be present in a supposedly 'true' proposition.

1   See Ellis (2015c).

274   *Archetypes in Religion and Beyond*

Figure 38. *Truth Presenting a Mirror to the Vanities of the World,*
unknown artist, ca. 1620–30. Ashmolean Museum, Oxford.
Reproduced by kind permission of the Ashmolean Museum.

Truth as an archetypal symbol can reflect any of the positive archetypal functions. Think first of a scientist, or detective, or a journalistic investigator who may be driven to expose 'the truth'. 'Truth' here is primarily a goal: the goal of sorting successfully between conflicting beliefs or claims, and in the process finding those that are much better justified, so as to discard those that are less so. When Sherlock Holmes finds who 'really' committed the crime, the 'really' is a contrast to a previously less justified claim about it, with the new claim having a clearer relationship to evidence, a consistent account of events, and a convincing account of motives. What drives the investigator to continue developing these things? An inspiration over time which offers continuing reminders of the goal and its value – 'the truth'! One can pursue the truth in a more or less integrated way, taking more or less into account, but it remains a heroic goal.

Archetypal Function in 'Secular' Concepts 275

Then think of the kind of truth we encounter in relationship. If a person is 'true', they are reliable and trustworthy, consistent in their words and deeds, and thus relatively integrated. We also find our own degree of 'truth' reflected by others, their degree of strangeness corresponding to the degree of objectivity of their standpoint. They can reflect awareness of ourselves back at us, as well as helping us to increase our general awareness of conditions. The other can thus act as a potent symbol of 'truth', constantly reminding us of a standpoint beyond our current assumptions. The more we integrate that standpoint, rather than projecting it by assuming, for instance, that another person has the total 'truth', the more we can integrate the anima/animus archetype.

Finally, there is truth as the transcendence function: reflected, for instance, in scientific truth, moral truth, and religious truth. It is here that we are probably most prone to thinking of 'truth' as a set of propositions. However, such 'truth' can only ever be a potentiality, and it is the value of that potentiality that moves us towards consistent justification of our beliefs. The potentiality engaged with in science is that of arriving at generalizations about a particular area of phenomena that remain consistent with all the evidence so far, and that continue to predict further fruitful lines of investigation. Whenever we arrive at such generalizations, there is always scope for improving them by investigating their consistency with further evidence, so the 'truth' continues to recede before us as we advance. Nevertheless, the ideal created by the total potentials beyond our current beliefs continues to offer an inspiring archetypal 'truth', which schematically links to the God function. Scientists may even have intuitions of the truth that inspire them to pursue their investigations over time, of a kind that have the same *function* as religious experiences, namely to provide a *gestalt* inspiration for a process that must be pursued piecemeal.

This version of 'truth' is of course easily interchangeable with a number of other kinds of archetypal symbol. A scientific 'truth' is identical to 'nature' or 'reality', either of which can be interpreted in very similar archetypal ways. Moral concepts of 'truth' are also equivalent to 'goodness' or 'the good', and religious ones to God, enlightenment, or revelation.

The most common response to the possibility of truth as an archetype is not a denial that the concept may have an inspirational function, but rather an insistence that the concept of truth as a representation of a state of affairs must be prior to its archetypal function. It is thus alleged that sceptical arguments of a kind that point out the limitations of truth-claims are themselves truth-claims, and thus that there is some version of the 'paradox of scepticism'. Such a paradox, however, is only created by the assumption that all justified beliefs must be implicit truth-claims, and that propositional 'truth' is the bedrock of all our other concepts, rather than our supposed 'truths' being an abstract metaphysical construction dependent on layers of formation in beliefs, cognitive models, metaphors, schemas, and associative processes in the brain and body. If we are to take embodied meaning seriously, we must stop putting the cart of propositions before the horse of bodily meaning and value. An archetypal interpretation of truth allows us to give full credit to the power of the concept in human affairs, whilst recognizing it as primarily a schematic value functioning similarly with many alternative symbols of the same schematic value. It is only by being inspired by that value first that we can even begin to start projecting it, let alone claiming the conceptual priority of that projection.

'Truth' as a projection is obviously one of the most damaging concepts in the world today. Everyone claims that what they believe is the 'truth', and that others' 'truth' is actually falsity, resulting in endless and intractable conflict. If that has been the case for a long time in moral debate and religious dissension, its use by populists to apply a wrecking ball to the social consensus on which democratic politics depends is one of the most worrying recent developments, extending that intractability to the social and political arena.[2]

The relativist use of 'truth' ('one's own truth') typically inspires absolutist responses, but this merely counters one projection with another, regardless of the substantially different degrees of justification each side may have for their beliefs. If we more widely understood 'truth' as an archetype, this could remove the power of the relativist populists just as much as that of the absolutist dogmatists, helping us to recognize that we all may be inspired by truth, but that inspiration in no way entitles us to claim to possess it.

There can be no such thing as either 'individual truth' or even 'provisional truth' without introducing a fatal ambiguity that

---

2   See, for instance, the 'alternative facts' controversy over the numbers attending President Trump's inauguration: https://www.washingtonpost.com/news/the-fix/wp/2017/01/22/kellyanne-conway-says-donald-trumps-team-has-alternate-facts-which-pretty-much-says-it-all/ (accessed 2020).

allows us to carry on importing an absolute sense into an incremental one. Ambiguity is an unavoidable feature of our embodied language, but the kind of ambiguity that allows us to maintain an absolute sense but superficially use it as though it was incremental is fatal. Practically speaking, provisional beliefs can be integrated, but 'truths' cannot, because they are not incrementally adjustable in response to new conditions. If it is a truth it is not provisional (in the sense that it is not *practically* provisional), and if it is provisional it is likewise not a truth.

Practical religion, as the integration of the archetypes, does need to take truth very seriously – so seriously that it would never claim to possess it. In this respect (practical) religion and science do not offer contrary 'truths' at all, but rather they value the same archetypal function of truth, and similarly recognize that their current beliefs must fall short of that truth. In both cases, a superficial acknowledgement that 'we're only human' is not enough: we need to follow through the implications of our embodied humanity rigorously, and in the process we can avoid creating unnecessary conflicts between scientific and religious perspectives. Just as both religion and science are inspired by truth, so do both, properly practised, acknowledge their inability to grasp it.

6.d. Beauty

There are some whose creative desire is of the soul, and who long to beget spiritually, not physically, the progeny which it is the nature of the soul to create and bring to birth. If you ask what that progeny is, it is wisdom and virtue in general.

Plato, Symposium 208e

The cult of beauty can take a variety of forms. The argument expressed by Socrates in Plato's *Symposium* is that beauty is a stimulus: not only to sexual propagation, but, in a sublimated form, to creativity. For the artist, the experience of beauty may offer an aesthetic type of integration (see 3.b), which is also a constant source of associative inspiration. For those who are themselves beautiful, or who in some sense have a regular relationship with someone or something beautiful, the experience of beauty either in oneself or in others (or in the world) may in itself be a direct source of continuing inspiration. However, the *idea* of beauty is more likely to betray us even whilst the experience inspires us. The experience of beauty will need to be interpreted in a way that allows us to integrate rather than merely project it.

There is long philosophical debate about whether beauty lies in an object itself or 'in the eye of the beholder' – a debate of a kind that, like many in philosophy, depends on an unnecessary dichotomy. Some more recent work has adopted a more helpful interactionist perspective, and particularly also taken neural factors into account. This has culminated in the processing fluency thesis: that what we find beautiful tends to be what we find it easiest to process.[1] What we find easiest to process is, in turn, affected by a complex mixture of genetic and cultural conditions. This theory can at least account for all the features we tend to experience as beautiful (e.g. strong contrasts, bright colours, bright light, symmetry, fitness for a perceived purpose, and – in a person – signs of health and fertility)[2] and does not have to be interpreted reductively. Rather, this is an indication that our response to beauty, like other kinds of meaning, emerges from embodiment, and provides a crucial condition for archetypal inspiration. Processing fluency may provide an access into experiences of more intense meaning, in which our

---

1 Reber, Schwarz, and Winkielman (2004).
2 Ibid.

ability to engage with a particular experience easily and strongly enables us to then engage with it more deeply, creating or developing new synaptic connections in relation to it as we do so.

Clearly beauty is *an experience* for the beholder, but that experience may be more easily stimulated by some types of object than others. We do not need to prove that any particular set of features 'creates' beauty, because their contribution is contingent. The sense of attraction and delight experienced by the viewer of visual beauty depends very much, not just on such features, but on the viewer's attentiveness and openness to new ways of seeing, making them able to explore a particular view with the eye. Similar points apply to aural, olfactory, tactile, or gustatory beauty.

Our capacity to continue to be delighted in this way is a source of inspiration, so that we could regard beautiful objects as schematic stimuli for archetypal functions. They could be schematic either in an aesthetic way (directly producing openness or attentiveness that is a source of inspiration) or in a symbolic way (beautiful objects reminding us of beauty, which is then schematically productive of archetypal functions). Those archetypal functions seem most likely to be those of the anima/animus or the God archetype, although it is also possible that beauty could provide continuing inspiration for a quest for its possession (the hero archetype).

Unless it is a somewhat narcissistic sense of being beautiful oneself, beauty always seems linked to some sense of the attractive other. Obviously, we may find this in the beauty of the opposite sex, but also in our own sex, and also in other kinds of animals, objects, works of art, or landscapes. The moral value of this experience of beauty, then, may be to continue to inspire us in our relationship to the other: whether this is a personal relationship with another human, or a sense of engagement with a whole environment.

However, beauty may also connect us to the God archetype by firing up our experience of potential. This may occur through what is sometimes called 'a sense of the sacred' – namely a sense of deeper meaning and significance in a particular object, place, or relationship. In a sense of the sacred, we glimpse a much bigger context, seeing a particular thing in the context of a much wider system. Religious experiences, as discussed in 4.f, may temporarily change our state of awareness in a way that opens up our capacity for beauty in a spectacular fashion. In these circumstances it is difficult to distinguish a capacity to appreciate beauty from a sense of

God – indeed, they are indistinguishable. If our experience of beauty settles on any particular object at all in these circumstances, it will probably not require a conventionally beautiful object to create an experience of beauty. I have heard different people describe, for instance, a flapping piece of corrugated iron roof, or the surface of a pan full of boiling beans, as sources of intense beauty when they were in a sufficiently mindful state.

The importance of the cultivation of the beautiful in religion, then, should become clear. For instance, some of the most intense experiences of beauty for me personally come from Renaissance paintings that depict scenes from Christian stories that are rich with archetypal significance, such as the Annunciation, the Transfiguration, or the Resurrection. Here aesthetic delight in the beauty of the forms combines with inspiration arising from my accretion of positive associations with the symbols, providing one of the most immediate sources of connection to the God archetype. The modern tendency to dichotomize religion as separate from 'secular' inspiration, however, often means that those who experience this kind of inspiration from religious art feel that they have to attribute it, not to 'God', but to 'beauty'. The difference between them is only one of false dichotomy once one starts to think in terms of archetypal functions: the function of beauty is the same as that of God, namely to provide schematic and diachronic inspiration connecting to our wider sense of potential. Romantic poets such as Wordsworth and Shelley particularly bring out this relationship. Wordsworth could almost have been directly expressing the relationship between the God archetype (particularly in the form of 'Nature') with beauty as he wrote his lines above Tintern Abbey:

> ...I have felt
> A presence that disturbs me with the joy
> Of elevated thoughts; a sense sublime
> Of something far more deeply interfused,
> Whose dwelling is the light of setting suns,
> And the round ocean and the living air,
> And the blue sky, and in the mind of man....[3]

However, once we turn 'beauty' into a concept thus separated from other such concepts, it can be readily projected, just like any other symbolic representation of the archetypes. When we project

---

3   Wordsworth (1994) p. 205.

it, beauty may become an abstract end in itself, may be pursued through obsessive relationships with people or things that are thought to embody it, or may even drive a desire to collect experiences of beauty that are more important in abstraction than in experiences. Perhaps your original motive for wanting to visit Florence and go round the Uffizi Gallery lay in an appreciation of beauty, but by the time you have exhaustedly checked off every famous painting, there is no longer any such experience: only a set of abstract shortcuts that substitute for it. Perhaps we may fall in love with another person because of a real appreciation of their beauty, but they very soon become a trophy, with their beauty an idea abstracted from the complexity of their character. Even religious beauty may readily turn from a highly meaningful experience in a complex context to a simplified substitute idea that has become decontextualized: the material of boring rituals, theological examinations, and over-habituated sights and sounds.

There is a strange flip here between beauty as we experience it, which demands an immediate aesthetic awareness, and beauty as we project it. As soon as we project beauty, it simultaneously ceases to be an experience of beauty. This is probably dependent on a move from right- to left-hemisphere dominance.[4] Whilst the right hemisphere is dominant, we are focusing on aesthetic experiences, and can thus allow them both to be integrated and to help integrate other judgements. Left-hemisphere dominance, however, creates 'flat' signs rather than living symbols. At that point we can 'know' conceptually that such-and-such is beautiful, but at the same time we cease to be integrated by that experience.

As a concept, too, beauty can vary from being merely associated with a right-hemisphere led experience, to becoming an apotheosized concept in a completely left-hemisphere dominant state. In that purely conceptual form, beauty can become an end in itself, as in the doctrine of 'art for art's sake' (a term particularly associated with Victorian critic Walter Pater[5]). It may become associated with aesthetic elitism of a kind that creates conflicts between those who appreciate beauty and those who prefer (or are obliged) to focus on more prosaic goals. The sacrifices made for beauty may then be off-stage: but the ugly factories will probably still be grinding away

4   McGilchrist (2009) pp. 478–9 (note 430).
5   Pater (1873) p. 213.

to provide the resources to support the aesthetes in their states of subtlety. The more it is repressed, the more likely it becomes that ugliness will break through into a life that takes beauty so much as an end in itself. Rather than projected in this way, then, beauty needs to be integrated with moral, political, and scientific values and concerns.

Practical religion, then, needs to support our engagement with beauty through the arts, but also to ensure that we integrate our sense of beauty with other types of value. If we identify the God archetype solely with beauty, we may end up with moral-aesthetic conflict of the kind illustrated by the officer in the Warsaw Ghetto (depicted in the film *Schindler's List*) who pauses for a few moments from massacring Jews to play some beautiful Mozart on a piano he stumbles upon. The archetype of beauty is not an end in itself, but a source of inspiration to moral judgement adequate to the situation we find ourselves in.

6.e. Rationality

Thinking begins only when we have come to know that reason, glorified for centuries, is the most stiff-necked adversary of thought.
Martin Heidegger, 'The word of Nietzsche: "God is dead"'
p. 61 (trans. Lovitt)

Rationality is probably the most overrated, projected concept since God. If we don't believe things on 'faith' (i.e. dogmatic belief), it is assumed, then, the alternative is 'rationality' (or 'reason', or 'logic'). As with the case of God, these terms are overwhelmingly assumed to have a representational rather than a functional role: i.e. that 'validly' used terms like 'implies' refer to a necessary 'true' relationship between concepts. The universe of Platonic rationalism, in which mathematics and logic somehow describe how things 'really are' as a set of necessary relationships, then follows.

Embodied meaning theory, however, shows the way in which these supposed necessary relationships merely form a consistent cognitive model, the meaning of which continues to depend on our bodily experience, however abstract it becomes. Cognitive models depend on metaphorical structures that are used to extend schemas, and schemas are meaningful because of their associative relationship to embodied experience.[1] We find both mathematical and logical language meaningful in dependence on these schemas, although we deploy them for specific purposes that may be framed by social goals that employ 'reason', from pure mathematical research to political attempts to persuade.

Just as we might project the shadow onto a potentially threatening person, then, we project the transcendence function onto 'reason', believing that the set of potentialities it describes are actually necessities. We believe, for instance, that if Fred is a rabbit, and rabbits are animals, then it is necessary that Fred is an animal. Within the cognitive model used to classify 'natural kinds' such as animals this is correct, but all it tells us is that it is useful for us to see these concepts consistently in such a relationship, whether it is used to help work out a solution to Fred's digestive problems by comparison with those of other animals, or to provide a philosophical example. The model depends on its consistency, so we cannot simply change it at will, but rather we use it to help us scaffold the

---

1   Lakoff and Johnson (1999) chs. 17, 18, 19 and 21; Lakoff and Nuñez (2000).

relationships between meaningful terms. None of this gives *necessity* to the model, any more than the projection of God as an 'existent' supernatural entity gives God any 'necessary' truth.[2]

It is, above all, the absoluteness of beliefs about rationality that should alert us to its status as a projected archetype. The rules of deductive logic, we are told, are either right or wrong, either found in a consistent set of logically valid relationships or not, rather than more or less justified. However, this absoluteness, as we have already seen, is a construction of the over-dominant left hemisphere in its attempt to represent the world, not a feature of our embodied relationship with the world, with its uncertainty and incrementality. Instead, *justification* is a matter of incremental support for a view taking uncertainty into account. Justification is not just 'inductive logic', but a matter of the assumptions we apply before we start reasoning. All accounts of 'logical' fallacies can be understood in terms of the unhelpful assumptions adopted, rather than of invalid logical forms.[3] We can be more or less *justified* in our assumptions, in a given embodied situation using particular models, depending on how much we take into account (the optionality of our judgement[4]). 'Reason', 'logic', and 'rationality' only tell us about the consistency of the claims made within a particular model, but nothing necessary about the *justification* of those claims.

There are also philosophical accounts of 'rationality', that try to distinguish it from mere reason (or, confusingly, vice-versa). Sometimes this amounts to a conception of 'rationality' as acting consistently in our own interests, but leaving unexamined the egoistic assumptions of 'our own interests'.[5] Sometimes it involves a systematic attempt to extend the core idea of reason to incorporate selected psychological insights – but it then becomes unclear what those insights have to do with the mere logical processing they are yoked to.[6] Sometimes it is even claimed that rationality is a completely separate quality from reason, with one or the other being based on a sense of proportionality, for instance.[7] But then it is even

2 In the infamously circular ontological argument for the existence of God, e.g. in Descartes (1968).
3 See Ellis (2015b); (2015a) section 3.
4 Ellis (2015a) 2.b.
5 E.g. Blackburn (1998).
6 E.g. Baggini (2016). Also see my response to Baggini, Ellis (2017).
7 E.g. McGilchrist (2009) pp. 330-1.

Archetypal Function in 'Secular' Concepts 285

less clear why we are using the labels 'rationality' or 'reason', unless it is just because Western academia is culturally obsessed with the idea. We are entitled to a stipulation of what it means, but the practical value of the stipulation needs to be clear. In this case, the endless appropriation of other features of psychological awareness and objectivity to 'rationality' tends to have the overwhelming effect of maintaining the deluded projection that mere logical processing is in some sense itself objective.

If we can let go of this projection, however, the concept of rationality can be recognized as having an archetypal function, acting as an inspiration over time dependent on the interpretation of an archetypal schema through certain specific symbols. The concept acting in this way does not have to *mean* any more than logic, even though the value of its archetypal functioning is not about logic, just as the *meaning* of God can remain one of infinity, even though the functioning of the God archetype takes place in a completely finite context. In both cases, an ability to rigorously separate meaning from belief is crucial.

I want to suggest that the archetypal function of the concept of rationality is either the heroic function or the God function. When we identify a potential for consistency in our beliefs, it can lead us to persevere in our pursuit of our goals, fulfilling the heroic function. Alternatively, it can lead us to build up new models from potential ones, creating the world for ourselves by developing a consistent account of it from a rough *gestalt* – a compressed vision without detail. Rationality, in the shape of an aspiration to consistency, inspires people, ironically enough through intuition. For example, it may inspire a scientist developing a new theory, an engineer developing a new solution to a technical problem, or indeed me in writing a book like this. I strive to make the arguments in this book consistent, not because I believe that there is a set of true consistent propositions describing the universe that I need to 'discover', but because I am inspired by the *value* of consistency.

Consistency is, for obvious reasons, self-reinforcing. The more consistently I believe what I believe, and the more it has been tested for consistency with the other things I believe, the more confidence I am likely to have in what I believe. We need that confidence as the internal requirement for justification, even though it is quite possible that a completely consistent view of the world is also totally deluded. However, it is the relationship with the phenomenal world that provides the only external basis for a reduction in the probability of delusion. That relationship with the phenomenal world comes not with reasoning or the left hemisphere but from the quality of our assumptions, depending on the level of awareness with which we have formed those assumptions.

Rationality is thus *inspiring* to us because it is a source of confidence over time. Once I have formed a consistent view, it becomes more likely that I will return to it, even if it is in conflict with some of my other views at other times. It is also *schematic*, because rationality itself does not offer a specific symbolic source of meaning, only a set of functional relationships between symbols. However, the *concept* of rationality, used explicitly, is a specific symbol, though that symbol only inspires us through its links to the function of rationality. Rationality fulfils archetypal functions by encouraging us to keep piecing together our view of the world, whether or not an explicit concept of rationality is part of the source of inspiration. We could be similarly inspired towards reasoning activity by other symbols for the hero or God archetypal functions: for example by the concept of God, by the concept of truth, the concept of nature, or any of the other concepts discussed in this section.

However, what rationality cannot do is what we tend to project it as doing: that is, telling us about the world. In this respect it is like any other projected archetype, such as God, in that it forms a shortcut or a substitution for the process of justification through attentive observation and reflection. Whenever we go through a process of reasoning and think that this justifies us in believing that our conclusions are 'correct', we are applying this projection, otherwise known as confirmation bias. This seems to be simply due to the fact that the more we think about something, the more we think it is true, whether we reason about it or not: a point supported by empirical psychology.[8]

When people claim that such-and-such a position is 'logical', the shortcut consists in merely invoking the concept of rationality in substitution for the more complex process of justification through observation and reflection. They may actually have a process of observation and reflection, but they believe that the justification is 'logical', even though it has nothing to do with logic. Negatively, this is also the case with 'logical' fallacies that actually have nothing

---

8   Hasher, Goldstein, and Toppino (1977).

to do with logic. The presence of a technically invalid connection tells us nothing about the justification of the associated belief. Instead, however, we talk about fallacious thinking being 'illogical' when instead it disobeys certain rules of social engagement that could enable us to reach agreement with others[9] (for instance, *ad hominem* argument that diverts from the issue by focusing on the person). The spurious distinction between formal and informal fallacies tries to rescue this association with logic: but 'formal' fallacies are not necessarily fallacious (they may be formally invalid whilst obeying the rules of engagement), whilst 'informal' ones are not illogical (they may be formally valid but still disobey the rules of engagement).

To integrate our archetypal projections of rationality, we need to recognize that however much we may have consciously considered our beliefs and linked them together in consistent patterns ('reasoned' them), their justification depends not on this, but on the breadth of options considered when we made a judgement about them. To keep extending that breadth, we need to maintain integrative practices: to become more aware of options through mindfulness, imagine more possibilities through the arts, and become more aware of the limited assumptions of our beliefs through critical thinking. The conflicts between different sets of assumptions that we may maintain at different times can only be integrated by reconsidering the limitations that surround those assumptions.

9   Walton (1987).

6.f. Humanity

I am endeavouring to see God through service of humanity; for I know that God is neither in heaven, nor down below, but in everyone.

Mahatma Gandhi

The use of 'humanity' as a symbol for the God archetype is well established, going back to the 19th century, when Ludwig Feuerbach recognized God as a projection of human features,[1] and Auguste Comte proposed a religion of humanity.[2] The assumption of humanism is generally that identifying God as human (or seeing humanity rather than God as the ideal) will rid us of projection – and it can indeed be the case that the awareness raised by questioning the supernatural projection of God helps to integrate the archetype. However, it is far from necessarily the case that by substituting 'humanity' for God we will thus avoid projection, given that it is not a precise metaphysical status that creates the projection, but a projective use of it that can take any of a number of metaphysical forms. It is much more relevant whether or not we attribute absolute features to either 'God' or 'humanity' that show that we think we have the whole story in some respect.

The use of 'humanity' as a positive ideal providing inspiration over time does not have to be an alternative to religion. If we understand 'humanity' as a vision of human potential (either in the developing individual or the harmonious society), it is found in all the non-theistic religious traditions of Asia: Buddhism, Jainism, Confucianism, and Daoism. It is also found in the Hellenistic philosophies of later classical times: Stoicism, Epicureanism, Aristotelianism, Pyrrhonism, and Neoplatonism. Since the 18th-century enlightenment, terms like 'humane' and 'humanitarian' have emerged as carriers of basic values of compassion and mutual respect that can be shared by religious 'believers' and 'non-believers' alike. In Thomist philosophy, these 'natural virtues' of humanity offer a first level potential for all human morality, which can then be supplemented by the superior revelatory ethics of Christianity.[3] Any of these traditions may thus use some form of the concept of 'humanity' as the symbol for an archetypal function.

1. Feuerbach (1989)
2. Comte (2009).
3. Aquinas (1920) I Q.1 and I–II Q.94.

Archetypal Function in 'Secular' Concepts

That archetypal function is most likely to be the God archetype, as the ideal of humanity symbolizes the most general potentiality. However, any of the other three archetypal functions might also be involved. We could be heroically driven to overcome difficulties by an ideal of humanity – for instance as a humanitarian doctor working as a volunteer in a distant war zone. We could be inspired by an ideal of humanity in our relationships that thus help us engage with the other: for instance, a sense of universal humanity may inspire us to persevere in befriending someone of a strange race, culture, or religion. A sense of humanity may also inspire us both in facing up to real threats against all humans (such as climate change) and avoiding unnecessary demonization of others. Jan Štursa's massive sculpture depicting 'Humanity' in Prague seems to emphasize qualities of mutual support and fully embodied solidarity (**figure 39**).

Figure 39. *Allegory of Humanity*, bronze statue by Jan Štursa, Prague. Photo by Jerzy Strzelecki (Wikimedia Commons).
Creative Commons Attribution Share-alike 4.0 International license.

However, modern humanism can also be interpreted as an antireligious movement. Humanists emphasize *this* world as opposed to a putative other world that they take to be offered by religion.[4] Humanist funerals allow a process of grieving without the interference of beliefs about the afterlife. Humanist movements engage in political campaigns against religious schools and for the separation of church and state. In taking these stances, humanists may argue that they are occupying the middle ground in some way, rejecting the absolutism associated with religion. Their religious opponents are also quite likely to assume that a book like this one that in any way questions supernaturalism in religion is 'humanist'.

On both sides, then, there is reactive projection creating conflict, mixed in complex ways with some genuine agnostic insights into the dispensability of absolutes. Humanism offers a reactive projection when its concern to avoid the negative effects of religious 'belief' leads it to accept aspects of the absolutist paradigm (e.g. that it is even relevant to assert one 'world' against another, or that science offers a 'truth' that religion is rejecting). Motte-and-bailey type arguments are often employed when humanists define humanism in agnostic ways but then slip into reactive projections, moving between a broader and a narrower position in an *ad hoc* fashion. Agnostic humanism thus needs to be clearly distinguished from anti-religious humanism, just as practical religion needs to be clearly distinguished from dogmatic religion.

The ideal of humanity can thus be as much a projection as any other use of the God archetype, whether this is a straightforward positive projection or a reactive projection. It is just as much of a mistake to think you can get away from God by relabelling him 'humanity', as it is to think that you can get away from humanity by relabelling it 'God'. The basis of the distinction is in many ways a displacement from the real issue of how these terms are used and how they relate to our experience. One of the key developments required for integrating the ideal of humanity is to recognize its relationship to religious ideals.

Some pointers for the integration of humanism are suggested by Jean-Paul Sartre's famous lecture 'Existentialism and Humanism'.[5] One of Sartre's key points in this lecture is our responsibility for

---

4 E.g. https://humanism.org.uk/humanism/ (accessed 2020).
5 Sartre (1980).

what we regard humanism as being. He recognizes that we could be 'humanist' in ways that are just as dogmatic as the religious beliefs that humanists are reacting against, but that a more helpful use of humanism is one in which we become aware of the choices we make both when we interpret humanism and when we interpret religion. Sartre distinguishes two senses of humanism, 'a theory that upholds man as the end-in-himself and as the supreme value'[6] (which Sartre says is 'absurd'), and a 'relation of transcendence as constitutive of man (not in the sense that God is transcendent, but in the sense of self-surpassing)'.[7] This may be no more than a glimpse of the potential for humanism to be interpreted as an integrative approach to the God archetype, but it seems to be present in Sartre's work.

The recollection of our humanity as a source of inspiration over time has such huge, open potential because it is no greater or less than the recollection of ourselves. We may be inspired to humility because we are *only* human, or to a healthy pride because of everything humans have achieved. We can be inspired to compassion in a spirit of solidarity as we recollect what we have in common with other humans. We may recollect the basis of more mindful, and thus integrated, states through embodiment as we recall our physical constitution as humans. We can look at great art that celebrates human beauty, philosophy that exercises human rationality, and stories that illustrate human virtue, all helping us to recall that as humans, we have all these potentials. The ambiguity that this gives to the concept of humanity can be dangerously misused, but as long as we accept that and allow for it, humanity offers an archetypal concept of an extremely powerful kind.

---

6   Ibid. p. 54.
7   Ibid. p. 55.

6.g. Democracy

> *The aristocratic ideal...has failed because it is found that the practical consequence of giving the few wise and good power is that they cease to remain wise and good. They become ignorant of the needs and requirement of the many; they leave the many outside the pale with no real share in the commonwealth.*
>
> John Dewey, 'The Ethics of Democracy'

You might think that democracy is a system of government, 'rule by the people', which of course is the origin of the word, but it has come to mean much more than that. It is the ideal in the name of which people rebel against totalitarian regimes. It is also the ideal that has been defended around the world, by force if necessary, by Western countries who call themselves democratic. There have even been attempts to impose it on others by force, as in Iraq in 2003. It is the object of appeal in a great number of arguments in Western countries: we need such-and-such new voting system, or interpretation of the duties of a representative, or party organization, or referendum, because it would be 'democratic'. At the time of writing, in 2019, the UK is convulsed by deep political divisions involving just such an appeal to 'democracy'. In a referendum in 2016, 52% of voters (over 48%) opted to leave the EU, though with almost no understanding in most cases of what the consequences of that might be, and amidst disagreement on what exactly it would mean. Whenever all the numerous drawbacks of following through this non-mandatory vote are argued, there is one central response from those who still wish to leave: 'anything else would be a betrayal of democracy'. That answer is supposed to be final. We are supposed to accept that 'democracy' must be the supreme good.[1]

In such cases, we are obviously no longer discussing a mere system of government, but rather an archetype. As with the concept of rationality, part of the appeal that makes it so tempting to adopt and project the archetype is that it superficially appears quite precise. Democracy is acting according to the will of the people: but how should that will be expressed, and what implications should it have? It is impracticable to have direct democracy in which all issues are voted upon by all people, so representatives are elected instead: but how far should the representatives be responsible for

---

1 E.g., see Rowson (2019).

exercising their own judgement? How far is the party system a distortion of democracy, or merely a way of making it practicable by giving voters a choice between coherent packages of policies? Should any decisions be made directly through a referendum, and if so, which? The huge variety of possibilities for what 'democracy' might mean make it clear that it is very far from precise. Rather, the ambiguous principle of consulting the people has become a concept that provides political inspiration over time, regardless of these variations. If we recognize the complexity of the relationship between that archetypal concept and the political systems it is associated with, it can serve us well: but if we project it, it produces conflict, like any other projected archetype.

As an archetype, however, democracy can be distinguished from the other concepts I have considered so far in working overwhelmingly at the social rather than the individual level. The potential that it reminds us of is a collective one, of how we can relate to each other in a larger, harmonious whole, resolving disagreement by distributing power amongst the people. The inspiring vision offered by democracy also tends to involve the rule of law, freedom of expression, other human rights, and a notion of responsible citizenship. In practice, all of these features of modern Western (or 'liberal') democracy are a matter of degree, and must often be traded off against each other (for instance, freedom of expression needs to be restricted when it causes harm). Nevertheless, each of these associated features interacts with democratic voting so as to allow informed collective judgements to be made peacefully, with opposing interests clashing only in debates that are capable of resolution, rather than resulting in intractable conflict. It is not surprising, then, that pragmatic philosopher John Dewey elevated democracy to not merely a system of government, but rather a whole principle for the dialectical resolution of social conflict.[2] We can resolve disputes at the social level by being forced to argue our case and to consider our assumptions when others oppose us.

However, democracy as a social system for resolving disputes in practice depends on some degree of the resolution of individual conflicts through integration. Voters and politicians who have not resolved their own conflicts are likely to perpetuate social conflict through democracy by projecting their absolutes onto parties,

2 Dewey (1993) and many other of his writings.

policies, and leaders, creating a reinforcing feedback loop between individual and social conflict. When individuals choose parties, leaders, or policies that reflect their projected archetypes rather than expressing archetypal aspirations themselves, these absolutized political forces will also tend to act in ways that maintain the support of individuals with those projections. These may project the hero archetype onto fallible leaders, the shadow onto internal or external 'enemies' of the nation-state, the anima/animus onto desirable future relational states (such as prosperity or unity), and the God archetype onto a vision of the idealized potential of a nation, class, or group that forms the basis of political identification. A reinforcing feedback loop is then created as politicians seek to play to these archetypes, so as to both maintain support and maintain their own projected ideas about themselves and their role, whilst individuals similarly become firmer in their support of such politicians as the dominance of the projected archetypes increases.

The projection of 'democracy' itself as a symbol of the God archetype thus tends to interact with other political projections. The more a particular social or political group becomes dominant, conflicting with other groups, the more a democratic system ceases to fulfil its potential for dialectical resolution, and 'democracy' merely becomes abstract grounds for an appeal to beliefs that maintain conflict, as in the arguments over Brexit. Socio-political conflict then becomes a further reason for individual stress, particularly for minorities, or for those who lose out by not being the dominant group. The stress of this position is more likely to produce anxious responses, which again increase the likelihood of projection, and reduce the likelihood of the open consideration of different possible options by voters.

Democracy experienced as a source of archetypal inspiration without projection, however, is entirely compatible with the more effective use of democracy as a political system to resolve social conflict. Security of life, relationships, and general well-being provide the basic conditions by which voters can start to use democracy, not to 'win' in internal or external conflicts, but to choose policies that allow the necessary re-framing that overcomes that conflict.

Those policies can't always be identified with one particular type of political value (such as equality, freedom, care, or authority[3]), but rather with the ability to look beyond a current clash of values

---

3   These are some of the values explained in Haidt (2012).

between groups, to see what other kinds of values can provide the basis of commonality. For instance, in some circumstances, the long-term well-being of all is greatly boosted by reducing the gap between rich and poor and thus the resentment and conflict over resources that this brings. However, in a relatively equal society where the state has been over-dominant, larger conflicts may be due to lack of freedom of the individual in relation to the all-controlling state. For citizens used to thinking in terms of the assumptions of their immediate interest group, however, it may take time and reflection to recognize that the kinds of political values that most immediately seem to serve their interests are not the whole story. In the long term the rich can benefit from greater relative equality, the dominant class benefit from greater freedom for all, and the over-opinionated can learn from the relative authority of expertise and experience. If citizens do not learn to reflect and be provisional, democracy can be merely a desperate conflict of opposed interests, but if they do, it has the potential to actually help those conflicts to reach long-term resolutions.

So, democracy as a concept symbolizing the God archetype can be an expression of the untapped potential of human solidarity, reflection, and consent: something we can vaguely sense in our positive relationship to democracy as an ideal. Commitment to that ideal, inspired over time by the concept of democracy, can help us to work in one way or another towards producing a more integrated society and world through the use of democracy. The projection of democracy, like the projection of any other symbol of the God archetype, though, can be a huge source of conflict, as people identify with a 'democracy' that they believe offers a shortcut answer, but that is reduced to mere concept, with little necessary relationship to liberal democracy as an effective system of government.

6.h. Health

Health is a state of complete physical, mental and social well-being, and not merely the absence of disease or infirmity.
World Health Organization

Health is the final concept I will examine here: one that often operates archetypally, because it is so ambiguous, but so strongly related to as an ideal. The concept may seem to have a relatively clear relationship to our bodily states, referring to a condition in which our bodies are operating normally or optimally, but both normality and optimality are vague concepts very subject to idealization. We may be inspired by an archetypal idea of health to continue in our recovery from illness or injury, or in our commitment to long-term bodily disciplines (such as dieting or exercise) that help our bodies and minds to operate better in the long term. Since we can so easily feel the effects directly in embodied experience, health possibly has a direct integrative power as an ideal that more completely abstract concepts such as rationality or humanity do not have. Nevertheless, the pursuit of idealized health as optimization may become just as hopelessly enmeshed in reinforcing feedback loops as the pursuit of any other integrative symbol – as obsessive dieters, exercisers, and vitamin pill poppers around the world may realize all too well. For those who are healers, on the other hand, health may be much more closely associated with the long-term perspective necessary to complete the process of healing, perhaps using dangerous treatments such as poisonous drugs that will nevertheless probably lead to benefit. The figure of health as the Greek goddess Hygeia seems to represent more the archetype for healers than for patients (**figure 40**).

It is important to approach this topic without presuppositions about the separation of body and mind, although those who idealize health may well have such presuppositions. Health is primarily thought of as a state of the 'body', despite the complete interdependence between the brain and nervous system with the rest of the body, with 'mental health' often assumed to be something separate from 'physical health', more an analogy than a different aspect of the same state. However, there are numerous instances of evidence of the interdependence of mental and physical health,[1] quite sufficient

---

1 E.g. Kershaw et al. (2016).

to warn us off this false dichotomy, if that dichotomy was not constantly reinforced by the illusion of the conceptual separateness of left pre-frontal cortex activity. Whatever our theoretical recognition that mind and body are interconnected, it is very easy to slip back into the unreflective assumption that our independent 'minds' can produce health in our 'bodies', as tools working on 'objective' matter. It is this assumption that we are in some sense not our bodies, even though we also continue to experience being our bodies, that corresponds to the absolutization of the ideal of health, and its projection onto a body that we assume merely needs to be repaired and adjusted like a faulty motor. Instead, however, we need to see conflicts in our minds as also conflicts in our bodies, and the degree of integration of our minds as also a degree of integration of our bodies. In this way, the concept of health can play a helpful role as an archetype inspiring us with a glimpse of a more integrated state.

Figure 40. *Hygeia* (Greek goddess of health) by Peter Paul Rubens, Detroit Institute of Art. Photographer unknown (Wikimedia Commons).
Public Domain picture.

To see states of ill-health as instances of bodily conflict only requires a little re-formatting of our conceptual model.[2] Ill-health can take the form of disease or injury, but in either case our body needs to put a lot of energy into responding to a more basic threat to its operation than the ones we are generally accustomed to dealing with. Thus, instead of dealing with our daily concerns of things like work, relationships, and political life, we are forced by ill-health to divert our bodily resources to dealing with more basic conditions – whether by merely resting or by seeking medical aid. This requirement to divert our resources conflicts with the normal and habitual focus of our energies, and with our assumptions about our basic duties and goals. It is a process of integration, resolving the conflict by addressing the new conditions that created it, that can deal with this situation. As we do so our priorities are likely to shift, reflecting the ways that ill-health can help to 'put things into perspective', forcing us to reconsider the basic conditions of our lives and give attention to things we have taken for granted.

Health can thus once again be seen primarily as a symbol for the God archetype, drawing on the glimpses of a less conflicted and more integrated state that we have experienced, not just abstractly but directly in bodily sensations. If we are relatively unhealthy, we may still be able to recall the bodily sensations of a more healthy state, for instance in childhood, together with the associated sensations of uninterrupted energy, clarity, creativity, and curiosity that can more easily arise in a healthy state. These recollections are, I think, an important constituent of the God archetype even when we do not directly associate it with health, as we are able to relate to the 'transcendent' only on the basis of a prior experience of bodily wholeness that we then abstract into a supreme meaning beyond our current state. As the idea of health gradually takes the place of the direct experience, the invalid can be deeply inspired by the concept of health even in the absence of a direct experience of it, but could hardly find that concept very meaningful without some past bodily experience to relate it to.

The archetypal projection of health is thus likely to be accompanied by complete abstraction from the bodily experience of health, whether in the past or the present. Instead, the idea of health becomes the focus of projection of the other three archetypes: an

---

2   Haig (2006); Ellis (2013a) 1.c.

obsessive heroic function, a longing for health as other, or a determination to conquer disease as the shadow. We could see the heroic function projected, for instance, in the obsessive dieter who is determined to reach a particular target weight, often ignoring some surrounding conditions, such as the tendency of the body to relapse to its previous weight after such diets are finished. An anticipation of oneself in an optimal state without current conflicts can form the basis of the projection, which becomes narrowly focused on weight to the exclusion of other conditions. An anima/animus projection regarding health might take the form of a longing to possess those who are healthier or more whole than oneself, perhaps by falling in love with them, allowing distraction from one's own state of health. An obsession with exemplars of health here may easily combine with an obsession with bodily beauty, as discussed above in 6.d. The desire to conquer ill-health is also likely to involve projections of the shadow that ignore its complexity: for instance latching onto a particular treatment as a hoped-for panacea, but ignoring the other factors that maintain a medical condition.

That health can be so easily projected in these forms so as to narrow our awareness of how it can be cultivated does not mean that we can't be genuinely inspired by any of these types of archetypal symbol in supporting and maintaining health. A person who 'battles against cancer' may have a projected heroism, but may also be inspired by the genuine sense of the meaning and value of health that helps to maintain their commitment to life in the face of immense pain and stress. Those who are inspired by the examples of health and bodily beauty set by athletes, models, or fitness instructors may be able to respond to that example so as to inspire them to work committedly on improving their own health and fitness. Those who search determinedly for new 'weapons' to 'fight' malaria, Alzheimer's, or alcoholism may succeed in making new discoveries that transform people's lives. The full enjoyment of health, though, is most of all an experience of a lack of conflict in the body for which the God archetype is the schematic source.

That the concept of health so often has an archetypal function does not, of course, prevent it from functioning in non-archetypal ways. However, it is overwhelmingly archetypal in many contexts, offering a strong source of positive value closely linked to our bodily experience. Health is nearly always positive, not because it is sufficient for the good, but because we nearly always experience it as good. Further goods such as those marked by more obviously ethical language are built on it, given that a sufficient degree of human health is the implicit condition of almost any other 'good' human judgement or activity. We cannot do these good things without working bodies. This does not always require that health is prioritized over other goods, but only that its central place is recognized. As we engage with that good as individuals or as social groups, the foundational value of health continues to inspire us time after time.

Conclusion

After the range of examples in the final two sections of this book, it remains for me to return to the central themes, and finally consider some of their implications.

The account of archetypes in this book stands or falls on its practical helpfulness. It is intended to relate to our experience of using archetypes in practice, for the purposes of inspiration. Any practical theory must also be provisional, and I'm sure that the account I have given here can be improved upon. However, I have tried to revise the limited practical basis I have found in Jung and Jungian thinking. I do think that Jung was probably actuated by practical considerations as well as other considerations. He was, after all, a practising therapist, as well as an individual practitioner who continually worked with his own experience. However, the lack of clear prioritization of practical bases of judgement in Jung is nevertheless a weak point.

I have tried to address what I see as the limitations in Jung's account without getting too bogged down in mere Jung scholarship, and primarily to provide an alternative, which is a far more important goal. Some of the key points of this alternative theory are that it treats universality as a practical (not descriptive) requirement, that it sets aside issues about the ultimate 'existence' or causes of archetypes to focus on their relationship to experience, and that it clearly separates archetypes as schemas from their specific symbolic (or metaphoric) expressions. Its practically oriented definition of archetypes is thus that they are schematic and also diachronic functions, specifically human because they support us in maintaining awareness of meaningful ideals over time.

The role of projection and integration, recognized but for some reason not fully applied by Jung and Jungians, is also crucial to my practical theoretical account of archetypes. They are helpful to us because they can help us to overcome conflict (internal or external) through integrative practices such as meditation, the arts, or critical thinking. To resolve conflict we need to be able to apply awareness so as to question the framing of opposed desires and beliefs, and to consider alternatives to the assumptions that are causing the conflict. This involves the application of the Middle Way at each point of judgement, and our ability to use it can be supported by integrative practices, which help to develop the conditions in which we can judge differently. To maintain integrative practice, however, we need sources of inspiration over time. This is why religions are most helpfully not about 'beliefs', but about providing continual archetypal inspiration for integrative practice.

However, this very source of archetypal inspiration can interfere with its own function through the process of projection. To project is to believe that a person or object 'really' has features that come from our own assumptions, and thus also to absolutize. I've referred to a wide body of work in cognitive psychology, linguistics, and neuroscience that can reinforce our basic experiential understanding of this projective process. Projection hijacks the helpful function of the archetypes and uses them, not to integrate, but to maintain our existing fixed beliefs, forcing our new perceptions to fit old assumptions and thus preventing adaptation to new conditions. It is this process that, I argue, lies behind justifiable criticism of the role of religion in human life. If we assume that religion is the source of inspiration and integration, it is a saviour, but if we assume that it consists essentially in projection, then it is a villain. Our task, then, is to constantly distinguish between the projective and integrative aspects of religious traditions – and indeed to treat all other human traditions even-handedly in the same way.

I have also offered an analysis of archetypal functions which leads me to suggest that there are four basic archetypes (hero, anima/animus, shadow, and God), rather than the indeterminate but consistently greater number suggested by Jung and Jungians. Each of these four archetypes corresponds to a basic function in human experience that can be schematically recognized and diachronically developed. Each also relates to different kinds of prioritization in moral judgement (consequence, virtue, avoidance of threat, imperative), and each can also be symbolized in a very wide range of ways varying in different cultural and individual contexts.

Any analysis is based on a particular view of specific phenomena and carves them up in one way, when there are likely to be other possible ways. However, I think my analysis of the four archetypal functions is at least adequate for the practical purposes I propose it for, even if it is improved on in future. I would be happy to revise it in future if others can offer better *practical* grounds for a different analysis, rather than merely an outraged appeal to Jung's authority, or an assertion of specific symbolic form rather than schema as the basis of archetypal distinctions.

Finally, then, I tried to engage with some of the complexity of the relationship between this theory and the wide range of symbols used in different religious and non-religious traditions. I have tried to analyse some of the key features of select traditions to show both the ways these four archetypal functions have been used, and how they have been projected or integrated, in those traditions. When it came to 'secular' traditions in the final part of the book, one of the key points was also that archetypal functions may emerge just as much in concepts as they may in mythic symbols, and that even concepts that we may regard as quite abstract and technical, such as rationality, can be used and abused in archetypal ways.

Along the way, in pursuing this basic argument, there have been a number of other sub-arguments. Some of these, such as those about scepticism and the Middle Way, are discussed in much more detail in my other books, but nevertheless need relating to the theory in this book to follow through the implications. If you have trouble with these arguments, I'd urge you to look at their fuller expression in my other books. There are other arguments, however, that have been included to help make sense of the theory here, but that are probably dispensable in the sense that they could be wrong in at least some respects without impacting on the whole argument in the book: for instance, the account of the differences between modernity and traditional society, or the argument about Islam, may be thus dispensable. I would urge readers to try to see the wood as well as the trees where these arguments are concerned.

If one adopts this basic way of understanding archetypes, however, I think that is only the first step in the wider range of work that needs to be done in understanding and acting on the implications. I will finish with some suggestions about the implications from three different perspectives: for individual practitioners, for religious traditions, and for academics.

I hope that this book may be of some use to individual practitioners in understanding how the symbols in their tradition can both help and hinder them in their development, and how they can be understood as relating to other traditions without recourse to naïve universalism. As an individual, it seems to me that when one recognizes that full potential practical value of archetypal symbols, one's responsibility is to find helpful ways of using them that recognize individual conditions rather than only depending on the authority of tradition. 'What works for me?' may not be a traditional religious question to ask, but is nevertheless a vital one in finding even-handed ways of working with religion rather than only uncritical or dismissive ones. What works for you will depend on whether, at a particular moment, your focus is on goals, relationships, threats, or wider potential. If you're working towards a goal, for instance, what is it that actually inspires you? That question needs to be distinct from assumptions about what you feel *ought* to inspire you given the traditions you may be embedded in. If, for instance, you're committed to Buddhist practices, but thousand-armed bodhisattvas leave you stone cold (an example from my own past experience), you might find it useful to seek out new symbols that you really respond to. Public art galleries are good places for this. Indeed, there have been creative proposals to recognize the religious function of art galleries more fully.[1] Seek out new symbols, or work creatively with the old ones, until they come alive. Then feed yourself with those symbols: they are the bread of life.

There are also implications for religious traditions (and also for other social traditions) at the institutional level. The helpful function of religion depends on it purposely adopting integrative interpretations of its symbols and avoiding projective ones. What is the point of religion otherwise, if it constantly sabotages its own best intentions? Of course, the same symbol (the same cross in the same church) may be simultaneously integrative for one person present and projective for another, but religious leaders and institutions need at all costs to stop simply assuming that the mere form or official intention of their symbols makes them integrative by definition. Instead, the conditions for greater integrative use of archetypal symbols can be developed. I'd suggest that this probably demands, initially, reformed training of religious leaders so that their grasp of the meaning of religious symbols is not merely formal and traditional, but also critical and psychological. At all points it needs to be borne in mind that the meaning of the symbols is created by

---

1 De Botton (2012) ch. 8.

the humans who experience them rather than only by the form of the symbols themselves. There may be many other reforms that are required in religious institutions, but perhaps it is the step of actually addressing the conditions for making the symbols live that is vital for enabling other kinds of reform to happen.

For academics, in the broadest sense, there are also wide implications of this approach to archetypes. One of them is that academics should stop wasting their time on elaborations of projective assumptions that in effect merely reinforce those projections, even when they are supposedly critical: for instance, endless debates about the 'existence' of God that merely recycle the same framing assumptions. More positively, however, there are a great many ways in which our understanding of the practical functioning of archetypes can be improved, extended, supported, and applied by further academic work. This work needs to be multidisciplinary, but can be understood in relation to a wide range of established disciplines, mainly but not entirely in the social sciences and humanities.

There is potentially an archetypal biology and neuroscience, studying the bodily and brain processes, not of archetypal symbols themselves (as in Goodwyn's recent approach[2]), but of the schemas that make those functions helpful to us for inspiring and shaping our judgement over time. Moral differentiation is crucial to this process, and often missing from scientific accounts. What is it that makes the difference to our judgement and therefore helps us to differentiate in practice? What does integration look like in neuroscientific terms, and how reliably does it relate to consistency of judgement?

This is obviously linked to an archetypal psychology that is not merely a Jungian psychology, but that investigates Jung's insights critically rather than dismissing him. There are cognitive, social, and developmental aspects to the use of archetypes that can connect with all these areas of psychology, showing how archetypal projection relates to biases, how social interactions both reinforce our projections and help maintain our inspirations, and how developmental staging relates to our ability to project or to integrate. What do the biology and psychology of religion start to look like when we stop assuming that all functions are evolutionary functions, and start to take seriously the ways that religious functions can fulfil a whole range of human needs?

2   Goodwyn (2012).

Beyond this, there is also an archetypal sociology and anthropology. How have different societies fulfilled archetypal functions, not only in their myths, symbols, and rituals, but also in their concepts? Can we trace continuity in the archetypal functions of pre-modern as opposed to modern societies? How different does the sociology and anthropology of religion look when we stop interpreting it through the all-pervasive framework of 'beliefs', and stop assuming that all the functions of religion are merely ones of social cohesion?

Then there is the linguistics and semantics of archetypes. What exactly do archetypes mean, in embodied rather than representational terms? What schemas enable archetypal functions to be meaningful to us, and how can we investigate these more closely? How do linguistic and other types of symbols vary in their inspirational effects?

Then there is archetypal theology. What would the study of God look like if we stopped worrying about his 'existence' and focused much more relevantly on his meaning? Every aspect of religious traditions seems concerned with archetypal functions in one way or another, but interpretations of those traditions, their scriptures and practices, all need to be developed that understand them in archetypal terms, and distinguish between projected and integrative forms. The kind of work I began in section 5 of this book is just an initial pointer, at best, to the huge task of interpreting the world's religious traditions in relation to the God archetype and the other archetypes.

There are similar questions to be asked in archetypal politics. My discussion of democracy in 6.g is, again, only a possible initial pointer to some of the questions that need to be asked in archetypal politics. A range of other important political concepts have archetypal functions: freedom, justice, and nationhood being amongst the most obvious. What determines people's responses to these concepts, or indeed to politicians or to other visual symbols? What does politics look like when we try to differentiate between the genuine inspiration that these political archetypes offer, and the abuse of power that tends to accompany their projection?

Archetypal history will attempt to plot the projection and integration of archetypal functions that has occurred in the past. Archetypal literary studies are not just a matter of analysing particular types of archetypal symbol in narrative, but rather of examining the schematic meaning linked to those symbols, and the ways that it can inspire readers or lead them to project onto characters. The same can be said for the study of any other artistic medium where archetypal figures appear: for instance film, portraiture, drama, or opera.

Finally, of course, there is archetypal philosophy. To understand archetypes and their functioning in a wide enough context, we need to recognize their relationship to all the major issues discussed in philosophy. Archetypal metaphysics investigates the relationship between metaphysical belief and projection. Archetypal epistemology considers the way that the justification of our judgements is impacted by archetypal inspiration, recognizing the role of psychological states in relation to judgement, and the ways that inspiration relates to provisionality. Archetypal ethics considers the ways that different kinds of archetypal inspiration are linked to different kinds of moral judgement, and how projection can interfere with moral judgement. Archetypal aesthetics does the same for aesthetic judgements, also taking into account the ways in which aesthetic (rather than symbolic) experiences of beauty can interact with archetypal practice.

If this book thus asks far more questions than it answers, then I consider this both practically necessary and salutary. For too long, our attitudes to religion, and to other related matters, have been tied up in assumptions that result only in circularity, conflict, and frustration. To breach the wall of dogmatic assumption results in the release of a torrent of new questions. However, these questions are not without potential answers.

Bibliography

Adair, Mark and Shimkunas, Algimantas (1973) 'Sublimation of sexual and aggressive drives' *Proceedings of the Annual Convention of the American Psychological Association* 169–70.
Ali, Abdullah Yusuf, trans. (2000) *The Holy Qur'an*. Wordsworth.
Anderson, Michael and seven others (2004) 'Neural systems underlying the suppression of unwanted memories' *Science* 303:5655, 232–5. https://doi.org/10.1126/science.1089504
Appleton, Jay (1975) *The Experience of Landscape*. Wiley.
Aquinas, St Thomas, trans. Fathers of the English Dominican Province (1920) *Summa Theologica*. http://www.newadvent.org/summa/index.html
Aristotle, trans. Hugh Tredennick and J.A.K. Thomson (1976) *Ethics*. Penguin.
Armstrong, Karen (2010) *The Case for God: What Religion Really Means*. Vintage.
Augustine of Hippo, St, trans. John Healey (1945) *City of God*. Dent.
Ault, James (2004) *Spirit and Flesh: Life in a Fundamentalist Baptist Church*. Vintage.
Awn, Peter J. (1983) *Satan's Tragedy and Redemption: Iblis in Sufi Psychology*. E.J. Brill. https://doi.org/10.1163/9789004378636
Baggini, Julian (2016) *The Edge of Reason: A Rational Skeptic in an Irrational World*. Yale University Press.
Bergen, Ben (2012) *Louder than Words: The New Science of How the Mind Makes Meaning*. Basic Books.
Berger, Pamela C. (1985) *The Goddess Obscured: Transformation of the Grain Protectress from Goddess to Saint*. Beacon Press.
Bernard of Clairvaux, trans. Marie-Bernard Saïd (1989) *Homilies in Praise of the Blessed Virgin Mary*. Cistercian Publications.
Bernard of Clairvaux, ed. M. Basil Pennington (1997) *Bernard of Clairvaux: A Lover Teaching the Way of Love*. New City Press.
Berto, Rita (2014) 'The role of nature in coping with psycho-physiological stress: A literature review on restorativeness' *Behavioral Sciences* 4:4, 394–409. https://doi.org/10.3390/bs4040394
Bertoloni, G., Anzola, G.A., Buchtel, H.A., and Rizzolatti, G. (1978) 'Hemispheric differences in the discrimination of the velocity and duration of a simple visual stimulus' *Neuropsychologia* 16:2, 213–20. https://doi.org/10.1016/0028-3932(78)90108-2
Bharati, Agehananda (1966) *The Tantric Tradition*. Rider.
Blackburn, Simon (1998) *Ruling Passions: A Theory of Practical Reasoning*. Oxford University Press.

Bodhi, Bhikkhu (2000) *The Connected Discourses of the Buddha: A New Translation of the Samyutta Nikaya* (2 vols). Wisdom Publications.

Bonner, Michael (2008) *Jihad in Islamic History: Doctrines and Practice*. Princeton University Press.

Buchtel, H.A., Rizzolatti, G., Anzola G.A., and Bertoloni, G. (1978) 'Right hemispheric superiority in discrimination of brief acoutic duration' *Neuropsychologia* 16:5, 643–7. https://doi.org/10.1016/0028-3932(78)90094-5

Cahill, Suzanne E. (1993) *Transcendence and Divine Passion: The Queen Mother of the West in Medieval China*. Stanford University Press.

Campbell, Joseph (2008, 3rd edn) *The Hero with a Thousand Faces*. New World Library.

Campbell, Keith and Sedikides, Constantine (1999) 'Self-threat magnifies the self-serving bias: A meta-analytic integration' *Review of General Psychology* 3:1, 23–43. https://doi.org/10.1037/1089-2680.3.1.23

Capra, Fritjof and Luisi, Pier Luigi (2014) *The Systems View of Life: A Unifying Vision*. Cambridge University Press. https://doi.org/10.1017/CBO9780511895555

Carozza, Paolo (2003) 'From conquest to constitutions: Retrieving a Latin American Tradition of the idea of human rights' *Human Rights Quarterly* 25, 281–313. https://doi.org/10.1353/hrq.2003.0023

Chechik, Gal, Meilijson, Isaac, and Ruppin, Eytan (1998) 'Synaptic pruning in development: A computational account' *Neural Computation* 10:7, 1759–77. https://doi.org/10.1162/089976698300017124

Comte, Auguste, trans. Richard Congreve (2009) *The Catechism of Positive Religion*. Cambridge University Press.

Confucius, trans. D.C. Lau (1979) *The Analects (Lun yü)*. Penguin.

Cook, Norman (1984) 'Callosal inhibition: The key to the brain code' *Behavioral Science* 29:2, 98–110. https://doi.org/10.1002/bs.3830290203

Csikszentmihályi, Mihaly (1990) *Flow: The Psychology of Optimal Experience*. Harper & Row.

Das, A. (2007) 'Masturbation in the United States' *Journal of Sex and Marital Therapy* 33, 301. https://doi.org/10.1080/00926230701385514

Dashu, Max (2017) 'Xi Wangmu, the shamanic great goddess of China'. http://suppressedhistories.net/goddess/xiwangmu.html (accessed 2019).

De Bono, Edward (1994) *De Bono's Thinking Course*. Facts on File.

De Botton, Alain (2012) *Religion for Atheists*. Penguin.

Depue, Richard and Morone-Strupinsky, Jeannine (2005) 'A neurobiological model of affiliative bonding' *Behavioral and Brain Sciences* 28, 313–95. https://doi.org/10.1017/S0140525X05000063

Descartes, René, trans. F.E. Sutcliffe (1968) *Discourse on Method and the Meditations*. Penguin.

Deutsch, Eliot (1996) *Advaita Vedanta: A Philosophical Reconstruction*. University of Hawaii Press.

Dewey, John (1993) 'The ethics of democracy' from Debra Morris and Ian Shapiro, eds., *The Political Writings*. Hackett.

Dion, Karen, Berscheid, Ellen, and Walster, Elaine (1972) 'What is beautiful is good' *Journal of Personality and Social Psychology* 24:3, 285–90. https://doi.org/10.1037/h0033731

Drake, Roger and Bingham, Brad (1985) 'Induced lateral orientation and persuasability' *Brain and Cognition* 4:2, 156–64.
https://doi.org/10.1016/0278-2626(85)90067-3
Eberlein, Johann Konrad (2006) 'Interpretatio Christiana', from *Brill's New Pauly*, ed. Hubert Cancik and Helmuth Schneider, trans. Christine F. Salazar. https://referenceworks.brillonline.com/entries/brill-s-new-pauly/interpretatio-christiana-ct-e1406540 (accessed 2019)
Eckhart, Meister, trans. Maurice O'C. Walshe (2009) *The Complete Mystical Works of Meister Eckhart*. Crossroad Publishing.
Edinger, Edward (1992) *Ego and Archetype: Individuation and the Religious Function of the Psyche*. Shambhala.
Ellis, Robert M. (1997) 'Revelation, wisdom, and learning from religion: A response to D. G. Attfield' *British Journal of Religious Education* 19:2.
https://doi.org/10.1080/0141620970190206
Ellis, Robert M. (2001a) *A [Buddhist] Theory of Moral Objectivity*. PhD thesis, Lancaster University. Published online by British Library and by Lulu (2011).
Ellis, Robert M. (2001b) 'How Buddhist was Plato?' *Western Buddhist Review* 3, 5–30.
Ellis, Robert M. (2012) *Middle Way Philosophy 1: The Path of Objectivity*. Lulu.
Ellis, Robert M. (2013a) *Middle Way Philosophy 2: The Integration of Desire*. Lulu.
Ellis, Robert M. (2013b) *Middle Way Philosophy 3: The Integration of Meaning*. Lulu.
Ellis, Robert M. (2015a) *Middle Way Philosophy 4: The Integration of Belief*. Lulu.
Ellis, Robert M. (2015b) 'Cognitive error as absolutization', available on Researchgate: https://www.researchgate.net/publication/283460051_Cognitive_error_as_absolutization
Ellis, Robert M. (2015c) 'Challenging misunderstandings of scepticism', available on Researchgate: https://www.researchgate.net/publication/283460128_Challenging_misunderstandings_of_scepticism
Ellis, Robert M. (2017) 'Reason is not objectivity: A response to Julian Baggini's narrowly rational criteria for objectivity', available on Researchgate: https://www.researchgate.net/publication/313696637_Reason_is_not_objectivity_A_response_to_Julian_Baggini's_narrowly_rational_criteria_for_objectivity
Ellis, Robert M. (2018) *The Christian Middle Way: The Case against Christian Belief but for Christian Faith*. Christian Alternative.
Ellis, Robert M. (2019) *The Buddha's Middle Way: Experiential Judgement in his Life and Teaching*. Equinox.
Ellis, Robert M. (2020) *Red Book, Middle Way: How Jung Parallels the Buddha's Method for Human Integration*. Equinox.
Ellis, Robert M. (2022) *Absolutization: The Source of Dogma, Repression and Conflict*. Equinox.
Ellis, Robert M. (forthcoming, 2023) *The Five Principles of Middle Way Philosophy: Living Experientially in a World of Uncertainty*. Equinox.
Ellis, Robert M. and Sheath, Peter (2016) 'The twelve steps of addiction recovery: Are they in the spirit of the Middle Way?' https://www.middlewaysociety.org/the-12-steps-of-addiction-recovery-are-they-in-the-spirit-of-the-middle-way/

Evans, J., Barston, Julie, and Pollard, Paul (1983) 'On the conflict between logic and belief in syllogistic reasoning' *Memory and Cognition* 11:3, 295–306. https://doi.org/10.3758/BF03196976
Fatoohi, Louay (2002) *Jihad in the Qur'an*. A.S. Noordeen.
Ferreiro, Emilia (1985) 'Literacy development', from David R. Olson, Nancy Torrance, and Angela Hildyard, eds., *Literacy, Language and Learning*. Cambridge University Press.
Festinger, Leon, Riecken, Henry, and Schachter, Stanley (1956) *When Prophecy Fails*. University of Minnesota Press. https://doi.org/10.1037/10030-000
Feuerbach, Ludwig, trans. George Eliot (1989) *The Essence of Christianity*. Prometheus Books.
Fondacaro, Rocco and Higgins, E. Tory (1985) 'Cognitive consequences of communication mode' from David R. Olson, Nancy Torrance, and Angela Hildyard, eds., *Literacy, Language and Learning*. Cambridge University Press.
Fordham, Frieda (1959) *An Introduction to Jung's Psychology*. Penguin.
Fox, Kieran and seven others (2014) 'Is meditation associated with altered brain structure? A systematic review and meta-analysis of morphometric neuroimaging in meditation practitioners' *Neuroscience and Behavioral Reviews* 43, 48–73. https://doi.org/10.1016/j.neubiorev.2014.03.016
Frazer, J.G. (1922) *The Golden Bough: A Study in Magic and Religion*. Macmillan. https://doi.org/10.1007/978-1-349-00400-3
French, Christopher (2005) 'Near death experiences in cardiac arrest survivors' *Progress in Brain Research* 150, 351–67. https://doi.org/10.1016/S0079-6123(05)50025-6
Fujita, Frank and Diener, Ed (2005) 'Life satisfaction set point: Stability and change' *Journal of Personality and Social Psychology* 88:1, 158–64. https://doi.org/10.1037/0022-3514.88.1.158
FWBO (1990, 5th edn) *The FWBO Puja Book*. Windhorse Publications.
Gabora, Liane, Rosch, Eleanor, and Aerts, Diederik (2008) 'Toward an ecological theory of concepts' *Ecological Psychology* 20:1, 84–116. https://doi.org/10.1080/10407410701766676
Ganguli, Kisari Mohan and Roy, Pratap Chandra (trans.) (2018) *The Mahabharata of Krishna-Dvaipayana Vyasa, vol. 12*. Franklin Classics Trade Press.
Garrison, Kathleen, Zefiro, Thomas, Scheinost, Dustin, Constable, R. Todd, and Brewer, Judson (2015) 'Meditation leads to reduced default mode network activity beyond an active task' *Cognitive, Affective and Behavioral Neuroscience* 15:3, 712–20. https://doi.org/10.3758/s13415-015-0358-3
Gazzaniga, Michael and Smylie, Charlotte (1990) 'Hemispheric mechanisms controlling voluntary and spontaneous facial expressions' *Journal of Cognitive Neuroscience* 2:3, 239–45. https://doi.org/10.1162/jocn.1990.2.3.239
Gilbert, Paul (2009) *The Compassionate Mind*. Constable.
Goethe, Johann Wolfgang von, trans. H.M. Waidson (2011) *Wilhelm Meister*. Alma Classics.
Goldberg, Aaron, Allis, C. David, and Bernstein, Emily (2007) 'Epigenetics: A landscape takes shape' *Cell* 128:4, 635–8. https://doi.org/10.1016/j.cell.2007.02.006
Goodwyn, Erik D. (2012) *The Neurobiology of the Gods: How Brain Physiology Shapes the Recurrent Imagery of Myth and Dreams*. Routledge. https://doi.org/10.4324/9780203141526

Goodwyn, Erik D. (2016) *Healing Symbols in Psychotherapy: A Ritual Approach.* Routledge. https://doi.org/10.4324/9781315651811

Govinda, Lama Anagarika (1969) *Foundations of Tibetan Mysticism.* Samuel Weiser.

Grossmann, Igor (2017) 'Wisdom and how to cultivate it: Review of emerging evidence for a constructivist model of wise thinking' *European Psychologist* 22, 233–46. https://doi.org/10.1027/1016-9040/a000302

Haidt, Jonathan (2007) 'Moral psychology and the misunderstanding of religion'. https://www.edge.org/conversation/moral-psychology-and-the-misunderstanding-of-religion (accessed 2019).

Haidt, Jonathan (2012) *The Righteous Mind: Why Good People are Divided by Politics and Religion.* Pantheon Books.

Haig, David (2006) 'Intrapersonal conflict' from M. Jones and A.C. Fabian, eds., *Conflict.* Cambridge University Press.

Halevi, Z'ev ben Shimon (2009) *Psychology and Kabbalah.* Kabbalah Society.

Halpern, Diane (1993) 'Assessing the effectiveness of critical thinking instruction' *Journal of General Education* 42:4, 238–54.

Hanslmayr, Simon, Leipold, Philipp, Pastötter, Bernhard, and Bäuml, Karl-Heinz (2009) 'Anticipatory signatures of voluntary memory suppression' *The Journal of Neuroscience* 29:9, 2742–7. https://doi.org/10.1523/JNEUROSCI.4703-08.2009

Harvey, Graham (1994) 'The roots of pagan ecology' *Religion Today* 9:3, 38–41. https://doi.org/10.1080/13537909408580720

Hasher, Lynn, Goldstein, David, and Toppino, Thomas (1977) 'Frequency and the conference of referential validity' *Journal of Verbal Learning and Verbal Behavior* 16:1, 107–12. https://doi.org/10.1016/S0022-5371(77)80012-1

Hebb, Donald (1949) *The Organization of Behavior: A Neuropsychological Theory.* John Wiley.

Heidegger, Martin, trans. William Lovitt (1977) 'The word of Nietzsche: "God is dead"', from *The Question Concerning Technology & Other Essays.* Harper Perennial.

Hildegard of Bingen, trans. Columba Hart and Jane Bishop (1990) *Scivias.* Paulist Press.

Homer, trans. Martin Hammond (1987) *The Iliad.* Penguin.

Homer, trans. E.V. Rieu (2003) *The Odyssey.* Penguin.

House, Adrian (2000) *Francis of Assisi.* Chatto & Windus.

Huettig, Falk and Mishra, Ramesh (2014) 'How literacy acquisition affects the illiterate mind – A critical examination of theories and evidence' *Language and Linguistics Compass* 8:10, 401–27. https://doi.org/10.1111/lnc3.12092

Hyden, Lars-Christer (2013) 'Bodies, embodiment and stories' from Molly Andrews, Corinne Squire, and Maria Tamboukou, eds., *Doing Narrative Research.* Sage Publications.

Ibn Ishaq, trans. A. Guillaume (1955) *The Life of Muhammad: A Translation of Isḥāq's 'Sirat Rasul Allah'.* Oxford University Press.

John of the Cross, trans. E. Allison-Peers (2003) *The Dark Night of the Soul.* Dover.

Johnson, Mark (2007) *The Meaning of the Body.* University of Chicago Press.

Johnson, Mark (2017) *Embodied Mind, Meaning and Reason.* University of Chicago Press. https://doi.org/10.7208/chicago/9780226500393.001.0001

Jones, Edward and Nisbett, Richard (1971) 'The actor and the observer: Divergent perceptions of the causes of behavior' from Edward Jones et al., eds. (1987) *Attribution: Perceiving the Causes of Behavior*, 79–94. Lawrence Erlbaum.

Jung, Carl Gustav, trans. W.S. Dell and Cary Baynes (1933) *Modern Man in Search of a Soul*. Kegan Paul.

Jung, Carl Gustav, trans. H. Godwin Baynes (1946) *Psychological Types*. Kegan Paul.

Jung, Carl Gustav, trans. R.F.C. Hull (1958) *Psychology and Religion: West & East* (Collected Works 11). Routledge.

Jung, Carl Gustav, trans. R.F.C. Hull (1959a) *The Archetypes and the Collective Unconscious* (Collected Works 9.1). Routledge.

Jung, Carl Gustav, trans. R.F.C. Hull (1959b) *Aion: Researches into the Phenomenology of the Self* (Collected Works 9.2). Routledge.

Jung, Carl Gustav, trans. R.F.C. Hull (1960) *The Structure and Dynamics of the Psyche* (Collected Works 8) Routledge.

Jung, Carl Gustav, ed. Sonu Shamdasani (2009) *The Red Book*. Norton.

Kaarby, Karen Marie Eid (2004) 'Children playing in Nature' from Heino Schonfeld, Sharon O'Brien, and Thomas Walsh, eds., *Questions of Quality: Proceedings of a Conference on Defining, Assessing and Supporting Quality in Early Childhood Care and Education*. Centre for Early Childhood Development and Education.

Kabat-Zinn, Jon (2013, 2nd edn) *Full Catastrophe Living: Using the wisdom of your body and mind to face stress, pain and illness*. Bantam.

Kahneman, Daniel (2011) *Thinking, Fast and Slow*. Penguin.

Kant, Immanuel, trans. Lewis White Beck (1995) *Foundations of the Metaphysics of Morals*. Prentice-Hall.

Kee, Alistair (1982) *Constantine versus Christ*. SCM Press.

Kegan, Robert (1982) *The Evolving Self: Problem and Process in Human Development*. Harvard University Press.

Kershaw, Trace and five others (2016) 'The interdependence of advanced cancer patients' and their family care-givers' mental health, physical health, and self-efficacy over time' *Annals of Behavioral Medicine* 49:6, 901–11. https://doi.org/10.1007/s12160-015-9743-y

King, Laura and Emmons, Robert (1990) 'Conflict over emotional expression: Psychological and physical correlates' *Journal of Personality and Social Psychology*, 58:5, 864–77. https://doi.org/10.1037/0022-3514.58.5.864

Klostermaier, Klaus K. (1994) *A Survey of Hinduism*. State University of New York Press.

Knox, Jean (2003) *Archetype, Attachment, Analysis: Jungian Psychology and the Emergent Mind*. Brunner-Routledge.
https://doi.org/10.4324/9780203391525

Koch, Kristof and Tsuchiya, Naotsugu (2007) 'Attention and consciousness: Two distinct brain processes' *Trends in Cognitive Sciences* 11:1, 16–22. https://doi.org/10.1016/j.tics.2006.10.012

Lakoff, George (1987) *Women, Fire and Dangerous Things: What Categories Reveal about the Mind*. University of Chicago Press.
https://doi.org/10.7208/chicago/9780226471013.001.0001

Lakoff, George (2007) 'Cognitive models and prototype theory' from V. Evans, B. Bergen, and J. Zinken, eds., *The Cognitive Linguistics Reader*. Equinox.

Lakoff, George and Johnson, Mark (1980) *Metaphors We Live by*. University of Chicago Press.

Lakoff, George and Johnson, Mark (1999) *Philosophy in the Flesh: The Embodied Mind and Its Challenge to Western Thought*. University of Chicago Press.

Lakoff, George and Nuñez, Rafael (2000) *Where Mathematics Comes From*. Basic Books.

Lent, Jeremy (2017) *The Patterning Instinct: A Cultural History of Humanity's Search for Meaning*. Prometheus Books.

Lomas, Tim (2016) 'Recontextualizing mindfulness: Theravada Buddhist perspectives on the ethical and spiritual dimensions of awareness' *Psychology of Religion and Spirituality* 9:2. https://doi.org/10.1037/rel0000080

Lueke, Adam and Gibson, Bryan (2014) 'Mindfulness meditation reduces implicit age and race bias: The role of reduced automaticity of responding' *Social, Psychological and Personality Science* 6:3, 284–91. https://doi.org/10.1177/1948550614559651

Lueke, Adam and Gibson, Bryan (2016) 'Brief mindfulness meditation reduces discrimination' *Psychology of Consciousness: Theory, Research and Practice* 3:1, 34–44. https://doi.org/10.1037/cns0000081

Luo Guanzhong, trans. Yu Sumei (2014) *The Three Kingdoms*. Tuttle Publishing. https://doi.org/10.1525/9780520957879

Maass, Anne, Salvi, Daniela, Arcuri, Luciano, and Semin, Gün (1989) 'Language use in intergroup contexts: The linguistic intergroup bias': *Journal of Personality and Social Psychology* 57:6, 981–93. https://doi.org/10.1037/0022-3514.57.6.981

Marinoff, Lou (2007) *The Middle Way: Finding Happiness in a World of Extremes*. Sterling Publishing.

Marx, Karl, ed. David McLellan (1977) *Selected Writings*. Oxford University Press.

Mashal, N., Faust, N., Hendler, T., and Jung-Beeman, M. (2007) 'An fMRI investigation of the neural correlates underlying the processing of novel metaphoric expressions' *Brain and Language* 100: 115–26. https://doi.org/10.1016/j.bandl.2005.10.005

Maslow, A.H. (1943) 'A theory of human motivation' *Psychological Review* 50: 370–96. https://doi.org/10.1037/h0054346

Maturana, Humberto and Varela, Francisco (1987) *The Tree of Knowledge: The Biological Roots of Human Understanding*. Shambhala.

McClellan, David (1971) *The Thought of Karl Marx*. Macmillan.

McGilchrist, Iain (2009) *The Master and His Emissary: The Divided Brain and the Making of the Western World*. Yale University Press.

McNamara, Patrick (2009) *The Neuroscience of Religious Experience*. Cambridge University Press. https://doi.org/10.1017/CBO9780511605529

Meadows, Donella (2008) *Thinking in Systems: A Primer*. Chelsea Green.

Mobbs, Dean and eight others (2009) 'From threat to fear: The neural organisation of defensive fear systems in humans' *The Journal of Neuroscience* 29:39, 12236–43. https://doi.org/10.1523/JNEUROSCI.2378-09.2009

Murata, Sachiko and Chittick, William (2000) *The Vision of Islam*. I.B. Tauris.

Myers, David G. (2002) *Intuition: Its Powers and Perils*. Yale University Press.
Nagarjuna, trans. Garfield (1995) *The Fundamental Wisdom of the Middle Way: Nagarjuna's Mulamadhyamikakarika*. Oxford University Press.
Nagy, Marilyn (1991) *Philosophical Issues in the Psychology of C.G. Jung*. State University of New York Press.
Ñanamoli, Bhikkhu and Bodhi, Bhikkhu (1995) *The Middle Length Discourses of the Buddha: A New Translation of the Majjhima Nikaya*. Wisdom Publications.
Neher, Andrew (1996) 'Jung's Theory of Archetypes: A critique' *Journal of Humanistic Psychology* 36:2, 61–91. https://doi.org/10.1177/00221678960362008
Nietzsche, Friedrich, trans. Douglas Smith (2008) *The Birth of Tragedy*. Oxford University Press.
Noorani, A.G. (2002) *Islam and Jihad: Prejudice versus Reality*. Zed Books.
Norwich, John Julius (2012) *The Popes: A History*. Chatto & Windus.
Olivelle, Patrick, trans. (2004) *The Law Code of Manu*. Oxford University Press.
Papadopoulos, Renos (2006) 'Jung's epistemology and methodology' from Renos Papadopoulos, ed., *Handbook of Jungian Psychology*. Routledge.
Pater, Walter (1873) *Studies in the History of the Renaissance*. Macmillan.
Perfetti, Charles A. and Goldman, Susan R. (1975) 'Discourse functions of thematization and topicalization' *Journal of Psycholinguistic Research*, 4:3, 257–71. https://doi.org/10.1007/BF01066930
Plato, trans. Lane Cooper (1961) 'Euthyphro' from *The Collected Dialogues*. Pantheon Books.
Plato, trans. Desmond Lee (1987) *The Republic*. Penguin.
Plato, trans. Hugh Tredennick and Harold Tarrant (1993) *The Last Days of Socrates*. Penguin.
Poloma, Margaret (2003) *Main Street Mystics: The Toronto Blessing and Reviving Pentecostalism*. Alta Mira Press.
Popper, Karl (1962) *The Open Society and Its Enemies*. Routledge.
Popper, Karl (1972) *Objective Knowledge*. Oxford University Press.
Prakash, Ruchika Shaurya, De Leon, Angeline, Klatt, Maryanna, Mallarkey, William, and Patterson, Beth (2013) 'Mindfulness disposition and default-mode network connectivity in older adults' *Social, Cognitive and Affective Neuroscience* 8:1, 112–17. https://doi.org/10.1093/scan/nss115
Pseudo-Dionysius, trans. John H. Parker (1924) *Mystic Theology*. https://en.wikisource.org/wiki/Dionysius_the_Areopagite,_Works/Mystic_Theology (accessed 2019).
Pychyl, Timothy (2019) 'Procrastination: Motivation deficit vs. regulation failure' *Psychology Today Blog*: https://www.psychologytoday.com/us/blog/dont-delay/201906/procrastination-motivation-deficit-vs-regulation-failure? (accessed 2019).
Ramachandran, V.S. and Blakeslee, S. (1998) *Phantoms in the Brain: Probing the Mysteries of the Human Mind*. William Morrow.
Ranke-Heinemann, Uta, trans. Peter Heinegg (1991) *Eunuchs for the Kingdom of Heaven: The Catholic Church and Sexuality*. Penguin.
Reber, Rolf (2016) *Critical Feeling: How to Use Feelings Strategically*. Cambridge University Press. https://doi.org/10.1017/CBO9781107446755

Reber, Rolf, Schwarz, Norbert, and Winkielman, Piotr (2004) 'Processing fluency and aesthetic pleasure: Is beauty in the perceiver's processing experience?' *Personality and Social Psychology Review* 8:4, 364–82.
https://doi.org/10.1207/s15327957pspr0804_3

Robin, Robert (1981) 'Revival movement hysteria in the southern highlands of Papua New Guinea' *Journal for the Scientific Study of Religion* 20:2, 150–63.
https://doi.org/10.2307/1385612

Robson, David (2019) *The Intelligence Trap: Why Smart People do Stupid things*. Hodder & Stoughton.

Rowson, Jonathan (2019) 'Brexit, democracy, and the sacred'. https://blogs.lse.ac.uk/religionglobalsociety/2019/01/brexit-democracy-and-the-sacred/ (accessed 2020).

Sangharakshita (1983) *Transcribed Seminar 118: Sigalovada Sutta*. https://www.freebuddhistaudio.com/text/read?num=SEM118 (accessed 2019).

Sangharakshita (2003) *Living with Awareness: A Guide to the Satipatthana Sutta*. Windhorse.

Sartre, Jean-Paul, trans. Bernard Frechtman (1963) *Genet: Actor and Martyr*. University of Minnesota Press. https://doi.org/10.2307/1125081

Sartre, Jean-Paul, trans. Philip Mairet (1980) *Existentialism and Humanism*. Methuen.

Scheid, John (2012) 'Roman animal sacrifice and the system of being' from Christopher A. Faraone and F.S. Naiden, eds., *Greek and Roman Animal Sacrifice*. Cambridge University Press.

Schlund, Michael, Hudgins, Caleb, Magee, Sandy, and Dymond, Simon (2013) 'Neuroimaging the temporal dynamics of human avoidance to sustained threat' *Behavioural Brain Research* 257: 148–55.
https://doi.org/10.1016/j.bbr.2013.09.042

Scholem, Gershom (1974) *Kabbalah*. Keter Publishing/Penguin.

Shapiro, Fred R. (2014) 'Who wrote the serenity prayer?' *Chronicle of Higher Education*: https://www.chronicle.com/article/Who-Wrote-the-Serenity-Prayer-/146159/ (accessed 2019).

Slingerland, Edward (2007) *Effortless Action: Wu Wei as Conceptual Metaphor and Spiritual Ideal in Early China*. Oxford University Press.

Smart, Ninian (1968) *Secular Education and the Logic of Religion*. Humanities Press.

Soldo, Mirjana, trans. Sean Bloomfield (2016) *My Heart Will Triumph*. Catholic Shop.

Soloviev, Vladimir, trans. Richard Gill (1935) *Plato*. Stanley Nott.

Sophocles, trans. H.D. F. Kitto (1962) *Antigone, Oedipus the King, Electra*. Oxford University Press.

Sperber, Dan and Wilson, Deirdre (2008) 'A deflationary account of metaphors' from Raymond Gibbs, ed., *The Cambridge Handbook of Metaphor and Thought*. Cambridge University Press.

Taleb, Nassim Nicholas (2018) *Skin in the Game: Hidden Asymmetries in Daily Life*. Penguin.

Teresa of Avila, trans. Allison Peers (2004) *Interior Castle*. Image/Doubleday.

Tertullian, trans. Peter Holmes (undated) 'The prescription against heretics' from Allan Menzies, ed., *Ante-Nicene Fathers Vol. 3*. Eerdmans.

Tolkien, J.R.R. (1954) *The Lord of the Rings*. Allen & Unwin.
Tolkien, J.R.R. (1964) 'On Fairy Stories' from *Tree and Leaf*. HarperCollins.
Tsang Nyön Heruka, trans. Nalanda Translation Committee (1995) *The Life of Marpa the Translator*. Shambhala.
Turcan, Robert, trans. Antonia Nevill (2001) *The Gods of Ancient Rome: Religion in Everyday Life from Archaic to Imperial Times*. Routledge.
Tweedy, Roderick (2013) *The God of the Left Hemisphere*. Karnac.
Unterman, Alan, trans. and ed. (2008) *The Kabbalistic Tradition: An Anthology of Jewish Mysticism*. Penguin.
Vaillant, George E. (1993) *The Wisdom of the Ego*. Harvard University Press.
Vessantara (1993) *Meeting the Buddhas: A Guide to Buddhas, Bodhisattvas and Tantric Deities*. Windhorse Publications.
Virgil, trans. David West (1991) *The Aeneid*. Penguin.
Von Glahn, Richard (2004) *The Sinister Way: The Divine and the Demonic in Chinese Religious Culture*. University of California Press. https://doi.org/10.1525/california/9780520234086.001.0001
Walton, Douglas (1987) *Informal Fallacies: Towards a Theory of Argument Criticisms*. John Betjemans. https://doi.org/10.1075/pbcs.4
Wason, P.C. (1960) 'On the failure to eliminate hypotheses in a conceptual task' *Quarterly Journal of Experimental Psychology* 12:3, 129–40. https://doi.org/10.1080/17470216008416717
Watt, W. Montgomery (1961) *Muhammad: Prophet and Statesman*. Oxford University Press.
Watts, Alan (2011) *Tao: The Watercourse Way*. Souvenir Press.
Wehr, Demaris (1988) *Jung and Feminism: Liberating Archetypes*. Routledge.
Wilber, Ken (2000) *Integral Psychology*. Shambhala.
Wordsworth, William (1994) *Collected Poems*. Wordsworth Editions.
Wu Cheng'en, trans. Arthur Waley (1942) *Monkey (Journey to the West)*. Grove Press.
Zaehner, R.C. (1966) *Hindu Scriptures*. Dent Dutton.
Zaehner, R.C. (1969) *The Bhagavad Gita*. Oxford University Press.
Zimmer, Herbert (1955) 'The roles of conflict and internalised demands in projection' *The Journal of Abnormal and Social Psychology* 50:2, 188–92. https://doi.org/10.1037/h0040713

Glossary

This glossary is intended to provide a ready reference for the uses of terms in this book that are in any way distinctive or technical.

Absolutization The assumption that a particular belief (explicit or implicit, positive or negative) is entirely true as represented.

Adaptation The adjustment of an organism (such as a human) to the surrounding conditions, by some sort of balancing feedback (q.v.) so that *all* the needs of the organism (not only survival and reproduction) can be fulfilled in the new conditions.

Agnosticism The recognition of uncertainty about both positive and negative absolutes, enabling belief in neither.

Allegory The interpretation of a symbol as having only one meaning, usually to fit an ideology.

Anima/Animus The archetype of the attractive other that inspires us over time with positive qualities that are beyond our current ones. This often, but not always, takes a feminine form (anima) for men and a masculine form (animus) for women.

Anima/Animus function The ways in which some symbols help us to fulfil the human need to develop relationships with those who are different from us.

Appropriative projection The assumption that an object has essential properties that support one's beliefs.

Archetype A schematic, diachronic function: i.e. any symbol that helps maintain meaningful inspiration over time.

Attraction-repulsion axis One of three bases for classifying archetypes, differentiated by whether the archetype attracts or repels us.

Authority Assumption of the value of a particular source in providing correct information or instruction.

Balancing feedback A cycle of causal relationships in a system that also allows new information to be brought into that system, so that it can maintain its stability in adjustment to the surrounding conditions (also known as *open* or *negative* feedback).

Glossary

Belief An assumed relationship between an explicit or implicit representation in our minds and a state of affairs, that we use as the basis of judgement.

Bias A tendency to adopt a less demanding belief instead of a more demanding one, when a more demanding one would be better adapted (q.v.) to the overall conditions.

Care Values of concern for the welfare of oneself and others.

Cognitive model A consistent set of assumptions that can enable symbols to be meaningful in relation to each other, but where the whole set requires underlying schemas and metaphors to be meaningful (e.g. the meaning of 'Tuesday' requires metaphorically interpreted schemas for time and a cognitive model of the relationships between days of the week).

Collective unconscious Jung's term for the shared sources of meaning for archetypes in the unconscious minds of all humans – argued here to be unnecessary.

Concept A term that is widely assumed to get its meaning abstractly through representation alone rather than being a symbol, even though words are dependent on embodied meaning (q.v.) just as much as other symbols are. Instead we need to see concepts as symbols that partly depend on cognitive models (q.v.).

Confidence The bodily state that allows us to perform accustomed actions, making accustomed assumptions, without difficulty.

Consequentialism The belief that morally correct judgement is determined by the likely effects of our actions.

Counter-projection The tendency of someone who is an object of projection to themselves also project onto the projector. This should not be confused with reactive projection (q.v.).

Credibility The application of critical thinking (q.v.) to assess the extent to which we can justify belief in the authority of a source.

Critical thinking The practice of applying wider awareness to assess our own or others' beliefs, comparing their degree of justification with that of other possible beliefs.

Critical universalism The belief that all traditions (q.v.) *can* offer justified beliefs that are adapted to conditions, but only if they are critically examined and sorted.

Dead metaphor Meaning of symbols that may in the past have been recognized as metaphorical, and is still dependent on metaphor and schema, but is now assumed to be representational.

Deontology The belief that morally correct judgement is determined by adherence to authoritative principles.

Determinism The belief that all causal relationships in the universe throughout time are fixed.

Diachronic Uniting perspectives over time by creating awareness of past or possible future states alongside present ones.

Dogma Beliefs that lack justification from experience because they are absolute (equivalent to absolutization (q.v.)).

Dogmatic religion Religion understood as essentially consisting in absolute beliefs, usually supported by appeals to authority or absolutely interpreted experience.

Embodied meaning The view that meaning combines cognitive and emotive elements, and is experienced through our bodies through associative links. Meaning becomes refined and differentiated through schemas and metaphors.

Embodiment The state, or recognition, that all our experience, desire, meaning, and belief is based in our whole bodies. This should *not* be confused with reductive physicalism or materialism.

Esotericism The restriction of the teaching of particular beliefs to a select group on the grounds that they are likely to be misunderstood beyond that group.

Essentialism The belief that a complex object can be adequately represented through the identification of certain definitive features.

Ethnic religion A form of religion that is primarily associated with a particular ethnic group and its culture.

Fallacy An argument that breaks particular identifiable social rules that might enable a basis of agreement to be reached, and thus makes conflict of belief intractable.

Feedback A repetitive causal process in which an initiating system maintains or changes its features through interaction with other systems. See *balancing* and *reinforcing* feedback.

Framing The basic assumptions made when we recognize and categorize an object, e.g. that tools have a purpose or that sexual difference is binary.

Freedom Values that prioritize our ability to fulfil our wishes without interference from others.

Function The value that a particular process has in fulfilling needs (q.v.).

Gestalt Experience that takes the form of an irreducible whole, not analysable conceptually, and that arises as intuition (q.v.).

Goal-oriented projection The tendency to understand an object solely in terms of its relationship to fulfilling our goals, i.e. as a tool.

God function The ways in which some symbols help us to fulfil the human need for reminders of greater potential over time.

Heroic function The ways in which some symbols help us to fulfil the human need for reminders of long-term goals and the means of fulfilling them.

Glossary

Iconoclasm The belief that archetypal images should be destroyed (or practice of destroying them) in reactive projection (q.v.) to idolatry (q.v.).

Ideology A fairly consistent set of beliefs held by a particular group.

Idolatry The projection of archetypal functions (especially the God function) onto an object, as distinct from the interactive process that fulfils the function. The object projected onto may be an image, a set of concepts, or a belief.

Image (1) Jung's term for a schema (q.v.). (2) A symbol that takes the form of a picture or other visual representation.

Incrementality The practice of conceptually adjusting our understanding of objects prior to judgement, so that their qualities are variables on a scale, rather than absolutes that are either present or absent.

Individuation Jungian term for integration (q.v.), specifically as applied to individuals.

Inspiration A motivating reminder from a symbol that has an archetypal function, enabling us to continue prioritizing that function.

Integration The resolution of conflict in either individuals or groups over time, so that desires, meanings, and beliefs are increasingly focused and increasingly adequate in response to conditions.

Integration-projection axis One of three bases for classifying archetypes, differentiated according to whether it is associated with experiences of genuine integration or of projection (as subsequently recognized in more integrated states).

Introjection Jung's term for 'the assimilation of the object into the subject' – in practice indistinguishable from projection.

Intuition Embodied experience taking a non-conceptual gestalt (q.v.) form. This is central to awareness and meaning, but does not justify absolute beliefs.

Jhana One of a number of levels of temporarily integrated state recognized in Buddhist tradition, and marked by intense and broad awareness, profound relaxation, and ecstatic emotional states.

Judgement The reflective processing of meaningful experience so as to arrive at beliefs, which offer an assumed representation of the environment for potential action.

Justice Values that prioritize the proportionate allocation of resources or of treatment by others.

Justification The incremental degree of adequacy of a judgement in addressing conditions, dependent on the degree of integration of that judgement in experience.

Loyalty Values that prioritize the welfare of others in our group or the interests of the group as a whole.

Meaning The association between symbols and embodied experience that enables us to respond similarly to each (e.g. the word 'dog', or a picture of a dog, stimulates some similar experienced responses to those we would have to an actual dog).

Metaphor An association between two symbols that allows the meaning of one to be shared with the other.

Metaphorical extension The use of a metaphor (q.v.) to extend the meaning of a symbol that is already meaningful in the schema in which it is used.

Metaphysics Beliefs about ultimate states of affairs beyond experience. As such beliefs have to be absolute to be ultimate, metaphysical beliefs are always absolutizations (q.v.).

Metonymy A form of metaphor (q.v.) in which part of something stands for the whole: e.g. 'Washington' for the US.

Middle Way The principle that more adequate judgements are reached by avoiding both positive and negative absolutizations (q.v.).

Modernity The condition in which archetypal functions are implicitly recognized as schematic but not diachronic.

Motif A consistent pattern of symbols (not necessarily an archetype).

Multivocality The property of a symbol of having multiple meanings.

Mysticism The strand of religious traditions that gives priority to direct archetypal experience and meaning over beliefs.

Naïve universalism The assumption that all traditions have the same essential value, without any attempt to discriminate between the practical effects of different elements of those traditions.

Naturalism Belief that scientific explanation can provide a representational account of 'nature' in the sense of ultimate states of affairs.

Needs Drives or desires of an organism that enable it to maintain itself and its kind, or to fulfil its potential in other respects.

Negative projection Assumption that an object is essentially bad.

Optionality The availability of different possibilities for consideration when we make a judgement.

Platonism The assumption that human meaning and judgement are essentially mental and are separated from the body.

Power (repressive sense only) The ability to make oneself or others act in accordance with one's current desires.

Practical religion Religion understood as practices that fulfil archetypal functions.

Glossary

Projection The assumption that a particular object consists solely in the archetypal function that it fulfils for us.

Prototype Primary association in experience that is extended in the meaning of a wider concept (q.v.) (e.g. robin for bird).

Provisionality The practice of maintaining awareness that a belief may need to be changed (requiring optionality – q.v.).

Psychological stage One of the five common differentiable periods in the development of humans, in which the value priorities used in judgement identifiably shift, as identified in the theory of Jean Piaget and Robert Kegan.

Purity Values that prioritize the maintenance of an object or person without interference because of the special status accorded to their current state.

Reactive projection Form of projection (q.v.) that over-reacts to the discovery of complexity and uncertainty by assuming the complete *absence* of an archetype in an object that was previously assumed to consist solely of it.

Reductionism A belief that assumes its own representational completeness and finality – most often applied to scientific theories that lack provisionality (q.v.) because of their naturalistic assumptions.

Reinforcing feedback A cycle of causal relationships in a system that maintains its current form without any adaptation, and thus creates increasing instability in relation to wider conditions (also called *closed* or *positive* feedback).

Religion The practice of integrating the archetypes, thus allowing their functions to operate.

Representation The relationship of formal identity between an image or verbal proposition and a state of affairs, creating an assumed basis for potential action.

Representationalism The belief that representation (q.v.), rather than embodiment (q.v.), forms the basis of meaning, and thus that it is primarily cognitive.

Responsibility Our experience of the meaning and value of acting in ways that are more aware and adequate in preference to those that are not.

Schema Basic association between a type of embodied experience and a set of symbols (e.g. between experiences of containment and the meaning of words associated with containers).

Schematic nature of archetypes Since the meaning of archetypes depends on schemas (q.v.), that meaning consists in a set of broad and universal functions for symbols rather than a representation (q.v.).

Self-other axis One of three bases for classifying archetypes, differentiated according to whether they are associated with self or other.

Shadow function The ways in which some symbols help us to fulfil the human need to avoid threats.

Sign An object that is assumed to have only one (representational) meaning, as distinct from the multivocality (q.v.) of symbols.

Soothing system The parts of the brain (particularly hippocampus) that can reduce stress by helping to give a wider context to our stressful experiences.

Soul Jung's alternative term for the anima/animus (q.v.).

Sublimation Process of developing dominant and obsessive desires and beliefs into more subtle, complex alternatives.

Symbol An object (most commonly a word or image) that has acquired meaning through association with a particular range of experiences. In contrast to a sign (q.v.), the meaning of a symbol is multivocal (q.v.).

System An object at any scale understood as a changing set of interrelated processes rather than as a discrete or fixed thing.

Third phase The condition in which archetypal functions are implicitly recognized as both schematic and diachronic, allowing those functions to be better fulfilled than in the previous two phases where only one or the other was recognized.

Tradition The process by which a group passes on cultural assumptions and habitual practices over time. Traditions can be categorized as religious, political, or artistic, for instance.

Traditional society The condition in which archetypal functions are implicitly recognized as diachronic but not schematic.

Transcendence projection The tendency to understand an object (e.g. a supernatural God) solely in terms of its relationship to maintaining our sense of wider potential.

Universal religion A form of religious tradition that can be adopted by anyone regardless of ethnicity.

Universalism The belief that we should maximize our capacity for consistency and sustainability. See *naïve* and *critical* forms.

Universality A maximized capacity for consistency and sustainability.

Univocality The property of only having one 'correct' meaning.

Value A pattern of beliefs about the most justified priorities in judgement and action.

Virtue A morally positive habitual quality contributing to the judgement of an individual or group (e.g. courage, wisdom).

Index

a priori (reasoning), 198, 227, 240
Abrahamic religions, 188, 200, 217, 221, 223, 256
absolute (belief), 2, 8, 32, 36, 43, 47, 68, 89, 91, 96, 98, 101, 104, 108–10, 115, 127, 130, 135, 152, 173, 179, 184, 193–5, 199–200, 202, 211, 220, 222–4, 227, 232, 234, 236, 238, 250, 251, 268, 270–1, 277, 288, 320–2, *see also* absolutization
absolutism, 41, 100, 247, 268, 290
absolutization, 15, 38, 45, **63**, 65–6, 72–4, 76, 79, 86, 88, 96–7, 100–2, 108–10, 113–14, 119, 124–5, 127, 135, 146, 162, 165–6, 169, 192–3, 198–9, 220, 227–8, 239, 255, 261, 297, 310, **318**, 320
abstraction, 12, 19–21, 25, 37–8, 41, 54, 59, 66, 70, 73, 76, 78, 97, 100, 118–19, 123, 125, 138, 164, 186, 219–20, 229, 238, 276, 281, 283, 294, 296, 298, 303
Achilles, 83–4
actor-observer bias, 87
ad hominem (fallacy), 65, 89, 106
Adam (Genesis), 222–3, 253, 258
Adam Kadmon (Kabbalah), 258
adaptation, 5, **318**
addiction, 113, 138, 180, 215, 310
adult development, 50, 54
Advaita Vedanta, 204, 309
aesthetics, 32–3, 121, 132, 156–9, 173, 264, 266–7, 279–82, 307, 316
agency, 28, 76, 86, 225, *see also* responsibility
agnosticism, 1, 8, 52, 104, 109–10, 242–3, 290, **318**
agreement, 126, 287, 320
Akhos (suffering), 225
Akshobhya, 202

Al-Ansari, 253
Alcoholics Anonymous, 180
alcoholism, 299
aliens, 18
Allah, 189, 247, 252, 254, 312, *see also* God
Al-Lat (goddess), 254
allegory, 144, 245, 263, 273, **318**
Al-Uzza (goddess), 254
ambiguity, 106, 129, 179–81, 183, 276–7, 291
Americas, 18
Amitabha, 197, 202
Amoghasiddhi, 203
amygdala, 82, 101, 113
Analects (Confucius), 210–11, 309
analogy, 78, 296
analysis, 72, 260
analytic psychology, 31, 57–8, 60, 137
anarchism, 234
ancestor worship, 210
androgyny, 180
angel, 238–9
anger, 11, 166
anima, 7, 14, 23–4, 29–30, 46, 52, 54–5, 57, 62, 70, 75, 96, 118, 121, 131, 136–40, 143, 145–6, **153–61**, 170, 178–9, 184, 196, 199–200, 206–8, 213, 215, 221–4, 235, 238–9, 243, 245, 254–6, 260–1, 264, 269, 275, 279, 294, 299, 302, **318**, 324
animals, 22–3, 137, 142, 147, 156, 158, 166, 206, 214–15, 264, 279, 283, 316
animation, 157
animus, 7, 14, 23–4, 29, 46, 55, 57, 70, 75, 96, 118, 121, 131, 136–40, 145–6, **153–61**, 170, 178–9, 184, 200, 213, 221–4, 235, 238–9, 245, 254, 260–1, 264, 269, 275, 279, 294, 299, 302, **318**, 324

Annunciation (to Mary), 238, 280
anthropology, 306
anxiety, 24, 77, 82, 114-15, 148
Aphrodite, 225
Apollonian, 225
apostates, 250
apostles, 235
appropriative projection, 75, 79, 87, 98, 102, **318**
Arabia, 247
archetype, *passim*, **4**, **318**
Ares, 225
argument structure, 128
Aristotle, 184, 257, 270, 288, 308
Arjuna, 205
Armstrong, Karen 54, 308
arrow, 83, 163-4, 245
art, 14, 46, 118, 120-1, 123, 134, 157, 159, 173, 177, 192, 197, 201, 214, 273-4, 278-9, 280-1, 291, 304, *see also* arts
art galleries, 304
artificiality, 264
artistic profundity, 23
arts, 47, **117-23**, 127, 224, 235, 250, 267, 282, 287, 301
asceticism, 151, 162, 166, 181-2, 191-3, 208, 232
association, 1, 4, 6-8, 10, 20-3, 25-7, 35, 46, 58, 61, 63, 78, 93, 108, 120-1, 125, 158-9, 170, 173, 241, 280, 287, 322-4
Assumption (of Mary), 238, 255
assumptions, 8, 30-1, 32, 34, 39-41, 45, 47, 52, 63, 65-6, 69, 72, 79-80, 85, 88, 93-4, 104-6, 109, 115, **124-9**, 134, 138-9, 151, 155, 162, 170, 175-6, 181, 191, 199, 206, 226-7, 231-2, 236, 244, 255, 257, 264, 266, 273, 275-6, 284, 286-8, 293, 295, 297-8, 302, 304, 307, 318-20, 322-4
astrology, 58, 65
Ate (blind folly), 225
atheism, 8, 30, 70-1, 94, 99, 110
Athena, 225
Athenians, 227
atonement, 233
attention, 11, 13, 19, 23, 33-4, 38, 44, 65-6, 89, 94, 113-15, 117, 124, 128, 133, 140, 158-9, 171-2, 219, 231-2, 249, 267, 273, 298
attraction, 7, 23-4, 29, 39, 115, 136, **137**, 139, 160, 166, 279

attraction-repulsion axis, **137**, 140, **318**
attribute substitution, 86
Augustine, St of Hippo, 104, 223, 30
Ault, James, 47, 308
austerity, 250, *see also* asceticism
authority, 3, **50-1**, 53-4, 57, 90, 94, 96-8, 119, 176, 195, 199, 204-5, 220, 250, 254, 295, 303-4, **318**, 319-20
Avalokiteshvara, 197, 199, 200
avarice, 240
awareness, 4-5, 18, 22, 27-9, 32, 34, 36, 38, 44-5, 52, 55, 77, 79-80, 83, 89, 99, 102, 105-7, 111-13, 115, 117, 124-5, 127-30, 132-3, 138, 148-9, 151, 158, 163-4, 172-3, 178-81, 184, 192-3, 196, 203, 208, 211-12, 223, 236, 246, 249, 260, 264, 266, 273, 275, 279, 281, 285-6, 288, 299, 301, 314, 319-21, 323
awe, 4, 115, **139**, 175, 217, 238-9, 242

Babylonian exile, 240
Bahai, 53
balance, 1, 6, 8, 47, 54, 93, 108, 110, 127, 134, 153, 160-1, 172, 178-9, 181, **193**, 206, 210, 241, 252-3, 260, 266, 269-70
Balance of Nature, 266, *see also* balancing feedback
balanced effort, 252
balancing feedback, **91-3**, 98, 104-5, 108, 168, 193, 238, **318**, 320
bao ying (moral reciprocity in the universe), 210
baptism, 230
basic level categories and schemas, **20-1**, 24-5, 27, 59, 80, 323
Batchelor, Stephen, 131, 190, 268
beauty, 8, 29, 72, 87-8, 158-9, 173, 260, 263, **278-82**, 291, 299, 307, 316
belief, 1-2, 8-9, 15, 28-31, 37-8, 41-8, 51, 53-5, 58, 60, 63, 65-6, 69-77, 79-80, 88, 92-4, 96, 98-101, 103-4, 109-10, 113, 117, 119, 123-7, 130, 134, 138, 147, 149-50, 152, 162-4, 170, 172-3, 175, 184, 187, 192, 194, 199, 208, 213, 221, 232-4, 236, 238, 243, 247, 255, 258, 263-4, 266, 268, 270-1, 273-7, 283-5, 287, 290, 294, 302, 306-7, 311, 318, **319**, 320-4
belief bias, 86
belief disconfirmation paradigm, 86

Bergen, Ben, 22, 308, 314
Bernard, St of Clairvaux, 237, 243–4, 246, 308
Bhagavad Gita, 205–6, 317
bias, 2, 6, 16, 18, 29, 39, 47, 57, 63, 74, 76, 82–3, **86–90**, 93–4, 97, 100, 105, 115, 129–30, 179, 212, 217, 286, 305, 309, 314, **319**
Bible, 75, 94, 186, 188, 217, 219–24, 231–2, 235–6, 237–8, 257
Bildungsroman, 121
binah (intellect), 260
biodiversity, 266
biology, 5, 12, 39, 145, 153, 305, *see also* physiology, neuroscience
Blake, William, 217–18
bodhisattva, 60, 196, 200, 213, *see separate entries for* individual names
body, 2, 11–12, 20–2, 25, 33–4, 36, 77, 79–80, 91, 101, 111, 113, 137, 151, 158, 184, 192, 204, 208, 219, 227, 230, 238–9, 242, 245, 257–8, 260, 273, 276, 296–9, 300, 302, 313, 320, 322, *see also* embodied meaning, embodiment
body language, 65
body-scanning, 111
Bosch, Hieronymous, 166–7
bounded rationality, 98
Brahman, 204–5
Brahminism, 206, 208, 229
brain, 23, 25–6, 45, 77, 80, **81**, 82–3, 86, 113–14, 119, 124, 138, 142, 144–5, 147, 157–8, 166, 178, 180, 184, 239, 260, 261, 276, 296, 305, 309, 311, 313, 324, *see separate entries for* specific regions and hormones, *see also* mind, neuroscience, neural links
Brexit, 294, 316
Brigid, St of Kildare, 235
Brihadaranyaka Upanishad, 204
Broca's Region, 25
Buddha, 3, 5, 7, 85, 139, 151, 163, 166, 170–1, 178–9, 181–2, 187–8, **190–5**, 196–7, 199–200, 202–3, 206, 209, 213, 219, 224, 232, 270, 309, 310, 315, 317, *see also* Gautama and other named Buddhas
Buddhism, 6, 16, 24, 34, 45, 53, 60, 112, 119–20, 131, 161, 166, 172–3, 175, 184, 187–8, **190–203**, 204, 206–7,
210, 213, 215, 229, 240, 252, 262, 268, 288, 304, 310, 314, 321

calculation, 83, 97
Campbell, Joseph, 87, 147–9, 191, 309
Canaan, 223
capitalism, 99
caprice, 249–50
Caravaggio, Michelangelo, 237
care, 11, 50–1, 54, 221, 229–30, 294, 313, **319**
Cartesian thinking, 31, 34, 81, *see also* Descartes
caste, 205–7, 209
catechism, 241
categorical imperative (Kant), 269
Catholicism, 61, 158, 161, 210, 239–41, 243, 315–16
causality, 72
cave art, 147
celibacy, 160–1, 239
Ceres, 225
certainty, 17, 43, 72, 108–9, 193, 211
chakras, 208
Chandogya Upanishad, 204
chaos, 164, 225
charity, principle of, 248
chemistry, 125
child, 7, 29, 140, 147, 154–5, 183, 231
children, 28, 137, 154–5, 172, 219, 231, 241, 265, 270
China, 29, 188, 196, 200, **210–16**, 219, 226, 253, 309, 316–17
Chipko Movement, 152
Christ, 7, 139, 151, 170, 179–80, 183, 187–8, 224, 228, **229–34**, 235–6, 238, 239, 242–5, 313, *see also* Jesus
Christianity, 2, 19, 35, 39, 45, 52–3, 60, 62, 98, 119, 131, 134–5, 156, 164, 170, 172, 183–4, 187–9, 200, 210, 221, 223–4, 228, **229–46**, 251–5, 257, 280, 288, 310–11
Christocentrism, 245
Christology, 184
chun tzu (Confucian gentleman), 210
church, 70, 134, 135, 158, 161, 174, 210, 236, 238, 240–1, 290, 304, 308, 315
church-going, 134, 177
churchmen, 235
citizenship, 293
civic tradition, 132
class oppression, 99

classical culture, *see* Graeco-Roman
cleverness, 153
climate change, 5, 289
cognitive biases, *see* bias
cognitive dissonance, 86, 98, 117, 172, 220, 255
cognitive linguistics, 47, 62, 77, *see also* embodied meaning
cognitive meaning, 10, 20, 77, 117–18, 164
cognitive models, 233, 276, 283, **319**
cognitive psychology, 6, 36, 62, 86, 88, 302, *see also* bias
collective unconscious, 3, **31–6**, 43, 49, 58, **319**
college education, 51
Columbus, Christopher, 212
comedy, 213, 224
coming of age rituals, 131
Communist Society, 99
compassion, 79, 95, 105, **119–20**, 156, 158, 196, 197, 200, 202, 239, 260, 288, 291
compensation, 93, 153
complexity, 4, 12, 24, 48, 50–1, 63, 64, 68, 73–4, 81, 97, 152–3, 172, 180, 196, 224, 241, 267, 281, 293, 299, 303, 323
Comte, Auguste, 288, 309
concentration, 114, *see also* attention
concept and conceptualization, 2, 8, 13, 25, 33–4, 70, 78, 80, 138, 145, 174–5, 184, 187–9, 217, 219, 220, **263**, 264, 266, 268, 270, 276, 281, 297–8, **319**
conditionality, 195
confabulation, 85
confidence, 17, 27–8, 55, 58, 70, 81, 131, 194, 234, 252, 285, **319**
confirmation bias, 16, 18, 29, 57, 63, 82–3, 86, 94, 100, 131, 212, 217, 286, *see also* bias
conflict, 2, 7–8, 18, 29, 43, **94–6**, 105–7, 117, 126, 138, 151, 166, 205, 221–3, 240, 249–50, 253, 255–6, 276, 282, 286, 293–5, 298–9, 301, 307, 311–12, 317, 320–1
Confucianism, 288
Confucius, 210–11, 309
conscience, 205, 268
consciousness, 31–5, 37–8, 43, 49, 234, 245, 313, *see also* awareness
consent, 295

consequentialism, 98, 108, 269–71, **319**
conservatism, 50–1, 132–3
consistency, 10–11, 17–18, 58, 61, 75, 135, 230, 247, 251, 267, 275, 283–5, 305, 324
consolation, 70
Constantine (Roman Emperor), 98, 313
container schema, 20–1, 25, 45
contemplation, 120, 211, 243
context and contextualization, 7, 44, 51, 74, 114–15, 125, 127–30, 139, 158, 159, 173, 191, 195, 219, 247, 263, 268, 299, 302, 314
contraception, 239, 264
conversion, 69, 236–7
copying, 158
Coronation (of Mary), 238, 255
corpus callosum, 82, 114
corroboration (credibility), 130
cortisol, 101, 162
counsel of perfection, 233, 269
counter-projection, 68, 95, **319**
courage, 164, 269, 324
cowardice, 269
craving, 24, 77, 79, 82, 215, *see also* desire
creation, 22, 55, 120, 124, 258
creativity, 14, 23, 46, 111, 119, 131, 176, 180, 189, 208, 242, 278, 298, 304
credibility, 65, **130**, **319**
creeds, 135
critical feeling, 128
critical thinking, 2, 6, 8, 15, 89, 115, **124–30**, 133, 199, 216, 228, 287, 301, 312, **319**
critical universalism, 124–30, **319**
criticality, 19, 58, 126, 194, *see also* critical thinking
crone, 140
crucifixion, 151, 230, 233, 235, 238
cruelty, 23, 102, 162, 164, 269
Crusades, 52
Csikszentmihályi, Mihaly, 171–2, 309
cultivation, 6, 89, 108, 111, 113, 120, 124, 242, 280
cultural chauvinism, 19
culture, 2–3, 8, 10, 16, 18, 27, 30, 36, 49, 60, 72, 95, 98, 131, 139, 142, 148, 160, 168, 169, 188, 212, 215–16, 226, 234, 250–1, 266, 289, 320
cunning, 166
curiosity, 223, 298

dakinis, 200
Dalai Lama, 199
Dalits, 209
Dante (Alighieri), 235
Dao, 210-11
Daoism, 210-11, 213, 215, 288
Dashu, Max, 213-15, 309
De, 210
De Botton, Alain, 49, 304, 309
De las Casas, Bartholome, 19
dead metaphor, 26-30, 83, 85, 144, **319**
death, 147, 150, 153, **162-8**, 170, 196, 227, 230, 233, 238, 240
de-automatization, 80
deception, 60, 106, 162
deduction, 36, 100, 126, *see also* reasoning
default mode network, 114, 311
defecation, 45
defences, 60
del Sarto, Andrea, 183
Demeter, 225
democracy, 8, 50, 70, 276, **292-5**, 306, 309, 316
demonization, 15, 102, 167, 216, 254, 289, *see also* shadow
demons, 43, 85, 166, 196, 215
denial, 30, 68, 69, 70, 74, 77-9, 109, 180, 233, 239, 245, 275
deontology, 241, 269-71, **319**
Descartes, René, 31-2, 284, 309
description, 12, 48, 64, 197, 301
design, 88
desire, 14, 51, 97, **106-7**, 139, 147, 151, 245, 249-50, 252, 254, 269, 278, 281, 299, 320, *see also* craving
destiny, 258
detective, 274
determinism, 12, 108, 110, 271, **319**
Devi, 206
devil, 85, 166, 245-6, 252, *see also* Satan
devotion, 2, 238, 246
Dewey, John, 292-3, 309
dharma, 205, 210
dharmapala, 213, 200
diachronicity, **3-4**, 13, 32, 35-6, 41, 44-5, 48-9, 51-4, 57-8, 60-2, 66, 69-70, 79, 84, 93, 107-9, 112, 114, 120-1, 126, 130, 132, 134, 137, 151, 155-6, 158, 160, 164, 171, 173, 176, 178, 185, 213, 219-220, 232, 243, 268-9, 280, 301, 318, **320**, 322, 324

dialectic, 37, **105-7**, 149, 170, 179, 184, 191, 227-8, 252, 293
dialogue, 35
Diana, 225
dieting, 296
dimensions of religion, seven (Smart), 46, 70
Dionysian, 225
direct democracy, 292
disassociation, 166
disciplines, 37, 296, 305
disease, 95, 166, 168, 296, 298, 299
disembodiment, 151
disgust, 166, 193
dissidents, 216
dissonance, 54, 223, *see also* cognitive dissonance
distraction, 7, 33, 39, 77, 299
Divine Comedy (Dante), 235
division of labour, 154
divorce, 47
doctrine, 5, 46, 175, 187, 198, 247, 261, 281
dogma, 39, 41, 43-4, 47, 50, 60-1, 63, 70, 80, 88, 94, 102, 132, 134-5, 161, 175, 184-5, 188, 194-5, 205, 209, 212, 223, 227, 238, 242, 283, 290-1, 307, 310, **320**
dogmatic religion, **47-8**, 61, 290, **320**
domain dependence, 74, 130
domestic abuse, 241
dominance, 38, 50, 74, 81-2, 96-7, 102, 111, 114, 138, 144, 148, 153, 179, 217, 222, 281, 294, *see also* power
dopamine, 22
Dormition (of Mary), 238
drama, 307
dream, 33, 35, 103, 142, 144, 173
duality, 190
Durga, 206, 208
Durkheim, Emile 45, 48

e gui (hungry ghosts), 215
early modern, 168, 246
earth, 6, 264
Eckhart, Meister, 52, 243, 310
economic exploitation, 234
ecosystems, 101, 266
ecstasy, 244
Eden, 222, 240
Edinger, Edward, 234, 310
education, 19, 37, 50, 65, 118, 127, 133

effort, 14, 21–2, 33, 36, 46, 53–4, 86, 87, 89, 96, 98, 108, 127, 137, 178, 213, 253
ego, 32, 54, 60–1, 137, 147–9, 151–2, 170, 233–4, 260, 284
egomania, 162, 164
eidos (Form), 227
Ein Sof (Kabbalah), 257, 258
elitism, 281, *see also* hierarchy
embodied meaning, 5, 12, **20–30**, 36, 38, 61, 63, 70, 77–80, 83, 85, 111–12, 125, 128, 142, 193, 207, 212, 223, 225, 276–7, 283–4, 306, 319, **320**, 322–3
embodiment, 74, **77–80**, 104, 109, 118, 150, 155, 162–3, 174, 181, 185, 191–2, 200, 208, 223, 232, 234, 245, 258, 265, 267, 270, 278, 289, 291, 296, 312, **320**
emotion, 6, 11, 23, 65, 68, 74, 80, 82–3, 89, 94, 111, 113–14, 117–18, 128–9, 163–4, 166, 172–3, 260, 313, 321
emotive meaning, 10, 20, 77, 118, 320
empathy, 79
empowerment, 23, 29
emptiness (Buddhist), 175, 198
energy, 11, 23, 63, 80, 86, 95, 106, 166, 208, 210–12, 229, 266, 298
Engels, Friedrich, 96
engineer, 285
Englander, Nathan, 16
enlightenment (Buddhist), 23, 29, 169, 175, 179, 190–1, 193–4, 199–200, 275
environment, 5–6, 12, 20, 48, 64, 91, 104, 113, 124, 148, 191, 249, 251, 260, 267, 279, 321
envy, 51, 166, 240
epic, 164, 205, 225
Epicureanism, 227, 288
epigenetics, 34–5
epoché, 135
equality, 53, 101, 188, 230, 273, 294, 295
Erebos (darkness), 225
eros, 153
esotericism, 257, 262, **320**
essentialism, 37–9, 41, 73, 153, **320**
eternal life (Christian), 232–3
eternalism (Buddhist), 193
eternality, 85, 232–3
ethics, 14, 46, 62, 71, 88, 100, 176, 195, 206, 221, 229–31, 256, 264, 267, **268–72**, 288, 292, 307, 308, 309, 314

ethnic religion, **186–9**, 204, 224, **320**
etymology, 21, 26
eucharist, 230
Europe, 134, 257
Euthyphro (Plato), 40–2, 315
Eve (Genesis), 222, 223
evidence, 8, 12, 17, **56–61**, 63, 65–6, 75, 78, 81, 83, 86, 94, 113–14, 142, 161, 212, 249, 265–6, 275, 296, 312
evil, 6, 28–9, 74, 79, **100–4**, 121, 138, 162, 164–6, 200, 206, 215, 222–4, 240–1, 245, 254, 261, 268
evil laugh, 104
exercise, 205, 296
Existentialism and Humanism (Sartre), 290, 316
Exodus, 217, 219–21, 247, 249
exoticism, 118, 160, 208
experience, *passim*
experiential dimension of religion, 46, 70
expertise, 65, 130, 295

fairy, 29
faith, 43, 53, 130, 139, 196, 219, 223, **234**, 283
fallacy, 65, **89–90**, 126, 129, 133, 284, 286–7, 317, **320**
false consensus, 97
false dichotomy, 34, 90, 100, 169, 232, 240, 280, 297
false emotion, 103–4
falsehood, 68, 70, 103, 126, 273
fast thinking (Kahneman), 63
fatalism, 66
father, 2, 29, 40–1, 140, 154, 220–1, 225, 231
fear, 24, 75, 139, 142, 147, 166, 215, 217, 238, 241, 314
feedback loops, 5, 6, **91–5**, 101, 104–5, 108, 113, 133, 163, 215, 245, 296, **320**, *see also* balancing feedback, reinforcing feedback
Feeding of the Five Thousand (Jesus), 232
female, 22, 62, 145, 152–3, 156, 159, 197, 200, 206, 208, 238–9, 244, 254–5, 273
femininity, 2, 29, 47, 54, 62, 139, 153–4, 156, 159, 200, 206, 210, 215, 225, 238–9, 243–4, 255, 259, 318, *see also* anima

fertility, 153, 156, 225, 239, 278
Feuerbach, Ludwig, 62, 288, 311
film, 14, 73, 120, 134, 165, 282, 307
fish, 206, 236
Five Buddha Mandala, 202–3
Five Principles of Middle Way Philosophy, 109–10
flow (Csikszentmihályi), 23, 80, 158, 171–2, 211
folk religion, 210, 213
food, 11, 13, 21, 137, 191–3, 232, 264
Fordham, Frieda 43, 311
Forest (life of Buddha), 181, 191
Form (Plato), 37, 227
Four Horsemen of the Apocalypse, 165
Fox, Kieran et al., 113–14, 311
fragility, 28, 55, 78, 115, 255–6, 261
fragmentation of meaning, 117–18
framing, 320, *see also* assumption
Francis, St of Assisi, 122–3, 235–6, 245, 312
Franklin, Benjamin, 124
freedom, 50–1, 53–4, 110, 208, 222, 233, 293–5, 306, **320**
freewill, 108–10
Freud, Sigmund, 144
Freudianism, 23, 245, 270
Frodo Baggins (Tolkien), 22, 150
function, archetypal, *passim*, **3–4**, *see also* anima/animus, God, hero, shadow
function (general), 4, **320**
fundamental attribution error, 87
fundamentalism, 47, 247, 254–5
funeral, 2, 290

Gaia, 264
game theory, 18
Gandhi, 288
Gautama, Siddhartha 190–5, *see also* Buddha, Shakyamuni
gedullah (love), 260
gender, 65, 146, 153, 169, 190, *see also* sexual difference
Genesis, 213, 222–3, 257
genetics, 34–5, 278, *see also* epigenetics
genocide, 19, 237
gentleman (Confucian), 210
gestalt, 38, 138, 157, 275, 285, **320**, 321
gevurah (judgement/power), 260
gharaniq (Numidian cranes), 254
ghosts, 215

Gideon, 222
gluttony, 240
Gnosticism, 37, 39, 165, 240
goal-oriented projection, **74**, 79, 87, 98–9, 102, 104, 107–8, 125, **320**
goals, 13–15, 17–18, 21, 27, 32, 74, 79, 87, 93–4, 96, 102, 106, 108–9, 125, 129, 132, 134, 137, **147–152**, 170, 178, 184, 205, 229, 231, 236, 261, 270, 281, 283, 285, 298, 304, 320
God, *passim*, *see also* following entries
God function, **15**, **23–4**, 29, 39, 46, 69, 75, 138–9, 145, 171, 173, 176, 181, 191, 212, 231, 260, 275, 285, **320**, 321
God of the Left Hemisphere, 217, 223, 317
God of the Right Hemisphere, 217
God's eye view, 174
God's kingdom, 230
goddess, 85, 139, 173, 206, 212–13, 225–6, 235, 254–5, 296–7, 308–9, *see also* individual names
Goethe, Johann, 117, 121, 311
golden mean (Aristotle), 184
good and goodness, 6, 8, 19, 37, 40, 56, 69, 72, 88, 100, 101–2, 104–5, 108, 133, 144, 162, 164–5, 169, 173, 185, 222, 224, 231, 240–1, 264, **268–72**, 275, 292, 299–300, 304, 309, *see also* ethics
Goodwyn, Erik, 44, 47, 142, 145, 153, 305, 311–12
gospel, 231–3, 236
government, 132, 292–3, 295
Graeco-Roman mythology, **224–8**, *see also* individual named gods, goddesses and heroes
Graeco-Roman philosophy, 224, **226–8**, 240
Graeco-Roman religion, 226
Graeco-Roman tradition, 8, 188, **224–8**, 229, 235, 240, 251, 275, 288
Greece, 4, 26, 29, 42, 72, 187, 189, 225–8, 296–7, 316
green environments, 177, 265
Grossmann, Igor, 61, 312
group, 28, 31, 45–8, 52, 55, 58, 63, 66, 74, 80, 95, **96–8**, 100–1, 106, 110, 131–5, 147–9, 152, 158, 172, 186–7, 193, 217, 225–6, 231, 236, 294–5, 320–1, 324

group biases, 97
groupthink, 97
growth, 91, 213, 223, 236, 258, 261
Guan Yu (*Romance of the Three Kingdoms*), 212-13
guru, 199, *see also* teacher

Haidt, Jonathan, 12, 45, 50, 53-4, 294, 312
halo effect, 6, 87-8, 115
Hanh, Thich Nhat, 111
Hanuman, 206
Harrowing of Hell, 235
Harry Potter, 270
hatred, 28, 79, 86, 106, 166
healers, 296
health, 263, 278, **296-300**, 313
heaven, 138, 162, 210, 213, 224, 238, 255, 288
Hebb, Donald, 119, 312
Hebrew Bible, 188, 217, 221-4, 235, 257, *see also* Genesis, Exodus
hedonic paradox/treadmill, 115, 150
Heidegger, Martin, 283, 312
hell, 162, 166-7, 180, 235, 240, 253
henotheism, 217
Henry V, 27
Hera, 225
Hercules (Heracles), 73, 170, 224
hermaphrodite, 180
hero and heroism, 1, 7, 10, 14, 21-2, 24, 27-8, 30, 36, 45-6, 48, 55, 57, 69-70, 73, 75, 85, 87, 96, 99, 102, 109, 115, 121, 129, 131, 136-8, 145, **147-52**, 164-5, 167, 170, 178, 179, 184, 189, 191, 199, 205-6, 215, 221-5, 230, 233, 235-7, 238, 245, 250, 252, 253, 256, 260-1, 269-71, 274, 279, 285-6, 294, 299, 302
heroic function, 14, 21-2, 24, 27, 57, 131, 137-8, 157, 170, 191, 252, 285, 299, **320**
hierarchy of needs, 12-13, 137
hierarchy of power, 97, 204, 206, 234, *see also* power
Hildegard of Bingen, 52, 245-6, 312
Himalaya, 196
Hinduism, 53, 98, 186, 188, **204-9**, 313, 317
hippocampus, 113-14, 324
Hira, Cave of (Islam), 251

historicity, 231
history, 69, 88, 99, 175, 186, 235, 240, 255
Hitler, Adolf, 100
hod (majesty), 260
hokhmah (wisdom), 260
holiness, 40-1
homosexuality, 154, 239, 266
honour, 205, 221
Hughes, Langston, 10
human rights, 50, 53, 293, 309
humanism, 288, 290-1
humanity, 8, 19, 157, 169, 183, 215, 230, 253, 258, 277, **288-91**, 296
humility, 138, 242, 244, 291
hungry ghosts, 215
hunting, 147
Hygeia, 296-7
hysteria, 172, 316

Iblis, 253, 308, *see also* Satan
Ibsen, Henrik, 152
icon, 23
iconoclasm, 69, 221, **321**
iconography, 196
ideal, 7, 29, 37, 40, 48, 54, 176, 191, 205, 210, 258, 268-9, 271, 275, 288-90, 292, 295-7
idealism, 38, 41
idealization, 15, 79, 161, 169, 180, 181, 230, 239
ideas, 2, 8, 10, 17, 31, 35, 37-8, 66, 78, 96, 102, 111, 148, 186, 268, 294
ideology, 96, 98, 110, 162, 247, 318, **321**
idol, 69, 221, 250
idolatry, 7, 69, 175, 217, **218-21**, 222, 234, 236, 249-50, 257, **321**
ignorance, 37, 208, 240, 269
ihsan (inspiration), 247-8
ill-health, 298-9
illiteracy, 219, 312
image, 2, 59, 69, 72, 117, 135, 142, 144-5, 156, 158, 173, 179, 190, 197, 201-2, 219, 233-4, 239, **321**, 323-4
imagination, 115, 118, 120, 128, 140
iman (belief), 247
imitation, 155
immortality, 73, 213
impatience, 10, 49, 269
incarnation, 7, 170, 199, 215, 233, 243
incrementality, 33-4, 63, 101, 109, 130, 134, 190, 277, 284, **321**

India, 11, 29, 72, 98, 182, 190, 192, 196, 207, 210, 213, 219, 225–7, 229, 233
individuality, 135
individuation, 106, 152, 233, 310, **321**, *see also* integration
infinite, 6, 54, 69, 72, 173–5, 187, 231, 249, 285
ingroup bias, 97
initiation, 149, 151, 196
innateness, 34, 36, 88, 153, 155
innocence, 29
inspiration, 1, 4, **7**, 8, 53, 55, 57, 66, 71, 98, 121, 123, 126, 134, 163, 173, 176–8, 179, 181, 185, 191, 194–5, 199, 205–6, 208, 210, 212, 215, 223, 227, 231–2, 235–6, 238, 246, 247, 251, 258, 267–76, 278–80, 282, 285–6, 288, 291, 293–4, 297, 301–2, 306–7, 318, **321**
instinct, 12
institutions, 44, 131–3, 304–5
instrumentality, 96, 102
integration, 2, 5, 7, 15, 29, 45, 55, 57, 60–2, 79, 88, 100, **105–8**, 109–11, 113–21, 123–5, 127, 129, 133, 135–6, 138–40, 143, 151, 155–8, 160, 163–4, 168–9, 173, 178–9, 184, 188, 194–5, 200–1, 204–6, 208–10, 212, 215, 217, 222–4, 227, 231, 238, 240, 242–3, 247, 249–50, 252–4, 256, 258, 260–2, 268–71, 277–8, 290–1, 293, 296–8, 301–2, 304–5, 310, **321**
integration of belief and judgement, 111, 124–30
integration of meaning, 117–20
integration-projection axis, 138–40, **321**
integrative practice, **111–35**, 168, 205, 212, 301–2, *see also* mindfulness, arts, critical thinking etc.
intellect, 260
interactionism, 278
inter-hemispheric connectivity, 114, *see also* corpus callosum
interpretatio Christiana, 235
interpretation, 2, 8, 9, 35–6, 39, 63–4, **128–9**, 132, 135, 139, 144, 195, 198–9, 209, 211, 219, 221, 233–4, 253, 259–60, 262, 270, 276, 285, 318
intolerance, 236
intractability, 276
intrinsic motivation, 171
introjection, 68, **321**

intuition, 4, 6, 12, 39, **56**, 57, 66, 97, 104, 130, 138–9, 162, 164, 210, 275, 285, 315, 320, **321**
Iraq, 292
Irenaean theodicy, 223
irrationality, 139
Isaiah, 220
Islam, 7, 35, 52, 69, 158, 187–9, 221, 223, 229, **247–56**, 303, 314–15
Islamic State, 47
Israel, 217, 254
Israelites, 175, 217, 219–22, 236, 247, 251

Jacob's ladder, 258
Jainism, 288
James, William, 47, 136
Japan, 117, 196, 200
Jason (hero), 149
Jeffrey, Scott, 142
Jesus, 48, 61, 170, 183, **230–3**, 236, 238–9, 252, 255, 269, *see also* Christ
jhana, 80, 172, 192, 321
Jibreel, 251
jihad, 252–4
Job, 223
John, St (gospel writer), 232
John of the Cross, St, 245, 312
Johnson, Mark, 5, 11, 20, 22, 25–6, 30, 38, 121, 283, 312, 314
Jonah, 236
Joshua, 222, 237
journalism, 274
Journey to the West, 213, 215, 317
joy, 66, 263, 280
Judaism, 132, 186–7, 189, 223, 229, 240, 251, 257, 262, 282, 317
judgement, 3, 17, 19, 36, 49–50, 52, 56, 66, 72, 101, 108, 111, 114–15, 124–6, 128, 133, 141, 162, 165, 178, 181, 184, 198, 204, 210, 212, 221, 231, 233, 240, 260–1, 268, 271, 282, 287, 293, 300–2, 305, 307, 319, **321**, 322–4
Judgement of Paris, 225–6
Jung, Carl **2–3**, 5, 10, 15, 20, 30, **31–42**, 43–4, 49, 51, 53, 57–8, 63–6, 68, 105–6, 137, 142–5, 150–5, 169–70, 173, 180, 202, 229, 233, 301–3, 305, 310–11, 313–15, 317, 319, 321, 324
Jungianism, 2–3, 5–7, 31, 39, 41, 43, 58, 68, 74, 136, 142, 153–4, 173, 233, 301–2, 305, 313, 315, 321

Juno, 225
Jupiter, 225
justice, 27, 49–51, 53–4, 110, 152, 230, 251, 306, **321**
justification, 17, 31, 50, 70, 72, 89, 94, 100, 102, 110, 127, 130, 132, 162, 211, 238, 264, 275, **284**, 285–7, 307, 319–20, **321**

Kabbalah, 189, **257–62**, 312, 316
Kahneman, Daniel, 56, 86–7, 313
Kali, 206, 208
Kampe (destruction), 225
Kannon, 200
Kant, Immanuel, 41, 269, 313
karma, 195
Keats, John, 169
Kegan, Robert, 50, 54, 313, 323
kelippah (shell), 261
keter (crown), 258, 260
killing, 151, 205, 250
kindness, 263, 269
king, 27
kingdom, 230, 271
Klostermaier, Klaus, 207, 313
knowledge, 38, 40, 65, 81, **92–3**, 109, 118, 175, 211, 222, 243
Knox, Jean, 37–9, 313
Korea, 196
Krishna, 205, 311
Kuan Yin, 200
kundalini, 207
Kunlun Mountains, 213, 215
Kyosai, Kawanabe, 194

La Yole (Renoir), 159
Lakoff, George, 5, 20, 25–6, 30, 38, 59, 283, 313, 314
Lamott, Anne, 43
landscape, 29, 156, 264, 267, 279
language, **20–2**, 25–6, 65, 118, 126, 128, 130, 147, 250, 277, 283, 300
Lanka, 206
lapis lazuli, 156, 158
lateralization (of brain), 82–3
law (human), 132, 217–18, 220, 229, 251, 269, 293
law (of logic), 125
law (of nature), 12, 111, 152, 176, 264, *see also* Natural Law
leaders and leadership, 97, 135, 212, 294, 304

left hemisphere (of brain), 27, 38, 74, **81–5**, 87, 103, 105, 148, 179, 217, 222, 239, 261, 281, 284, 286
left pre-frontal cortex, 25, 26, 82, 93, 113, 147, 297
Lent, Jeremy, 211–12, 314
li (natural system), 210–11
liberalism, 47, 50–1, 221, 295
libertarianism, 110
lifetime, 58, 60, 106, 131
likelihood, *see* probability
limbic system, 172, *see* amygdala, corpus callosum, hippocampus
lingam, 208
linguistics, **20–30**, 38, 59, 62, 72, 77, 82, 117, 120, 220, 302, 306, 314
liquid, 230, 261
literacy, 175, **219–21**, 250, 312
literalism, **25–6**, 27, 54, 83, 85, 199, 233, 247
liturgy, 190
logic, 85, 118, 125–6, 128, **283–7**, 307, 311
logos, 153, 169
Loki, 151
lotus, 24, 207
love, 6, 14, 29, 44, 57, 79, 119–20, 126, 208, 219, 231–2, 235, 237–8, 242, 245, 253, 260, 281, 299, *see also* compassion
lover, 7, 15, 75, 154
loving-kindness, 120
loyalty, 51, 53–4, 86, **321**
Lucifer, 164, *see also* Satan
Luria, Isaac, 257–8
lust, 24, 216, 240

Madhyamaka, 198
Madonna, 159
magic, 73, **152**, 219
magician, 7, 140, 152
Mahabharata, 205, 311
Mahakala, 200–1
Mahavajrabhairava, 16
Mahayana Buddhism, 119, 188, 190, **196–203**, 206
male, 10, 152–4, 156, 158, 206, 215, 225, 235, 239, 254–5
malkhut (embodied state), 258, 260
Manasa, 206
Manat (goddess), 254
mandala, 29, 173, 174, 179, **201–2**

Index

Manichaeism, 165, 168
manipulation, 102-3
Mara, 60, 166, 200, 215, 240
marginality, 179, 181
Marinoff, Lou, 184, 314
marriage, 131-2, 138, 160, 244
Mars, 225
martial arts, 212
martyrdom, 162, 227, 235, **238**, 252
Marx, Karl, 96, 99, 314
Marxism, 96, 99
Mary (mother of Jesus), 6, 52, 61, **156-8**, 170, 172, 238-9, 243-4, 246, 255, 308
masculinity, 29, 47, 63, 139, 153-6, 200, 206, 210, 244, 253, 259, 318
Maslow, Abraham, 12-13, 314
masturbation, 239, 241
material dimension of religion, 46
materialism, 227, 320, *see also* determinism, mechanism, reductionism
mathematics, 37-8, 125, 227, 283
maturation, 60
maturity, 50, 222
MBSR (mindfulness based stress reduction), 114
McGilchrist, Iain, 25-6, 38, 81-3, 97, 147, 157, 281, 284, 314
McNamara, Patrick, 176, 314
Meadows, Donella, 91, 314
meaning, *passim*, **20-30**, **322**, *see* cognitive meaning, embodied meaning, emotive meaning, meaningfulness, representationalism
meaningfulness, 4, **11**, 12, 15, 21, 23, 25-6, 28-30, 41, 43-4, 47, 62, 70, 77, 80, 93, 119-20, 127, 131, 149, 225, 281, 283-4, 298, 301, 306, 318-19, 321-2
meat, 206, 266
Mecca, 251, 254
mechanism, 83, 158, *see also* determinism, reductionism
mediation, 229
medieval period, 27, 52, 168, 189, 235, 246, 257
meditation, 5, 32-3, 46, 79, **111-16**, 120, 127, 158, 177, 192, 198, 207-8, 301, 311, 314
Medjugorje, 172
men, 29, 35, 37, 49, 73, 153-6, 190, 215, 238-9, 243, 318, *see also* masculinity

mental health, 166, 296
mental state, 158, 178, 180, 184
mercy, 237, 253
mermaid, 29
Merton, Thomas, 243
messiah, 126, *see also* Christ
metaphor, 2, 5, 12, 20-2, **25-30**, 38, 52, 77-8, 83, 85, 117-18, 120, 144, 166, 179, 193, 276, 293, 316, 319-20, **322**
metaphorical extension, 25, **322**
metaphysics, 1, 19, 30, 35, 37-9, 42, 62, **72-6**, 77, 79, 99, 104-5, 109-10, 151, 162, 169, 184, 198, 204, 211, 227, 236, 238, 262, 264, 276, 288, 307, 313, **322**
metonymy, 59, **322**
metta-bhavana (loving-kindness meditation), 120
Middle Way, 3, 5, 7, 105, **108-10**, 119, 121, 151, 161, 178-81, 183-5, 188, 190-5, 198-9, 203, 204-6, 210, 213, 219, 227-30, 232, 242, 260-1, 269, 270, 302-3, 310, 314-15, **322**
Mill, John Stuart, 68
Milton, John, 103, 162, 164-5, 235
mimesis, 158
mind, 14, 19, 31, 34, 37, 40, 43, 81-2, 86, 91, 121, 124, 138, 149, 151-2, 159, 166, 179-80, 196, 211, 219, 223, 236, 239, 242, 263, 280, 296-7, 304, 313, *see also* brain
mindfulness, 2, 5, 23, 34, 77, **111-16**, 117, 119, 127, 133, 158, 160, 163, 172, 194, 267, 280, 287, 291, 314
Minerva, 225
miracles, 231-2
mirror neurons, 155
misogyny, 239
missionary, 235-6
modernity, 8, 12, 24, 29, 32, **49-55**, 57, 69, 70, 93, 99, 122, 131-2, 134, 142, 160, 196, 210-12, 216, 219, 222, 243, 254, 256, 280, 290, 293, 303, 306, **322**
mogui (ghosts), 215
monastics, 97, 239
Monet, Claude, 123
monism, 188, 204-5
monotheism, 29, 217, 251
Monroe, Marilyn, 30
moral experience, 100
moral rules, 46

morality, *see* ethics
mortal sin, 240–1
Moses, 217–18, 220, 222
mother, 7, 12, 29, 40, 140–1, **144–5**, 154–5, 206, 214, 220–1, 238–9, 255
Mother Nature, 264
motif, 10–11, 151, **322**
motte-and-bailey fallacy, 290
Mozart, Wolfgang, 282
MRI (magnetic resonance imaging), 81
Muhammad, 139, 189, 250–2, 254–5, 312, 317
multiple personality disorder, 166
multivocality, 10, **322**, 324
Murata, Sachiko, and Chittick, William, 249, 253, 314
mushriks, 250
music, 117, 120–1, 173
Muslim tradition, *see* Islam
mysticism, 8, 23, 52, 188–9, 221, 235, 237, **242–6**, 249, 257, 312, 317, **322**
myth, 51, 70, 144, 147–8, 303, 306
mythology, 151, 166, 213, 215, **224–6**, 227, 229, **235–41**

Nagarjuna, 198, 315
naïve universalism, 127, 304, **322**, *see also* critical universalism, monism, universalism
narrative, 22, 46, 47, 70, 120, 137, 191, 206, 225, 233, 235, 247, 306, *see also* story
National Gallery (London), 123, 157, 159, 232
nationalism, 271
nations, 137, 271
native Americans, 212
natural environments, *see* green environments
Natural Law, 210, 263–4, 266, *see also* law (of nature)
naturalism, 264, **322**, *see also* law (of nature)
nature, 8, 29–30, 34, 41, 81, 111, 125, 169, 176, 188, 190, 210–12, 216, 227, **263–7**, 275, 286, 308, 312–13, 322
Nature Red in Tooth and Claw, 264
near-death experiences, 172, 311
needs, **12–14**, 15, 17, 102, 107, 109, 119, 131, 136–7, 292, 305, 318, 320, **322**
nefesh (personhood), 257
negation, 73, 96, 109, 180, *see also* denial

negative projection, 68, 74, **322**
Neher, Andrew, 31, 34, 315
Neo-Confucianism, 211
neomania, 93
Neoplatonism, 288
neshamah (life-principle), 257
neural connections, *see* neural links
neural links, 11, 20–1, 34, 108, **119**, 144, 158, 279
neuroscience, 30, 33, 47, **81**, 302, 305, *see also* brain and its specific regions, links, or hormones
New Age, 7, 53
New Testament, 235, *see also* Bible, gospel
Newton, Isaac, 3
nezah (endurance), 260
Nicene Creed, 183
Niebuhr, Reinhold, 163–4, 169
Nietzsche, Friedrich, 162, 225, 273, 283, 312, 315
Nihilism (Buddhist sense), 193
Nineveh, 236
nirvana, 193–4
nixie, 29
Noble Eightfold Path, 194
nomadism, 251
nominalism, 38
Norse, 151, 213
novel, 73, 120–1, 165
nuns, 239
nurturance, 29

object (thing), 2, 10–11, 20, 23–4, 28–9, 32–3, 38, 43, 53, 59, 62–6, 68–9, 73–9, 83, 86, 89, 94, 97, 111, 113, 117, 137, 147, 157–8, 160, 162, 164, 166, 168, 175, 222, 242, 252, 278–80, 292, 302, 318–24
objectivity, **125–6**, 273, 275, 285, 310
obsession, 15, 23, 77, 102, 113, 148, 240, 244, 281, 296, 299, 324, *see also* craving, addiction
Odysseus, 22, 151, 224
Oedipus, 224, 316
Oizys (misery), 225
Old Testament, *see* Hebrew Bible
omniscience, 223
ontology, 268, 284, *see also* metaphysics
openness, 24, 66, 83, 86, 104, 111, 158–9, 171, 173, 230, 243, 279
opera, 307

optimality, 296
optionality, 104, 124, 180, 284, **322**, 323
orbitofrontal cortex, 113
order, 104, **164-5**, 210-11, 225-6
Original Sin, 223, 233
Orwell, George, 86
others, the other, otherness, 7, 18, 23, 29, 44, 96-8, 102-4, 118-20, 128-9, 132, 136-8, 141, 143, 145, 147, 149-50, **155-61**, 166-7, 170, 177, 180, 206, 208, 215, 222, 225, 238, 244, 255, 261, 264-6, 269, 275-6, 278, 287, 289, 292, 299, 318-19, 323
other-shadow, 138, 140
overspecialization, 74, 88, 155
oxytocin, 145

pacifism, 107, 234
Padmasambhava, 200, 202
paganism, 29, 235, 267, 312
pain, 114, 168, 223, 225, 245, 299, 313
painting, 120-1, 132, 148, 159, 267
Palace (Buddha's life), 181, 191
Pali Canon, 190
pantheon, 226, 254
Papadopoulos, Renos, 37, 64, 315
Paradise Lost, 103, 162, 164-5, 235
paradox of scepticism, 276
participation mystique, 49, 51
particularity, 41
parties (political), 51, 292-4
passions, 240
passivity, 45, 60, 211, 239
Pater, Walter, 281, 315
path, 26-7, 64, 149, 179, 184, 193-4, 200, 205, 210, 212, 238, 268, *see also* Middle Way
patience, 269
patriarchy, 156, 250, 255
Paul, St, 69, 186, 229, 236, 238
peace dividend, 106
perception, 64, 208
Perseus, 224
Persia, 233
personal unconscious, 31
Peter, St, 238
Philemon (Jung), 152
philosophy, 41, 47, 74, 89, 125, 188, 198, 204, 226, 227-9, 278, 288, 291, 307, *see also* individual topics, schools, and philosophers
physical health, 296, 313

physiology, 12, 163, 208, 308
Piaget, Jean, 50, 54, 220, 323
Pirsig, Robert, 56
Plato, **37-42**, 77, 224, 227, 268, 272, 278, 310, 315-16
Platonism, 3, 5, **37-42**, 43, 80, 151, 227-8, 240, 257-8, 283, **322**
playfulness, 29
plays, 36-7, 120
plurality, 134
policy, 236, 293-4
politician, 28, 106
politics, 15, 47, 51, 62, 95-6, 276, 292-5, 306, *see also* socio-political tradition, democracy
polytheism, 247
Popper, Karl, 64, 99, 315
populism, 276
portraiture, 307
possessions, 137
potential and potentiality (integrative), 7, 10, 15, 17-18, **23-4**, 29-30, 75, 79, 93, 97, 99, 101, 105-6, 108, 113-14, 119, 121, 123, 125-6, 130, 132, 138-9, 143-4, 157-60, 164, **169-74**, 176, 178, 180, 184-5, 190-1, 217, 222, 238, 251, 258, 264, 266-7, 269-70, 275, 279-80, 288-9, 291, 293-5, 304, 320-2, 324
power (repressive sense only), 47, 54, 74, 88, **96-9**, 102-3, 105, 165-6, 204, 206, 208-9, 211, 215-17, 234, 250, 255, 261, 293, 306, **322**
practical religion, **47**, 58, 60-1, 80, 117, 121, 130, 134, 161, 164, 175, 184, 194-5, 277, 282, 290, **322**
practicality, 17
practice, 3, 4, 5, 6, 8, 33, 35, **44-7**, 57, 59, 77, 79, 105, 108, **111-35** *passim*, 137, 146, 160-1, 163-4, 168, 176-7, 180, 184, 188, 195, 197-9, 205, 207-8, 212, 231, 242-3, 246, 253, 263, 271, 293, 301-2, 305, 307, 319, 321, 323
Prague, 289
Prajñaparamita, 198, 200
prayer, 46, 53, 156, 164, 230-1, 236, 238, 248, 250
precepts, 195, 199
prejudice, 6, 66, 125, *see also* bias
prescription, 48, 64, 316, *see also* ethics
pride, 240, 291

priests, 239
principles, 14, 17, 38, 98, 110, 210, 269, 319, *see also* deontology
probability, 17, 38-9, 65, 72, 108, 110
process (as opposed to object), 64, 78, 83, 93 149-50, **178-9**, 184, 191
processing fluency (beauty), 278
procrastination, 93, 129, 315
progressives, 50
projection, *passim*, **62-7**, **323** and more broadly **67-104**, *see also* reactive projection, counter-projection, introjection
proletariat, 99
Promised Land, 222
prophet, 189, 221, 235-6, 250
propositions, 73, 78, 220, 273, 323
propriocentric awareness, 77
Protestantism, 69, 221, 243
prototypes and prototype theory, **58-9**, 97, 314, **323**
Proust, Marcel, 65
provisionality, 45, 54, 65, 72-3, 81, 94, 101, **108-9**, 127, 129, 135, 173, 178, 198, 231-2, 260, 276-7, 295, 301, 307, **323**
pruning, synaptic, 119, *see also* neural links
Pseudo-Dionysius, 243, 315
psychoanalysis, 31, 60
psychology, 2, 4, 6, 12, 36, 50, 54-5, 58, 62, 70, 74, 86, 88-9, 105, 106, 142, 148, 155, 163, 196, 198, 212, 220, 233, 249, 262, 284-6, 302, 304-5, 312
psychological stage, 50-1, 54, **323**
Puligo, Domenico, 243-4
pulse, 61, 120
punishment, 219, 240-1
puritanism, 221, 250
purity, 5, 10-11, 24, 50-1, 53-4, 206, 257, **323**
Pyrrhonism, 227, 288

qi (energy) 210-11
Quakers, 47, 107, 135, 243
Qur'an, 247, 250-5, 308, 311

race, 6, 98, 289, 314
rain, 150, 231
Rama, 206
Ramayana, 206

Ranke-Heinemann, Ute, 239, 315
Raphael (Raffaello Santi). 159
rationality, 8, 19, 41, 53, 70, 83, 89, 125-6, 137, 139, 263, **283-7**, 291-2, 296, 303, 310, *see also* reason
Ratnasambhava, 202
Ravana, 206
reactive projection, **68-71**, 75, 87, 89, 99, 108, 151, 162, 233, 290, 319, 323
reality, 6, 20, 38, 62-3, 73, 79, 89, 93, 105, 117, 124, 169, 175, 199, 202, 257, 275, *see also* metaphysics, nature
reason and reasoning, 38-9, 53, 64, 74, 82, 86, 89-90, 94, 125-6, 128-9, 133, 139, 227, 240, 272, **283-7**, 308, 310-12, *see also* rationality, logic
Reber, Rolf, 128, 278, 315-16
rebirth, 170, 195, *see also* reincarnation
Red Book (Jung), 39, 105, 143, 150, 152-3, 229, 310, 313
reductionism, 4, 34, 227, 323, *see also* determinism, materialism, mechanism
referendum, 292
reflection, 13, 19, 24, 27, 46, 57, 97, 109, 129, 132, 137, 178-9, 181, 233, 286, 295
reformers, 133, 221, 235
re-framing, 47, 107, 109, 149-51, 170, 252, 294, *see also* integration
regulatory idea, 41
reincarnation, 199, 258, *see also* rebirth
reinforcing feedback, 5, 74, **91-5**, 101, 104-5, 108, 111, 113, 131, 133, 148, 163, 215, 217, 240, 245, 294, 296, 320, **323**
relationship (personal), 6, 14-15, 17-18, 24, 66, 68, 93, 95-7, 102, 104, 130, 131, 138, 141, **154-61**, 178, 180, 223, 229, 253, 269, 275, 278-9, 281, 289, 294, 298, 304, 318
relativism, 100, 126, 188, 224, 227, **268**, 271, 276
relaxation, 111, 172, 321
religion, *passim*, **43-8**, **323**, *see also* following entries, and those for specific religions
religion, seven dimensions of (Smart), *see* dimensions of religion, seven
religious beliefs, 1, 291
Religious Education, 44, 310

religious experience, 23, 45, 66, 80, 135, **171-7**, 217, 228, 236, 243, 245, 249, 251-2, 279, 314
religious groups, 45-8
religious organizations, 96
religious synthesis, 226
Renaissance, 123, 238, 263, 280, 315
Renoir, Auguste, 123, 159
representation, 10, 20, 25-6, 28, 38, 59, 82, 147-9, 173-4, 183, 190, 219-20, 250-1, 257, 260-1, 276, 280, 283, 319, 321-2, **323**, 324
representationalism, 52, **77-80**, 92-3, 175, 217, 239, 240, **323**
representative (political), 205, 292
repression, 7, 18, 47, 60, 63, **95**, 209, 211-12, 237, 239, 247, 249-55, *see also* power, suppression
reproduction, 23, 137, 318
repulsion, 7, 136-9, 166, 245
responsibility, 18, 55, 87, 88, 108-9, 127, 129, 161, 176, 221, 225, 233, 243, 271, 273, 290, 304, **323**
resurrection, 151, 230, 233, 235, 238, 280
revelation, 63, 176, 198-9, 236, 243, 250-1, 272, 275, 288
Revelations, Book of, 165
right hemisphere (of brain), 26, 82-3, 85, 105, 157, 281
rigidity, 5, 23, 47, 124
rites of passage, 135
ritual, 2, 46, 47, 60, 70, 131, 133, 135, 176, 198, 206, 208, 210, 217, 226, 230, 248, 281, 306
Robin Hood, 27, 30
Rohr, Richard, 242, 243
Roman tradition, 29, 161, 188, 224-9, 235, 251, 257, 316, *see also* Graeco-Roman tradition, mythology, philosophy, religion
Roman Empire, 226, 229
Romance of the Three Kingdoms, 212
Rosch, Eleanor, 59, 311
Rovan, Ruggiero, 264, 265
Rowling, J.K., 102
ṛta, 210
ruach, 257
Rubens, Peter, 297
Rubin, Marty, 72
Rumi, Jalal Ad-din, 25
Rushdie, Salman, 252

sacred, 60, 279, 316
sacrifice, 151, 226, 252
sacrilege, 156
sadhana (meditation), 196
saints, 235, 239
Salafism, 247
salat (prayer), 248
sampajana (awareness over time), 34, 113
Samson, 222
San Damiano, Church of, 236
Sangharama, 213
Sartre, Jean-Paul, 100, 290-1, 316
Sassetta (Stephano di Giovanni), 122-3
Satan, 28, 52, 55, 59-61, 75, 102-4, 164-6, 215, 222-3, 225, 240-1, 253, 255, 308
Satanic Verses, 254
sati (awareness in present), 34, 113
Saturn, 225
Sauron, 102
scepticism, 41, 72, 109, 175, 226, 273, 276, 303, 310, *see also* Pyrrhonism
schema, 3-5, 12-13, **20-4**, 25-8, 30, 36, 39, 41, 45-6, 49, 51-4, 58-62, 69, 77-8, 85, 93, 112, 117-18, 120-1, 126, 130, 136-7, 140, 142, 144, 155-6, 158-9, 164, 171, 176, 178, 181, 185, 187-8, 193, 212, 219, 243, 250, 259, 263-4, 268, 270, 276, 279-80, 283, 285-6, 299, 301, 303, 305-6, 318-22, **323**, 324
Schindler's List, 282
Scholem, Gerschom, 257, 261, 316
Schopenhauer, Arthur, 38
science, 8, 9, 45, 47, 51, 56-8, 61, 78, 82, 125, 176-7, 208, 241, 263-4, 266-7, **274**, 275, 277, 282, 285, 290, 305, 322, 323
Scivias (Hildegard), 245, 312
scripture, 63, 213, 236, 306
sculpture, 16, 121, 171, 264-5, 289
Second Crusade, 237, 246
secular, 8, 24, 53, 70, 115-16, 122-3, 159, 169, 175, 185, 210, 227, 263, 271-2, 280, 303
seduction, 223
sefirot (kabbalah), 258-61
self, 3, 7, 60, 72-3, 136, **137-8**, 140, 143, 145, 153, 160, 166, 170, 176, 180, 204, 233, 236, 242, 323

Self, 137, 169, 176, 204, 234, 313, *see also* God, God function
self-actualization, 13
self-existence, 198
self-indulgence, 181, 236, 266
self-mortification, 178, 181, *see also* asceticism
self-other axis, **137-8**, 140, 166, **323**
self-preservation, 137
self-serving bias, 87
self-shadow, 138
semantics, 78, *see also* meaning, language, linguistics
sensual experience, 10, 25, *see also* experience
Serenity Prayer, 163, 170
Sermon on the Mount, 231
serpent, 222, 240
seven deadly sins, 240
seven dimensions of religion, *see* dimensions of religion
Seven Sermons to the Dead, 39
sex and sexuality, 11, **23**, 29, 68, 70, 132, 137, 139, 145, 153-5, 160-1, 199, 206-8, 214, 225, 239-40, 244-5, 255, 257, 266, 278, 308, 320, *see also* homosexuality, trans-sexuality
sexual abuse, 161, 199, 234
sexual difference, 145, 153, 167, 254-5, 279, 320, *see also* gender
shadow, 6, 7, 14, 16, 22-4, 28, 46, 52, 55, 59, 68-70, 74-5, 79, 87, 90, 94-6, **100-4**, 105, 107, 114-15, 118, 121, 136-9, 142-3, 145, 147, **162-8**, 170, 172, 178-80, 184, 196, 200, 206, 208-9, 212, 215-16, 222-5, 235, 240-1, 245, 253-4, 256, 261, 264-5, 283, 294, 299, 302
shadow function, 14, 16, **22-3**, 28, 74-5, 101-2, 142, 163, 240-1, **323**
shadow-other, 166
shadow-self, 166
shahadah (Muslim declaration), 248, 250
Shaivism, 206
Shakti, 206, 208
Shakyamuni, 194, 196, 199, 200, *see also* Gautama, Buddha
shaman, 214
shell, 261
Shelley, Percy, 280
Sherlock Holmes, 274

shirk (idolatry), 221, 249-50, 253
Shitala, 206
Shiva, 206-9
shunyata (emptiness), 198
Siegfried (hero), 150
sign, **10**, 13, 25, 49, 173, 232, 281, **324**
simplicity, 96, 153
sin, 52, 218, 233, 240-1, 249, 253
Sinai, 217, 223
single cause fallacy, 90
singularity, 221-2
Sita, 206
sitra ahra (evil), 261
slavery, 222, 241
sloth, 240
Smart, Ninian, 46, 70, 316
Smith, Adam, 74
snake, 142-3, 166, 206-7
social conflict, 105-6, 305, *see also* conflict, socio-political tradition
social dimension of religion, 46, 70
social integration, 44, 126, 132, *see also* integration, socio-political tradition
social proof, 97
social sciences 45, 48, 305, *see also* sociology, psychology
socialism, 110
sociology, 306
socio-political tradition, 47, 50-1, 62, 70, 95-9, 106, 110, 118, 132, 204-6, 211, 230, 234, 271, 276, 282-3, 290, 292-5, 298, 306, 324
Socrates, 40-1, 42, 227, 278, 315
Socratic dialogues, 39
solemn ban, 237
solidarity, 132, 135, 172, 289, 291, 295
solitude, 251
soothing system, 113, **324**
soul, 73, 75, 77, 117, 124, 143, 151, 153, 170, 227, 236, 243, 245, 257, 278, **324**
sound, 10, 126
source-path-goal schema, 27
sources (of justification), 76, 86, 94, 109, 130
space, 10, **26-7**, 72, 76, 83-4, 152, 172, 174, 193
Spanish, 212
specialization, 82, 154-5
spirit guides, 214-15
spirituality, 45, 134, 230

split-brain effects, 81, 85, *see also* lateralization, left hemisphere, right hemisphere
splittists, 216
spouse, 139, 154, 160
state (political), 86, 216, 290, 294-5
statuary, 53
Stephen, St, 238
Stoicism, 227-8, 240, 288
story, 1, 16, 22, 28, 36, 44-6, 48, 57, 70, 77, 100, 135, 148, 164, 166, 181, 191, 193, 213, 222-3, 230, 233, 235, 245, 255, 269, 280, 288, 291, 312, *see also* narrative
storytelling, 22
straw man (fallacy), 89
strength, 114, 119, 166, 226, 254, 273
stress, 60, 95, 113-14, 198, 249, 265, 267, 294, 299, 308, 313, 324
striatum, 82, 113
Štursa, Jan, 289
subject (experiencer), 63-4, 66, 68, 76, 86, 321
subjectivity, 44, 68, 125, 145
sublimation, 23-4, 29, 60, 161, 245, 308, **324**
subservience, 153
substitution, 63, 100, 175, 286
suffering, 28, 162-4, 168, 170-1, 219, 223, 225, 233, 245
Sufism, 249, 253, 256, 308
sun, 231
sunk costs fallacy, 87, 93
superego, 270
supernatural, 28, 70, 73, 75, 85, 101, 156, 198, 212, 215, 232, 263, 268, 284
supervenience, 74
suppression, 95
survivorship bias, 93
sustainability, 18, 22, 24, 93, 104, 148, 251, 324
svabhava, 198
symbol and symbology, *passim*, **10**, **324**
symmetry, 278
Symposium (Plato), 278
synaptic connections/links, *see* neural links
synchronicity, 38
synthesis, 30, 74, 81, 106, 189, 229, 260, 267
system, 3-4, **5-6**, 16, 26, 28, 36, 63-4, 71, 73, 77, 80, 91, 98, 113, 125, 132-4, 168, 209, 211, 257, 279, 292-6, 318, 320, 323, **324**
systems theory, 5, 47, 62, 91, 93, 211, *see also* balancing feedback and reinforcing feedback

tail risk, 93
Taleb, Nassim Nicholas, 93, 316
Tantrism, 206-7, 308, 317
tanzih (incompatibility with God), 253
Tara, 6, 174, 197, 200
tashbih (compatibility with God), 253
task-positive network, 114, 158
tawhid (God's singularity), 221, 247-51, 254-5
taxonomy, 7
teacher, 40, 118-19, 127, 155-6, 181, 191, 197, 199
television, 134
temporality, 23, 76, 85, 157, 168, 172, 316
temporal lobe, 23, 172
temporary integration, 80, see also *jhana*
temptation, 139, 166, 222-3, 240
Teresa, St of Avila, 244, 316
theism, 71, 162, 288
thematization, 220
theology, 98, 174, 188, 227-8, 235, 252-3, 281, 306
theory-ladenness, 64
therapy, 42, 301
third phase, 51, 54-5, **324**
Thomism, 288
threat system, 162
threats, 6, 14-15, 17-18, 22-4, 46, 79, 93-4, 96, **101-2**, 104-5, 107, 113, 115, 130-2, 137, 142-3, **162-4**, 166, 168, 172, 180, 200, 223, 235, 240-1, 261-2, 264, 283, 289, 304, 323
tian (heaven), 210
Tibet, 16, 196, 197, 199, 200-2, 212, 312
tiferet (compassion), 260
tiger, 215
Tillich, Paul, 100
time, 4, 10, 13, 19, 21-2, 26-7, 32-4, 36, 38, 46-8, 53-4, 56-7, 60-1, 70, 72, 76, 79, **83-5**, 86, 93, 106-8, 113, 117, 120-1, 127, 131-2, 134-5, 138, 144, 147-9, 151-3, 155-6, 161, 163-4, 170, 172, 174, 188, 193, 195, 206, 210, 214, 219, 250, 256, 260-1, 263,

342 *Archetypes in Religion and Beyond*

267–70, 272, 274–5, 285–8, 291, 293, 295, 301–2, 305, 313, 318–21, 324
timelessness, 73, *see also* eternality
tolerance, 50, 53, 135, 187, 212, 226, 243
Tolkien, J.R.R. 1, 102–3, 150, 317
tool-using, 147
Torah, 258
Toronto Blessing, 172, 315
torture, 234, 237
tourism, 160
trade, 251
tradition, 5, 24, 26, 29, 41–2, 45–7, **49–55**, 57, 70–1, 77, 80, 93, 111, 121–2, 130, **131–5**, 149, 156, 165–6, 170, 173, 175, 185, 187–9, 193, 195, 198–200, 202–5, 208–13, 215, 221, 223–4, 228–30, 233, 242–4, 246–7, 249, 253, 256–7, 262, 271, 288, 302–4, 308–9, 317, 321, **324**
traditional society, 49–55, 303, **324**
tragedy, 224–5, 308, 315
transcendence, 54, 75, 88, 97, 99, 102, 115, 125–6, 131, 180, 275, 283, 291
transcendence projection, 75, 97, 99, 125, **324**
Transfiguration (of Christ), 280
trans-sexuality, 154
Tree of Life, 179, 213, 258
trickster, 7, 27, 140, 151
Troy, 224
truth, 8, 17, 29–30, 40–1, 52–3, 56, 68, 70, 75, 77–9, 89, 109, 111, 124, 126, 136, 169, 175, 184, 204, 250, 263, **273–7**, 284, 286, 290
truth-dependent theory of meaning, 77
tu quoque (fallacy), 90
Turner, J.M.W., 123
Tweedy, Roderick, 217, 317
two mules, 106–7
two truths (Nagarjuna), 198
Typhaeus (storm), 225

Uffizi Gallery, 281
ugliness, 282
UK Parliament, 132
ultimate concern (Tillich), 169
uncertain, 22, 72, 164
uncertainty, 22, 68, 72–3, 109, 138, 152, 161, 164, 192, 198, 211, 273, 284, 318, 323
unconscious (the), 26, **31–6**, 38, 45, 49, 64, 137, 144, 233

understanding, 2–3, 12, 14, 16–17, 19–21, 24, 26, 30, 35–6, 39, 43, 45, 48, 52, 56, 59, 62, 64–6, 72, 77–8, 80, 83, 100, 119, 127, 130, 141, 149–50, 164, 169, 174, 176, 184, 187, 199, 205, 211, 219, 221, 241–2, 246, 250, 252, 258, 260–1, 267, 292, 302–3, 305, 321
unholy alliance, 44
Unitarianism, 53, 243
universality, 2, 12, **16–19**, 36–7, 41–2, 52–4, 126–7, 136, 149, 164, 173, 175, 186–90, 193, 219, 224, 226–7, 229, 231, 233, 247, 268–9, 289, 301, 323, **324**
universal religion, 186–9, 204, 229, 247, **324**
universalism, 37, 53, 124, 127, 304, **324**, *see also* critical universalism, naïve universalism
universalizability, 269
univocality, 10, **324**
US, 254
utilitarianism, 133–4, 269

vagueness, 129
Vaillant, George, 60–1, 317
Vajrayana, 200
validity, 126, 128, 284, 287
values, 18–19, 46, 50–1, 53–4, 69, 76, 86, 98, 100, 110, 124, 127, 149–50, 156, 188, 201, 211–12, 238, 251, 264, 282, 288, 294–5, **324**, *see also* ethics
varna (class), 98
Vedas, 204
vengeful ghosts, 215
venial sins, 240
Venus, 225
vested interest (credibility), 130
via negativa, 242–3, 257
video gaming, 134
villain, 104, 165, 167
Vimalakirti Nirdesha, 196
violence, 209, 233, 236
virginity, 10–11, 225, 239, 244, 255
virtue, 108, 210, 227, 263, 269, 271, 278, 291, 302, **324**
virtue ethics, 108, 269
Vishnu, 205, 206
voice-tones, 121
Voldemort (Rowling character), 102

von Glahn, Richard, 215
voting, 51, 292-3
Vulture's Peak, 213

war, 98, 234, 236, 250, 252-3, 289
Waraqa, 251
Warsaw Ghetto, 282
washing, 248
wealth, 86, 215-16
Wheel of the Year, 267
whore, 239
wilful effort, 252
wisdom, **14**, 29, 61, 137, 163-4, 194, 198, 200, 203, 225, 242, 251, 260, 269, 278, 310, 313, 324
wise old man, 29, 173
wise old woman 173
wishful thinking, 17, 32
witch, 167
woman, 6, 29, 153-5, 158, 160, 167, 173, 200, 222, 230, 238-9, 243-4, 255, 273, 318
Wordsworth, William, 263, 280, 308, 317
work (employment), 96, 98, 119, 298
World Health Organization, 296

worship, 35, 44, 79, 131, 135, 164, 175-6, 186, 206, 219-21, 249-50, 254-5
wrath, 240
wrathful deities, 200
wu wei (effortless action), 210-11, 316
Wutong, 215

Xi Wangmu, 213-15, 309
Xuanzang, 213

Yahweh, 188, 217, 223
Yamantaka, 200
yang, 210, 212, 253
yesod (foundation), 260
yin, 210, 212, 215, 253
yoga, 111, 205, 207-8, 225
yoga-yukta, 205
yoginis, 200
yoni, 208
yuan gui (vengeful ghosts), 215

Zeus, 225
Zheng, Admiral, 212
Zhuge Liang (*Romance of the Three Kingdoms*), 212
Zoroastrianism, 165, 222, 240

www.ingramcontent.com/pod-product-compliance
Lightning Source LLC
Chambersburg PA
CBHW042041240426
43667CB00047B/2935